THE WORLD'S CLASSICS

A MAD WORLD, MY MASTERS, AND OTHER PLAYS

THOMAS MIDDLETON was born in 1580 and died in 1627. His career as a London dramatist therefore spans the most productive, innovative, and exciting period of theatrical activity in the history of English drama. Middleton wrote nearly fifty plays during these years, either alone or in collaboration with other Jacobean dramatists. His greatest play, written in collaboration with William Rowley, is *The Changeling* (1622), a superb and tragic rendering of the pathology of sexual obsession. In his City Comedies, Middleton replays this and other pathologies in robustly comic vein. By the time of his death, Middleton was reasonably well-to-do, having been appointed the City Chronologer for London in 1620, a post which obliged him to keep records of important civic events and organize public entertainments and pageants.

MICHAEL TAYLOR is an independent scholar living in Ottawa, Canada. He has published extensively on Renaissance drama (mainly on Shakespeare) and on the novel.

MICHAEL CORDNER is a Senior Lecturer in the Department of English and Related Literature at the University of York. He has edited George Farquhar's *The Beaux' Stratagem*, the *Complete Plays* of Sir George Etherege, *Four Comedies* of Sir John Vanbrugh and, for the World's Classics series, *Four Restoration Marriage Comedies*. He has also co-edited *English Comedy* (Cambridge, 1994) and is completing a book on *The Comedy of Marriage 1660–1737*.

PETER HOLLAND is Judith E. Wilson University Lecturer in Drama in the Faculty of English, at the University of Cambridge.

MARTIN WIGGINS is a Fellow of the Shakespeare Institute and Lecturer in English at the University of Birmingham.

D1473946

DRAMA IN WORLD'S CLASSICS

THE WORLD'S CLASSICS

THOMAS MIDDLETON

A Mad World, My Masters
Michaelmas Term
A Trick to Catch the Old One
No Wit, No Help Like a Woman's

Edited with an Introduction by
MICHAEL TAYLOR

General Editor
MICHAEL CORDNER
Associate General Editors
PETER HOLLAND   MARTIN WIGGINS

Oxford   New York
OXFORD UNIVERSITY PRESS
1995

Oxford University Press, Walton Street, Oxford OX2 6DP

Oxford New York
Athens Auckland Bangkok Bombay
Calcutta Cape Town Dar es Salaam Delhi
Florence Hong Kong Istanbul Karachi
Kuala Lumpur Madras Madrid Melbourne
Mexico City Nairobi Paris Singapore
Taipei Tokyo Toronto
and associated companies in
Berlin Ibadan

Oxford is a trade mark of Oxford University Press

© Michael Taylor 1995

First published as a World's Classics paperback 1995

All rights reserved. No part of this publication may be reproduced,
stored in a retrieval system, or transmitted, in any form or by any means,
without the prior permission in writing of Oxford University Press.
Within the UK, exceptions are allowed in respect of any fair dealing for the
purpose of research or private study, or criticism or review, as permitted
under the Copyright, Designs and Patents Act, 1988, or in the case of
reprographic reproduction in accordance with the terms of the licences
issued by the Copyright Licensing Agency. Enquiries concerning
reproduction outside these terms and in other countries should be
sent to the Rights Department, Oxford University Press,
at the address above

This book is sold subject to the condition that it shall not, by way
of trade or otherwise, be lent, re-sold, hired out or otherwise circulated
without the publisher's prior consent in any form of binding or cover
other than that in which it is published and without a similar condition
including this condition being imposed on the subsequent purchaser

British Library Cataloguing in Publication Data
Data available

Library of Congress Cataloging in Publication Data
Middleton, Thomas, d. 1627
[Plays. Selections]
A mad world, my masters; Michaelmas term; A trick to catch the
old one; No wit, no help like a woman's / Thomas Middleton; edited
with an introduction by Michael Taylor; general editor, Michael
Cordner; associate general editors, Peter Holland, Martin Wiggins.
1. City and town life—England—London—Drama.   2. London
(England)—Drama.   I. Taylor, Michael.   II. Cordner, Michael.
III. Title.   IV. Series.
PR2712.T39 1996   822'.3—dc20   95-4309
ISBN 0-19-282255-1

1 3 5 7 9 10 8 6 4 2

Typeset by Pure Tech India Ltd., Pondicherry
Printed in Great Britain
by Biddles Ltd.
Guildford and King's Lynn

CONTENTS

ACKNOWLEDGEMENTS

I would like to thank the Faculty of Arts of the University of New Brunswick (Fredericton, Canada) for relieving me of some teaching duties so that I could begin work on this edition. Special thanks are owed to the General Editor of this series, Michael Cordner, for much good advice and encouragement.

INTRODUCTION

MIDDLETON'S 'city comedies' are a response to the bitter romance
of London bourgeois life in the early seventeenth century. They
celebrate and castigate the magnetism of this 'man-devouring city'
(*Michaelmas Term*, 2.2.21), and are dominated by two of the great
themes of literature dealing with the city, sex and money. Of the two,
money—and the real estate that advertises its possession—is ultim-
ately the more important, especially at a time of rampant inflation.
One of Middleton's more perceptive critics, Charles Barber, focuses
upon a revealing moment in this competition between sex and money
for the souls of Middleton's characters in his observation about Witgood at the end of *A Trick to Catch the Old One*: 'his rapture on the
recovery of his estate is much more heartfelt than anything he ever
says about the woman he marries'.[1] A similar response from another
of Middleton's cynical protagonists, Richard Easy, at the conclusion
of *Michaelmas Term*, leaves some readers uncertain as to the fate of
Thomasine, Quomodo's 'widow', whom Easy has recently married.
They have so much difficulty in believing Easy's easy-come, easy-go
acceptance of the Judge's decision to return Thomasine to Quomodo
that they wonder if something that happened so casually and so
swiftly ever really happened at all. But such lack of enthusiasm for
the claims of romantic love on the part of the principals involved
(except Thomasine, of course) is a good example of the way in which
most of the characters in Middleton's early comedies value the energy
involved in money-making more highly than that involved in love-
making. Quomodo himself believes that the two are incompatible: 'to
get riches and children too, 'tis more than one man can do' (*Term*,
4.1.33–4). Often in these comedies the act of making money is a
substitute for the act of making love; it may even, more perversely,
actually become the act of making love, as in, for instance, Witgood's
desire to 'hug four hundred a year' (*A Trick*, 1.2.44).

Making love to money does not seem so bizarre in the world of
these comedies, a world that has so remorselessly substituted its own
unnatural laws for natural ones. Or, rather, its unnatural laws seem
inevitable and natural to the city's inhabitants: 'the pox [*the* city

[1] Charles Barber (ed.), *A Trick to Catch the Old One*, Fountainwell Drama Texts
(Berkeley, 1968), 4.

vii

disease] is as natural now as an ague in the springtime' (*Mad World*, 4.2.24–5), observes Sir Bounteous Progress wryly. And Onesiphorus Hoard's explanation—' 'Tis as natural for old folks to fall out as for young to fall in' (*A Trick*, 1.1.122–3)—for the conflict between those 'mortal adversaries' (1.1.107), Walkadine Hoard and Pecunius Lucre, perceives their quarrel merely as age's natural and inevitable ague. In fact, the city, a (teeming) world unto itself, is seen throughout these comedies as the creator and dispenser of 'natural agues', a merciless tutor, a subculture with absurd and rigid 'observances' (*Term*, 2.1.93) where 'a man must not so much as spit but within line and fashion' (*Term*, 2.1.93–4). So palpable is London's presence in these comedies that the city can be thought of as Middleton's Marlovian protagonist: 'The city's power is a product of the greediness of the city's embrace, because the city is a version of the Renaissance overreacher, unwilling to let anyone or anything go.'[2] The city's most pernicious observance turns nature on its head by making it a 'principle in usury' (*A Trick*, 1.1.17) to victimize family members, especially the weaker ones:

> He that doth his youth expose
> To brothel, drink, and danger,
> Let him that is his nearest kin
> Cheat him before a stranger.
> (*A Trick*, 1.1.13–16)

The plays are full of conflict between members of the same family: in *No Wit, No Help Like a Woman's*, for instance, Sir Oliver Twilight talks of the 'sophistic faith of natural sons' (4.1.15), while the Dutch Merchant earlier had broadened the indictment to take in not only a man's natural sons but all his dependants: 'what worse knave to a man | Than he that eats his meat?' (1.3.78–9).

On the principle that 'All sins are venial but venereal' (*Mad World*, 1.2.137), a worse knave to a man than his son, his brother, or his servant, is his wife or his mistress. As many of Middleton's critics have pointed out, Middleton treats marriage in an irreverent and cynical fashion. Richard Horwich notes that in Middleton marriage is 'not an alternative to or an escape from the predatory marketplace, but a marketplace itself';[3] he contrasts Middleton's plays with those

[2] G. K. Paster, *The Idea of the City in the Age of Shakespeare* (Athens, Ga., 1985), 177.
[3] Richard Horwich, 'Wives, Courtesans, and the Economics of Love in Jacobean City Comedy', *Comparative Drama*, 7 (1973–4), 291–309, 306.

of Dekker, Heywood, and Marston where marriage functions in a gentler, more Shakespearian mode: 'Middleton's courtesans are indeed courtesans, not innocent girls mistaken for fallen women, and they marry to be reclaimed, but these cheerful and mettlesome women are never reformed by marriage, only enriched, and remain throughout superior in every respect to the fools who marry them.'[4]

Fear of women in general is rife in Middleton's comedies. ' 'Tis an Amazonian time; you shall have women shortly tread their husbands' (*Mad World*, 3.3.105–6), Follywit bawdily prophesies, little imagining that he will be trodden down by one very shortly, fulfilling thereby the promise of his name. The plays are full of male characters nervously looking over their shoulders for looming female predators: roaring girls, witty squalls, weak and sinful creatures, slaves to vanity, 'deluding shadows begot between tirewomen and tailors' (*Term*, 3.1.4–5), as Hellgill memorably dismisses them, who will do anything for a satin gown. What they mostly do in these plays for satin gowns or country estates or simply to satisfy their own physical appetites involves the sexual enslavement of men. Even Lethe's old mother in *Michaelmas Term* imagines that London will provide her with young courtiers who 'will be hungry upon an old woman' (1.1.307). Small wonder then that Sir Gilbert Lambston in *No Wit* peoples his rogues' gallery with 'clap-fallen daughters, | Night-walking wives . . . libidinous widows' (4.3.52–3). Women-beware-women with a vengeance.

As is the case with many of Middleton's positions, it is not entirely clear just how far this misogyny is the target of his satire and how far the instrument. (It is not until *No Wit, No Help Like a Woman's* (*c*.1611–12) that Middleton's women begin to bear any resemblance to the providential agents we find in Shakespeare's Romances.) Certainly, Follywit's diatribe in *Mad World* against the unnaturalness of women—'And is not most they do against kind, I prithee?' (3.3.91)—resonates with the measured contempt endemic to the plays on this subject, while managing to avoid the fanaticism of Penitent Brothel's hysterical response after he has fulfilled the prediction in *his* name: 'To dote on weakness, slime, corruption, woman!' (4.1.18). The subject of woman produces many a weighty apophthegm of the Follywit variety: 'Man's never at high height of madness full | Until he love and prove a woman's gull'

---

[4] Ibid. 302.

(*Mad World*, 4.5.12–13). Indeed, in this sporting life, the sophistic-ated gallant ruefully anticipates a final reckoning from one of these immensely resourceful creatures, whose 'wit is ever at full moon' (*Mad World*, 3.2.160), as perhaps Middleton himself did on more than one occasion—he a fatherless boy, brought up by an emotionally unstable mother and married at the age of 22 or 23. In any case, the unnaturalness of women, like all the other unnatural-nesses in the city comedies, is fundamentally the product of the wicked city: as Hellgill remarks, 'Virginity is no city trade' (*Term*, 1.2.41). And men, as Hellgill, Lethe, Follywit, and Witgood exem-plify, are quick to seize the chance to become pimps, procurers, perverters of innocence. 'What strange impudence | Governs in man when lust is lord of him' (*No Wit*, 1.2.74–5), Mistress Low-water observes.

All city trades demand resourcefulness, wit, ruthlessness, and energy. The tricksters in Middleton's city comedies have to operate in a world growing ever more deceitful and devious (or so they claim); in their commentaries on the *Zeitgeist* they repeatedly use words like 'subtlety' and 'cunning'. (The fact that their tricks are sometimes transparent and would not deceive a simpleton is a stage convention.) Whores and tricksters in the plays practise a 'politic conveyance' (*Mad World*, 1.1.156), a 'sincere carriage', a 'religious eyebrow' (1.1.157). Even the 'shallow ploughman', the Courtesan's mother claims in *Mad World*, can now distinguish ' 'Twixt simple truth and a dissembling brow' (1.1.140). Hence the need felt on the part of virtually all the plays' characters to practise the art of dissimulation, from the straightforward counterfeiting of unfelt emotion (as when Thomasine acts like a 'hanging moon, a little waterish awhile' (*Term*, 4.3.42) at Quomodo's 'death') to the elaborate shifts of the quick-change artist, as illustrated in the careers of Follywit, Shortyard, Quomodo, and Mistress Low-water. Country wenches transform themselves into aristocratic whores with the aid of 'wires and tires, bents and bums, felts and falls' (*Term*, 1.2.13–14); fathers and mothers are not able to recognize their own children because of their fancy attire and city ways; all these self-fashioners are in the grip of the city compulsion to make money or to cut a figure, and they are the fic-tional representatives of their real counterparts in Jacobean society, a status society, obsessed with role-playing, as we can see from the huge number of self-making manuals churned out by the printing presses every year. 'What base birth does not raiment make glorious?' (*Term*, 3.1.1–2), muses Hellgill.

Such self-making is essentially a city pursuit, of course, as only the city offers the possibility of making oneself over in desirable terms, as a gallant or gentlewoman (or trickster and whore). The 'city powd'ring' (*Term*, 1.1.56), as Cockstone calls it. *Michaelmas Term*, in particular, dramatizes the extraordinary appeal of the city for the inhabitants of rural society; London's numbers rose from some 120,000 in 1550 to 375,000 by 1650. *Michaelmas Term*'s formal, symbolic induction lays stress on the conflict between the city and country, while demonstrating at the same time their perverse symbiosis, as do the events of the play—Quomodo, the city merchant, talks of the country gentry being 'busy 'bout our wives, we 'bout their lands' (*Term*, 1.1.109). Hence the use of a metaphor whereby, for instance, the exploitation of the country litigants is seen in terms of a harvest for London lawyers, giving rise to one of those memorable Middleton couplets: 'And so through wealthy variance and fat brawl | The barn is made but steward to the hall' (*Induction*, 13–14). The 'clients' are seen as 'fools', 'asses', 'lambs', 'dried straws', and the 'writs' are like 'wild-fowl'. In an extended metaphor, the Boy vividly portrays the plight of the country innocents: 'Alas, poor birds that cannot keep the sweet country where they fly at pleasure, but must needs come to London to have their wings clipped and are fain to go hopping home again' (3.2.19–21).

At times, and anticipating the later tragedies, subtlety, role-playing, and cunning seem fiendish to their practitioners and victims. ' 'Tis an age for cloven creatures' (*Term*, 1.2.9), observes Dick Hellgill (a prototype for De Flores), and even in the Fletcherian *No Wit*, Mistress Low-water asks herself, 'Is the world's lease from hell, the devil head-landlord?' (1.2.4). When Witgood seems to be cornered by his sadistic creditors, his response acknowledges the city's spiritual hegemony: 'I am in hell here and the devils will not let me come to thee' (*A Trick*, 4.3.58–9). There is a whiff of sulphur in the air of most of Middleton's city comedies: the Succubus and Penitent Brothel in *Mad World*; Hellgill and the disturbing Dampit and Gulf in *Term*; Lethe in *Trick*—even *No Wit* has its benign, whimsical version of the devilish arts in the presentation of Weatherwise, lost in the fatuities of his almanac. Middleton is clearly fascinated by the possibility of damnation, and a character such as Dampit, once thought to be incoherent and extraneous to the world of his play, now threatens to monopolize critical attention. This 'famous, infamous trampler of time' (*A Trick*, 1.4.10)—and of language—is troublingly fantastic, unnervingly himself, his collapse looking forward to the 'particularly disturbing sense of emptiness that lies at the heart of Middleton's tragedies'.[5] As Richard Levin suggests,[6] Dampit's career offers a paradigmatic rogue's progress for the economic activities of the Hoards and Lucres of all the city comedies, an observation we should put into a larger cultural context: 'From about the end of the sixteenth century devils appear not, as in *Doctor Faustus* (1588–92), as tempters of a great man's soul, but as metaphors for the uncontrollable forces of the city economy.'[7]

To be in hell here reminds us of Mephistopheles' reply in Marlowe's *Doctor Faustus* to Faustus's naïve belief that hell has geographical (or cosmological) boundaries: 'Why, this is hell, nor am I out of it.'[8] Middleton's characters are not out of hell because hell is here in the city—is the city. At other times, even more pessimistically, characters in these city comedies tend to think of hell as the natural human condition in or out of cities. Such an extreme position is masked by an urbane (and urban) appeal to the cynicism of 'common reason', as the Courtesan calls it: 'And in common reason one keeper cannot be enough for so proud a park as a woman' (*Mad World*, 1.1.131–3). Although such a belief may be preferable to, say, Harebrain's pathological jealousy in which his wife's 'very dreams are answerable' (*Mad World*, 1.2.53), the Courtesan herself acknowledges how short the step is from a belief in the primacy of common reason to a fatalistic recognition of the inevitable corruption of human nature—'This natural drunkard that undoes us all' (*Mad World*, 4.1.9) as Penitent Brothel puts it—especially female human nature: 'for since we were made for a weak, imperfect creature, we can fit that best that we are made for' (*Mad World*, 2.5.33–4). Given this emphasis on natural corruption in the plays, it is no mere coincidence that the 'device' that Beveril manufactures for the celebration of Lady Goldenfleece's 'marriage' to Mistress Low-water in *No Wit* should involve the 'natural opposition | And untruced war' (3.1.229–30) between the four elements themselves.

[5] P. K. Ayers, 'Plot, Subplot, and the Uses of Dramatic Discord in *A Mad World, My Masters* and *A Trick to Catch the Old One*', *Modern Language Quarterly*, 47 (1986), 3–18, 15.

[6] Richard Levin, 'The Dampit Scenes in *A Trick to Catch the Old One*', *Modern Language Quarterly*, 25 (1964), 140–52.

[7] Michael Hattaway, 'Drama and Society', in R. A. Braunmuller and Michael Hattaway (eds.), *The Cambridge Companion to English Renaissance Drama* (Cambridge, 1990), 91–126, 105.

[8] Christopher Marlowe, *The Tragical History of the Life and Death of Doctor Faustus*, ed. J. D. Jump, The Revels Plays (London, 1962), III. 78.

A fascination with damnation (however melodramatically conceived), the body's natural drunkenness, and the way things fall apart, hardly suggest a writer indifferent to the corruption he satirizes. And yet the traditional assessment of Middleton talks of his detachment, his ability to render his world in vivid colours without giving anything of himself away, least of all his moral position. Recent criticism has taken issue with this line of reasoning (heavily influenced as it was by the *obiter dicta* of T. S. Eliot) and has tended to go to the other extreme, presenting Middleton in earnest, not to say, donnish terms, or, even more startlingly, as a seventeenth-century Ibsen, Brecht, or Zola. Farley-Hills thinks *Mad World* an 'outstanding example of Calvinistically inspired satirical comedy',[9] and R. B. Parker believes Middleton's comic world has 'a more than Calvinistically determined scheme of retribution'.[10] George Rowe acknowledges the presence of a moral concern but thinks the plays full of irreconcilable clashes due to a contradictory mixture of traditional and contemporary material.[11] The moralism, in other words, does not sit easily with what Parker calls an 'amoral vitalism'.[12] None the less, the plays are full of quasi-apophthegms like Easy's in *Michaelmas Term*: 'Man is ne'er healthful till his follies bleed' (5.1.15), and all of them (more or less) subscribe to Lucre's conception of the retributive cycle: 'Does not he return wisest that comes home whipped with his own follies?' (*A Trick*, 2.1.77–8). Paster sees the city itself as the whipper: 'The city exacts a brutal justice in the self-perpetuating order of the predatory cycle.'[13] And Susan Wells concludes that city comedy as a genre is traditionally moral: 'city comedy is an orthodox instance of corrective moral comedy, liberally salted, perhaps, especially in Middleton's practice, with moral ambiguity.'[14]

Sometimes the whipping is self-inflicted. As in Jonson, we are dealing here with the notion, essentially a moralistic one, of the comic overreacher, whose infinite capacity for invention finally brings the complicated edifice he has laboriously constructed crashing down

[9] David Farley-Hills, *The Comic in Renaissance Comedy* (London, 1981), 102.

[10] R. B. Parker, 'Middleton's Experiments with Comedy and Judgment', *Jacobean Theatre*, Stratford-upon-Avon Studies, 1 (New York, 1960), 179–200, 199.

[11] George E. Rowe, Jr., *Thomas Middleton and the New Comedy Tradition* (Lincoln, Nebr., 1979).

[12] Parker, 'Middleton's Experiments', 199.

[13] Paster, *The Idea*, 159.

[14] Susan Wells, 'Jacobean City Comedy and the Ideology of the City', *English Literary History*, 48 (1981), 37–60, 37.

around him. The duper outdupes himself. According to Leinwand,[15] these overreachers are 'caricatures of anti-comic types' and provide a kind of self-regulating mechanism for the enormities they practise: 'wit destroys wit' (*Term*, 5.1.44), as Shortyard ruefully concludes. The most notorious example of a trickster out-Volponing Volpone is Quomodo, who indulges the 'sweet inventions' (*Term*, 4.1.78–9) of his reckless egotism with a self-destructive abandon that is in vivid contrast to his performance as the patient, wily cony catcher pursuing the intricacies of his plot against Easy. In talking about his grand-father's punishment, Richard Follywit in *Mad World* sums up Quomodo's plight (and his own, did he but know it): 'craft recoils in the end, like an overcharged musket, and maims the very hand that puts fire to't' (3.3.10–11). Passing a somewhat more far-reaching ontological judgement on Quomodo, the Judge tells him at the end of the play: 'Thou art thine own affliction' (5.3.163).

A less convincing, more troublesome, version of the self-destructive retributive cycle involves a sudden Pauline conversion in mid-sinning career. The extreme case is Penitent Brothel in *Mad World*, whose 'sin-shaking sinews' (4.1.72) summon up the dance of the Succubus and force him to forgo the pleasures of his affair with Mistress Harebrain, converting her in the process to the higher pleasures of the chaste life. 'Sin's hate is the best gift that sin bestows' (4.1.28) is his contribution to the list of sonorous dicta in these maxim-haunted plays. Even less convincing, perhaps, is the occa-sional choric moralist, like the Country Wench's Father in *Michaelmas Term*, who, once a Penitent Brothel himself, now spends his time looking for his corrupted daughter and commenting on the city's depravity in familiar scene-closing sententiae: 'We're bad by nature, but by custom [i.e. habit] worse' (4.2.27). Much more convincing than any variety of self-inflicted punishment is the one governed by the traditional biter-bit formula—equally Jonsonian—where the trick-sters are out-tricked by superior strategists (often women, as we have seen), as is Follywit in *Mad World*, outmanœuvred by the Courtesan in her role as a demure virgin. It is left to Sir Bounteous Progress to enjoy the play's last moral word at Follywit's expense: 'Who lives by cunning, mark it, his fate's cast; | When he has gulled all then is himself the last' (*Mad World*, 5.2.282–3).

Although the sources of these city comedies are primarily the ephemera of city life—cony-catching pamphlets, jest books, the

[15] T. B. Leinwand, *The City Staged: Jacobean Comedy, 1603–1613* (Madison, Wis., 1986), 60.

routine business of the law courts, the 'rough texture of daily life on the city streets'[16]—the moral criteria they appeal to are traditional and conventional. These plays tend to be nostalgic, dreaming of 'life as it ought to be lived by the standards of a traditional, largely pre-urban frame of reference'.[17] In *Michaelmas Term*, the Father clings to a notion of a sexually pristine time past where the truly human (the truly natural), what he calls the 'human stroke' (3.1.264), ensured the production of moral progeny; in *Mad World* Sir Bounteous Progress looks back to a mythical time when aristocrats, governed by the hospitality embodied in his name, dispensed largesse with open-handed liberality. In *No Wit*, Master Pepperton looks back with the Father's eyes when he says: 'Saucy courting has brought all modest wooing clean out of fashion' (2.1.39–40), and even the malicious and parodic performance by the four rejected and bitter suitors takes the form of the four elements having been corrupted from a pristine past to scandalously evil ways in the present. Sir Bounteous would have especially applauded Fire's presentation: 'I was once a name of comfort, warmed great houses | When charity was landlord' (*No Wit*, 4.3.59–60). Lady Goldenfleece records the decline (disingenuously, no doubt) in linguistic terms: 'How many honest words have suffered corruption since Chaucer's days?' (*No Wit*, 2.1.77–8).

These Edenic fantasies of a lost golden culture animate fugitive yearnings in the present. The obsession, for instance, with 'city powd'ring' sometimes manifests itself in ways that subscribe to a kind of furtive idealism. Quomodo, for example, in *Michaelmas Term*, rejects Rearage as a possible son-in-law despite the fact that he is more obviously desirable in economic—and all other—terms than the candidate whom Thomasine (and Susan) favours, the absurd Lethe. (Although Rearage may be in arrears, at least he still owns the land to be in arrears over.) Quomodo seems to be simply and uncharacteristically dazzled by Lethe's putative Court connections. His scorn for Rearage is all the more remarkable given the fact that the play's main plot follows the labyrinthine intricacies of Quomodo's gulling of Easy out of his country estate, the rural equivalent for the city merchant of a city powdering. The longest speech in the play records Quomodo's raptures at the 'very thought of green fields' (4.1.78) as he subscribes to the popular view in London at the time of Essex as a

---

[16] G. K. Paster, 'The City in Plautus and Middleton', *Renaissance Drama*, 6 (1973), 29–44, 31.

[17] Ayers, 'Plot, Subplot', 6.

distant Arcadia distinct from the likes of Cheapside, Clerkenwell, and Brentford. The same motivation inspires a similar speech from Hoard in *A Trick to Catch the Old One* as he imagines himself and his retinue riding down to the country to enjoy Witgood's estate. The sweet inventions that contemplation of these rural paradises inspires in Quomodo and Hoard have something in common with the occasional moments in these plays when a desire for the respectability of marriage (the goal of many a whore) takes on a certain ineffable, effulgent quality. Follywit's hunger for the perfect virgin, a chaste maid in Cheapside, 'a woman's simple modesty' (*Mad World*, 4.5.63), reads like a purified version of the 'venereal dreams' he wishes for Sir Bounteous.

These yearnings when fulfilled are the hallmark of romance. *A Mad World, Michaelmas Term*, and *A Trick to Catch the Old One*, all written between 1604 and 1606, appeared at a time when satirical drama, beginning with Jonson's *Every Man Out of His Humour* in 1599, was the dominant form. Between 1599 and 1613 all but twelve of the fifty-five extant plays are satiric comedies. However, with Fletcher's *The Faithful Shepherdess* (1608) we enter a period of the theatre dominated by the plays of Beaumont and Fletcher and the genre of romance. Consequently, *No Wit, No Help Like a Woman's* (*c.*1611–12) is—superficially anyway—a different kind of play from the earlier three. It belongs to a group of plays broadly in the tragicomic mould, *More Dissemblers Besides Women* (*c.*1614–15), *A Fair Quarrel* (*c.*1615–17), *The Witch* (*c.*1615) and *The Widow* (*c.*1616), and it might best be seen as a transitional piece between satire and romance, rendering the fugitive expressions of romantic feeling in the earlier city comedies in a much more expansive and celebratory manner. It also appears just before Middleton took up the writing of city pageants in a serious way in 1613, the year of *A Chaste Maid in Cheapside*. At the same time, *No Wit*, like *A Chaste Maid*, has many of the characteristics of satiric city comedy; George Rowe argues, in fact, that *No Wit*, despite its New Comedy plot, has more cynicism in it than any of Middleton's other city comedies, with the exception of *A Chaste Maid*.[18]

Cynicism notwithstanding, *No Wit* is clearly in the grip of the workings of a preposterous history whose strange coincidences obey the iron laws of romance's beneficent destiny, 'The secret powers [that] work wondrously and duly' (1.2.146), as Mistress Low-water

[18] Rowe, *Thomas Middleton*, 173.

reverentially informs us. Middleton feels obliged to match sentiments with language in this play and so he largely abandons his normal racy prose for a verse that is the vehicle for oracular statement: 'I feel a hand of mercy lift me up | Out of a world of waters' (2.3.252–3). Weatherwise provides a parodic instance of this reliance on a beneficent destiny in the absurd way he subjects himself (and anyone else who will listen to him) to the inscrutable sayings of his almanac, and he warns his sceptical interlocutors that, without the guiding posies his almanac provides, they 'may wander like masterless men' (3.1.129).

On the other hand, despite Sir Oliver Twilight's respectful surrender to the secret workings of this implacable force in their lives—'We must not be our own choosers in our fortunes' (1.3.114)—*No Wit* resembles the other three city comedies (and much romance also, for that matter) in its equal emphasis on the contribution made by individual resolve. 'Wake, wake, and let not patience keep thee poor' (1.2.148), Mistress Low-water urges her stricken husband. Indeed, the play's title celebrates the help (as well as the wit) of women in particular to bring about the desired conclusion: that there is no help like a woman's presumably includes the helping hand of providence. In Mistress Low-water's resourcefulness and Lady Twilight's extraordinary magnanimity we find the potent combination that characterizes the wonder-working heroines of Shakespeare's Romances. And the play makes much of the concept of the mother-healer (shades of *Pericles* and *The Winter's Tale*). When all seems lost, Savourwit recommends to Philip Twilight that he 'fly to your mother's pity' (2.2.88); the romantic idealism that suffuses this play is especially articulate (*pace* the city comedy scepticism about the 'sophistic' relationship between the generations) on the subject of the reciprocal obligations of mothers and sons: 'Love is a mother's duty to a son, | As a son's duty is both love and fear' (4.1.169–70) in Lady Twilight's words (not that Philip ever inspires much confidence as a model son).

One of the abiding delights of Middleton's city comedies lies in another potent combination in which satire and festivity are in creative tension. His art 'accommodates both satiric critique and festive celebration, severely scrutinizing commercial urban society while retaining a comic tone'.[19] The plays celebrate those who 'sojourn upon their brain and make their wits their mercers' (*A Trick*,

---

[19] Mary Beth Rose, *The Expense of Spirit: Love and Sexuality in English Renaissance Drama* (Ithaca, NY, 1988), 46.

1.1.22–3). Hence the frequency with which their main characters are given those potent Wit combinations as names, Follywit, Witgood, Savourwit. They work hard for their living, laying their wits upon the tenters (as Follywit puts it), but wit gets them most things and into most places: 'he's welcome for's wit' (*Mad World*, 5.1.17) says the connoisseur of hospitality, Sir Bounteous. In Pecunius Lucre's eyes, Witgood is a 'brotheller, a wastethrift, a common surfeiter' (*A Trick*, 2.1.3–4), but Witgood demonstrates, as do the other wits, including the Wit characters' adversaries, a necessary wit-in-adversity, the city comedy counterpart of Hemingway's grace-under-pressure: 'I perceive there's nothing conjures up wit sooner than poverty, and nothing lays it down sooner than wealth and lechery!' (*A Trick*, 3.1.85–7).

In these comedies, at their most robust, life calls to both sexes: 'If men be wags, are there not women wagtails?' (*A Trick*, 2.1.75). Even hatred can be life-enhancing: 'I think their anger be the very fire | That keeps their age alive' (*A Trick*, 1.1.110–11) says Onesiphorus Hoard about the vendetta between the old usurers, Hoard and Lucre, one of the more extreme examples of Parker's amoral vitalism. And there is something to be said even for someone like Dampit in *A Trick to Catch the Old One* when he can induce a description of himself as the 'most notorious, usuring, blasphemous, atheistical, brothel-vomiting rascal' (1.4.12–13). *A Mad World*, in particular, celebrates what Sir Bounteous describes as a 'jovial season' (5.1.112). And *No Wit* ends as all romances should in what Lady Twilight calls 'a feast of marriages' (4.1.153). At their most robust, also, the plays' language and dramaturgy are correspondingly kinaesthetic: a remark such as 'I have rinsed the whoreson's gums in mull-sack many a time and often' (*A Trick*, 1.1.66–7) has a Falstaffian vigour and flavour (or a Poinsian at least) and there is much wit in such astute observations as Salewood's in *Michaelmas Term*: 'I have known a virgin of five bastards wedded' (1.1.16). 'Did the plot want either life or art?' (*Mad World*, 3.3.1–2), Follywit asks his henchmen, to which we may well respond as approvingly as they do. All Middleton's city comedies employ a racy, idiomatic, witty and pun-filled prose in a dialogue full of smart retorts and witticisms, only occasionally sinking to the level of vaudevillean repartee (of the 'pray-be-patient . . . I-cannot-be-patient-and-a-physician-too' school). They also make lively, if frequently cryptic, use of city slang—'the last translation' (*A Trick*, 2.1.11) as Lucre calls it—especially smutty city slang, Master Pepperton's 'bawdy ranks of his discourse' (*No Wit*, 2.1.51) and 'libidinous whispers' (2.1.52).

If Middleton is a master of a casual, gossipy, cynical, and witty conversation (an enjoyable proposition for any actor), he has a less certain touch at this stage in his career with verse. One of the difficulties for any editor of Middleton is the way in which verse elides into prose and vice versa, but when Middleton's verse is undeniably, not to say ostentatiously, verse, it is so usually for the wrong reasons, an efflorescence of literary figure, tendentious sentiment, and clotted syntax. Even the later *No Wit*—verse-ridden as it is—frequently displays a ripeness of effect comparable to the properties of the Widow Medlar; in particular, a straining of invention in which vehicle overwhelms tenor, as in Sir Oliver Twilight's description of the physical attractiveness of the girl he imagines to be Jane Sunset: 'As fine a body, wife, as e'er was measured | With an indenture cut in farthing steaks' (4.1.143–4), or in Savourwit's unsavoury gothic depiction of his response to the renewal of Sandfield's and Philip Twilight's friendship: 'Then thus the marigold opens at the splendour | Of a hot constant friendship 'twixt you both' (1.1.59–60). Such lapses are venial, however (and frequently venereal), so that we are much more inclined in the last analysis to think of Middleton's city comedies in the terms Easy uses to praise Shortyard in *Michaelmas Term*: 'full of nimble wit, various discourse, pregnant apprehension, and uncommon entertainment' (3.2.11–12).

NOTE ON THE TEXTS

COPY-TEXTS for the four plays are as follows: *A Mad World, My Masters*, the Bodleian Library copy of the 1608 first quarto (Q); *Michaelmas Term*, the Henry E. Huntington Library copy of the 1607 first quarto (Q); *A Trick to Catch the Old One*, the Bodleian Library copy of the 1608 first quarto (Q); *No Wit, No Help Like a Woman's*, the Shakespeare Folger Library copy of the 1657 first edition in octavo (O). I have recorded and discussed any substantive emendations to the copy-texts in the Explanatory Notes.

Modernizing the copy-text has been done silently most of the time. On occasion I have retained Q punctuation when its archaic placement makes a clear difference in meaning, otherwise I have modernized it, though I doubt that total consistency here has been achieved. Spelling has also been modernized and standardized and any interpretative problems as a consequence have been dealt with in the *Notes*. Stage directions have been standardized and, where helpful, expanded; there are a number of new ones, designed usually to clarify where characters are on (or off) the stage or what they are doing. Speech prefixes have been regularized and printed in full. The past participle or preterite ending in 'ed' has a grave accent over the 'e' when the syllable is stressed.

As the original editions of Middleton's plays were not divided into scenes, the location of each scene is a matter of inference and conjecture. I have given the probable location for these scenes in square brackets, but the reader should bear in mind that the Jacobean stage was non-locational and relatively bare of scenery or any other indication of place.

There is always a difficulty in editing Middleton to know at times whether a passage (or even a single line) should be in verse or prose. The problem is no doubt due in part to Middleton's habits as a writer of manuscripts. He uses small capitals or minuscules at the heads of lines, crowds lines into a small space, and occasionally completes verse lines at the left margin. But I suspect that the compositors' confusion was mainly caused by a general tendency in Middleton to write a prose that often sounds like indifferent verse and a verse that would have been better off for having been prose. Suffice to say that I have followed the practice of more recent editors in rendering suspect passages in prose rather than verse.

SELECT BIBLIOGRAPHY

Although there have been a number of interesting books and articles in recent years dealing with different aspects of Middleton's drama, the most rewarding work has been done in attempts to see him, his contemporaries, and their plays as part of the larger cultural, literary, and theatrical environment. (An exemplary instance of this inclusive approach is the collection of essays by Kastan and Stallybrass.) In particular, there have been a number of provocative discussions of genre: what is city comedy, why did it become for a while the dominant form for comedy, what version of it did Middleton write, why did romance snuff it out? Anatomists of the genre owe a debt to the earlier work of Knights, Bradbrook, and Gibbons. In the early 1970s, two important books appeared, Covatta's *Thomas Middleton's City Comedies* and Leggatt's *Citizen Comedy in the Age of Shakespeare*. The first attacked the common misconception of Middleton as essentially a realistic writer, made interesting connections between the city comedies and Middleton's later comedy, and forcefully argued for Middleton as an ironist rather than a satirist. The second placed Middleton's city comedy in the context of the genre as it was practised by Middleton's contemporaries.

From these treatments of the topic sprang a number of other perspicacious works on city comedies: Carrithers's article on the ambiguous status of literacy in them; Horwich's on their economics of love; Wells's on their city ideology; and a highly readable book by G. K. Paster, *The Idea of the City in the Age of Shakespeare*, an impressive theoretical work exploring the notion of the city in the drama as a 'parodic form of inverted community' (p. 156). An interesting book along these lines is Leinwand's, although he may exaggerate the plays' capacity to arouse an audience's scepticism about the London they dramatize. Indeed, the most recent work to deal with Jacobean city comedy questions the emphasis traditionally placed by critics since Knights on the excoriating function of the drama, and also the usefulness of the term 'city comedy' itself. Instead, Douglas Bruster's book, while acknowledging the plays' satiric drive, elevates comedy's carnivalesque treatment of London life into what he calls the 'materialist vision' (p. 38) in which the triumph of the commodification of urban life is (largely) celebrated.

More generally, casting the net into deeper cultural waters, there have been a number of provocative theoretical and/or historical discussions recently of great value for a deeper understanding of Middleton's work. An impressive piece from a theoretical point of view is Michael Bristol's *Carnival and Theatre* which offers us a new and more convincing Elizabethan World Picture under the tutelage of Bakhtin rather than Tillyard. Mary Beth Rose writes cogently about the 'eros-as-lust and lust-as-commodity' (p. 48) version of love and sexuality in the city comedies. This should be read in tandem with Gail Paster's other important book on the representations of the body in Renaissance drama and the collection of essays by Susan Zimmerman. An extremely important book for an understanding of the vexed question of Middleton's moral and religious positions is Margot Heinemann's. George Rowe's *Thomas Middleton and the New Comedy Tradition* addresses large and important issues of lineage for the city comedies in a convincing and arresting manner. *The Cambridge Companion to English Renaissance Drama* (1990) has a number of important articles, especially those by Braunmuller and Hattaway. Articles by Bruster, Maus, and Slights make impressive reading. The older theoretical work by the iconoclastic Richard Levin has not lost its capacity to arouse fear and admiration.

On Middleton more directly, there are good introductions by Mulryne and Brittin. A useful collection of essays, '*Accompaninge the players*', edited by Kenneth Friedenreich, appeared in 1983, which includes the impressive essay by Roma Gill, 'The World of Thomas Middleton'. David Holmes's book is still very readable and so too is Hallett's, though his emphasis on Middleton's inadequacies as a writer and his contention that Middleton has only one subject, 'the baseness of the urban middle class' (p. 5), seem rather grudging and simplistic. There is an interesting and useful collection of responses to Middleton from readers, editors, playgoers, and critics in the seventeenth, eighteenth, and nineteenth centuries, collected by Sara Steen. Rereading Parker's seminal essay is always worth while and there are a couple of helpful bibliographies by Brooks and Steen. Finally, a word should be said about a number of editions of Middleton's city comedies which I have found particularly helpful in their annotation and sophisticated in their critical approaches. Especially impressive are those by Loughrey and Taylor, Frost, Price, Salgado, and Levin.

City Comedy

Bradbrook, M. C., 'The Anatomy of Knavery: Jonson, Marston, Middleton', in id. *The Growth and Structure of Elizabethan Comedy*, London: Chatto & Windus, 1955, 136–64.

Bruster, Douglas, *Drama and the Market in the Age of Shakespeare*, Cambridge: Cambridge University Press, 1992.

Carrithers, Gale H. Jr., 'City-Comedy's Sardonic Hierarchy of Literacy', *Studies in English Literature*, 29 (1989), 337–55.

Covatta, Anthony, *Thomas Middleton's City Comedies*, Lewisburg, Pa.: Bucknell University Press, 1973.

Gibbons, Brian, *Jacobean City Comedy: A Study of Satiric Plays by Jonson, Marston and Middleton*, Cambridge, Mass.: Harvard University Press, 1968.

Horwich, Richard, 'Wives, Courtesans, and the Economics of Love in Jacobean City Comedy', *Comparative Drama*, 7 (1973–4), 291–309.

Knights, L. C., *Drama and Society in the Age of Jonson*. New York: Stewart, 1937.

Leinwand, T. B., *The City Staged: Jacobean Comedy, 1603–1613*, Madison, Wis.: University of Wisconsin Press, 1986.

Leggatt, Alexander, *Citizen Comedy in the Age of Shakespeare*, Toronto: University of Toronto Press, 1973.

Paster, G. K., *The Idea of the City in the Age of Shakespeare*, Athens, Ga.: University of Georgia Press, 1985.

Wells, Susan, 'Jacobean City Comedy and the Ideology of the City', *English Literary History*, 48 (1981), 37–60.

General

Braunmuller, R. A. and Hattaway, Michael (eds.), *The Cambridge Companion to English Renaissance Drama*, Cambridge: Cambridge University Press, 1990.

Bristol, Michael D., *Carnival and Theater: Plebeian Culture and the Structure of Authority in Renaissance England*, New York: Methuen, 1985.

Bruster, Douglas, 'The Horn of Plenty: Cuckoldry and Capital in the Drama in the Age of Shakespeare', *Studies in English Literature*, 30 (1990), 195–215.

Heinemann, Margot, *Puritanism and Theatre: Thomas Middleton and Opposition Drama under the Early Stuarts*, Past and Present Publications, Cambridge: Cambridge University Press, 1980.

Kastan, David Scott and Stallybrass, Peter (eds.), *Staging the Renaissance: Reinterpretations of Elizabethan and Jacobean Drama*, New York: Routledge, 1991.

Levin, Richard, *The Multiple Plot in English Renaissance Drama*, Chicago: University of Chicago Press, 1971.

—— *New Readings v. Old Plays*, Chicago: University of Chicago Press, 1979.

Maus, Katharin E., 'Horns of Dilemma: Jealousy, Gender, and Spectatorship in English Renaissance Drama', *English Literary History*, 54 (1981), 561–83.

Paster, G. K., *The Body Embarrassed: Drama and the Disciplines of Shame in Early Modern England*, Ithaca, NY: Cornell University Press, 1993.

Rose, Mary Beth, *The Expense of Spirit: Love and Sexuality in English Renaissance Drama*, Ithaca, NY: Cornell University Press, 1988.

Rowe, George E., Jr., *Thomas Middleton and the New Comedy Tradition*, Lincoln, Nebr.: University of Nebraska Press, 1979.

Slights, William W. E., 'Unfashioning the Man of Mode: A Comic Countergenre in Marston, Jonson, and Middleton', *Renaissance Drama*, NS 15 (1984), 69–91.

Zimmerman, Susan (ed.), *Erotic Politics: Desire on the Renaissance Stage*, New York: Routledge, 1992.

Middleton

Brittin, Norman A., *Thomas Middleton*, Twayne's English Authors Series, 139, New York: Twayne, 1972.

Brooks, John B., 'Recent Studies in Middleton (1971–1981)', *English Literary Renaissance*, 14 (1984), 114–28.

Friedenreich, Kenneth (ed.), *'Accompaninge the players': Essays Celebrating Thomas Middleton, 1580–1980*, New York: AMS Press, 1983.

Gill, Roma, 'The World of Thomas Middleton', in Kenneth Friedenreich (ed.), *'Accompaninge the players': Essays Celebrating Thomas Middleton, 1580–1980* (New York, 1983), 15–38.

Hallett, C. A., *Middleton's Cynics: A Study of Middleton's Insight into the Moral Psychology of the Mediocre Mind*, Jacobean Drama Studies, 47, Salzburg: Institut für Englische Sprache und Literatur, 1975.

Holmes, David M., *The Art of Thomas Middleton*, Oxford: Oxford University Press, 1970.

Mulryne, J. R., *Thomas Middleton*, Writers and their Work, 268, Cardiff: Longman, 1979.

Parker, R. B., 'Middleton's Experiments with Comedy and Judgement', *Jacobean Theatre*, Stratford-upon-Avon Studies, 1, New York: St Martin's Press, 1960, 179–200.

Steen, Sara Jane, *Thomas Middleton: a Reference Guide*, Boston: G. K. Hall, 1984.

——*Ambrosia in An Earthern Vessel: Three Centuries of Audience and Reader Response to the Works of Thomas Middleton*, New York: AMS Press, 1993.

Editions

Frost, David L. (ed.), *The Selected Plays of Thomas Middleton*, Cambridge: Cambridge University Press, 1978.

Levin, Richard (ed.), *Michaelmas Term*, Regents Renaissance Drama Series, Lincoln, Nebr.: University of Nebraska Press, 1966.

Loughrey, Bryan and Taylor, Neil (eds.), *Thomas Middleton: Five Plays*, Penguin Classics, Harmondsworth: Penguin, 1988.

Price, G. R. (ed.), *Thomas Middleton: Michaelmas Term and A Trick to Catch the Old One*, Studies in English Literature, 91, The Hague: Mouton, 1976.

Salgado, Gamini (ed.), *Four Jacobean City Comedies*, Harmondsworth: Penguin, 1975.

A CHRONOLOGY OF
THOMAS MIDDLETON

1580 Birth of Thomas Middleton.

1597 *The Wisdom of Solomon Paraphrased* (poem) published.

1598 Matriculates at Queen's College, Oxford, April 9.

1599 *Micro-Cynicon: Six Snarling Satires* (poem) published.

1600 *Ghost of Lucrece* (poem) published.

c.1602 Marries Mary Marbeck; *The Chester Tragedy, or Randall Earl of Chester* (lost); *The Family of Love*; *Blurt Master Constable*; *Caesar's Fall* (with Dekker, Drayton, Munday, and Webster) (lost).

c.1603 *The Phoenix*; *The True Narration of the Entertainment of His Royal Majesty from Edinburgh till London* (pamphlet).

c.1604 Son, Edward, born; *The Ant and the Nightingale, or Father Hubbard's Tales* (pamphlet) published; *The Black Book* (pamphlet) published; *The Puritan, or The Widow of Watling Street*; *The Honest Whore, Part I* (with Dekker).

c.1605 *A Mad World, My Masters*; *Michaelmas Term*; *A Trick to Catch the Old One*.

1606 *The Viper and Her Brood* (lost).

c.1607 *Your Five Gallants*.

c.1608 *The Roaring Girl* (with Dekker).

1609 *Sir Robert Sherley's Entertainment in Cracovia* (pamphlet).

c.1611 *A Chaste Maid in Cheapside*; *The Second Maiden's Tragedy*; *Wit at Several Weapons* (with Rowley).

1612 *No Wit, No Help Like a Woman's*.

1613 *The New River Entertainment* (pageant); *The Triumphs of Truth* (pageant).

1614 *The Masque of Cupid* (lost).

c.1615 *The Witch*; *More Dissemblers Besides Women*.

c.1616 *The Mayor of Quinborough or Hengist King of Kent*; *The Widow*; *The Nice Valour* (with Fletcher?); *Civitatis Amor* (pageant).

1617 *A Fair Quarrel* (with Rowley); *The Triumphs of Honour and Industry* (pageant).

c.1618 *The Old Law* (with Massinger and Rowley); *The Peacemaker* (pamphlet).

1619 *Inner Temple Masque or Masque of Heroes*; *The World Tossed at Tennis* (with Rowley); *The Triumphs of Love and Antiquity* (pageant); *On the Death of Richard Burbage* (poem).

1620 Appointed City Chronologer; *The Marriage of the Old and New Testament* (pamphlet).

A MAD WORLD, MY MASTERS

THE ACTORS IN THE COMEDY

Sir Bounteous Progress,° an old rich knight
Richard Follywit,° Sir Bounteous Progress's nephew°
Penitent Brothel,° a country gentleman
Mawworm,° a lieutenant ⎱ comrades to Follywit
Hoboy,° an ancient   ⎰   5
Inesse   ⎱ two elder brothers°
Possibility ⎰
Harebrain,° a citizen
Gunwater,° Sir Bounteous's man
Jasper, Penitent's man   10
Rafe,° Harebrain's man
Two Knights
A Constable
A Succubus [as Mistress Harebrain]
Watchmen   15
A Footman
An Old Gentlewoman, mother to the courtesan
Mistress Harebrain, the citizen's wife
Frank° Gullman, the courtesan
Attendants   20

[1.1]

Enter Dick Follywit, and his consorts, Lieutenant Mawworm,
Ancient Hoboy, and others his comrades°

MAWWORM Oh captain, regent, principal!

HOBOY What shall I call thee? The noble spark of bounty, the
lifeblood of society.

FOLLYWIT Call me your forecast,° you whoresons. When you come
drunk out of a tavern, 'tis I must cast your plots into form still;   5
'tis I must manage the prank, or I'll not give a louse for the
proceeding; I must let fly my civil fortunes,° turn wild-brain, lay
my wits upo'th'tenters,° you rascals, to maintain a company of
villains, whom I love in my very soul and conscience.

MAWWORM Aha, our little forecast.   10

FOLLYWIT Hang you, you have bewitched me among you. I was as
well given° till I fell to be wicked, my grandsire had hope of me;
I went all in black,° swore but o'Sundays,° never came home drunk
but upon fasting nights to cleanse my stomach;° 'slid, now I'm
quite altered, blown into light colours,° let out oaths by th'minute,   15
sit up late till it be early, drink drunk till I am sober, sink down
dead in a tavern, and rise in a tobacco shop. Here's a transformation. I was wont yet to pity the simple, and leave 'em some
money; 'slid, now I gull 'em without conscience; I go without
order, swear without number, gull without mercy, and drink   20
without measure.

MAWWORM I deny the last, for if you drink ne'er so much, you drink
within measure.

FOLLYWIT How prove you that, sir?

MAWWORM Because the drawers never fill their pots.   25

FOLLYWIT Mass,° that was well found out; all drunkards may
lawfully say they drink within measure by that trick. And now
I'm put i'th'mind of a trick, can you keep your countenance,
villains? Yet I am a fool to ask that, for how can they keep their
countenance,° that have lost their credits?   30

HOBOY I warrant you for blushing,° captain.

FOLLYWIT I easily believe that, ancient, for thou lost thy colours°
once. Nay, faith, as for blushing, I think there's grace little enough
amongst you all; 'tis Lent in your cheeks, the flag's down.° Well,
your blushing face I suspect not, nor indeed greatly your laughing   35

3

face, unless you had more money in your purses.° Then thus
compendiously now. You all know the possibilities of my hereafter
fortunes, and the humour of my frolic grandsire, Sir Bounteous
Progress, whose death makes all possible to me: I shall have all
when he has nothing; but now he has all I shall have nothing. I   40
think one mind runs through a million of 'em; they love to keep
us sober all the while they're alive, that when they're dead we may
drink to their healths; they cannot abide to see us merry all the
while they're above ground, and that makes so many laugh at their
fathers' funerals. I know my grandsire has his will in a box, and   45
has bequeathed all to me when he can carry nothing away; but
stood I in need of poor° ten pounds now, by his will I should hang
myself ere I should get it. There's no such word in his will, I
warrant you, nor no such thought in his mind.

MAWWORM You may build upon that, captain.   50

FOLLYWIT Then since he has no will to do me good as long as he
lives, by mine own will I'll do myself good before he dies. And
now I arrive at the purpose. You are not ignorant, I'm sure, you
true and necessary implements of mischief, first, that my grandsire
Sir Bounteous Progress is a knight of thousands, and therefore   55
no knight since one thousand six hundred;° next, that he keeps a
house like his name, bounteous, open for all comers; thirdly and
lastly, that he stands much upon the glory of his complement,
variety of entertainment, together with the largeness of his kitchen, longitude of his buttery, and fecundity of his larder, and   60
thinks himself never happier than when some stiff lord or great
countess alights to make light his dishes. These being well
mixed together may give my project better encouragement, and
make my purpose spring forth more fortunate. To be short, and
cut off a great deal of dirty way,° I'll down° to my grandsire like   65
a lord.

MAWWORM How, captain?

FOLLYWIT A French ruff,° a thin beard, and a strong perfume will
do't. I can hire blue coats for you all by Westminster clock,° and
that colour° will be soonest believed.   70

MAWWORM But prithee, captain—

FOLLYWIT Push, I reach past your fathoms;° you desire crowns.

MAWWORM From the crown of our head, to the sole of our foot,
bully.

FOLLYWIT Why, carry yourselves but probably,° and carry away   75
enough with yourselves.

4

HOBOY Why, there spoke a Roman captain.°
       Enter Master Penitent Brothel
    Master Penitent Brothel.
PENITENT Sweet Master Follywit.
       Exeunt [all but Penitent Brothel]
    Here's a mad-brain o'th'first,° whose pranks° scorn to have preced-   80
    ents, to be second to any, or walk beneath any mad-cap's inventions;
    he's played more tricks° than the cards can allow a man, and of the
    last stamp° too, hating imitation; a fellow whose only glory is to be
    prime of the company, to be sure of which, he maintains all the rest.
    He's the carrion and they the kites that gorge upon him.   85
    But why in others do I check wild passions
    And retain deadly follies in myself?
    I tax his youth of common received riot,°
    Time's comic flashes, and the fruits of blood;°
    And in myself soothe up adulterous motions,   90
    And such an appetite that I know damns me,
    Yet willingly embrace it—love to Harebrain's wife,
    Over whose hours and pleasures her sick husband,
    With a fantastic but deserved suspect,°
    Bestows his serious time in watch and ward.°   95
    And therefore I'm constrained to use the means
    Of one that knows no mean, a courtesan,
    One poison for another, whom her husband°
    Without suspicion innocently admits
    Into her company, who with tried art°   100
    Corrupts and loosens her most constant powers,
    Making his jealousy more than half a wittol,
    Before his face plotting his own abuse
    To which himself gives aim,°
    Whilst the broad arrow with the forkèd head°   105
    Misses his brow but narrowly.
       Enter Courtesan
                        See, here she comes,
    The close courtesan, whose mother is her bawd.°
COURTESAN Master Penitent Brothel.
PENITENT My little pretty Lady Gullman, the news, the comfort?
COURTESAN Y'are the fortunate man, sir, Knight o'th'Holland   110
    Skirt.° There wants but opportunity, and she's wax of your own
    fashioning. She had wrought herself into the form of your love,
    before my art set finger to her.

PENITENT Did our affections meet, our thoughts keep time?

COURTESAN So it should seem by the music. The only jar is in the   115
grumbling bass° viol, her husband.

PENITENT Oh, his waking suspicion!

COURTESAN Sigh not, Master Penitent, trust the managing of the
business with me; 'tis for my credit now to see't well finished. If
I do you no good, sir, you shall give me no money, sir.   120

PENITENT I am arrived at the court of conscience.° A courtesan!
Oh admirable times! Honesty is removed to the common place.°
Farewell, lady.

Exit Penitent. Enter Mother

MOTHER How now, daughter?

COURTESAN What news, mother?   125

MOTHER A token from thy keeper.

COURTESAN Oh, from Sir Bounteous Progress. He's my keeper
indeed, but there's many a piece of venison stolen that my
keeper° wots not on; there's no park kept so warily but loses flesh
one time or other, and no woman kept so privately, but may watch   130
advantage to make the best of her pleasure. And in common
reason one keeper cannot be enough for so proud° a park as a
woman.

MOTHER Hold thee there, girl.

COURTESAN Fear not me, mother.   135

MOTHER Every part of the world shoots up daily into more subtlety.
The very spider weaves her cauls with more art and cunning to
entrap the fly.
The shallow ploughman can distinguish now
'Twixt simple truth and a dissembling brow.   140
Your base mechanic fellow can spy out
A weakness in a lord, and learns to flout.
How does't behoove us then that live by sleight,
To have our wits wound up to their stretched height!
Fifteen times thou know'st I have sold thy maidenhead,   145
To make up a dowry for thy marriage, and yet
There's maidenhead enough for old Sir Bounteous still;
He'll be all his lifetime about it yet,
And be as far to seek when he has done.°
The sums that I have told upon thy pillow!   150
I shall once see those golden days again;°
Though fifteen, all thy maidenheads are not gone.°
The Italian is not served yet, nor the French;

6

The British men come for a dozen at once,°
They engross all the market. Tut, my girl,   155
'Tis nothing but a politic conveyance,°
A sincere carriage, a religious eyebrow,°
That throws their charms over the worldlings' senses;
And when thou spiest a fool that truly pities
The false springs of thine eyes,   160
And honourably dotes upon thy love,
If he be rich set him by for a husband.
Be wisely tempered and learn this, my wench:
Who gets th'opinion for a virtuous name,
May sin at pleasure and ne'er think of shame.   165
COURTESAN Mother, I am too deep a scholar grown
     To learn my first rules now.
MOTHER   'Twill be thy own.°
     I say no more. Peace, hark, remove thyself.
          [*Exit Courtesan*]
     Oh, the two elder brothers.
          Enter Inesse and Possibility
POSSIBILITY A fair hour, sweet lady.   170
MOTHER Good morrow, gentlemen, Master Inesse and Master
     Possibility.
INESSE Where's the little sweet lady your daughter?
MOTHER Even at her book, sir.
POSSIBILITY So religious?   175
MOTHER 'Tis no new motion, sir; she's took it from an infant.
POSSIBILITY May we deserve a sight of her, lady?
MOTHER Upon that condition you will promise me, gentlemen, to
     avoid all profane talk, wanton compliments, undecent phrases, and
     lascivious courtings (which I know my daughter will sooner die   180
     than endure), I am contented your suits shall be granted.
POSSIBILITY Not a bawdy syllable, I protest.
INESSE Syllable was well-placed° there, for, indeed, your one syl-
     lables are your bawdiest words: prick° that down.
          Exeunt

[1.2]

Enter Master Harebrain

HAREBRAIN She may make nightwork on't; 'twas well recovered.°
He-cats and courtesans stroll most i'th'night;°
Her friend may be received and conveyed forth nightly.
I'll be at charge for watch and ward, for watch and ward i'faith;°
And here they come.   5
    Enter two or three [Watchmen]

FIRST WATCHMAN Give your worship good even.

HAREBRAIN Welcome, my friends. I must deserve your diligence in
an employment serious. The truth is, there is a cunning plot laid,
but happily discovered, to rob my house, the night uncertain when
but fixed within the circle of this month.°   10
Nor does this villainy consist in numbers
Or many partners; only someone
Shall, in the form of my familiar friend,
Be received privately into my house
By some perfidious servant of mine own   15
Addressed fit for the practice.

FIRST WATCHMAN   Oh abominable!°

HAREBRAIN If you be faithful watchmen show your goodness,
And with these angels shore up your eyelids.
    [Gives them money]
Let me not be purloined°—[*aside*] purloined indeed, the merry
Greeks° conceive me.—There is a gem I would not lose, kept by   20
the Italian under lock and key;° we Englishmen are careless
creatures. Well, I have said enough.

SECOND WATCHMAN And we will do enough, sir.

HAREBRAIN Why, well said, watch me a good turn now.
    Exeunt [Watchmen]
So, so, so.   25
Rise villainy with the lark, why, 'tis prevented,
Or steal't by with the leather-wingèd bat,
The evening cannot save it. Peace—°
    [Enter Courtesan]
Oh, Lady Gullman, my wife's only company, welcome. And how
does the virtuous matron, that good old gentlewoman, thy mother?   30
I persuade myself, if modesty be in the world she has part on't. A

8

woman of an excellent carriage all her lifetime, in court, city, and
country.

COURTESAN She's always carried it well° in those places, sir—[*aside*]
witness three bastards apiece.—How does your sweet bedfellow,   35
sir? You see I'm her boldest visitant.

HAREBRAIN And welcome, sweet virgin, the only companion my soul
wishes for her. I left her within at her lute; prithee give her good
counsel.

COURTESAN Alas, she needs none, sir.   40

HAREBRAIN Yet, yet, yet, a little of thy instructions will not come
amiss to her.

COURTESAN I'll bestow my labour, sir.

HAREBRAIN Do, labour her prithee; I have conveyed away all her
wanton pamphlets, as *Hero and Leander, Venus and Adonis*;° oh,   45
two luscious mary-bone° pies for a young married wife. Here,
here, prithee take the *Resolution*° and read to her a little.

COURTESAN She's set up her resolution already, sir.

HAREBRAIN True, true, and this will confirm it the more. There's a
chapter of hell, 'tis good to read this cold weather. Terrify her,   50
terrify her; go, read to her the horrible punishments for itching
wantonness, the pains allotted for adultery; tell her her thoughts,
her very dreams, are answerable, say so; rip up the life of a courtesan
and show how loathsome 'tis.

COURTESAN [*aside*] The gentleman would persuade me in time to   55
disgrace myself and speak ill of mine own function.

    Exit [Courtesan]

HAREBRAIN This is the course I take; I'll teach the married man
A new selected strain. I admit none°
But this pure virgin to her company;
Puh, that's enough. I'll keep her to her stint,°   60
I'll put her to her pension;°
She gets but her allowance, that's a bare one;°
Few women but have that beside their own.°
Ha, ha, ha, nay, I'll put her hard to't.

    Enter Wife [Mistress Harebrain] and Courtesan

MISTRESS HAREBRAIN Fain would I meet the gentleman.   65

COURTESAN Push, fain would you meet him! Why, you do not take
the course.

HAREBRAIN [*aside*] How earnestly she labours her, like a good
wholesome sister of the Family.° She will prevail, I hope.

COURTESAN Is that the means?   70

MISTRESS HAREBRAIN What is the means? I would as gladly, to
  enjoy his sight, embrace it as the—
COURTESAN Shall I have hearing? Listen—
HAREBRAIN [*aside*] She's round with her i'faith.
COURTESAN When husbands in their rank'st suspicions dwell,   75
  Then 'tis our best art to dissemble well.
  Put but these notes in use that I'll direct you,
  He'li curse himself that e'er he did suspect you.
  Perhaps he will solicit you, as in trial,
  To visit such and such; still give denial,   80
  Let no persuasions sway you; they are but fetches
  Set to betray you, jealousies, sleights, and reaches.
  Seem in his sight to endure the sight of no man;
  Put by all kisses till you kiss in common;
  Neglect all entertain; if he bring in   85
  Strangers, keep you your chamber, be not seen;
  If he chance steal upon you, let him find
  Some book lie open 'gainst an unchaste mind
  And coted scriptures, though for your own pleasure°
  You read some stirring pamphlet and convey it   90
  Under your skirt, the fittest place to lay it.
  This is the course, my wench, to enjoy thy wishes;
  Here you perform best when you most neglect;
  The way to daunt is to outvie suspect.
  Manage these principles but with art and life;   95
  Welcome all nations, thou'rt an honest wife.°
HAREBRAIN [*aside*] She puts it home i'faith, even to the quick;°
  From her elaborate action I reach that.°
  I must requite this maid—faith, I'm forgetful.
MISTRESS HAREBRAIN Here, lady,   100
  Convey my heart unto him in this jewel.
  Against you see me next you shall perceive°
  I have profited. In the mean season, tell him
  I am a prisoner yet a'th'master's side:°
  My husband's jealousy,   105
  That masters him as he doth master me,
  And as a keeper that locks prisoners up
  Is himself prisoned under his own key,
  Even so my husband, in restraining me,
  With the same ward bars his own liberty.   110
COURTESAN I'll tell him how you wish it, and I'll wear

My wits to the third pile but all shall clear.°

MISTRESS HAREBRAIN I owe you more than thanks, but that I hope
My husband will requite you.

COURTESAN Think you so, lady? He has small reason for't.   115

HAREBRAIN [joining them] What, done so soon? Away, to't again, to't
again, good wench, to't again; leave her not so. Where left you?
Come—

COURTESAN Faith, I am weary, sir.
I cannot draw her from her strict opinion   120
With all the arguments that sense can frame.°

HAREBRAIN No? Let me come. Fie, wife, you must consent.
What opinion is't? Let's hear.

COURTESAN Fondly and wilfully she retains that thought
That every sin is damned.   125

HAREBRAIN Oh, fie, fie, wife! Pea, pea, pea, pea, how have you lost
your time? For shame, be converted. There's a diabolical opinion
indeed. Then you may think that usury were damned; you're a fine
merchant i'faith. Or bribery? you know the law well. Or sloth?
would some of the clergy heard you i'faith. Or pride? you come at   130
court! Or gluttony? you're not worthy to dine at an alderman's
table.
Your only deadly sin's adultery,
That villainous ringworm, woman's worst requital.°
'Tis only lechery that's damned to th'pit-hole;°   135
Ah, that's an arch-offence; believe it, squall,
All sins are venial but venereal.

COURTESAN I've said enough to her.

HAREBRAIN And she will be ruled by you.

COURTESAN Fah!   140

HAREBRAIN I'll pawn my credit on't. Come hither, lady,
I will not altogether rest ingrateful.
Here, wear this ruby for thy pains and counsel.

COURTESAN It is not so much worth, sir. I am a very ill counsellor,
truly.   145

HAREBRAIN Go to, I say.

COURTESAN Y'are too blame, i'faith, sir; I shall ne'er deserve it.

HAREBRAIN Thou hast done't already. Farewell, sweet virgin, prithee
let's see thee oftener.

COURTESAN [aside] Such gifts will soon entreat me.   150
        Exit [Courtesan]

HAREBRAIN Wife, as thou lov'st the quiet of my breast,

Embrace her counsel, yield to her advices;
Thou wilt find comfort in 'em in the end,°
Thou'lt feel an alteration; prithee think on't.°
Mine eyes can scarce refrain.°   155

MISTRESS HAREBRAIN Keep in your dew, sir, lest when you would
you want it.

HAREBRAIN I've pawned my credit on't. Ah, didst thou know
The sweet fruit once, thou'dst never let it go.°

MISTRESS HAREBRAIN 'Tis that I strive to get.

HAREBRAIN   And still do so.   160

    Exeunt

[2.1]

Enter Sir Bounteous with Two Knights [Sir Andrew Polcut and Sir Aquitaine Colewort]

SIR ANDREW You have been too much like your name, Sir Bounteous.

SIR BOUNTEOUS Oh, not so, good knights, not so, you know my humour; most welcome, good Sir Andrew Polcut, Sir Aquitaine Colewort,° most welcome.

BOTH Thanks, good Sir Bounteous.

Exeunt at one door [Sir Andrew and Sir Aquitaine.] At the other, enter in haste a Footman

FOOTMAN Oh, cry your worship heartily mercy, sir.

SIR BOUNTEOUS How now, linen stockings° and threescore-mile-a-day,° whose footman art thou?

FOOTMAN Pray can your worship tell me—[*panting*] hoh, hoh, hoh—if my lord be come in yet?

SIR BOUNTEOUS Thy lord! What lord?

FOOTMAN My Lord Owemuch, sir.

SIR BOUNTEOUS My Lord Owemuch! I have heard much speech of that lord; h'as great acquaintance in the city.° That lord has been much followed.°

FOOTMAN And is still, sir; he wants no company when he's in London. He's free of the mercers,° and there's none of 'em all dare cross° him.

SIR BOUNTEOUS An they did, he'd turn over a new leaf° with 'em; he would make 'em all weary on't i'th'end. Much fine rumour have I heard of that lord, yet had I never the fortune to set eye upon him. Art sure he will alight here, footman? I am afraid thou'rt mistook.

FOOTMAN Thinks your worship so, sir? [*Going*] By your leave, sir.

SIR BOUNTEOUS Puh! Passion of me, footman! Why, pumps, I say come back.

FOOTMAN Does your worship call?

SIR BOUNTEOUS Come hither, I say. I am but afraid on't; would it might happen so well. How dost know? Did he name the house with the great turret a'th'top?

FOOTMAN No, faith, did he not, sir. [*Going*]

SIR BOUNTEOUS Come hither, I say. Did he speak of a cloth o'gold chamber?

FOOTMAN Not one word, by my troth, sir. [*Going*]

SIR BOUNTEOUS Come again, you lousy seven-mile-an-hour.°   35

FOOTMAN I beseech your worship, detain me not.

SIR BOUNTEOUS Was there no talk of a fair pair of organs, a great gilt candlestick, and a pair of silver snuffers?

FOOTMAN 'Twere sin to belie my lord; I heard no such words, sir. [*Going*]   40

SIR BOUNTEOUS A pox confine° thee, come again! Puh!

FOOTMAN Your worship will undo me, sir.

SIR BOUNTEOUS Was there no speech of a long dining room, a huge kitchen, large° meat, and a broad dresser board?

FOOTMAN I have a greater maw to that, indeed, an't please your   45
worship.

SIR BOUNTEOUS Whom did he name?

FOOTMAN Why, one Sir Bounteous Progress.

SIR BOUNTEOUS Ah, a, a, I am that Sir Bounteous, you progressive°
round-about rascal.   50

FOOTMAN (*laughs*) Puh.

SIR BOUNTEOUS I knew I should have him i'th'end; there's not a
lord will miss me, I thank their good honours; 'tis a fortune laid
upon me, they can scent out their best entertainment; I have a
kind of complimental gift given me above ordinary country   55
knights, and how soon 'tis smelt out! I warrant ye there's not
one knight i'th'shire able to entertain a lord i'th'cue, or a lady
i'th'nick,° like me.° There's a kind of grace belongs to't, a kind
of art which naturally slips from me, I know not on't, I promise
you, 'tis gone before I'm aware on't.° Cuds me, I forget myself.   60
Where!
          [*Enter two Servants*]

FIRST SERVANT Does your worship call?

SIR BOUNTEOUS Run, sirrah, call in my chief gentleman i'th'chain
of gold;° expedite.
          [*Exit First Servant*]
And how does my good lord? I never saw him before in my   65
life.—A cup of bastard for this footman.

FOOTMAN My lord has travelled this five year, sir.

SIR BOUNTEOUS Travailed° this five year? How many children has
he?—Some bastard I say!

FOOTMAN No bastard,° an't please your worship.   70

SIR BOUNTEOUS A cup of sack to strengthen his wit.
          [*Exit Second Servant*]

The footman's a fool.

    [Enter Gunwater]

Oh, come hither, Master Gunwater, come hither. Send presently
to Master Pheasant for one of his hens; there's partridge i'th'house.

GUNWATER And wild duck, an't please your worship.   75

SIR BOUNTEOUS And woodcock,° an't please thy worship.

GUNWATER And woodcock, an't please your worship. I had thought
to have spoke before you.

SIR BOUNTEOUS Remember the pheasant, down with some plover,
clap down six woodcocks: my lord's° coming. Now, sir?   80

GUNWATER An't please your worship, there's a lord and his followers
newly alighted.

SIR BOUNTEOUS Dispatch, I say, dispatch! Why, where's my music?°
He's come indeed.

    *[Exit Gunwater.] Enter Follywit like a lord with his comrades
    in blue coats*

FOLLYWIT Footman.   85

FOOTMAN My lord?

FOLLYWIT Run swiftly with my commendations to Sir Jasper
Topaz; we'll ride and visit him i'th'morning, say.

FOOTMAN Your lordship's charge shall be effected.°

    Exit [Footman]

FOLLYWIT That courtly, comely form should present to me Sir   90
Bounteous Progress.

SIR BOUNTEOUS Y'ave found me out, my lord; I cannot hide myself.
Your honour is most spaciously welcome.

FOLLYWIT In this forgive me, sir,
That being a stranger to your houses and you,   95
I make my way so bold, and presume
Rather upon your kindness than your knowledge;°
Only your bounteous disposition
Fame hath divulged, and is to me well known.

SIR BOUNTEOUS Nay, an your lordship know my disposition, you   100
know me better than they that know my person; your honour is so
much the welcomer for that.

FOLLYWIT Thanks, good Sir Bounteous.

SIR BOUNTEOUS Pray pardon me, it has been often my ambition, my
lord, both in respect of your honourable presence, and the prodigal   105
fame that keeps even stroke with your unbounded worthiness, to
have wished your lordship where your lordship is, a noble guest in
this unworthy seat. Your lordship ne'er heard my organs?

FOLLYWIT Heard of 'em, Sir Bounteous, but never heard 'em.

SIR BOUNTEOUS They're but double gilt, my lord; some hundred   110
and fifty pound will fit your lordship with such another pair.

FOLLYWIT Indeed, Sir Bounteous?

SIR BOUNTEOUS Oh, my lord, I have a present suit° to you.

FOLLYWIT To me, Sir Bounteous? And you could ne'er speak at
fitter time, for I'm here present to grant you.   115

SIR BOUNTEOUS Your lordship has been a traveller?

FOLLYWIT Some five year, sir.

SIR BOUNTEOUS I have a grandchild, my lord. I love him, and when
I die I'll do somewhat for him. I'll tell your honour the worst of
him: a wild lad he has been.   120

FOLLYWIT So we have been all, sir.

SIR BOUNTEOUS So we have been all indeed, my lord, I thank your
lordship's assistance. Some comic pranks he has been guilty of, but
I'll pawn my credit for him, an honest, trusty bosom.

FOLLYWIT And that's worth all, sir.   125

SIR BOUNTEOUS And that's worth all, indeed, my lord, for he's like
to have all when I die. *Imberbis juvenis*,° his chin has no more
prickles yet than a midwife's;° there's great hope of his wit, his
hair's so long a-coming.° Shall I be bold with your honour to prefer
this aforesaid Ganymede to hold a plate under your lordship's cup?   130

FOLLYWIT You wrong both his worth and your bounty, an you
call that boldness. Sir, I have heard much good of that young
gentleman.

SIR BOUNTEOUS Nay, h'as a good wit i'faith, my lord.

FOLLYWIT He's carried himself always generously.°   135

SIR BOUNTEOUS Are you advised of that, my lord? He's carried
many things cleanly.° I'll show your lordship my will; I keep it
above in an outlandish box. The whoreson boy must have all; I
love him, yet he shall ne'er find it as long as I live.

FOLLYWIT Well, sir, for your sake and his own deserving, I'll reserve   140
a place for him nearest to my secrets.

SIR BOUNTEOUS I understand your good lordship, you'll make him
your secretary. My music, give my lord a taste of his welcome.

*A strain played by the consort, Sir Bounteous makes a courtly
honour° to that lord and seems to foot° the tune°*

SIR BOUNTEOUS So how like you our airs, my lord? Are they choice?

FOLLYWIT They're seldom matched, believe it.   145

SIR BOUNTEOUS The consort of mine own household.

FOLLYWIT Yea, sir.

SIR BOUNTEOUS The musicians are in ordinary,° yet no ordinary
    musicians. Your lordship shall hear my organs now.

FOLLYWIT Oh, I beseech you, Sir Bounteous.   150

SIR BOUNTEOUS My organist!

    The organs play, and [*servants carrying*] *covered dishes march*
    over the stage

Come, my lord, how does your honour relish my organ?

FOLLYWIT A very proud air i'faith, sir.

SIR BOUNTEOUS Oh, how can't choose? A Walloon plays upon 'em,
    and a Welshman° blows wind in their breech.   155

    Exeunt. A song to the organs°

[2.2]

    Enter Sir Bounteous with Follywit and his consorts
    [*Mawworm, Hoboy and others*] *toward his lodging*

SIR BOUNTEOUS You must pardon us, my lord, hasty cates. Your
    honour has had even a hunting meal on't; and now I am as like to
    bring your lordship to as mean a lodging—a hard down bed i'faith,
    my lord, poor cambric sheets, and a cloth o'tissue canopy. The
    curtains° indeed were wrought in Venice with the story of the   5
    prodigal child° in silk and gold; only the swine are left out, my
    lord, for spoiling the curtains.

FOLLYWIT 'Twas well prevented, sir.

SIR BOUNTEOUS Silken rest, harmonious slumbers, and venereal
    dreams to your lordship.   10

FOLLYWIT The like to kind Sir Bounteous.

SIR BOUNTEOUS Fie, not to me, my lord. I'm old, past dreaming of
    such vanities.

FOLLYWIT Old men should dream best.

SIR BOUNTEOUS They're dreamers° indeed, my lord, y'ave gi'n't°   15
    us. Tomorrow your lordship shall see my cocks, my fish ponds,
    my park, my champion grounds; I keep chambers° in my house
    can show your lordship some pleasure.

FOLLYWIT Sir Bounteous, you even° whelm me with delights.

SIR BOUNTEOUS Once again a musical night to your honour; I'll   20
    trouble your lordship no more.

FOLLYWIT Good rest, Sir Bounteous.

    Exit [*Sir Bounteous*]

So, come, the vizards; where be the masquing suits?

MAWWORM In your lordship's portmantua.

FOLLYWIT Peace, lieutenant.   25

MAWWORM I had rather have war, captain.

FOLLYWIT Puh, the plot's ripe. Come, to our business, lad;
  Though guilt condemns, 'tis gilt must make us glad.

MAWWORM Nay, an you be at your distinctions,° captain,
  I'll follow behind no longer.   30

FOLLYWIT Get you before then and whelm your nose with your
  vizard—go.
      [*Exeunt Mawworm, Hoboy, and others*]
  Now, grandsire, you that hold me at hard meat,°
  And keep me out at the dag's end, I'll fit you.°
  Under his lordship's leave all must be mine,°   35
  He and his will confesses. What I take, then,
  Is but a borrowing of so much beforehand.
  I'll pay him again, when he dies, in so many blacks;
  I'll have the church hung round with a noble a yard,
  Or requite him in scutcheons. Let him trap me   40
  In gold, and I'll lap him in lead: *quid pro quo*. I°
  Must look none of his angels in the face, forsooth,
  Until his face be not worth looking on. Tut, lads,
  Let sires and grandsires keep us low, we must
  Live when they're flesh as well as when they're dust.   45
      Exit

[2.3]

Enter Courtesan with her man

COURTESAN Go, sirrah, run presently to Master Penitent Brothel;
  you know his lodging, knock him up. I know he cannot sleep for
  sighing.
  Tell him I've happily bethought a mean
  To make his purpose prosper in each limb,   5
  Which only rests to be approved by him.
  Make haste, I know he thirsts for't.
      Exeunt

[2.4]

Enter, in a masking suit with a vizard in his hand, Follywit

[GUNWATER] WITHIN Oh!

FOLLYWIT Hark, they're at their business.

[GUNWATER]° WITHIN Thieves, thieves!

FOLLYWIT Gag that gaping rascal! Though he be my grandsire's chief gentleman i'th'chain of gold, I'll have no pity of him.   5

Enter the rest [Mawworm, Hoboy and others] vizarded

How now, lads?

MAWWORM All's sure and safe. On with your vizard, sir; the servants are all bound.

FOLLYWIT There's one care past then. Come follow me, lads, I'll lead you now to th'point and top of all your fortunes. Yon lodging   10
is my grandsire's.

MAWWORM So, so, lead on, on.

HOBOY Here's a captain worth the following, and a wit worth a man's love and admiring!

Exeunt [Follywit, Mawworm, Hoboy and others] [Re-]enter [Follywit, Mawworm, Hoboy and others] with Sir Bounteous in his nightgown

SIR BOUNTEOUS Oh, gentlemen, an you be kind gentlemen, what   15
countrymen are you?

FOLLYWIT Lincolnshire men, sir.

SIR BOUNTEOUS I am glad of that i'faith.

FOLLYWIT And why should you be glad of that?

SIR BOUNTEOUS Oh, the honestest thieves of all come out of   20
Lincolnshire,° the kindest-natured gentlemen; they'll rob a man with conscience; they have a feeling of what they go about, and will steal with tears in their eyes. Ah, pitiful gentlemen.

FOLLYWIT Push! Money, money, we come for money.

SIR BOUNTEOUS Is that all you come for? Ah, what a beast was I to   25
put out my money t'other day. Alas, good gentlemen, what shift shall I make for you? Pray come again another time.

FOLLYWIT Tut, tut, sir, money.

SIR BOUNTEOUS Oh, not so loud, sir, you're too shrill a gentleman. I have a lord lies in my house; I would not for the world his honour   30
should be disquieted.

FOLLYWIT Who, my Lord Owemuch? We have took order with him beforehand; he lies bound in his bed and all his followers.

SIR BOUNTEOUS Who, my lord? Bound my lord? Alas, what did you
  mean to bind my lord? He could keep his bed well enough without   35
  binding. Y'ave undone me in't already, you need rob me no farther.

FOLLYWIT Which is the key? Come.

SIR BOUNTEOUS Ah, I perceive now y'are no true Lincolnshire
  spirits; you come rather out of Bedfordshire: we cannot lie quiet
  in our beds for you. So, take enough, my masters; spur a free   40
  horse,° my name's Sir Bounteous. A merry world i'faith; what
  knight but I keep open house at midnight? Well, there should be
  a conscience° if one could hit upon't.

FOLLYWIT Away now; seize upon him, bind him.

SIR BOUNTEOUS Is this your court of equity? Why should I be   45
  bound° for mine own money? But come, come, bind me, I have
  need on't; I have been too liberal tonight. Keep in my hands; nay,
  as hard as you list, I am [not]° too good to bear my lord company.
  You have watched your time, my masters; I was knighted at
  Westminster° but many of these nights will make me a knight of   50
  Windsor.° Y'ave deserved so well, my masters, I bid you all to
  dinner tomorrow; I would I might have your companies i'faith; I
  desire no more.

FOLLYWIT Oh ho, sir!

    [*Follywit finds more booty*]

SIR BOUNTEOUS Pray meddle not with my organs, to put 'em out of   55
  tune.

FOLLYWIT Oh no, here's better music, sir.

SIR BOUNTEOUS Ah, pox feast you!

FOLLYWIT Dispatch with him, away.

    [*Exeunt Hoboy and others carrying Sir Bounteous*]
  So, thank you, good grandsire; this was bounteously done of him   60
  i'faith. It came somewhat hard from him at first, for indeed
  nothing comes stiff from an old man but money; and he may well
  stand upon° that when he has nothing else to stand upon. Where's
  our portmantua?

MAWWORM Here, bully captain.   65

FOLLYWIT In with the purchase, 'twill lie safe enough there under's
  nose, I warrant you.

    Enter [Hoboy and others]
  What, is all sure?

HOBOY All's sure, captain.

FOLLYWIT You know what follows now; one villain binds his   70
  fellows. Go, we must be all bound for our own securities,° rascals,

there's no dallying upo'th'point. You conceit me. There is a lord
to be found bound in the morning, and all his followers; can you
pick out that lord now?

MAWWORM Oh admirable spirit!   75

FOLLYWIT You ne'er plot for your safeties, so your wants be
satisfied.

HOBOY But if we bind one another, how shall the last man be bound?

FOLLYWIT Pox on't, I'll have the footman 'scape.

FOOTMAN That's I; I thank you, sir.   80

FOLLYWIT The footman, of all other,° will be supposed to 'scape,
for he comes in no bed all night, but lies in's clothes to be first
ready i'th'morning. The horse and he lies in litter together; that's
the right fashion of your bonny footman. And his freedom will
make the better for our purpose, for we must have one i'th'morn-   85
ing to unbind the knight, that we may have our sport within
ourselves. We now arrive at the most ticklish point, to rob and take
our ease, to be thieves and lie by't.° Look to't, lads, it concerns
every man's gullet; I'll not have the jest spoiled, that's certain,
though it hazard a windpipe.° I'll either go like a lord as I came,   90
or be hanged like a thief as I am; and that's my resolution.

MAWWORM Troth, a match, captain, of all hands.

        Exeunt

[2.5]

Enter Courtesan with Master Penitent Brothel

COURTESAN Oh, Master Penitent Brothel!

PENITENT What is't, sweet Lady Gullman, that so seizes on thee
with rapture and admiration?

COURTESAN A thought, a trick, to make you, sir, especially happy,
and yet I myself a saver° by it.   5

PENITENT I would embrace that, lady, with such courage I would
not leave you on the losing hand.

COURTESAN I will give trust to you, sir, the cause then why I raised
you from your bed so soon, wherein I know sighs would not let
you sleep; thus understand it.   10
You love that woman, Master Harebrain's wife,
Which no invented means can crown with freedom
For your desires and your own wish° but this,

Which in my slumbers did present itself.

PENITENT I'm covetous, lady.   15

COURTESAN You know her husband, ling'ring in suspect,
Locks her from all society but mine.

PENITENT Most true.

COURTESAN I only am admitted, yet hitherto that has done you no
real happiness; by my admittance I cannot perform that deed that   20
should please you, you know. Wherefore thus I've conveyed° it,
I'll counterfeit a fit of violent sickness.

PENITENT Good.

COURTESAN Nay, 'tis not so good, by my faith, but to do you good.

PENITENT And in that sense I called it. But take me with you,°   25
lady, would it be probable enough to have a sickness so suddenly
violent?

COURTESAN Puh, all the world knows women are soon down; we can
be sick when we have a mind to't, catch an ague with the wind of
our fans, surfeit upon the rump of a lark, and bestow ten pound in   30
physic upon't; we're likest ourselves when we're down. 'Tis the
easiest art and cunning for our sect to counterfeit sick, that are
always full of fits when we are well; for since we were made for a
weak, imperfect creature, we can fit that best that we are made for.
I thus translated, and yourself slipped into the form of a physician—   35

PENITENT I a physician, lady? Talk not on't, I beseech you; I shall
shame the whole college.°

COURTESAN Tut, man, any quacksalving terms will serve for this
purpose; for I am pitifully haunted with a brace of elder brothers,
new perfumed in the first of their fortunes, and I shall see how   40
forward their purses will be to the pleasing of my palate, and
restoring of my health. Lay on load enough upon 'em and spare
'em not, for they're good plump fleshly asses, and may well enough
bear it. Let gold, amber and dissolved pearl be common ingredients,
and that you cannot compose a cullis without 'em. Put but this   45
cunningly in practice, it shall be both a sufficient recompense for
all my pains in your love, and the ready means to make Mistress
Harebrain way, by the visiting of me, to your mutual desired
company.°

PENITENT I applaud thee, kiss thee, and will constantly embrace it.   50
Exeunt

[2.6]

[Sir Bounteous] within. [Follywit, bound, on stage behind curtains]°

SIR BOUNTEOUS Ho, Gunwater!°

FOLLYWIT Singlestone!°

SIR BOUNTEOUS Jenkin, wa, ha, ho!

FOLLYWIT Ewen!°

SIR BOUNTEOUS Simcod!°   5

FOLLYWIT Footman! Whew!

> *Enter Sir Bounteous with a cord, half unbound, Footman with him*

FOOTMAN Oh, good your worship, let me help your good old worship.

SIR BOUNTEOUS Ah, poor honest footman, how didst thou 'scape this massacre?   10

FOOTMAN E'en by miracle, and lying in my clothes, sir.

SIR BOUNTEOUS I think so; I would I had lain in my clothes too, footman, so I had 'scaped 'em; I could have but risse like a beggar then, and so I do now, till more money come in. But nothing afflicts me so much, my poor geometrical footman, as that the   15
barbarous villains should lay violence upon my lord. Ah, the binding of my lord cuts my heart in two pieces.

> *[Footman releases him]*

So, so, 'tis well, I thank thee; run to thy fellows, undo 'em, undo 'em, undo 'em.

FOOTMAN Alas, if my lord should miscarry, they're unbound   20
already, sir; they have no occupation but sleep, feed, and fart.

> *Exit [Footman]*

SIR BOUNTEOUS If I be not ashamed to look my lord i'th'face, I'm a Saracen. My lord—

FOLLYWIT *[behind curtains]* Who's that?

SIR BOUNTEOUS One may see he's been scarred, a pox on 'em for   25
their labours.

FOLLYWIT Singlestone!

SIR BOUNTEOUS Singlestone? I'll ne'er answer to that i'faith.

FOLLYWIT Suchman!

SIR BOUNTEOUS Suchman?° Nor that neither i'faith; I am not   30
brought so low though I be old.

FOLLYWIT Who's that i'th'chamber?

SIR BOUNTEOUS [*opens curtains*] Good morrow, my lord, 'tis I.

FOLLYWIT Sir Bounteous, good morrow. I would give you my hand, sir, but I cannot come at it. Is this the courtesy o'th'country, Sir Bounteous? 35

SIR BOUNTEOUS Your lordship grieves me more than all my loss;
'Tis the unnatural'st sight that can be found,
To see a noble gentleman hard bound.°

FOLLYWIT Trust me, I thought you had been better beloved, Sir Bounteous; but I see you have enemies, sir, and your friends fare the worse for 'em. I like your talk better than your lodging; I ne'er lay harder in a bed of down; I have had a mad night's rest on't. Can you not guess what they should be, Sir Bounteous? 40

SIR BOUNTEOUS Faith, Lincolnshire men, my lord. 45

FOLLYWIT How? Fie, fie, believe it not, sir; these lie not far off, I warrant you.

SIR BOUNTEOUS Think you so, my lord?

FOLLYWIT I'll be burnt, an they do; some that use to° your house, sir, and are familiar with all the conveyances.° 50

SIR BOUNTEOUS This is the commodity of keeping open house, my lord, that makes so many shut their doors about dinner time.

FOLLYWIT They were resolute villains. I made myself known to 'em, told 'em what I was, gave 'em my honourable word not to disclose 'em— 55

SIR BOUNTEOUS Oh saucy, unmannerly villains!

FOLLYWIT And think you the slaves would trust me upon my word?

SIR BOUNTEOUS They would not?

FOLLYWIT Forsooth, no. I must pardon 'em, they told me lords' promises were mortal, and commonly die within half an hour after they are spoken; they were but gristles, and not one amongst a hundred come to any full growth or perfection, and therefore, though I were a lord, I must enter into bond.° 60

SIR BOUNTEOUS Insupportable rascals!

FOLLYWIT Troth, I'm of that mind, Sir Bounteous. You fared the worse for my coming hither. 65

SIR BOUNTEOUS Ah, good my lord, but I'm sure your lordship fared the worse.

FOLLYWIT Pray pity not me, sir.

SIR BOUNTEOUS Is not your honour sore about the brawn of the arm? A murrain meet 'em, I feel it. 70

FOLLYWIT About this place, Sir Bounteous?

SIR BOUNTEOUS You feel as it were a twinge, my lord?

24

FOLLYWIT Ay, e'en a twinge; you say right.

SIR BOUNTEOUS A pox discover 'em, that twinge I feel too. 75

FOLLYWIT But that which disturbs me most, Sir Bounteous, lies here.

SIR BOUNTEOUS True, about the wrist a kind of tumid numbness.

FOLLYWIT You say true, sir.

SIR BOUNTEOUS The reason of that, my lord, is the pulses had no play. 80

FOLLYWIT Mass, so I guessed it.

SIR BOUNTEOUS A mischief swell 'em, for I feel that too.

    [*Enter Mawworm*]

MAWWORM 'Slid, here's a house haunted indeed.

SIR BOUNTEOUS [*to Mawworm*] A word with you, sir.

FOLLYWIT How now, Singlestone? 85

MAWWORM I'm sorry, my lord, your lordship has lost—

SIR BOUNTEOUS [*to Mawworm*] Pup, pup, pup, pup, pup!

FOLLYWIT What have I lost? Speak!

SIR BOUNTEOUS [*to Mawworm*] A good night's sleep, say.

FOLLYWIT Speak, what have I lost, I say. 90

MAWWORM A good night's sleep, my lord, nothing else.

FOLLYWIT That's true. My clothes, come!

MAWWORM My lord's clothes! His honour's rising.

    [*Enter Hoboy and others with clothes.*] Curtains drawn.
    [*Follywit, Hoboy and others retire behind the curtains*]

SIR BOUNTEOUS Hist, well said. Come hither; what has my lord lost? Tell me. Speak softly. 95

MAWWORM His lordship must know that, sir.

SIR BOUNTEOUS Hush, prithee tell me.

MAWWORM 'Twill do you no pleasure to know't, sir.

SIR BOUNTEOUS Yet again? I desire it, I say.

MAWWORM Since your worship will needs know't, they have stolen 100
away a jewel in a blue silk ribbon of a hundred pound price, beside some hundred pounds in fair spur-royals.

SIR BOUNTEOUS That's some two hundred i'th'total.

MAWWORM Your worship's much about it, sir.

SIR BOUNTEOUS Come, follow me; I'll make that whole again in so 105
much money. Let not my lord know on't.

MAWWORM Oh, pardon me, Sir Bounteous, that were a dishonour to my lord; should it come to his ear, I should hazard my undoing by it.

SIR BOUNTEOUS How should it come to his ear? If you be my lord's 110
chief man about him, I hope you do not use to speak unless you

be paid for't; and I had rather give you a counsellor's double fee°
to hold your peace. Come, go to; follow me, I say.

MAWWORM There will be scarce time to tell it, sir; my lord will away
instantly.   115

SIR BOUNTEOUS His honour shall stay dinner, by his leave; I'll
prevail with him so far. And now I remember a jest; I bade the
whoreson thieves to dinner last night. I would I might have their
companies, a pox poison 'em!

   Exit [Sir Bounteous]

MAWWORM Faith, and you are like to have no other guests, Sir   120
Bounteous, if you have none but us; I'll give you that gift i'faith.

   Exit

[3.1]

Enter Master Harebrain with two elder brothers, Master Inesse and Master Possibility

POSSIBILITY You see bold guests, Master Harebrain.

HAREBRAIN You're kindly welcome to my house, good Master Inesse and Master Possibility.

INESSE That's our presumption, sir.

HAREBRAIN Rafe!   5

    [Enter Rafe]

RAFE Here, sir.

HAREBRAIN Call down your mistress to welcome these two gentlemen, my friends.

RAFE I shall, sir.

    Exit [Rafe]

HAREBRAIN *[aside]* I will observe her carriage and watch   10
  The slippery revolutions of her eye;
  I'll lie in wait for every glance she gives,
  And poise her words i'th'balance of suspect;
  If she but swag, she's gone, either on this hand
  Overfamiliar, or this too neglectful;   15
  It does behoove her carry herself even.

POSSIBILITY But Master Harebrain—

HAREBRAIN True, I hear you, sir; was't you said?

POSSIBILITY I have not spoke it yet, sir.

HAREBRAIN Right, so I say.   20

POSSIBILITY Is it not strange that in so short a time my little Lady Gullman should be so violently handled?

HAREBRAIN Oh, sickness has no mercy, sir.
  It neither pities ladies' lip nor eye;
  It crops the rose out of the virgin's cheek   25
  And so deflowers her that was ne'er deflowered.°
  Fools, then, are maids to lock from men that treasure
  Which death will pluck and never yield 'em pleasure.
  Ah, gentlemen, though I shadow it, that sweet virgin's sickness grieves me not lightly; she was my wife's only delight and   30
company. Did you not hear her, gentlemen, i'th'midst of her most extremest fit, still how she called upon my wife, remembered still my wife, sweet Mistress Harebrain? When she sent for me, o'one

side of her bed stood the physician, the scrivener° on the other;
two horrible objects, but mere opposites in the course of their   35
lives, for the scrivener binds folks, and the physician makes them
loose.°

POSSIBILITY But not loose of their bonds, sir?

HAREBRAIN No, by my faith, sir, I say not so. If the physician could
make 'em loose of their bonds, there's many a one would take   40
physic that dares not now for° poisoning. But as I was telling of
you, her will was fashioning wherein I found her best and richest
jewel given as a legacy unto my wife. When I read that, I could
not refrain weeping. Well, of all other, my wife has most reason to
visit her; if she have any good nature in her, she'll show it there.   45
    [Enter Rafe]
Now, sir, where's your mistress?

RAFE She desires you and the gentlemen your friends to hold her
excused; sh'as a fit of an ague now upon her, which begins to
shake her.

HAREBRAIN Where does it shake her most?   50

RAFE All over her body, sir.

HAREBRAIN Shake all her body? 'Tis a saucy fit; I'm jealous of that
ague. Pray walk in, gentlemen, I'll see you instantly.
    [Exeunt Inesse and Possibility]

RAFE Now that they are absent, sir, 'tis no such thing.

HAREBRAIN What?   55

RAFE My mistress has her health, sir,
But 'tis her suit she may confine herself
From sight of all men but your own dear self, sir;
For since the sickness of that modest virgin,
Her only company, she delights in none.   60

HAREBRAIN No? Visit her again, commend me to her,
Tell her they're gone and only I myself
Walk here to exchange a word or two with her.

RAFE I'll tell her so, sir.
    Exit [Rafe]

HAREBRAIN Fool that I am, and madman, beast! What worse?   65
Suspicious o'er a creature that deserves
The best opinion and the purest thought;
Watchful o'er her that is her watch herself;
To doubt her ways that looks too narrowly
Into her own defects. I, foolish-fearful,   70
Have often rudely, out of giddy flames,°

Barred her those objects which she shuns herself.
Thrice I've had proof of her most constant temper;°
Come I at unawares by stealth upon her,
I find her circled in with divine writs   75
Of heavenly meditations; here and there
Chapters with leaves tucked up, which when I see,
They either tax pride or adultery.
Ah, let me curse myself that could be jealous
Of her whose mind no sin can make rebellious.   80
And here the unmatched comes.
    [*Enter Mistress Harebrain*]
                             Now, wife, i'faith they're gone.
Push, see how fearful 'tis; will you not credit me?°
They're gone i'faith; why, think you I'll betray you?
Come, come, thy delight and mine, thy only virtuous friend, thy
  sweet instructress, is violently taken, grievous sick, and which is   85
  worse, she mends not.

MISTRESS HAREBRAIN Her friends are sorry for that, sir.

HAREBRAIN She calls upon thee, poor soul, remembers thee still,
  thy name whirls in her breath. 'Where's Mistress Harebrain?' says
  she.   90

MISTRESS HAREBRAIN Alas, good soul.

HAREBRAIN She made me weep thrice; she's put thee in a jewel in
  her will.

MISTRESS HAREBRAIN E'en to the last gasp a kind soul.

HAREBRAIN Take my man, go, visit her.   95

MISTRESS HAREBRAIN Pray pardon me, sir; alas, my visitation
  cannot help her.

HAREBRAIN Oh, yet the kindness of a thing, wife.—[*Aside*] Still she
  holds the same rare temper.—Take my man, I say.

MISTRESS HAREBRAIN I would not take your man, sir, though I did   100
  purpose going.

HAREBRAIN No? Thy reason?

MISTRESS HAREBRAIN The world's condition is itself so vile, sir,
  'Tis apt to judge the worse of those deserve not;
  'Tis an ill-thinking age, and does apply   105
  All to the form of it own luxury.°
  This censure flies from one, that from another;
  That man's her squire, says he; her pimp, the t'other;°
  She's of the stamp, a third; fourth, I ha' known her.°
  I've heard this not without a burning cheek.   110

Then our attires are taxed, our very gait
Is called in question, where a husband's presence
Scatters such thoughts, or makes 'em sink for fear
Into the hearts that breed 'em. Nay, surely,
If I went, sir, I would entreat your company.   115

HAREBRAIN Mine? Prithee, wife, I have been there already.

MISTRESS HAREBRAIN That's all one; although you bring me but to
th'door, sir, I would entreat no farther.

HAREBRAIN Thou'rt such a wife! Why, I will bring thee thither,
then, but not go up, I swear.   120

MISTRESS HAREBRAIN I'faith you shall not; I do not desire it, sir.

HAREBRAIN Why then, content.

MISTRESS HAREBRAIN Give me your hand you will do so, sir.

HAREBRAIN Why, [kissing her] there's my lip, I will.

MISTRESS HAREBRAIN Why then, I go, sir.   125

HAREBRAIN With me or no man, incomparable such a woman.

    Exeunt

[3.2]

*Viols, gallipots,° plate,° and an hourglass by her. The
Courtesan on a bed for her counterfeit fit. To her, Master
Penitent Brothel, like a doctor of physic*

PENITENT Lady!

COURTESAN Ha, what news?

PENITENT There's one Sir Bounteous Progress newly alighted from
his foot-cloth, and his mare waits at door as the fashion is.

COURTESAN 'Slid, 'tis the knight that privately maintains me; a little   5
short old spiny gentleman in a great doublet.

PENITENT The same; I know'm.

COURTESAN He's my sole revenue, meat, drink, and raiment. My
good physician, work upon him; I'm weak.

PENITENT Enough.   10

    [Enter Sir Bounteous]

SIR BOUNTEOUS Why, where be these ladies, these plump, soft,
delicate creatures? Ha?

PENITENT Who would you visit, sir?

SIR BOUNTEOUS Visit, who? What are you with the plague in your
mouth?   15

PENITENT A physician, sir.

SIR BOUNTEOUS Then you are a loose liver,° sir; I have put you to your purgation.°

PENITENT [*aside*] But you need none, you're purged in a worse fashion.

COURTESAN Ah, Sir Bounteous.

SIR BOUNTEOUS How now? What art thou?°

COURTESAN Sweet Sir Bounteous.

SIR BOUNTEOUS Passion of me, what an alteration's here! Rosamond sick, old Harry?° Here's a sight able to make an old man shrink; I was lusty when I came in, but I am down now i'faith. Mortality! Yea, this puts me in mind of a hole seven foot deep, my grave, my grave, my grave. Hist, master doctor, a word, sir; hark, 'tis not the plague, is't?

PENITENT The plague, sir? No.

SIR BOUNTEOUS Good.

PENITENT [*aside*] He ne'er asks whether it be the pox or no, and of the twain that had been more likely.

SIR BOUNTEOUS How now, my wench? How dost?

COURTESAN [*coughs*] Huh—weak, knight—huh.

PENITENT [*aside*] She says true; he's a weak knight indeed.

SIR BOUNTEOUS Where does it hold thee most, wench?

COURTESAN All parts alike, sir.

PENITENT [*aside*] She says true, still, for it holds her in none.

SIR BOUNTEOUS Hark in thine ear, thou'rt breeding of young bones; I am afraid I have got thee with child i'faith.

COURTESAN I fear that much, sir.

SIR BOUNTEOUS Oh, oh, if it should! A young Progress when all's done.

COURTESAN You have done your good will,° sir.

SIR BOUNTEOUS [*aside*] I see by her 'tis nothing but a surfeit of Venus,° i'faith, and though I be old I have gi'n't her.—But since I had the power to make thee sick, I'll have the purse to make thee whole, that's certain.—Master doctor.

PENITENT Sir?

SIR BOUNTEOUS Let's hear, I pray, what is't you minister to her.

PENITENT Marry, sir, some precious cordial, some costly refocillation, a composure comfortable and restorative.

SIR BOUNTEOUS Ay, ay, that, that, that.

PENITENT No poorer ingredients° than the liquor of coral;° clear amber, or *succinum;*° unicorn's horn,° six grains; *magisterium perlarum,*° one scruple.

SIR BOUNTEOUS Ah!

PENITENT *Ossis de corde cervi*,° half a scruple; *aurum potabile*° or his
tincture.

SIR BOUNTEOUS Very precious, sir.   60

PENITENT All of which being finely contunded and mixed in a stone
or glass mortar with the spirit of diamber°—

SIR BOUNTEOUS Nay, pray be patient, sir.

PENITENT That's impossible; I cannot be patient and a physician
too, sir.   65

SIR BOUNTEOUS Oh, cry you mercy, that's true, sir.

PENITENT All which aforesaid—

SIR BOUNTEOUS Ay, there you left, sir.

PENITENT When it is almost exsiccate or dry I add thereto *olei*
succini, *olei masi*, and *cinnamoni*.°   70

SIR BOUNTEOUS So, sir, *olei masi*; that same oil of mace° is a great
comfort to both the Counters.

PENITENT And has been of a long time, sir.

SIR BOUNTEOUS Well, be of good cheer, wench; there's gold for
thee.—Huh, let her want for nothing, master doctor; a poor   75
kinswoman of mine; nature binds me to have a care of her.—
[*Aside*] There I gulled you, master doctor.—Gather up a good
spirit, wench, the fit will away; 'tis but a surfeit of gristles.—Ha,
ha, I have fitted her;° an old knight and a cock o'th'game° still; I
have not spurs° for nothing, I see.   80

PENITENT No, by my faith, they're hatched;° they cost you an
angel,° sir.

SIR BOUNTEOUS Look to her, good master doctor, let her want
nothing. I've given her enough already, ha, ha, ha!

    Exit [*Sir Bounteous*]

COURTESAN So, is he gone?   85

PENITENT He's like himself, gone.

COURTESAN Here's somewhat to set up with. How soon he took
occasion to slip into his own flattery, soothing his own defects. He
only fears he has done that deed which I ne'er feared to come from
him in my life. This purchase came unlooked for.   90

PENITENT Hist! The pair of sons and heirs.

COURTESAN Oh, they're welcome; they bring money.

    Enter Master Inesse and Possibility

POSSIBILITY Master doctor.

PENITENT I come to you, gentlemen.

POSSIBILITY How does she now?   95

PENITENT Faith, much after one fashion, sir.

INESSE There's hope of life, sir?

PENITENT I see no signs of death of her.°

POSSIBILITY That's some comfort. Will she take anything yet?

PENITENT Yes, yes, yes, she'll take still; sh'as a kind of facility in   100
taking.° How comes your band bloody, sir?

INESSE You may see I met with a scab, sir.

PENITENT *Diversa genera scabierum*,° as Pliny reports, 'there are
divers kind of scabs'.

INESSE Pray let's hear 'em, sir.   105

PENITENT An itching scab, that is your harlot; a sore scab, your
usurer; a running scab,° your promoter; a broad° scab, your
intelligencer; but a white scab, that's a scald° knave and a pander.
But to speak truth, the only scabs we are nowadays troubled withal
are new officers.   110

INESSE Why, now you come to mine,° sir, for I'll be sworn one of
them was very busy about my head° this morning; and he should
be a scab by that, for they are ambitious and covet the head.°

PENITENT Why, you saw I derived him,° sir.

INESSE You physicians are mad gentlemen.   115

PENITENT We physicians see the most sights of any men living.
Your astronomers look upward into th'air, we look downward into
th'body, and indeed we have power upward and downward.°

INESSE That you have, i'faith, sir.

POSSIBILITY Lady, how cheer you now?   120

COURTESAN The same woman still—huh.

POSSIBILITY That's not good.
        [*Gives money*]

COURTESAN Little alteration. Fie, fie, you have been too lavish,
gentlemen.

INESSE Puh, talk not of that, lady, thy health's worth a million. Here,   125
master doctor, spare for no cost.
        [*Gives money*]

POSSIBILITY Look what you find there, sir.

COURTESAN What do you mean, gentlemen? Put up,° put up; you
see I'm down and cannot strive with you; I would rule you else.
You have me at advantage, but if ever I live I will requite it deeply.   130

INESSE Tut, an't come to that once° we'll requite ourselves well
enough.

POSSIBILITY Mistress Harebrain, lady, is setting forth to visit you
too.

33

COURTESAN Ha!—huh.   135

PENITENT [*aside*] There struck the minute that brings forth the birth
of all my joys and wishes. But see the jar now. How shall I rid
these from her?

COURTESAN Pray, gentlemen, stay not above an hour from my sight.

INESSE 'Sfoot, we are not going, lady.   140

PENITENT [*aside*] Subtly brought about, yet 'twill not do; they'll
stick by it.—A word with you, gentlemen.

BOTH What says master doctor?

PENITENT She wants but settling of her sense with rest. One hour's
sleep, gentlemen, would set all parts in tune.   145

POSSIBILITY He says true i'faith.

INESSE Get her to sleep, master doctor; we'll both sit here and watch
by her.

PENITENT [*aside*] Hell's angels watch you! No art can prevail with
'em. What with the thought of joys, and sight of crosses, my wits   150
are at Hercules' Pillars,° *non plus ultra*.

COURTESAN Master doctor, master doctor!

PENITENT Here, lady.

COURTESAN Your physic works; lend me your hand.
          [*She is placed upon a bed pan*]

POSSIBILITY Farewell, sweet lady.   155

INESSE Adieu, master doctor.
          [*Exeunt Inesse and Possibility*]

COURTESAN So.

PENITENT Let me admire thee!
    The wit of man wanes and decreases soon,
    But women's wit is ever at full moon.   160
          Enter Mistress Harebrain
    There shot a star from heaven;
    I dare not yet behold my happiness,
    The splendour is so glorious and so piercing.

COURTESAN Mistress Harebrain, give my wit thanks hereafter; your
wishes are in sight, your opportunity spacious.   165

MISTRESS HAREBRAIN Will you but hear a word from me?

COURTESAN Whooh!

MISTRESS HAREBRAIN My husband himself brought me to th'door,
walks below for my return. Jealousy is prick-eared and will hear
the wagging of a hair.°   170

COURTESAN Pish, y'are a faint liver.° Trust yourself with your
pleasure and me with your security; go.

34

PENITENT The fullness of my wish!
MISTRESS HAREBRAIN   Of my desire!
PENITENT Beyond this sphere I never will aspire.
  [*Exeunt Penitent and Mistress Harebrain.*] *Enter Master Hare-*
  brain listening°
HAREBRAIN I'll listen, now the flesh draws nigh her end;°   175
 At such a time women exchange their secrets
 And ransack the close corners of their hearts.
 What many years hath whelmed, this hour imparts.
COURTESAN Pray sit down, there's a low stool. Good Mistress
 Harebrain, this was kindly done;—huh—give me your hand;—   180
 huh—alas, how cold you are. Even so is your husband, that
 worthy, wise gentleman; as comfortable a man to woman in my
 case as ever trod°—huh—shoe-leather. Love him, honour him,
 stick by him; he lets you want nothing that's fit for a woman; and
 to be sure on't he will see himself that you want it not.   185
HAREBRAIN And so I do, i'faith, 'tis right my humour.°
COURTESAN You live a lady's life with him, go where you will, ride°
 when you will, and do what you will.
HAREBRAIN Not so, not so neither; she's better looked to.
COURTESAN I know you do, you need not tell me that.° 'Twere   190
 e'en pity of your life, i'faith, if ever you should wrong such
 an innocent gentleman. Fie, Mistress Harebrain, what do you
 mean? Come you to discomfort me? Nothing but weeping with
 you?
HAREBRAIN She's weeping, 't'as made her weep. My wife shows her   195
 good nature already.
COURTESAN Still, still weeping? Huff, huff, huff. Why, how now,
 woman? Hey, hy, hy, for shame, leave. Suh, suh, she cannot
 answer me for snobbing.
HAREBRAIN All this does her good. Beshrew my heart, and I pity   200
 her; let her shed tears till morning. I'll stay for her. She shall have
 enough on't by my good will; I'll not be her hindrance.
COURTESAN Oh no, lay your hand here, Mistress Harebrain. Ay,
 there; oh, there, there lies my pain, good gentlewoman. Sore? Oh,
 ay, I can scarce endure your hand upon't.°   205
HAREBRAIN Poor soul, how she's tormented.
COURTESAN Yes, yes, I ate a cullis an hour since.
HAREBRAIN There's some comfort in that yet; she may 'scape it.
COURTESAN Oh, it lies about my heart much.
HAREBRAIN I'm sorry for that i'faith; she'll hardly 'scape it.   210

COURTESAN Bound?° No, no, I'd a very comfortable stool this morning.

HAREBRAIN I'm glad of that, i'faith, that's a good sign; I smell she'll 'scape it now.

COURTESAN Will you be going then? 215

HAREBRAIN Fall back, she's coming.

COURTESAN Thanks, good Mistress Harebrain; welcome, sweet Mistress Harebrain; pray commend me to the good gentleman your husband—

HAREBRAIN I could do that myself now. 220

COURTESAN And to my Uncle Winchcomb, and to my Aunt Lipsalve, and to my Cousin Falsetop, and to my Cousin Lickit, and to my Cousin Horseman, and to all my good cousins in Clerkenwell and St. John's.°

Enter Wife [Mistress Harebrain] with Master Penitent

MISTRESS HAREBRAIN At three days' end my husband takes a 225
journey.

PENITENT Oh, thence I derive a second meeting.

MISTRESS HAREBRAIN May it prosper still;
Till then I rest a captive to his will.

Once again, health, rest, and strength to thee, sweet lady. Farewell, 230
you witty squall.—Good master doctor, have a care to her body;
if you stand her friend I know you can do her good.

COURTESAN Take pity of your waiter, go. Farewell, sweet Mistress
Harebrain.

[Curtains around the bed are drawn]

HAREBRAIN Welcome, sweet wife, alight upon my lip. Never was 235
hour spent better.

MISTRESS HAREBRAIN Why, were you within the hearing, sir?

HAREBRAIN Ay, that I was i'faith, to my great comfort; I deceived
you there, wife, ha, ha!

I do entreat thee, nay, conjure thee, wife,° 240
Upon my love, or what can more be said,
Oft'ner to visit this sick, virtuous maid.

MISTRESS HAREBRAIN Be not so fierce; your will shall be obeyed.

HAREBRAIN Why then, I see thou lov'st me.

Exeunt [all but Penitent Brothel]

PENITENT Art of ladies! 245
When plots are e'en past hope and hang their head,
Set with a woman's hand, they thrive and spread.°

Exit

[3.3]

*Enter Follywit with Lieutenant Mawworm, Ancient Hoboy,
and the rest of his consorts*

FOLLYWIT Was't not well managed, you necessary mischiefs? Did
the plot want either life or art?

MAWWORM 'Twas so well, captain, I would you could make such
another muss at all adventures.°

FOLLYWIT Dost call't a muss? I am sure my grandsire ne'er got his   5
money worse in his life than I got it from him. If ever he did cozen
the simple, why, I was born to revenge their quarrel; if ever
oppress the widow, I, a fatherless child, have done as much for
him; and so 'tis through the world either in jest or earnest. Let the
usurer look for't; for craft recoils in the end like an overcharged   10
musket and maims the very hand that puts fire to't. There needs
no more but a usurer's own blow to strike him from hence to hell;
'twill set him forward° with a vengeance. But here lay the jest,
whoresons; my grandsire, thinking in his conscience that we
had not robbed him enough o'ernight, must needs pity me   15
i'th'morning and give me the rest.

MAWWORM Two hundred pounds in fair rose nobles, I protest.

FOLLYWIT Push, I knew he could not sleep quietly till he had paid
me for robbing of him too; 'tis his humour and the humour of
most of your rich men in the course of their lives; for you know   20
they always feast those mouths that are least needy, and give them
more that have too much already. And what call you that but
robbing of themselves a courtlier way? Oh!

MAWWORM Cuds me, how now, captain?

FOLLYWIT A cold fit that comes over my memory and has a shrode   25
pull° at my fortunes.

MAWWORM What's that, sir?

FOLLYWIT Is it for certain, lieutenant, that my grandsire keeps an
uncertain creature, a quean?

MAWWORM Ay, that's too true, sir.   30

FOLLYWIT So much the more preposterous° for me; I shall hop
shorter by that trick; she carries away the thirds° at least. 'Twill
prove entailed land,° I am afraid, when all's done i'faith.
Nay, I have known
A vicious, old, thought-acting father,°   35
Damned only in his dreams, thirsting for game

37

(When his best parts hung down their heads for shame),°
For his blanched harlot dispossess his son°
And make the pox his heir; 'twas gravely done.°
How hadst thou first knowledge on't, lieutenant?   40
MAWWORM Faith, from discourse; yet all the policy
That I could use I could not get her name.
FOLLYWIT Dull slave that ne'er couldst spy it!
MAWWORM But the manner of her coming was described to me.
FOLLYWIT How is the manner prithee?   45
MAWWORM Marry, sir, she comes most commonly coached.
FOLLYWIT Most commonly coached indeed;° for coaches are as
    common nowadays as some that ride in 'em. She comes most
    commonly coached—
MAWWORM True, there I left, sir;—guarded with some leash of   50
    pimps.
FOLLYWIT Beside the coachman?
MAWWORM Right, sir. Then alighting, she's privately received by
    Master Gunwater.
FOLLYWIT That's my grandsire's chief gentleman i'th'chain of gold. 55
    That he should live to be a pander and yet look upon his chain
    and his velvet jacket!
MAWWORM Then is your grandsire rounded i'th'ear, the key given
    after the Italian fashion, backward,° she closely conveyed into
    his closet, there remaining till either opportunity smile upon his 60
    credit, or he send down° some hot caudle to take order in his
    performance.°
FOLLYWIT Peace, 'tis mine own i'faith; I ha't.°
MAWWORM How now, sir?
FOLLYWIT   Thanks, thanks to any spirit
    That mingled it 'mongst my inventions.   65
HOBOY Why, Master Follywit!
ALL Captain!
FOLLYWIT Give me scope and hear me.
    I have begot that means which will both furnish me,
    And make that quean walk under his conceit.°   70
MAWWORM That were double happiness, to put thyself into money
    and her out of favour.
FOLLYWIT And all at one dealing.
HOBOY 'Sfoot, I long to see that hand played.
FOLLYWIT And thou shalt see't quickly i'faith; nay, 'tis in grain,° I 75
    warrant it hold colour. Lieutenant, step behind yon hanging; if

I mistook not at my entrance there hangs the lower part of a
gentlewoman's gown with a mask and a chin-clout; bring all this
way. Nay, but do't cunningly now; 'tis a friend's house,° and I'd
use it so—there's a taste for you.°   80
    [*Exit Mawworm*]

HOBOY But prithee what wilt thou do with a gentlewoman's lower
part?

FOLLYWIT Why, use it.

HOBOY Y'ave answered me indeed in that; I can demand no farther.

FOLLYWIT Well said. Lieutenant!   85
    [*Enter Mawworm with clothes*]

MAWWORM What will you do now, sir?

FOLLYWIT Come, come, thou shalt see a woman quickly made up
here.

MAWWORM But that's against kind, captain, for they are always long
a-making ready.   90

FOLLYWIT And is not most they do against kind, I prithee? To lie
with their horse-keeper,° is not that against kind? To wear
half-moons made of another's hair, is not that against kind? To
drink down a man, she that should set him up,° pray is not that
monstrously against kind now? Nay, over with it, lieutenant, over   95
with it; ever while you live put a woman's clothes over her head.
Cupid plays best at blindman buff.

MAWWORM [*dressing Follywit*] You shall have your will, maintenance; I love mad tricks as well as you for your heart, sir. But what
shift will you make for upper bodies,° captain?   100

FOLLYWIT I see now thou'rt an ass. Why, I'm ready.

MAWWORM Ready?

FOLLYWIT Why, the doublet serves as well as the best and is most
in fashion. We're all male to th'middle, mankind from the beaver
to th'bum.° 'Tis an Amazonian time;° you shall have women   105
shortly tread° their husbands. I should have a couple of locks
behind;° prithee, lieutenant, find 'em out for me and wind 'em
about my hatband. Nay, you shall see, we'll be in fashion to a hair°
and become all with probability; the most musty-visage critic shall
not except against me.   110

MAWWORM Nay, I'll give thee thy due behind thy back;° thou art as
mad a piece of clay—

FOLLYWIT Clay! Dost call thy captain clay?° Indeed, clay was made
to stop holes,° he says true. Did not I tell you rascals you should
see a woman quickly made up?   115

HOBOY I'll swear for't, captain.

FOLLYWIT Come, come, my mask and my chin-clout. Come into th'court.

MAWWORM Nay, they were both i'th'court° long ago, sir.

FOLLYWIT Let me see; where shall I choose two or three for pimps   120
now? But I cannot choose amiss amongst you all, that's the best.
Well, as I am a quean you were best have a care of me and guard
me sure; I give you warning beforehand, 'tis a monkey-tailed age.
Life, you shall go nigh° to have half a dozen blithe fellows surprise
me cowardly, carry me away with a pair of oars and put in° at   125
Putney.

MAWWORM We should laugh at that i'faith.

FOLLYWIT Or shoot in upo'th'coast of Cue.

MAWWORM Two notable fit landing places for lechers, P. and C.,
Putney and Cue.°   130

FOLLYWIT Well, say you have fair warning on't. The hair about the
hat is as good as a flag upo'th'pole at a common playhouse to waft
company, and a chin-clout is of that powerful attraction, I can tell
you, 'twill draw more linen to't.

MAWWORM Fear not us, captain; there's none here but can fight for   135
a whore as well as some Inns o'Court man.°

FOLLYWIT Why then, set forward, and as you scorn two-shilling°
brothel,
Twelve-penny panderism, and such base bribes,
Guard me from bonny scribs and bony scribes.°   140

MAWWORM Hang 'em, pensions and allowances, fourpence half-
penny a meal, hang 'em!°

Exeunt

[4.1]

*Enter in his chamber out of his study, Master Penitent
Brothel, a book in his hand, reading*

PENITENT Ha! Read that place again. 'Adultery
    Draws the divorce 'twixt heaven and the soul.'
    Accursèd man that stand'st divorced from heaven,
    Thou wretched unthrift that hast played away
    Thy eternal portion at a minute's game,   5
    To please the flesh hast blotted out thy name.
    Where were thy nobler meditations busied
    That they durst trust this body with itself,
    This natural drunkard that undoes us all
    And makes our shame apparent in our fall?   10
    Then let my blood pay for't and vex and boil.
    My soul, I know, would never grieve to th'death
    The eternal spirit that feeds her with his breath.
    Nay, I that knew the price of life and sin,
    What crown is kept for continence, what for lust,   15
    The end of man, and glory of that end
    As endless as the giver,
    To dote on weakness, slime, corruption, woman!
    What is she took asunder from her clothes?
    Being ready, she consists of a hundred pieces,°   20
    Much like your German clock, and near allied:°
    Both are so nice they cannot go for pride,
    Beside a greater fault, but too well known,
    They'll strike to ten when they should stop at one.°
    Within these three days the next meeting's fixed;   25
    If I meet then hell and my soul be mixed.
    My lodging I know constantly, she not knows.°
    Sin's hate is the best gift that sin bestows;
    I'll ne'er embrace her more; never, bear witness, never.°
      Enter the devil [as a Succubus] in her [Mistress Harebrain's]
      shape, claps him on the shoulder
SUCCUBUS What, at a stand? The fitter for my company.°   30
PENITENT Celestial soldiers guard me!
SUCCUBUS   How now, man?
    'Las, did the quickness of my presence fright thee?

41

PENITENT Shield me you ministers of faith and grace!
SUCCUBUS Leave, leave; are you not ashamed to use
    Such words to a woman?
PENITENT   Th'art a devil.
SUCCUBUS   A devil?   35
    Feel, feel, man; has a devil flesh and bone?°
PENITENT I do conjure thee by that dreadful power—
SUCCUBUS The man has a delight to make me tremble.
    Are these the fruits of thy adventurous love?
    Was I enticed for this? To be soon rejected?   40
    Come, what has changed thee so, delight?
PENITENT   Away!°
SUCCUBUS Remember—
PENITENT   Leave my sight!
SUCCUBUS Have I this meeting wrought with cunning
    Which, when I come, I find thee shunning?
    Rouse thy amorous thoughts and twine me;   45
    All my interest I resign thee.°
    Shall we let slip this mutual hour
    Comes so seldom in our power?°
    Where's thy lip, thy clip, thy fadom?°
    Had women such loves, would't not mad 'em?   50
    Art a man? or dost abuse one?
    A love? and know'st not how to use one?
    Come, I'll teach thee.
PENITENT   Do not follow!
SUCCUBUS Once so firm and now so hollow?
    When was place and season sweeter?   55
    Thy bliss in sight, and dar'st not meet her?
    Where's thy courage, youth, and vigour?
    Love's best pleased, when 't's seared with rigour;
    Sear me then with veins most cheerful,°
    Women love no flesh that's fearful.   60
    'Tis but a fit, come, drink't away,
    And dance and sing and kiss and play.
      [*She sings and dances around him*]
    Fa le la, le la, fa le la, le la la,
    Fa le la, fa la le, la le la!
PENITENT Torment me not!   65
SUCCUBUS Fa le la, fa le la, fa la la loh!
PENITENT Fury!

SUCCUBUS Fa le la, fa le la, fa la la loh!

PENITENT Devil! I do conjure thee once again°
  By that soul-quaking thunder to depart   70
  And leave this chamber freed from thy damned art.
      Succubus stamps and exit,° [*descending through the trap-
      door*]

PENITENT It has prevailed. Oh, my sin-shaking sinews! What should
  I think? Jasper, why, Jasper!
      [*Enter Jasper*]

JASPER Sir. How now? What has disturbed you, sir?

PENITENT A fit, a qualm. Is Mistress Harebrain gone?   75

JASPER Who, sir? Mistress Harebrain?

PENITENT Is she gone, I say?

JASPER Gone? Why, she was never here yet.

PENITENT No?

JASPER Why no, sir.   80

PENITENT Art sure on't?

JASPER Sure on't? If I be sure I breathe and am myself.

PENITENT I like it not. Where kept'st thou?

JASPER I'th'next room, sir.

PENITENT Why, she struck by thee, man.   85

JASPER You'd make one mad, sir; that a gentlewoman should steal
  by me and I not hear her. 'Sfoot, one may hear the ruffling of their
  bums almost an hour before we see 'em.

PENITENT I will be satisfied, although to hazard;
  What though her husband meet me? I am honest.   90
  When men's intents are wicked, their guilt haunts 'em;
  But when they're just, they're armed and nothing daunts 'em.

JASPER [*aside*] What strange humour call you this? He dreams of
  women, and both his eyes broad open!
      Exeunt

[4.2]

Enter at one door Sir Bounteous, at another Gunwater

SIR BOUNTEOUS Why, how now, Master Gunwater? What's the
  news with your haste?

GUNWATER I have a thing to tell your worship.

SIR BOUNTEOUS Why, prithee tell me; speak, man.

GUNWATER Your worship shall pardon me, I have better bringing up   5
    than so.

SIR BOUNTEOUS How, sir?

GUNWATER 'Tis a thing made fit for your ear,° sir.

SIR BOUNTEOUS Oh, oh, oh, cry you mercy; now I begin to taste°
    you. Is she come?   10

GUNWATER She's come, sir.

SIR BOUNTEOUS Recovered, well, and sound° again?

GUNWATER That's to be feared,° sir.

SIR BOUNTEOUS Why, sir?

GUNWATER She wears a linen cloth about her jaw.°   15

SIR BOUNTEOUS Ha, ha, haw! Why, that's the fashion, you whoreson
    Gunwater.

GUNWATER The fashion, sir?
    Live I so long time to see that a fashion
    Which rather was an emblem of dispraise?   20
    It was suspected much in Monsieur's days.°

SIR BOUNTEOUS Ay, ay, in those days; that was a queasy time. Our
    age is better hardened now and put oftener in the fire;° we are tried°
    what we are. Tut, the pox is as natural now as an ague in the spring-
    time; we seldom take physic without it.° Here, take this key, you   25
    know what duties belong to't. Go, give order for a cullis; let there
    be a good fire made i'th'matted chamber, do you hear, sir?

GUNWATER I know my office, sir.
    Exit [Gunwater]

SIR BOUNTEOUS [*to the audience*] An old man's venery is very
    chargeable, my masters; there's much cookery belongs to't.   30
    Exit

[4.3]

Enter Gunwater with Follywit in courtesan's disguise, and masked

GUNWATER Come, lady, you know where you are now?

FOLLYWIT Yes, good Master Gunwater.

GUNWATER This is the old closet, you know.

FOLLYWIT I remember it well, sir.

GUNWATER There stands a casket. I would my yearly revenue were   5
    but worth the wealth that's locked in't, lady; yet I have fifty pound
    a year, wench.

FOLLYWIT Beside your apparel, sir?

GUNWATER Yes, faith, have I.

FOLLYWIT But then you reckon your chain, sir.   10

GUNWATER No, by my troth, do I not neither. Faith, and you
    consider me rightly, sweet lady, you might admit a choice gentle-
    man into your service.°

FOLLYWIT Oh, pray away, sir.

GUNWATER Pusha, come, come, you do but hinder your fortunes   15
    i'faith. I have the command of all the house; I can tell you, nothing
    comes into th'kitchen but comes through my hands.

FOLLYWIT Pray do not handle me, sir.

GUNWATER Faith, y'are too nice, lady. And as for my secrecy, you
    know I have vowed it often to you.   20

FOLLYWIT Vowed it? No, no, you men are fickle.

GUNWATER Fickle? 'Sfoot, bind me, lady.

FOLLYWIT Why, I bind you by virtue of this chain to meet me
    tomorrow at the Flower-de-luce° yonder between nine and ten.

GUNWATER And if I do not, lady, let me lose it, thy love, and my   25
    best fortunes.

            [Gives Follywit the chain]

FOLLYWIT Why now, I'll try you; go to.

GUNWATER Farewell, sweet lady.

        Kisses her, and exit [Gunwater]

FOLLYWIT Welcome, sweet coxcomb; by my faith, a good induc-
    tion.° I perceive by his overworn phrase and his action toward the   30
    middle region° still, there has been some saucy nibbling motion,°
    and no doubt the cunning quean waited but for her prey; and I
    think 'tis better bestowed upon me for his soul's health and his
    body's too. I'll teach the slave to be so bold yet as once to offer to
    vault into his master's saddle i'faith. Now, casket, by your leave; I   35
    have seen your outside oft but that's no proof; some have fair
    outsides that are nothing worth. [He opens the casket] Ha! Now,
    by my faith, a gentlewoman of very good parts: diamond, ruby,
    sapphire, onyx cum prole silexque.° If I do not wonder how the
    quean 'scaped tempting I'm an hermaphrodite. Sure she could lack   40
    nothing but the devil to point to't, and I wonder that he should be
    missing. Well, 'tis better as it is; this is the fruit of old grunting
    venery. Grandsire, you may thank your drab for this; oh fie, in
    your crinkling days, grandsire, keep a courtesan to hinder your
    grandchild! 'Tis against nature, i'faith, and I hope you'll be weary   45
    on't. Now to my villains that lurk close below.

Who keeps a harlot, tell him this from me,
He needs nor thief, disease, nor enemy.
            Exit [Follywit.] Enter Sir Bounteous

SIR BOUNTEOUS Ah, sirrah,° methink I feel myself well toasted,
bumbasted,° scrubbed, and refreshed. But, i'faith, I cannot forget   50
to think how soon sickness has altered her to my taste. I gave her
a kiss at bottom o'th'stairs, and by th'mass, methought her breath
had much ado to be sweet, like a thing compounded, methought,
of wine, beer, and tobacco. I smelt much pudding in't.
It may be but my fancy or her physic;   55
For this I know, her health gave such content,
The fault rests in her sickness or my scent.°
How dost thou now, sweet girl; what, well recovered?
Sickness quite gone, ha? Speak! Ha? Wench? Frank Gullman!
Why, body of me, what's here? My casket wide open, broke open,   60
    my jewels stolen. Why, Gunwater!

GUNWATER [*within*] Anon, anon, sir.

SIR BOUNTEOUS Come hither, Gunwater.

GUNWATER [*within*] That were small manners, sir, i'faith; I'll find a
time anon. Your worship's busy yet.   65

SIR BOUNTEOUS Why, Gunwater!

GUNWATER [*within*] Foh, nay then, you'll make me blush i'faith, sir.
            [*Enter Gunwater*]

SIR BOUNTEOUS Where's this creature?

GUNWATER What creature is't you'd have, sir?

SIR BOUNTEOUS The worst that ever breathes.   70

GUNWATER That's a wild boar,° sir.

SIR BOUNTEOUS That's a vild whore, sir. Where didst thou leave
her, rascal?

GUNWATER Who, your recreation, sir?

SIR BOUNTEOUS My execration, sir!   75

GUNWATER Where I was wont, in your worship's closet.

SIR BOUNTEOUS A pox engross her,° it appears too true. See you
this casket, sir?

GUNWATER My chain, my chain, my chain, my one and only chain!
            Exit [Gunwater]

SIR BOUNTEOUS Thou run'st to much purpose now, Gunwater,   80
yea? Is not a quean enough to answer for, but she must join a
thief to't? A thieving quean! Nay, I have done with her i'faith; 'tis
a sign she's been sick o'late, for she's a great deal worse than she
was.

By my troth, I would have pawned my life upon't. 85
Did she want anything? Was she not supplied?°
Nay, and liberally, for that's an old man's sin;
We'll feast our lechery though we starve our kin.
Is not my name Sir Bounteous? Am I not expressed there?
Ah, fie, fie, fie, fie, fie, but I perceive 90
Though she have never so complete a friend
A strumpet's love will have a waft i'th'end°
And distaste the vessel. I can hardly bear this.°
But say I should complain, perhaps she has pawned 'em.
'Sfoot, the judges will but laugh at it and bid her borrow more money 95
of 'em. 'Make the old fellow pay for's lechery', that's all the mends I
get. I have seen the same case tried at Newbury the last 'sizes.
Well, things must slip and sleep; I will dissemble it
Because my credit shall not lose her lustre;
But whilst I live I'll neither love nor trust her. 100
I ha' done, I ha' done, I ha' done with her i'faith.
       Exit

[4.4]

Master Penitent Brothel knocking within; enter a Servant

SERVANT Who's that knocks?
PENITENT [*within*] A friend.
       Enter Master Penitent
SERVANT What's your will, sir?
PENITENT Is Master Harebrain at home?
SERVANT No, newly gone from it, sir. 5
PENITENT Where's the gentlewoman his wife?
SERVANT My mistress is within, sir.
PENITENT When came she in, I pray?
SERVANT Who, my mistress? She was not out these two days to my
    knowledge. 10
PENITENT No? Trust me, I'd thought I'd seen her. I would request
    a word with her.
SERVANT I'll tell her, sir.
       [*Exit Servant*]
PENITENT I thank you. It likes me worse and worse.
       Enter Mistress Harebrain

47

MISTRESS HAREBRAIN Why, how now, sir? 'Twas desperately ad- 15
   ventured; I little looked for you until the morrow.
PENITENT No? Why, what made you at my chamber then even now?
MISTRESS HAREBRAIN I, at your chamber?
PENITENT Puh, dissemble not; come, come, you were there.
MISTRESS HAREBRAIN By my life, you wrong me, sir. 20
PENITENT What?
MISTRESS HAREBRAIN First, y'are not ignorant what watch keeps
   o'er me;
  And for your chamber, as I live, I know't not.
PENITENT Burst into sorrow then, and grief's extremes,
  Whilst I beat on this flesh!
MISTRESS HAREBRAIN   What is't disturbs you, sir? 25
PENITENT Then was the devil in your likeness there.
MISTRESS HAREBRAIN Ha?
PENITENT The very devil assumed thee formally,
  That face, that voice, that gesture, that attire,
  E'en as it sits on thee, not a pleat altered, 30
  That beaver band, the colour of that periwig,°
  The farthingale above the navel, all,
  As if the fashion were his own invention.
MISTRESS HAREBRAIN Mercy defend me!
PENITENT   To beguile me more,
  The cunning succubus told me that meeting 35
  Was wrought o'purpose by much wit and art,
  Wept to me, laid my vows before me, urged me,
  Gave me the private marks of all our love,
  Wooed me in wanton and effeminate rhymes,
  And sung and danced about me like a fairy; 40
  And had not worthier cogitations blessed me
  Thy form and his enchantments had possessed me.
MISTRESS HAREBRAIN What shall become of me? My own thoughts
   doom me!
PENITENT Be honest; then the devil will ne'er assume thee.
  He has no pleasure in that shape to abide 45
  Where these two sisters reign not, lust or pride.
  He as much trembles at a constant mind
  As looser flesh at him. Be not dismayed;
  Spring souls for joy, his policies are betrayed.°
  Forgive me, Mistress Harebrain, on whose soul° 50
  The guilt hangs double,

My lust and thy enticement; both I challenge,°
And therefore of due vengeance it appeared
To none but me to whom both sins inhered.
What knows the lecher when he clips his whore   55
Whether it be the devil his parts adore?
They're both so like, that, in our natural sense,
I could discern no change nor difference.
No marvel then times should so stretch and turn;
None for religion, all for pleasure burn.   60
Hot zeal into hot lust is now transformed,
Grace into painting, charity into clothes,
Faith into false hair, and put off as often.
There's nothing but our virtue knows a mean;
He that kept open house now keeps a quean.   65
He will keep open still that he commends,°
And there he keeps a table for his friends;
And she consumes more than her sire could hoard,
Being more common than his house or board.
        Enter Harebrain [unnoticed]
Live honest and live happy, keep thy vows;   70
She's part a virgin, whom but one man knows.
Embrace thy husband, and beside him none;
Having but one heart, give it but to one.
MISTRESS HAREBRAIN I vow it on my knees, with tears true bred,
No man shall ever wrong my husband's bed.   75
PENITENT Rise, I'm thy friend forever.
HAREBRAIN [*comes forward*] And I thine forever and ever.
Let me embrace thee, sir, whom I will love
Even next unto my soul, and that's my wife;
Two dear rare gems this hour presents me with,   80
A wife that's modest, and a friend that's right.°
Idle suspect and fear now take your flight.
PENITENT A happy inward peace crown both your joys.
HAREBRAIN Thanks above utterance to you.
        [*Enter Servant*]
                                        Now, the news?
SERVANT Sir Bounteous Progress, sir,   85
Invites you and my mistress to a feast
On Tuesday next; his man attends without.
HAREBRAIN Return both with our willingness and thanks.
        [*Exit Servant*]

I will entreat you, sir, to be my guest.
PENITENT   Who, I, sir?
HAREBRAIN   Faith, you shall.
PENITENT   Well, I'll break strife.°   90
HAREBRAIN   A friend's so rare, I'll sooner part from life.
        Exeunt

[4.5]

        Enter Follywit, the Courtesan striving from him

FOLLYWIT   What, so coy, so strict? Come, come.
COURTESAN   Pray change your opinion, sir; I am not for that use.
FOLLYWIT   Will you but hear me?
COURTESAN   I shall hear that° I would not.
        Exit [Courtesan]
FOLLYWIT   'Sfoot, this is strange. I've seldom seen a wench stand   5
    upon stricter points; life, she will not endure to be courted. Does
    she e'er think to prosper? I'll ne'er believe that tree can bring forth
    fruit that never bears a blossom; courtship's a blossom and often
    brings forth fruit in forty weeks. 'Twere a mad part in me now to
    turn over;° if ever there were any hope on't, 'tis at this instant. Shall   10
    I be madder now than ever I have been? I'm in the way i'faith.
    Man's never at high height of madness full
    Until he love and prove a woman's gull.
    I do protest in earnest, I ne'er knew
    At which end to begin to affect a woman   15
    Till this bewitching minute; I ne'er saw
    Face worth my object, till mine eye met hers.°
    I should laugh, an I were caught i'faith; I'll see her again, that's
    certain, whate'er comes on't.
        Enter the Mother
    By your favour, lady.°   20
MOTHER   You're welcome, sir.
FOLLYWIT   Know you the young gentlewoman that went in lately?
MOTHER   I have best cause to know her; I'm her mother, sir.
FOLLYWIT   Oh, in good time.° I like the gentlewoman well; a
    pretty-contrived beauty.   25
MOTHER   Ay, nature has done her part, sir.
FOLLYWIT   But she has one uncomely quality.

MOTHER What's that, sir?

FOLLYWIT 'Sfoot, she's afraid of a man.

MOTHER Alas, impute it to her bashful spirit; she's fearful of her   30
honour.

FOLLYWIT Of her honour? 'Slid, I'm sure I cannot get her maidenhead with breathing upon her, nor can she lose her honour in her
tongue.

MOTHER True, and I have often told her so. But what would you   35
have of a foolish virgin, sir, a wilful virgin? I tell you, sir, I need
not have been in that solitary estate that I am, had she had grace
and boldness to have put herself forward. Always timorsome,
always backward; ah, that same peevish honour of hers has undone
her and me both, good gentleman. The suitors, the jewels, the   40
jointures that has been offered her! We had been made° women
forever, but what was her fashion? She could not endure the sight
of a man, forsooth, but run and hole° herself presently. So choice
of° her honour, I am persuaded whene'er she has husband
She will e'en be a precedent for all married wives,   45
How to direct their actions and their lives.

FOLLYWIT Have you not so much power with her to command her
presence?

MOTHER You shall see straight what I can do, sir.
        Exit [Mother]

FOLLYWIT Would I might be hanged if my love do not stretch to   50
her deeper and deeper; those bashful maiden humours take me
prisoner. When there comes a restraint on't, upon flesh, we are
always most greedy upon't, and that makes your merchant's wife
oftentimes pay so dear for a mouthful.° Give me a woman as
she was made at first,° simple of herself,° without sophistication,   55
like this wench; I cannot abide them when they have tricks, set
speeches, and artful entertainments. You shall have some so
impudently aspected they will outcry the forehead of a man,°
make him blush first and talk him into silence, and this is
counted manly in a woman. It may hold so; sure, womanly it is   60
not; no,
If e'er I love, or anything move me,
'Twill be a woman's simple modesty.
        Enter Mother bringing in strivingly the Courtesan

COURTESAN Pray let me go; why, mother, what do you mean? I
beseech you, mother! Is this your conquest now? Great glory 'tis   65
to overcome a poor and silly virgin.

FOLLYWIT The wonder of our time sits in that brow;
    I ne'er beheld a perfect maid till now.°
MOTHER Thou childish thing, more bashful than thou'rt wise,
    Why dost thou turn aside and drown thine eyes?   70
    Look, fearful fool, there's no temptation near thee;
    Art not ashamed that any flesh should fear thee?°
    Why, I durst pawn my life the gentleman means no other but
    honest and pure love to thee. How say you, sir?
FOLLYWIT By my faith, not I, lady.   75
MOTHER Hark you there? What think you now, forsooth?
    What grieves your honour now?
    Or what lascivious breath intends to rear
    Against that maiden organ, your chaste ear?
    Are you resolved now better of men's hearts,   80
    Their faith, and their affections? With you none,°
    Or at most few, whose tongues and minds are one.
    Repent you now of your opinion past;
    Men love as purely as you can be chaste.
    To her yourself, sir, the way's broke before you;°   85
    You have the easier passage.
FOLLYWIT   Fear not; come,
    Erect thy happy graces in thy look.
    I am no curious° wooer, but, in faith,
    I love thee honourably.
COURTESAN   How mean you that, sir?
FOLLYWIT 'Sfoot, as one loves a woman for a wife.   90
MOTHER Has the gentleman answered you, trow?
FOLLYWIT I do confess it truly to you both,
    My estate is yet but sickly; but I've a grandsire
    Will make me lord of thousands at his death.
MOTHER I know your grandsire well; she knows him better.   95
FOLLYWIT Why then, you know no fiction. My state then°
    Will be a long day's journey 'bove the waste, wench.°
MOTHER Nay, daughter, he says true.
FOLLYWIT And thou shalt often measure it in thy coach
    And with the wheels' tract make a girdle for't.   100
MOTHER Ah, 'twill be a merry journey.
FOLLYWIT What, is't a match? If't be, clap hands and lips.°
MOTHER 'Tis done, there's witness on't.
FOLLYWIT Why then, mother, I salute you.
        [Kisses her]

MOTHER Thanks, sweet son. Son Follywit, come hither; if I might   105
    counsel thee, we'll e'en take her while the good mood's upon her.
    Send for a priest and clap't up° within this hour.

FOLLYWIT By my troth, agreed, mother.

MOTHER Nor does her wealth consist all in her flesh,
    Though beauty be enough wealth for a woman;   110
    She brings a dowry of three hundred pound with her.

FOLLYWIT 'Sfoot, that will serve till my grandsire dies; I warrant
    you he'll drop away at fall o'th'leaf. If ever he reach to All
    Hollantide I'll be hanged.

MOTHER Oh yes, son, he's a lusty old gentleman.   115

FOLLYWIT Ah, pox, he's given to women; he keeps a quean at this
    present.

MOTHER Fie!

FOLLYWIT Do not tell my wife on't.

MOTHER That were needless i'faith.   120

FOLLYWIT He makes a great feast upon the 'leventh of this month,
    Tuesday next, and you shall see players there. I have one trick
    more to put upon him. My wife and yourself shall go thither
    before as my guests and prove his entertainment; I'll meet you
    there at night. The jest will be here: that feast which he makes will,   125
    unknown to him, serve fitly for our wedding dinner. We shall be
    royally furnished and get some charges° by't.

MOTHER An excellent course, i'faith, and a thrifty. Why, son,
    methinks you begin to thrive before y'are married.

FOLLYWIT We shall thrive one day, wench, and clip enough;°   130
    Between our hopes there's but a grandsire's puff.
        Exit [Follywit]

MOTHER So, girl, here was a bird well caught.

COURTESAN If ever, here;
    But what for's grandsire? 'Twill scarce please him well.

MOTHER Who covets fruit ne'er cares from whence it fell;   135
    Thou'st wedded youth and strength, and wealth will fall.
    Last, thou'rt made honest.

COURTESAN   And that's worth 'em all.
        Exeunt

[5.1]

Enter busily Sir Bounteous Progress [with Gunwater and servants] for the feast

SIR BOUNTEOUS Have a care, blue coats.° Bestir yourself, Master Gunwater, cast an eye into th'kitchen, o'erlook the knaves a little. Every jack has his friend° today, this cousin and that cousin puts in° for a dish of meat; a man knows not till he make a feast how many varlets he feeds; acquaintances swarm in every corner 5 like flies at Barthol'mew-tide that come up with drovers. 'Sfoot, I think they smell my kitchen seven mile about.

[Enter Harebrain, Mistress Harebrain and Penitent Brothel]

Master Harebrain° and his sweet bedfellow, y'are very copiously° welcome.

HAREBRAIN Sir, here's an especial dear friend of ours; we were bold 10 to make his way to your table.

SIR BOUNTEOUS Thanks for that boldness ever, good Master Harebrain.° Is this your friend, sir?

HAREBRAIN Both my wife's friend and mine, sir.

SIR BOUNTEOUS Why then compendiously, sir, y'are welcome. 15

PENITENT In octavo° I thank you, sir.

SIR BOUNTEOUS Excellently retorted i'faith; he's welcome for's wit. I have my sorts of salutes and know how to place 'em courtly. Walk in, sweet gentlemen, walk in, there's a good fire i'th'hall. You shall have my sweet company instantly. 20

HAREBRAIN Ay, good Sir Bounteous.

SIR BOUNTEOUS You shall indeed, gentlemen.

[Exeunt Harebrain, Mistress Harebrain and Penitent Brothel]
Enter Servant

How now, what news brings thee in stumbling now?

SERVANT There are certain players come to town, sir, and desire to interlude before your worship. 25

SIR BOUNTEOUS Players? By the mass, they are welcome; they'll grace my entertainment well. But for certain players, there thou liest, boy; they were never more uncertain in their lives. Now up and now down, they know not when to play, where to play, nor what to play; not when to play for fearful fools,° where to play° 30 for Puritan fools, nor what to play for critical fools. Go, call 'em in.

[Exit Servant]

How fitly the whoresons come upo'th'feast; troth, I was e'en
wishing for 'em.

[*Re-enter Servant with Follywit, Mawworm, Hoboy and others
dressed as players*]

Oh, welcome, welcome, my friends!

FOLLYWIT The month of May delights not in her flowers   35
More than we joy in that sweet sight of yours.

SIR BOUNTEOUS Well acted, o'my credit; I perceive he's your best
actor.

[MAWWORM]° He has greatest share,° sir, and may live of himself,
sir.   40

SIR BOUNTEOUS What, what? [*To Follywit*] Put on your hat,° sir,
pray put on. Go to, wealth must be respected; let those that have
least feathers° stand bare. And whose men are you, I pray? Nay,
keep on your hat still.

FOLLYWIT We serve my Lord Owemuch, sir.   45

SIR BOUNTEOUS My Lord Owemuch? By my troth, the welcom'st
men alive! Give me all your hands at once. That honourable
gentleman? He lay at my house in a robbery once and took all
quietly,° went away cheerfully. I made a very good feast for him.
I never saw a man of honour bear things bravelier away. Serve   50
my Lord Owemuch? Welcome i'faith. Some bastard for my lord's
players!

[*Exit Servant*]

Where be your boys?°

FOLLYWIT They come along with the wagon, sir.

SIR BOUNTEOUS Good, good; and which is your politician amongst   55
you? Now, i'faith, he that works out restraints,° makes best legs° at
court, and has a suit made of purpose for the company's business,
which is he? Come, be not afraid of° him.

FOLLYWIT I am he, sir.

SIR BOUNTEOUS Art thou he? Give me thy hand. Hark in thine ear;   60
thou rollest too fast to gather so much moss as thy fellows° there;
champ upon that. Ah, and what play shall we have, my masters?

FOLLYWIT A pleasant witty comedy, sir.

SIR BOUNTEOUS Ay, ay, ay, a comedy in any case, that I and my
guests may laugh a little. What's the name on't?   65

FOLLYWIT 'Tis called *The Slip*.°

SIR BOUNTEOUS *The Slip*? By my troth, a pretty name and a glib
one. Go all and slip into't as fast as you can.—Cover° a table for
the players.—First take heed of a lurcher;° he cuts deep, he will

eat up all from you.—Some sherry for my lord's players there,   70
sirrah!—Why, this will be a true feast, a right Mitre supper, a play
and all.
      [*Exeunt Follywit and the others*]
More lights!
      Enter Mother and Courtesan
I called for light; here come in two are light° enough for a whole
house i'faith. Dare the thief look me i'th'face? Oh impudent times!   75
Go to, dissemble it!°
MOTHER Bless you, Sir Bounteous!
SIR BOUNTEOUS Oh, welcome, welcome, thief, quean, and bawd,
      welcome all three!
MOTHER Nay here's but two on's, sir.   80
SIR BOUNTEOUS O'my troth, I took her for a couple; I'd have sworn
      there had been two faces there.
MOTHER Not all under one hood,° sir.
SIR BOUNTEOUS Yes, faith, would I, to see mine eyes bear
      double.°   85
MOTHER I'll make it hold, sir; my daughter is a couple. She was
      married yesterday.
SIR BOUNTEOUS Buz!
MOTHER Nay, to no buzzard neither; a right hawk whene'er you
      know him.   90
SIR BOUNTEOUS Away! He cannot be but a rascal. Walk in, walk in,
      bold guests that come unsent for.
      [*Exit Mother*]
[*To the Courtesan*] Soft.° [*Aside*] I perceive how my jewels went
now: to grace her marriage.
COURTESAN Would you with me,° sir?   95
SIR BOUNTEOUS Ay; how happed it, wench, you put the slip upon
      me
   Not three nights since? I name it gently to you;
   I term it neither pilfer, cheat, nor shark.
COURTESAN Y'are past my reach.
SIR BOUNTEOUS I'm old and past your reach, very good; but you   100
      will not deny this, I trust.
COURTESAN With a safe conscience, sir.
SIR BOUNTEOUS Yea? Give me thy hand; fare thee well. I have done
      with her.
COURTESAN Give me your hand, sir; you ne'er yet begun with me.°   105
      Exit [*Courtesan*]

56

SIR BOUNTEOUS Whew, whew! Oh audacious age!
    She denies me and all, when on her fingers
    I spied the ruby sit that does betray her
    And blushes for her fact. Well, there's a time for't,
    For all's too little now for entertainment,°   110
    Feast, mirth, ay, harmony, and the play to boot.
    A jovial season.
            Enter Follywit
                    How now, are you ready?
FOLLYWIT Even upon readiness, sir.
            Takes hat off
SIR BOUNTEOUS Keep you your hat on.
FOLLYWIT I have a suit to your worship.   115
SIR BOUNTEOUS Oh, cry you mercy; then you must stand bare.°
FOLLYWIT We could do all to the life of action, sir, both for the
    credit of your worship's house and the grace of our comedy—
SIR BOUNTEOUS Cuds me, what else, sir?
FOLLYWIT And° for some defects, as the custom is, we would be   120
    bold to require your worship's assistance.
SIR BOUNTEOUS Why, with all my heart; what is't you want?
    Speak.
FOLLYWIT One's a chain for a justice's hat, sir.
SIR BOUNTEOUS [*handing Follywit his chain*] Why, here, here, here,   125
    here, whoreson, will this serve your turn?
FOLLYWIT Excellent well, sir.°
SIR BOUNTEOUS What else lack you?
FOLLYWIT We should use a ring with a stone in't.
SIR BOUNTEOUS Nay, whoops, I have given too many rings already;   130
    talk no more of rings, I pray you. Here, here, here, make this jewel
    serve for once.
FOLLYWIT Oh, this will serve, sir.
SIR BOUNTEOUS What, have you all now?
FOLLYWIT All now, sir. Only Time is brought i'th'middle of the   135
    play, and I would desire your worship's watch.
SIR BOUNTEOUS My watch? With all my heart; only give Time a
    charge that he be not fiddling with it.
FOLLYWIT You shall ne'er see that, sir.
SIR BOUNTEOUS Well, now you are furnished, sir, make haste,   140
    away.
FOLLYWIT E'en as fast as I can, sir.
        [*Exit Sir Bounteous*]

I'll set my fellows going first; they must have aim and leisure, or
they're dull else. I'll stay and speak a prologue, yet o'ertake 'em; I
cannot have conscience, i'faith, to go away and speak ne'er a word   145
to 'em. My grandsire has given me three shares here; sure I'll do
somewhat for 'em.

  Exit

[5.2]

*Enter Sir Bounteous and all the guests [Harebrain, Mistress
Harebrain, Penitent Brothel, Frank Gullman and her
Mother, and other guests; Gunwater and servants]*

SIR BOUNTEOUS More lights! More stools! Sit, sit, the play begins.
HAREBRAIN Have you players here, Sir Bounteous?
SIR BOUNTEOUS We have 'em for you, sir; fine, nimble comedians,
 proper actors most of them.
PENITENT Whose men, I pray you, sir?   5
SIR BOUNTEOUS Oh, there's their credit, sir, they serve an honour-
 able popular gentleman yclipped my Lord Owemuch.
HAREBRAIN My Lord Owemuch? He was in Ireland° lately.
SIR BOUNTEOUS Oh, you ne'er knew any of the name but were great
 travellers.   10
HAREBRAIN How is the comedy called, Sir Bounteous?
SIR BOUNTEOUS Marry, sir, *The Slip*.
HAREBRAIN *The Slip*?
SIR BOUNTEOUS Ay, and here the Prologue begins to slip in
 upon's.   15
HAREBRAIN 'Tis so indeed, Sir Bounteous.
  Enter, for a Prologue, Follywit
      PROLOGUE
FOLLYWIT 'We sing of wand'ring knights, what them betide
 Who nor in one place nor one shape abide;
 They're here now, and anon no scouts can reach 'em,   20
 Being every man well-horsed like a bold Beacham.°
 The play which we present no fault shall meet
 But one: you'll say 'tis short, we'll say 'tis sweet.
 'Tis given much to dumb shows, which some praise,
 And like the Term, delights much in delays.°   25
 So to conclude, and give the name her due,

The play being called *The Slip*, I vanish too.'
    Exit [Follywit]

SIR BOUNTEOUS Excellently well acted and a nimble conceit.°

HAREBRAIN The Prologue's pretty i'faith.

PENITENT And went off well.   30

SIR BOUNTEOUS Ay, that's the grace of all, when they go away
    well, ah!

COURTESAN [*aside*] O'my troth, an I were not married, I could find
    in my heart to fall in love with that player now and send for him
    to a supper.° I know some i'th'town that have done as much, and 35
    there took such a good conceit° of their parts° into th'two-penny
    room° that the actors have been found i'th'morning in a less compass
    than their stage, though 'twere ne'er so full of gentlemen.°

SIR BOUNTEOUS But, passion of me, where be these knaves? Will
    they not come away? Methinks they stay very long.   40

PENITENT Oh, you must bear a little, sir; they have many shifts° to
    run into.

SIR BOUNTEOUS Shifts call you 'em? They're horrible long things.
    Follywit returns in a fury

FOLLYWIT [*aside*] A pox of such fortune! The plot's betrayed! All will
    come out; yonder they come, taken upon suspicion and brought 45
    back by a constable. I was accursed to hold society with such
    coxcombs! What's to be done? I shall be shamed forever, my wife
    here and all. Ah pox! By light, happily thought upon: the chain!
    Invention stick to me this once and fail me ever hereafter. So, so.

SIR BOUNTEOUS Life, I say, where be these players? Oh, are you   50
    come? Troth, it's time; I was e'en sending for you.

HAREBRAIN How moodily he walks; what plays he, trow?

SIR BOUNTEOUS A justice upon my credit; I know by the chain
    there.

FOLLYWIT 'Unfortunate justice!'   55

SIR BOUNTEOUS Ah, a, a.

FOLLYWIT 'In thy kin unfortunate!
    Here comes thy nephew now upon suspicion,
    Brought by a constable before thee, his vile
    Associates with him,   60
    But so disguised none knows him but myself.
    Twice have I set him free from officers' fangs,
    And, for his sake, his fellows. Let him look to't;
    My conscience will permit but one wink more.'

SIR BOUNTEOUS Yea, shall we take justice winking?   65

FOLLYWIT   'For this time
    I have bethought a means to work thy freedom,
    Though hazarding myself; should the law seize him,
    Being kin to me, 'twould blemish much my name.
    No, I'd rather lean to danger than to shame.'
SIR BOUNTEOUS A very explete justice.   70
CONSTABLE [*within*] Thank you, good neighbours; let me alone with
    'em now.
            Enter Constable with them [*i.e. Mawworm, Hoboy, and others,*
            and citizens]
MAWWORM [*aside*] 'Sfoot, who's yonder?
HOBOY [*aside*] Dare he sit there?
FIRST COMPANION Follywit!   75
SECOND COMPANION Captain! Puh!
FOLLYWIT 'How now, constable, what news with thee?'
CONSTABLE [*to Sir Bounteous*] May it please your worship, here are
    a company of auspicious° fellows.
SIR BOUNTEOUS To me? Puh! Turn to th'justice, you whoreson   80
    hobbyhorse!—This is some new player now; they put all their fools
    to the constable's part still.
FOLLYWIT 'What's the matter, constable, what's the matter?'
CONSTABLE I have nothing to say to your worship. [*To Sir Boun-*
    teous] They were all riding a-horseback, an't please your worship.   85
SIR BOUNTEOUS Yet again? A pox of all asses still! They could not
    ride afoot unless 'twere in a bawdy house.
CONSTABLE The ostler told me they were all unstable fellows, sir.
FOLLYWIT 'Why, sure the fellow's drunk!'
MAWWORM 'We spied that weakness in him long ago, sir. Your   90
    worship must bear with him; the man's much o'erseen. Only in
    respect of his office we obeyed him, both to appear comfortable
    to law and clear of all offence. For I protest, sir, he found us but
    a-horseback.'
FOLLYWIT 'What, he did?'   95
MAWWORM 'As I have a soul, that's all, and all he can lay° to us.'
CONSTABLE I'faith, you were not all riding away then?
MAWWORM ''Sfoot, being a-horseback, sir, that must needs follow.'
FOLLYWIT 'Why true, sir.'
SIR BOUNTEOUS Well said, justice. He helps his kinsman well.   100
FOLLYWIT 'Why, sirrah, do you use to bring gentlemen before us
    for riding away? What, will you have 'em stand still when they're
    up like Smug upo'th'white horse° yonder? Are your wits steeped?

I'll make you an example for all dizzy constables. How they abuse
justice! Here, bind him to this chair.'   105
    [*They bind him*]
CONSTABLE Ha, bind him? Ho!
FOLLYWIT 'If you want cords, use garters.'
CONSTABLE Help, help, gentlemen!
MAWWORM 'As fast as we can, sir.'
CONSTABLE Thieves, thieves!   110
FOLLYWIT 'A gag will help all this. Keep less noise, you knave!'
CONSTABLE Oh help, rescue the constable! Oh, oh!
    [*They gag him*]
SIR BOUNTEOUS Ho, ho, ho, ho!
FOLLYWIT 'Why, la you, who lets you now?°
You may ride quietly; I'll see you to   115
Take horse myself; I have nothing else to do.'
    [*Exeunt Follywit and his companions*]
CONSTABLE Oh, oh, oh!
SIR BOUNTEOUS Ha, ha, ha! By my troth, the maddest piece of
   justice, gentlemen, that ever was committed!
HAREBRAIN I'll be sworn for the madness on't, sir.   120
SIR BOUNTEOUS I am deceived if this prove not a merry comedy and
   a witty.
PENITENT Alas, poor constable, his mouth's open and ne'er a wise
   word.
SIR BOUNTEOUS Faith, he speaks now e'en as many as he has done;   125
   he seems wisest when he gapes and says nothing. Ha, ha, he turns
   and tells his tale to me like an ass. What have I to do with their
   riding away? They may ride for me, thou whoreson coxcomb, thou;
   nay, thou art well enough served i'faith.
PENITENT But what follows all this while, sir? Methinks some   130
   should pass by before this time and pity the constable.
SIR BOUNTEOUS By th'mass, and you say true, sir. Go, sirrah, step
   in; I think they have forgot themselves. Call the knaves away;
   they're in a wood, I believe.
    [*Exit Servant*]
CONSTABLE Ay, ay, ay!   135
SIR BOUNTEOUS Hark, the constable says ay, they're in a wood.°
   Ha, ha!
[HAREBRAIN]° He thinks long of the time, Sir Bounteous.
    [*Enter Servant*]
SIR BOUNTEOUS How now? When come they?

SERVANT Alas, an't please your worship, there's not one of them to   140
    be found, sir.

SIR BOUNTEOUS How?

HAREBRAIN What says the fellow?

SERVANT Neither horse nor man, sir.

SIR BOUNTEOUS Body of me, thou liest!   145

SERVANT Not a hair of either, sir.

HAREBRAIN How now, Sir Bounteous?

SIR BOUNTEOUS Cheated and defeated! Ungag that rascal; I'll hang
    him for's fellows, I'll make him bring 'em out.
        [*They untie him*]

CONSTABLE Did not I tell your worship this before? Brought 'em   150
    before you for suspected persons? Stayed 'em at town's end upon
    warning given? Made signs that my very jawbone aches? Your
    worship would not hear me, called me ass, saving your worship's
    presence, laughed at me.

SIR BOUNTEOUS Ha?   155

HAREBRAIN I begin to taste° it.

SIR BOUNTEOUS Give me leave, give me leave. Why, art not thou
    the constable i'th'comedy?

CONSTABLE I'th'comedy? Why, I am the constable i'th'common-
    wealth, sir.   160

SIR BOUNTEOUS I am gulled, i'faith, I am gulled! When wast thou chose?

CONSTABLE On Thursday last, sir.

SIR BOUNTEOUS A pox go with't, there't goes!

PENITENT I seldom heard jest match it.

HAREBRAIN Nor I i'faith.   165

SIR BOUNTEOUS Gentlemen, shall I entreat a courtesy?

HAREBRAIN What is't, sir?

SIR BOUNTEOUS Do not laugh at me seven year hence.

PENITENT We should betray and laugh at our own folly then, for of
    my troth none here but was deceived in't.   170

SIR BOUNTEOUS Faith, that's some comfort yet. Ha, ha, it was featly
    carried. Troth, I commend their wits. Before our faces make us
    asses, while we sit still and only laugh at ourselves.

PENITENT Faith, they were some counterfeit rogues, sir.

SIR BOUNTEOUS Why, they confessed so much themselves; they said   175
    they'd play *The Slip*; they should be men of their words. I hope
    the justice will have more conscience, i'faith, than to carry away a
    chain of a hundred mark of that fashion.

HAREBRAIN What, sir?

SIR BOUNTEOUS Ay, by my troth, sir; besides a jewel and a jewel's 180
fellow, a good fair watch that hung about my neck, sir.

HAREBRAIN 'Sfoot, what did you mean, sir?

SIR BOUNTEOUS Methinks my Lord Owemuch's players should not
scorn me so i'faith; they will come and bring all again, I know.
Push, they will, i'faith; but a jest, certainly. 185

    Enter Follywit in his own shape, and all the rest [Mawworm,
    Hoboy and others]

FOLLYWIT Pray, grandsire, give me your blessing.
    [Follywit kneels]

SIR BOUNTEOUS Who? Son Follywit?

FOLLYWIT *[aside]* This shows like kneeling after the play,° I praying
for my Lord Owemuch and his good countess, our honourable lady
and mistress. 190

SIR BOUNTEOUS Rise richer by a blessing; thou art welcome.

FOLLYWIT Thanks, good grandsire. I was bold to bring those
gentlemen, my friends.

SIR BOUNTEOUS They're all welcome. Salute you that side, and I'll
welcome this side. 195

    [Follywit greets Sir Bounteous's guests; Sir Bounteous greets
    Follywit's companions]

Sir, to begin with you.

HAREBRAIN Master Follywit.

FOLLYWIT I am glad 'tis our fortune so happily to meet, sir.

SIR BOUNTEOUS *[to Hoboy]* Nay, then you know me not, sir.

FOLLYWIT Sweet Mistress Harebrain. 200

SIR BOUNTEOUS *[to Mawworm]* You cannot be too bold, sir.

FOLLYWIT Our marriage known?

COURTESAN Not a word yet.

FOLLYWIT The better.

SIR BOUNTEOUS Faith, son, would you had come sooner with these 205
gentlemen.

FOLLYWIT Why, grandsire?

SIR BOUNTEOUS We had a play here.

FOLLYWIT A play, sir? No.

SIR BOUNTEOUS Yes, faith, a pox o'th'author! 210

FOLLYWIT Bless us all! Why, were they such vile ones, sir?

SIR BOUNTEOUS I am sure villainous ones, sir.

FOLLYWIT Some raw, simple fools?

SIR BOUNTEOUS Nay, by th'mass, these were enough for thievish
knaves. 215

63

FOLLYWIT What, sir?

SIR BOUNTEOUS Which way came you, gentlemen? You could not choose but meet 'em.

FOLLYWIT We met a company with hampers after 'em.

SIR BOUNTEOUS Oh, those were they, those were they, a pox   220
hamper 'em!

FOLLYWIT Bless us all again!

SIR BOUNTEOUS They have hampered me finely, sirrah.

FOLLYWIT How, sir?

SIR BOUNTEOUS How, sir? I lent the rascals properties to furnish out   225
their play, a chain, a jewel, and a watch, and they watched their time and rid quite away with 'em.

FOLLYWIT Are they such creatures?

[*The watch rings in Follywit's pocket*]

SIR BOUNTEOUS Hark, hark, gentlemen! By this light, the watch rings alarum in his pocket! There's my watch come again, or the   230
very cousin-german to't. Whose is't, whose is't? By th'mass, 'tis he; hast thou one, son? Prithee bestow it upon thy grandsire. I now look for mine again i'faith.

[*He searches Follywit's pockets*]

Nay, come with a good will or not at all;° I'll give thee a better thing. A prize,° a prize, gentlemen!   235

HAREBRAIN Great or small?

SIR BOUNTEOUS At once I have drawn chain, jewel, watch, and all!

PENITENT By my faith, you have a fortunate hand, sir.

HAREBRAIN Nay, all to come at once.

MAWWORM A vengeance of this foolery!   240

FOLLYWIT Have I 'scaped the constable to be brought in by the watch?

COURTESAN Oh destiny! Have I married a thief, mother?

MOTHER Comfort thyself; thou art beforehand with him,° daughter.

SIR BOUNTEOUS Why son, why gentlemen, how long have you been my Lord Owemuch his° servants i'faith?   245

FOLLYWIT Faith, grandsire, shall I be true to you?

SIR BOUNTEOUS I think 'tis time; thou'st been a thief already.

FOLLYWIT I, knowing the day of your feast and the natural inclination you have to pleasure and pastime, presumed upon your patience for a jest, as well to prolong your days as—   250

SIR BOUNTEOUS Whoop! Why, then you took my chain along with you to prolong my days, did you?

FOLLYWIT Not so neither, sir; and that you may be seriously assured of my hereafter stableness of life, I have took another course.

SIR BOUNTEOUS What?   255
FOLLYWIT Took a wife.
SIR BOUNTEOUS A wife? 'Sfoot, what is she for a fool° would marry
 thee, a madman? When was the wedding kept in Bedlam?
FOLLYWIT She's both a gentlewoman and a virgin.
SIR BOUNTEOUS Stop there, stop there; would I might see her!   260
FOLLYWIT You have your wish; she's here.
          [*Follywit points out the Courtesan*]
SIR BOUNTEOUS Ah, ha, ha, ha! This makes amends for all.
FOLLYWIT How now?
MAWWORM Captain, do you hear? Is she your wife in earnest?
FOLLYWIT How then?   265
MAWWORM Nothing but pity you, sir.
SIR BOUNTEOUS Speak, son, is't true?
    Can you gull us and let a quean gull you?
FOLLYWIT Ha!
COURTESAN What I have been is past; be that forgiven,   270
    And have a soul true both to thee and heaven.
FOLLYWIT Is't come about? Tricks are repaid, I see.
SIR BOUNTEOUS The best is, sirrah, you pledge° none but me;
    And since I drink the top, take her; and hark,
    I spice the bottom with a thousand mark.   275
FOLLYWIT By my troth, she is as good a cup of nectar as any
 bachelor needs to sip at.
    Tut, give me gold, it makes amends for vice;
    Maids without coin are caudles without spice.
SIR BOUNTEOUS Come, gentlemen, to th'feast, let not time waste;   280
    We have pleased our ear, now let us please our taste.
    Who lives by cunning, mark it, his fate's cast;
    When he has gulled all, then is himself the last.
          [*Exeunt*]

MICHAELMAS TERM

THE ACTORS IN THE COMEDY°

Richard Easy,° a gentleman of Essex
Rearage°
Salewood°   London gallants
Cockstone°
Ephestian Quomodo,° a woollen draper°   5
Sim, his son
Shortyard, alias John Blastfield,° etc.
Falselight,° alias Idem,° etc.   } Quomodo's accomplices
Andrew Lethe,° born Andrew Gruel, an upstart adventurer
Dick Hellgill, Lethe's pander   10
Country Wench's Father
Dustbox, a scrivener°
Boy, Quomodo's servant
Thomasine,° Quomodo's wife
Susan, their daughter   15
Country Wench,° Lethe's mistress
Mother Gruel, Lethe's mother
Old Woman, Thomasine's friend
Winnifred, Thomasine's maid
Mistress Comings, a tirewoman°   20
Judge,° Tailor, Drawer, Officers, Mourners, Servants, etc.
Michaelmas Term
Boy, his servant   } In the Induction
Hilary Term, Easter Term, Trinity Term°
Poor Fellow, Page, Pander, in the dumb show   25

Induction

Enter Michaelmas Term in a whitish cloak, new come up out of the country, a Boy bringing his gown after him

MICHAELMAS TERM Boy!

BOY Here, sir.

MICHAELMAS TERM Lay by my conscience, give me my gown,
    That weed is for the country;°
    We must be civil now and match our evil;°   5
    Who first made civil black he pleased the devil.°
    So now know I where I am, methinks already
    I grasp best part of the autumnian blessing
    In my contentious fathom; my hand's free,°
    From wronger and from wrongèd I have fee,   10
    And what by sweat from the rough earth they draw
    Is to enrich this silver harvest, Law;
    And so through wealthy variance and fat brawl°
    The barn is made but steward to the hall.°
    Come they up thick enough?°   15

BOY Oh, like hops and harlots, sir.

MICHAELMAS TERM Why dost thou couple them?

BOY Oh, very aptly, for as the hop well boiled° will make a man not stand upon his legs, so the harlot in time will leave a man no legs° to stand upon.   20

MICHAELMAS TERM Such another, and be my heir. I have no child,°
    Yet have I wealth would redeem beggary.
    I think it be a curse both here and foreign,
    Where bags are fruitful'st there the womb's most barren;
    The poor has all our children, we their wealth.   25
    Shall I be prodigal when my life cools,°
    Make those my heirs whom I have beggared, fools?°
    It would be wondrous; rather beggar more;
    Thou shalt have heirs enow, thou keep'st a whore.°
    And here comes kindred too with no mean purses,   30
    Yet strive to be still blest with clients' curses.

        Music playing. Enter the other three Terms, the first bringing in
        a fellow poor,° which the other two advanceth, giving him rich
        apparel, a page, and a pander. Exit [fellow]

MICHAELMAS TERM What subtlety have we here? A fellow
   Shrugging for° life's kind benefits, shift and heat,
   Crept up in three Terms,° wrapped in silk and silver,
   So well appointed too with page and pander;   35
   It was a happy gale that blew him hither.°
FIRST TERM Thou father of the Terms, hail to thee.
SECOND TERM May much contention still keep with thee.
THIRD TERM Many new fools come up and fee thee.
SECOND TERM Let 'em pay dear enough that see thee.   40
FIRST TERM And like asses use such men;
   When their load's off turn 'em to graze again.°
SECOND TERM And may our wish have full effect,
   Many a suit and much neglect.°
THIRD TERM And as it hath been often found,   45
   Let the clients' cups come round.
SECOND TERM Help your poor kinsmen when you ha' got 'em;°
   You may drink deep, leave us the bottom.°
THIRD TERM Or when there is a lamb fallen in,°
   Take you the lamb, leave us the skin.°   50
MICHAELMAS TERM Your duty and regard hath moved us,
   Never till now we thought you loved us;
   Take comfort from our words, and make no doubt
   You shall have suits come sixteen times about.°
ALL THREE TERMS We humbly thank the patron of our hopes.   55
      Exeunt [*the Three Terms*]
MICHAELMAS TERM With what a vassal-appetite they gnaw
   On our reversions, and are proud
   Coldly to taste our meats, which eight returns°
   Serve in to us as courses.
   One day our writs, like wild-fowl, fly abroad,   60
   And then return o'er cities, towns, and hills,
   With clients, like dried straws, between their bills;
   And 'tis no few, birds pick to build their nests,°
   Nor no small money that keeps drabs and feasts!°
   But, gentlemen,° to spread myself open unto you, in cheaper   65
   Terms I salute you; for ours° have but sixpenny fees° all the year
   long, yet we dispatch you in two hours° without demur. Your
   suits° hang° not long here after candles be lighted. Why call we°
   this play by such a dear and chargeable title, *Michaelmas Term*?
   Know it consents happily to our purpose, though perhaps faintly   70
   to the interpretation of many, for he that expects any great quarrels

in law to be handled here will be fondly deceived; this only presents those familiar accidents which happened in town in the circumference of those six weeks whereof Michaelmas Term is lord. *Sat sapienti*;° I hope there's no fools i'th'house.   75
       [*Exeunt*]

[1.1]

Enter at one door Master Rearage, meeting Master Salewood°

SALEWOOD What, Master Rearage?

REARAGE Master Salewood? Exceedingly well met in town. Comes your father up this Term?

SALEWOOD Why, he was here three days before the Exchequer gaped.   5

REARAGE Fie, such an early Termer?

SALEWOOD He's not to be spoke withal; I dare not ask him blessing till the last of November.°

REARAGE And how looks thy little venturing° cousin?

SALEWOOD Faith, like a lute that has all the strings broke; nobody   10
will meddle with° her.

REARAGE Fie, there are doctors enow in town will string her again and make her sound as sweet as e'er she did. Is she not married yet?

SALEWOOD Sh'as no luck; some may better steal a horse than others   15
look on.° I have known a virgin of five bastards wedded. Faith, when all's done we must be fain to marry her into the North,° I'm afraid.

REARAGE But will she pass so,° think you?

SALEWOOD Puh, any thing that is warm enough is good enough for   20
them; so it come in the likeness, though the devil be in't, they'll venture the firing.°

REARAGE They're worthy spirits i'faith. Heard you the news?

SALEWOOD Not yet.

REARAGE Mistress Difficult is newly fallen° a widow.   25

SALEWOOD Say true, is Master Difficult, the lawyer, dead?

REARAGE Easily dead, sir.

SALEWOOD Pray, when died he?

REARAGE What a question's that! When should a lawyer die but in the vacation?° He has no leisure to die in the Term-time; beside,   30
the noise there would fetch him° again.

SALEWOOD Knew you the nature of his disease?

REARAGE Faith, some say he died of an old grief he had that the vacation was fourteen weeks long.

SALEWOOD And very likely. I knew 'twould kill him at last; 't'as   35
troubled him a long time. He was one of those that would fain have

72

brought in the heresy of a fifth Term, often crying with a loud
voice, 'Oh, why should we lose Barthol'mew week?'

REARAGE He savours; stop your nose; no more of him.

    Enter Master Cockstone, a gentleman [at the other door],
    meeting Master Easy of Essex

COCKSTONE Young Master Easy, let me salute you, sir. When came you?   40

EASY I have but inned° my horse since,° Master Cockstone.

COCKSTONE You seldom visit London, Master Easy,
  But now your father's dead 'tis your only course;
  Here's gallants of all sizes, of all lasts;
  Here you may fit your foot, make choice of those   45
  Whom your affection may rejoice in.

EASY You have easily possessed me, I am free;°
  Let those live hinds that know not liberty.

    [*Cockstone takes Rearage aside; Easy takes Salewood*]

COCKSTONE Master Rearage?

EASY Good Master Salewood, I am proud of your society.   50

REARAGE What gentleman might that be?

COCKSTONE One Master Easy; h'as good land in Essex,°
  A fair free-breasted gentleman, somewhat too open,
  Bad in man, worse in woman,
  The gentry-fault at first; he is yet fresh°   55
  And wants the city powd'ring. But what news?
  Is't yet a match 'twixt Master Quomodo's
  The rich draper's daughter and yourself?

REARAGE Faith, sir, I am vilely rivalled!

COCKSTONE Vilely? By whom?   60

REARAGE One Andrew Lethe, crept to a little warmth,°
  And now so proud that he forgets all storms;
  One that ne'er wore apparel but, like ditches,
  'Twas cast before he had it, now shines bright°
  In rich embroideries. Him Master Quomodo affects,   65
  The daughter him, the mother only me;°
  I rest most doubtful, my side being weakest.

COCKSTONE Yet the mother's side,
  Being surer than the father's, it may prove,°
  'Men plead for money best, women for love'.°   70

REARAGE 'Slid, Master Quomodo!

COCKSTONE How then, afraid of a woollen draper?

REARAGE He warned me° his house, and I hate he should see me
  abroad.

[Rearage and Cockstone move aside.]° [Enter] Quomodo with his
two spirits, Shortyard and Falselight

QUOMODO Oh, my two spirits,° Shortyard and Falselight, you that   75
have so enriched me. I have industry for you both.

SHORTYARD Then do you please us best, sir.

QUOMODO Wealthy employment.

SHORTYARD You make me itch, sir.

QUOMODO You, Falselight, as I have directed you.   80

FALSELIGHT I am nimble.

QUOMODO Go, make my coarse commodities look sleek, with subtle
art beguile the honest eye. Be near to my trap-window, cunning
Falselight.

FALSELIGHT I never failed it yet.   85

QUOMODO I know thou didst not.

    Exit Falselight

But now to thee my true and secret Shortyard,
Whom I dare trust e'en with my wife;°
Thou ne'er didst mistress harm, but master good;
There are too few of thy name gentlemen,   90
And that we feel, but citizens in abundance.°
I have a task for thee, my pregnant spirit,
To exercise thy pointed wits upon.

SHORTYARD Give it me, for I thirst.

QUOMODO   Thine ear shall drink it.
Know then I have not spent this long vacation   95
Only for pleasure's sake. Give me the man
Who out of recreation culls advantage,
Dives into seasons, never walks but thinks,°
Ne rides but plots. My journey was toward Essex—

SHORTYARD Most true.

QUOMODO   Where I have seen what I desire.   100

SHORTYARD A woman?

QUOMODO   Puh, a woman! Yet beneath her,
That which she often treads on, yet commands her:
Land, fair neat land.

SHORTYARD   What is the mark you shoot at?°

QUOMODO Why, the fairest to cleave the heir in twain,°
I mean his title, to murder his estate,°   105
Stifle his right in some detested prison.°
There are means and ways enow to hook in gentry,
Besides our deadly enmity, which thus stands:

74

They're busy 'bout our wives, we 'bout their lands.

SHORTYARD Your revenge is more glorious: 110
To be a cuckold is but for one life,
When land remains to you, your heir, or wife.

QUOMODO Ah, sirrah, do we sting 'em? This fresh gallant rode
newly up before me.

SHORTYARD I beseech his name.   115

QUOMODO Young Master Easy.

SHORTYARD Easy? It may fall right.

QUOMODO I have inquired his haunt.—Stay, hah! Ay, that 'tis,°
that's he, that's he!

SHORTYARD Happily!   120

QUOMODO Observe, take surely note of him, he's fresh and free;
Shift thyself speedily into the shape of gallantry;°
I'll swell thy purse with angels.
Keep foot by foot with him, out-dare his expenses,°
Flatter, dice, and brothel to him;   125
Give him a sweet taste of sensuality,
Train him to every wasteful sin that he
May quickly need health, but especially money;
Ravish him with a dame or two, be his bawd for once,
I'll be thine forever;   130
Drink drunk with him, creep into bed to him,°
Kiss him and undo him, my sweet spirit.

SHORTYARD Let your care dwell in me, soon shall it shine;
What subtlety is in man, that is not mine.
            Exit [Shortyard]

QUOMODO Oh, my most cheerful spirit, go, dispatch!   135
Gentry is the chief fish we tradesmen catch.
            Exit [Quomodo]

EASY [*pointing to the rental notices*] What's here?

SALEWOOD Oh, they are bills for chambers.

EASY [*reading bill*] 'Against° Saint Andrew's,° at a painter's house,
there's a fair chamber ready furnished to be let, the house not only   140
endued with a new fashion forepart, but, which is more convenient
for a gentleman, with a very provident back door'.°

SALEWOOD Why, here's virtue still; I like that thing that's necessary°
as well as pleasant.
            [*Enter Lethe studying the bills*]

COCKSTONE What news in yonder paper?   145

REARAGE Hah! Seek you for news? There's for you!

SALEWOOD Who's this?° In the name of the black angels,° Andrew
  Gruel!

REARAGE No, Andrew Lethe.

SALEWOOD Lethe? 150

REARAGE He's forgot his father's name, poor Walter° Gruel, that
  begot him, fed him, and brought him up.

SALEWOOD Not hither?°

REARAGE No, 'twas from his thoughts; he brought him up below.°

SALEWOOD But does he pass for Lethe?

REARAGE   'Mongst strange eyes° 155
  That no more know him than he knows himself,
  That's nothing now, for Master Andrew Lethe,
  A gentleman of most receivèd parts,°
  Forgetfulness, lust, impudence, and falsehood,
  And one especial courtly quality, 160
  To wit, no wit at all. I am his rival
  For Quomodo's daughter, but he knows it not.

SALEWOOD He's spied us o'er his paper.

REARAGE Oh, that's a warning to make our duties ready.°

COCKSTONE Salute him? Hang him! 165

REARAGE Puh, wish his health awhile, he'll be laid° shortly. Let
  him gorge venison for a time, our doctors will bring him to dry
  mutton.° Seem respective, to make his pride swell like a toad° with
  dew.

SALEWOOD Master Lethe. 170

REARAGE Sweet Master Lethe.

LETHE Gentlemen, your pardon; I remember you not.

SALEWOOD Why, we supped with you last night, sir!

LETHE Oh, cry you mercy, 'tis so long ago
  I had quite forgot you; I must be forgiven. 175
  Acquaintance, dear society, suits, and things,°
  Do so flow to me,
  That had I not the better memory,
  'Twould be a wonder I should know myself.
  'Esteem is made of such a dizzy metal.'° 180
  I have received of many, gifts o'er night,
  Whom I have forgot ere morning; meeting the men,
  I wished 'em to remember me again;°
  They do so, then if I forget again
  I know what helped before, that will help then. 185
  This is my course, for memory I have been told

Twenty preserves, the best I find is gold.
Ay, truly! Are you not knights yet, gentlemen?°
SALEWOOD Not yet.
LETHE No? That must be looked into, 'tis your own fault. I have   190
some store of venison; where shall we devour it, gentlemen?
SALEWOOD The Horn were a fit place.
LETHE For venison fit,
The horn having chased it,°
At the Horn we'll—   195
Rhyme to that—
COCKSTONE Taste it.
SALEWOOD   Waste it.
REARAGE   Cast it.
LETHE That's the true rhyme indeed.
We hunt our venison twice, I tell you,
First out o'th'park, next out o'th'belly.   200
COCKSTONE First dogs take pains to make it fit for men,°
Then men take pain to make it fit for dogs.°
LETHE Right.
COCKSTONE Why, this is kindness; a kind gallant, you,
And love to give the dogs more than their due.   205
We shall attend you, sir.
LETHE   I pray do so.
SALEWOOD The Horn.
LETHE   Easily remembered that, you know!°
Exeunt [all but Lethe]
But now unto my present business. The daughter yields and
Quomodo consents; only my Mistress Quomodo, her mother, without
regard runs full against° me and sticks hard. Is there no law for a   210
woman that will run upon° a man at her own apperil? Why should
not she consent, knowing my state, my sudden fortunes? I can
command° a custard and other bake-meats, death of sturgeon;° I
could keep house with nothing. What friends have I! How well am I
beloved, e'en quite throughout the scullery.° Not consent? 'Tis e'en   215
as I have writ; I'll be hanged, an she love me not herself, and would
rather preserve me as a private friend° to her own pleasures than any
way advance her daughter upon me to beguile herself. Then how
have I relieved her in that point? Let me peruse this letter.
[Reads the letter]
'Good Mistress Quomodo—or rather, as I hope ere the Term end,   220
Mother Quomodo, since only your consent keeps aloof off° and

hinders the copulation° of your daughter—what may I think but
that it is a mere° affection in you, doting upon some small inferior
virtue of mine, to draw me in upon yourself? If the case stand so,
I have comfort for you; for this you may well assure yourself, that   225
by the marriage of your daughter I have the better means and
opportunity to yourself and without the least suspicion.' This is
moving stuff, and that works best with a citizen's wife. But who
shall I get to convey this now? My page I ha' lent forth; my pander
I have employed about the country to look out some third sister,°   230
or entice some discontented gentlewoman from her husband,
whom the laying out of my appetite shall maintain. Nay, I'll deal
like an honourable gentleman, I'll be kind to women; that which I
gather i'th'day I'll put into their purses at night.° You shall have
no cause to rail at me; no, faith, I'll keep you in good fashion,   235
ladies; no meaner men than knights shall ransom home° your
gowns and recover your smocks.° I'll not dally with you!° Some
poor widow woman would come as a necessary bawd now; and see
where fitly comes—

    [*Enter Mother Gruel*]

My mother! Curse of poverty! Does she come up to shame me,   240
to betray my birth, and cast soil upon my new suit? Let her pass
me, I'll take no notice of her. Scurvy murrey kersey!

MOTHER GRUEL By your leave, an like your worship—

LETHE [*aside*] Then I must proudly venture it.—To me, good
    woman?   245

MOTHER GRUEL I beseech one word with your worship.

LETHE Prithee be brief then.

MOTHER GRUEL Pray can your worship tell me any tidings of one
    Andrew Gruel, a poor son of mine own?

LETHE I know a gallant gentleman of the name, one Master Andrew   250
    Gruel, and well received amongst ladies.

MOTHER GRUEL That's not he then. He is no gentleman that I mean.

LETHE Good woman, if he be a Gruel, he's a gentleman i'th'morn-
    ings,° that's a gentleman o'th'first;° you cannot tell me.

MOTHER GRUEL No, truly, his father was an honest upright tooth-   255
    drawer.°

LETHE Oh my teeth!

MOTHER GRUEL An't please your worship, I have made a sore
    journey on't,° all this vacant time,° to come up and see my
    son Andrew. Poor Walter Gruel, his father, has laid his life°   260
    and left me a lone woman; I have not one husband in all the

world. Therefore my coming up is for relief, an't like your
worship, hoping that my son Andrew is in some place° about the
kitchen.

LETHE Kitchen! Puh, fah!   265

MOTHER GRUEL Or a servingman to some knight of worship.°

LETHE [aside] Oh, let me not endure her!—Know you not me, good
woman?

MOTHER GRUEL Alas, an't please your worship, I never saw such a
glorious suit since the hour I was kersened.   270

LETHE [aside] Good, she knows me not, my glory does disguise
    me;
Beside, my poorer name being drenched in Lethe,°
She'll hardly understand me. What a fresh air can do!°
I may employ her as a private drudge
To pass my letters and secure my lust,°   275
And ne'er be noted mine to shame my blood,
And drop my staining birth upon my raiment.°
—Faith, good woman, you will hardly get to the speech of
Master Andrew, I tell you.

MOTHER GRUEL No? Marry, hang him, an like your worship, I have 280
known the day when nobody cared to speak to him.

LETHE You must take heed how you speak ill of him now, I can tell
you; he's so employed.

MOTHER GRUEL Employed for what?

LETHE For his behaviour, wisdom, and other virtues.   285

MOTHER GRUEL His virtues? No, 'tis well known his father was too
poor a man to bring him up to any virtues; he can scarce write and
read.

LETHE He's the better regarded for that amongst courtiers, for that's
but a needy quality.°   290

MOTHER GRUEL If it be so, then he'll be great shortly, for he has no
good parts about him.

LETHE Well, good woman, or mother, or what you will.

MOTHER GRUEL Alack the day, I know your worship scorns to call
me mother; 'tis not a thing fit for your worship indeed, such a   295
simple old woman as I am.

LETHE In pity of thy long journey, there's sixpence British.° Tend
upon me, I have business for you.

MOTHER GRUEL I'll wait upon your worship.

LETHE Two pole off at least.   300

MOTHER GRUEL I am a clean old woman, an't like your worship.

LETHE It goes not by cleanness here, good woman; if you were
fouler, so° you were braver,° you might come nearer.
Exit [Lethe]

MOTHER GRUEL Nay, an that be the fashion, I hope I shall get it
shortly; there's no woman so old but she may learn, and as an old   305
lady delights in a young page or monkey, so there are young
courtiers will be hungry upon an old woman, I warrant you.
Exit

[1.2]

Enter Lethe's pander [Hellgill], with a Country Wench

HELLGILL Come, leave your puling and sighing.

COUNTRY WENCH Beshrew you now, why did you entice me from
my father?

HELLGILL Why? To thy better advancement. Wouldst thou, a
pretty, beautiful, juicy squall, live in a poor thrummed house   5
i'th'country in such servile habiliments and may well pass for a
gentlewoman i'th'city? Does not five hundred do so, think'st
thou, and with worse faces? Oh, now in these latter days,° the
devil reigning, 'tis an age for cloven creatures! But why sad now?
Yet indeed 'tis the fashion of any courtesan to be seasick i'th'first   10
voyage, but at next she proclaims open wars° like a beaten° soldier.
Why, Northamptonshire lass, dost dream of virginity now? Remember a loose-bodied° gown, wench, and let it go; wires and tires,
bents and bums, felts and falls, thou shalt° deceive the world that
gentlewomen indeed shall not be known from others. I have a   15
master to whom I must prefer thee after the aforesaid decking,
Lethe by name, a man of one most admired property: he can both
love thee, and for thy better advancement be thy pander himself,
an excellent spark of humility.°

COUNTRY WENCH Well, heaven forgive you, you train me up to't.   20

HELLGILL Why, I do acknowledge it, and I think I do you a pleasure
in't.

COUNTRY WENCH And if I should prove a harlot now, I should be
bound to curse you.

HELLGILL Bound?° Nay, an you prove a harlot you'll be loose enough.   25

COUNTRY WENCH If I had not a desire to go° like a gentlewoman,
you should be hanged ere you should get me to't, I warrant you.

HELLGILL Nay, that's certain, nor a thousand more of you;° I know
  you are all chaste enough till one thing or other tempt you! Deny°
  a satin gown, an you dare now?   30
COUNTRY WENCH You know I have no power to do't, and that
  makes you so wilful; for what woman is there such a beast that will
  deny any thing that is good?
HELLGILL True, they will not, most dissemble.°
COUNTRY WENCH No, an she bear a brave mind, she will not, I   35
  warrant you.
HELLGILL Why, therefore take heart, faint not at all,
  Women ne'er rise but when they fall;
  Let a man break, he's gone, blown up,°
  A woman's breaking sets her up;   40
  Virginity is no city trade,
  You're out o'th'freedom when you're a maid;°
  Down with the lattice, 'tis but thin,°
  Let coarser beauties work within,°
  Whom the light mocks; thou art fair and fresh,   45
  The gilded flies will light upon thy flesh.°
COUNTRY WENCH Beshrew your sweet enchantments, you have
  won.
HELLGILL [aside] How easily soft women are undone.
  So farewell wholesome weeds, where treasure pants,°
  And welcome silks, where lies disease and wants.   50
  —Come, wench, now flow thy fortunes in to bless thee;
  I'll bring thee where thou shalt be taught to dress thee.
COUNTRY WENCH Oh, as soon as may be! I am in a swoon till I be
  a gentlewoman; and you know what flesh is man's meat till it
  be dressed.°   55
HELLGILL Most certain; no more: a woman.
  Exeunt

[2.1]

Enter Rearage, Salewood, Lethe, Easy, with Shortyard, alias Blastfield [and his Boy], at dice

REARAGE Gentlemen, I ha' sworn I'll change the room.° Dice? Devils!

LETHE You see I'm patient, gentlemen.

SALEWOOD Ay, the fiend's in't. You're patient, you put up all.°

REARAGE Come, set me, gentlemen.   5

SHORTYARD [*to Easy*] An Essex gentleman, sir?

EASY An unfortunate one, sir.

SHORTYARD I'm bold to salute you, sir.
          [*He doffs his hat*]
     You know not Master Alsup° there?

EASY Oh, entirely well.   10

SHORTYARD Indeed, sir?

EASY He's second to° my bosom.

SHORTYARD I'll give you that comfort then, sir, you must not want money as long as you are in town, sir.

EASY No, sir?   15

SHORTYARD I am bound in my love to him to see you furnished, and in that comfort I recover my salute again, sir.
          [*He puts on his hat again*]

EASY Then I desire to be more dear unto you.

SHORTYARD I rather study to be dear° unto you.—Boy, fill some wine.—I knew not what fair impressier I received at first, but I   20
began to affect your society very speedily.

EASY I count myself the happier.

SHORTYARD To Master Alsup, sir, to whose remembrance I could love to drink till I were past remembrance.
          [*Drinks*]

EASY I shall keep Christmas with him, sir, where your health shall   25
likewise undoubtedly be remembered, and thereupon I pledge you.
          [*Drinks*]
     I would sue for your name, sir.

SHORTYARD Your suit shall end in one Term, sir; my name is Blastfield.

EASY Kind Master Blastfield, your dearer acquaintance.   30
          [*Drinks*]

82

REARAGE Nay, come, will ye draw in, gentlemen? Set me.

EASY Faith, I'm scattered.

SHORTYARD Sir, you shall not give out so meanly of yourself in my
company for a million. Make such° privy to your disgrace? You're
a gentleman of fair fortunes; keep me° your reputation. Set 'em   35
all;° there's crowns for you.

EASY Sir, you bind me infinitely in these courtesies.

SHORTYARD You must always have a care of your reputation here
in town, Master Easy; although you ride down° with nothing, it
skills not.   40

EASY I'm glad you tell me that yet, then I'm indifferent.
Well, come, who throws? I set all these.

SHORTYARD Why, well said.

SALEWOOD This same Master Lethe here begins to undo us again.

LETHE Ah, sir, I came not hither but to win.   45

SHORTYARD And then you'll leave us, that's your fashion.

LETHE He's base that visits not his friends.°

SHORTYARD But he's more base that carries out his winnings;
None will do so but those have base beginnings.

LETHE It is a thing in use and ever was.   50
I pass° this time.

SHORTYARD   I wonder you should pass,
And that you're suffered.

LETHE   Tut, the dice are ours,
Then wonder not at those that have most powers.

REARAGE The devil and his angels!°

LETHE   Are these they?
Welcome, dear angels, where y'are cursed, ne'er stay.°   55
[*He moves to another part of the stage*]

SALEWOOD Here's luck!

EASY Let's search him, gentlemen, I think he wears a smock.°

SHORTYARD I knew the time he wore not half a shirt, just like a pea.°

EASY No! How did he for the rest?

SHORTYARD Faith, he compounded with a couple of napkins at   60
Barnet and so trussed up the lower parts.

EASY 'Twas a pretty shift° i'faith.

SHORTYARD But Master Lethe has forgot that too.

EASY A mischief on't, to lose all! I could—°

SHORTYARD Nay, but good Master Easy, do not do yourself that   65
tyranny, I beseech you. I must not ha' you alter your body now
for the purge° of a little money; you undo me, an you do.

EASY 'Twas all I brought up° with me, I protest, Master Blastfield; all my rent till next quarter.°

SHORTYARD Pox of money, talk not on't, I beseech you. What said   70
I to you? Mass, I am out of cash myself too.—Boy!

BOY Anon, sir.

SHORTYARD Run presently to Master Gum° the mercer and will him to tell out two or three hundred pound for me, or more, according as he is furnished. I'll visit him i'th'morning, say.   75

BOY [*pretending to leave*] It shall be said,° sir.

SHORTYARD [*calling him back*] Do you hear, boy?

BOY [*returning*] Yes, sir.

SHORTYARD If Master Gum be not sufficiently ready, call upon Master Profit the goldsmith.   80

BOY [*pretending to leave*] It shall be done, sir.

SHORTYARD Boy!

BOY [*aside*] I knew° I was not sent yet; now is the time.

SHORTYARD Let them both rest till another occasion. You shall not need to run so far at this time. Take one nigher hand; go to Master   85
Quomodo the draper and will° him to furnish me instantly.

BOY Now I go, sir.
         [*Exit Boy*]

EASY It seems y'are well known, Master Blastfield, and your credit very spacious here i'th'city.

SHORTYARD Master Easy, let a man bear himself portly, the whore-   90
sons° will creep to him o'their bellies, and their wives o'their backs; there's a kind of bold grace expected throughout all the parts of a gentleman. Then, for your observances, a man must not so much as spit but within line and fashion. I tell you what I ha' done: sometimes I carry my water all London over only to deliver it   95
proudly at the Standard; and do I pass altogether unnoted, think you? No, a man can no sooner peep out his head, but there's a bow bent at him out of some watchtower or other.

EASY So readily, sir?

SHORTYARD Push, you know a bow's quickly ready, though a gun   100
be long a-charging and will shoot five times to his once.° Come, you shall bear yourself jovially. Take heed of setting your looks to your losses,° but rather smile upon your ill luck and invite 'em tomorrow to another breakfast of bones.°

EASY Nay, I'll forswear dicing.   105

SHORTYARD What? Peace, I am ashamed to hear you. Will you cease in the first loss? Show me one gentleman that e'er did it! Fie

upon't, I must use° you to company, I perceive; you'd be spoiled
else. Forswear dice? I would your friends heard you i'faith.

EASY Nay, I was but in jest, sir.   110

SHORTYARD I hope so; what would gentlemen say of you? 'There
goes a gull that keeps his money'. I would not have such a report
go on you for the world as long as you are in my company. Why,
man, fortune alters in a minute. I ha' known those have recovered
so much in an hour their purses were never sick after.   115

REARAGE Oh, worse than consumption of the liver!
Consumption of the patrimony!

SHORTYARD How now? Mark their humours, Master Easy.

REARAGE Forgive me, my posterity yet ungotten.

SHORTYARD That's a penitent maudlin dicer.   120

REARAGE Few know the sweets that the plain life allows;
Vile son that surfeits of his father's brows!°

SHORTYARD Laugh at him, Master Easy.

EASY Ha, ha, ha!

SALEWOOD I'll be damned, an these be not the bones of some quean   125
that cozened me in her life and now consumes me after her death.

SHORTYARD That's the true wicked, blasphemous, and soul-
shuddering dicer, that will curse you all service time,° and
attribute his ill luck always to one drab or other.

[Enter Hellgill to Lethe; they talk apart]

LETHE Dick Hellgill, the happy news?   130

HELLGILL I have her for you, sir.

LETHE Peace, what is she?

HELLGILL Young, beautiful, and plump; a delicate piece of sin.

LETHE Of what parentage?

HELLGILL Oh, a gentlewoman of a great house.   135

LETHE Fie, fie!

HELLGILL [aside] She newly came out of a barn, yet too good for a
tooth-drawer's son.

LETHE Is she wife or maid?

HELLGILL That which is daintiest, maid.   140

LETHE I'd rather she'd been a wife.

HELLGILL A wife, sir? Why?

LETHE Oh, adultery is a great deal sweeter in my mind.

HELLGILL [aside] Diseases° gnaw thy bones!—I think she has deserved
to be a wife, sir.   145

LETHE That will move well.

HELLGILL [aside]   Her firstlings shall be thine.°

85

Swine look but for the husks; the meat be mine.°
[*Enter Boy to Shortyard and Easy; they talk apart*]

SHORTYARD How now, boy?

BOY Master Quomodo takes your worship's greeting exceeding
kindly, and in his commendations returns this answer that your   150
worship shall not be so apt to receive it, as he willing to lend it.

SHORTYARD Why, we thank him i'faith.

EASY Troth, an you ha' reason to thank him, sir; 'twas a very friendly
answer.

SHORTYARD Push, a gentleman that keeps his days even° here   155
i'th'city, as I myself watch° to do, shall have many of those
answers in a twelvemonth, Master Easy.

EASY I promise you, sir, I admire your carriage and begin to hold a
more rev'rend respect of you.

SHORTYARD Not so, I beseech you; I give my friends leave to be   160
inward with me.—Will you walk, gentlemen?

LETHE We're for you. [*To Hellgill*] Present her with this jewel, my
first token.

                    Enter a Drawer

DRAWER There are certain countrymen without, enquiring for
Master Rearage and Master Salewood.   165

REARAGE Tenants!°

SALEWOOD Thou reviv'st us, rascal.

REARAGE When's our next meeting, gentlemen.

SHORTYARD   Tomorrow night;
This gentleman, by me, invites you all.
Do you not, Master Easy?

EASY   Freely, sir.   170

SALEWOOD We do embrace your love. [*Aside*] A pure, fresh gull.

SHORTYARD Thus make you men at parting dutiful
And rest beholding to you; 'tis the sleight°
To be remembered when you're out of sight.

EASY A pretty virtue.   175

                    Exeunt

[2.2]

Enter the Country Wench's Father, that° was enticed for
Lethe

FATHER Where shall I seek her now? Oh, if she knew
The dangers that attend on women's lives,
She would rather lodge under a poor thatched roof
Than under carved ceilings. She was my joy°
And all content that I received from life,   5
My dear and only daughter.
What says the note she left? Let me again
With staider grief peruse it.
    [*Reads*] 'Father, wonder not at my so sudden departure with-
out your leave or knowledge. Thus, under pardon, I excuse it;   10
had you had knowledge of it I know you would have sought
to restrain it, and hinder me from what I have long desired,
being now happily preferred to a gentleman's service in Lon-
don about Holborn. If you please to send, you may hear well
of me.'   15
As false as she is disobedient!
I've made larger inquiry, left no place
Where gentry keeps unsought, yet cannot hear,°
Which drives me most into a shameful fear.
Woe worth th'infected cause that makes me visit°   20
This man-devouring city, where I spent
My unshapen youth, to be my age's curse,
And surfeited away my name and state
In swinish riots, that now, being sober,
I do awake a beggar. I may hate her.   25
Whose youth voids wine, his age is cursed with water.
Oh heavens! I know the price of ill too well,
What the confusions are, in whom they dwell,
And how soon maids are to their ruins won;
One minute, and eternally undone;°   30
So in mine may it, may it not be thus!°
Though she be poor, her honour's precious.
May be my present form, and her fond fear,°
May chase her from me if her eye should get me;
And therefore, as my love and wants advise,   35
I'll serve, until I find her, in disguise.°

Such is my care to fright her from base evils,
I leave calm state to live amongst you, devils.
    Exit

[2.3]

*Lethe's Mother enters with Quomodo's wife [Thomasine], with
the letter [from Lethe]*

THOMASINE Were these fit words, think you, to be sent to any
citizen's wife: to enjoy the daughter and love the mother too for a
need?° I would foully scorn that man that should love me only
for a need, I tell you. And here the knave writes again, that by the
marriage of my daughter 'a has the better means and opportunity   5
to myself. He lies in his throat like a villain; he has no opportunity of me, for all that; 'tis for his betters to have opportunity of
me, and that he shall well know. A base, proud knave! 'A has forgot
how he came up° and brought two of his countrymen° to give their
words° to my husband for a suit of green kersey; 'a has forgot all   10
this. And how does he appear to me when his white satin suit's on,
but like a maggot crept out of a nutshell, a fair body and a foul
neck; those parts that are covered of him looks indifferent well
because we cannot see 'em; else, for all his cleansing, pruning, and
paring, he's not worthy a broker's° daughter, and so tell him.   15
MOTHER GRUEL I will indeed forsooth.
THOMASINE And as for my child, I hope she'll be ruled in time,
though she be foolish yet, and not be carried away with a cast of
manchets,° a bottle of wine, or a custard, and so, I pray, certify him.
MOTHER GRUEL I'll do your errand° effectually.   20
THOMASINE Art thou his aunt, or his—
MOTHER GRUEL Alas, I am a poor drudge of his.
THOMASINE Faith, an thou wert his mother, he would make thee his
drudge, I warrant him.
MOTHER GRUEL Marry, out upon him,° sir-reverence of your   25
mistress-ship.
THOMASINE Here's somewhat for thy pains, fare thee well.
    [*Gives money*]
MOTHER GRUEL 'Tis more than he gave me since I came to him.
    [*Exit Mother Gruel.*] *Enter Quomodo and his daughter*
    Su[san]

QUOMODO How now, what prating have we here? Whispers? Dumb shows? Why, Thomasine, go to; my shop is not altogether 30
so dark as some of my neighbours', where a man may be made cuckold at one end while he's measuring with his yard at t'other.

THOMASINE Only commendations sent from Master Lethe, your worshipful son-in-law that should be. 35

QUOMODO Oh, and that you like not. He that can make us rich in custom, strong in friends, happy in suits,° bring us into all the rooms° o'Sundays from the leads to the cellar, pop us in with venison till we crack again,° and send home the rest in an honourable napkin;° this man you like not forsooth! 40

SUSAN But I like him, father.

QUOMODO My blessing go with thy liking.

SUSAN A number of our citizens hold our credit° by't, to come home drunk and say we ha' been at Court; then how much more credit is't to be drunk there indeed! 45

QUOMODO Tut, thy mother's a fool.—Pray, what's Master Rearage whom you plead for so?

THOMASINE Why, first, he is a gentleman.

QUOMODO Ay, he's often first a gentleman that's last a beggar.

SUSAN My father tells you true. What should I do with a gentleman? 50
I know not which way to lie with him.

QUOMODO 'Tis true too. Thou know'st, beside, we undo gentlemen daily.

THOMASINE That makes so few of 'em marry with our daughters unless it be one green fool° or other. Next, Master Rearage has 55
land and living,° t'other but his walk i'th'street and his snatching diet;° he's able to entertain you in a fair house of his own, t'other in some nook or corner, or place us behind the cloth° like a company of puppets;° at his house you shall be served curiously, sit down and eat your meat with leisure; there° we must be glad 60
to take it standing and without either salt, cloth, or trencher, and say we are befriended too.

QUOMODO Oh, that gives a citizen a better appetite than his garden.°

SUSAN So say I, father; methinks it does me most good when I take 65
it standing;° I know not how all women's minds are.

    Enter Falselight

QUOMODO Faith, I think they are all of thy mind for that thing.— How now, Falselight?

FALSELIGHT I have descried my fellow, Shortyard, alias Blastfield,
    at hand with the gentleman.   70

QUOMODO Oh, my sweet Shortyard!—Daughter, get you up to your
    virginals.
       [*Exit Susan*]
    By your leave,° Mistress Quomodo—

THOMASINE Why, I hope I may sit i'th'shop, may I not?

QUOMODO That you may, and welcome, sweet honey-thigh, but not   75
    at this season; there's a buck to be struck.°

THOMASINE [*aside*] Well, since I'm so expressly forbidden, I'll watch
    above i'th'gallery, but I'll see your knavery.
       Exit [*Thomasine*]

QUOMODO Be you prepared as I tell you.

FALSELIGHT You ne'er feared me.°   80
       Exit [*Falselight*]

QUOMODO Oh, that sweet, neat, comely, proper, delicate parcel of
    land, like a fine gentlewoman i'th'waist, not so great as pretty,
    pretty: the trees in summer whistling, the silver waters by the
    banks harmoniously gliding. I should have been a scholar;° an
    excellent place for a student, fit for my son that lately commenced   85
    at Cambridge, whom now I have placed at Inns of Court. Thus
    we that seldom get lands honestly must leave our heirs to in-
    herit our knavery. But whist, one turn about my shop and meet
    with 'em.
       Enter Master Easy with Shortyard, alias Blastfield [*and his
       Boy*]

EASY Is this it, sir?   90

SHORTYARD Ay, let me see, this is it; sign of Three Knaves,° 'tis it.

QUOMODO [*into the shop*] Do you hear, sir?—What lack you,°
    gentlemen? See good kerseys or broadcloths here; I pray come
    near.—Master Blastfield!°

SHORTYARD I thought you would know me anon.   95
       [*Enter Thomasine above*]°

QUOMODO You're exceeding welcome to town, sir. Your worship must
    pardon me, 'tis always misty weather in our shops here; we are a
    nation the sun ne'er shines upon. Came this gentleman with you?

SHORTYARD Oh, salute him fairly, he's a kind gentleman, a very
    inward of mine.   100

QUOMODO Then I cry you mercy, sir, y'are especially welcome.

EASY I return you thanks, sir.

QUOMODO But how shall I do for you now, Master Blastfield?

SHORTYARD Why, what's the matter?

QUOMODO It is my greatest affliction at this instant, I am not able to   105
furnish you.

SHORTYARD How, Master Quomodo? Pray say not so; 'slud, you
undo me then.

QUOMODO Upon my religion, Master Blastfield, bonds lie forfeit° in
my hands; I expect the receipt of a thousand every hour and cannot   110
yet set eye of a penny.

SHORTYARD That's strange, methinks.

QUOMODO 'Tis mine own pity that plots against me, Master Blastfield; they know I have no conscience to take the forfeiture° and
that makes 'em so bold with my mercy.   115

EASY I am sorry for this.

QUOMODO Nevertheless, if I might entreat your delay but the age°
of three days, to express my sorrow now, I would double the sum
and supply you with four or five hundred.

SHORTYARD Let me see, three days?   120

QUOMODO Ay, good sir, an it may be possible.

EASY Do you hear, Master Blastfield?
          [Takes him to one side]

SHORTYARD Hah?

EASY You know I've already invited all the gallants to sup with me
tonight.   125

SHORTYARD That's true i'faith.

EASY 'Twill be my everlasting shame if I have no money to maintain
my bounty.

SHORTYARD I ne'er thought upon that.—[Aside] I looked still when
that should come from him.°—We have strictly examined our   130
expenses; it must not be three days, Master Quomodo.

QUOMODO No? Then I'm afraid 'twill be my grief, sir.

EASY Master Blastfield, I'll tell you what you may do now.

SHORTYARD What, good sweet bedfellow?°

EASY Send to Master Gum or Master Profit, the mercer and   135
goldsmith.

SHORTYARD Mass, that was well remembered of thee.—[Aside] I perceive the trout will be a little troublesome ere he be catched.—Boy!

BOY Here, sir.

SHORTYARD Run to Master Gum, or Master Profit, and carry my   140
present occasion° of money to 'em.

BOY I run, sir.
          [Exit Boy]

QUOMODO Methinks, Master Blastfield, you might easily attain to
the satisfaction of three days; here's a gentleman, your friend, I
dare say will see you sufficiently possessed till then.   145

EASY Not I, sir, by no means; Master Blastfield knows I'm further in
want than himself. My hope rests all upon him; it stands upon the
loss of my credit tonight if I walk° without money.

SHORTYARD Why, Master Quomodo, what a fruitless motion have
you put forth! You might well assure yourself this gentleman had   150
it not if I wanted it. Why, our purses are brothers; we desire but
equal fortunes; in a word, w'are man and wife; they can but lie
together and so do we.

EASY As near as can be i'faith.

SHORTYARD And to say truth, 'tis more for the continuing of this   155
gentleman's credit in town than any incitement from mine own
want only, that I covet to be so immediately furnished. You shall
hear him confess as much himself.

EASY 'Tis most certain, Master Quomodo.

       Enter Boy

SHORTYARD Oh, here comes the boy now.—How now, boy, what   160
says Master Gum or Master Profit?

BOY Sir, they're both walked forth this frosty morning to Brentford°
to see a nurse-child.

SHORTYARD A bastard be it! Spite and shame!

EASY Nay, never vex yourself, sweet Master Blastfield.   165

SHORTYARD Bewitched, I think!

QUOMODO Do you hear, sir? [*Takes Easy to one side*] You can
persuade with him?

EASY A little, sir.

QUOMODO Rather than he should be altogether destitute, or be too   170
much a vexation to himself, he shall take up a commodity of cloth°
of me, tell him.

EASY Why la! By my troth, 'twas kindly spoken.

QUOMODO Two hundred pounds' worth, upon my religion, say.

SHORTYARD So disastrously!   175

EASY Nay, Master Blastfield, you do not hear what Master Quomodo
said since, like an honest, true citizen i'faith. Rather than you
should grow diseased° upon't, you shall take up a commodity of
two hundred pounds' worth of cloth.

SHORTYARD The mealy moth consume it! Would he ha' me turn   180
peddler now? What should I do with cloth?

QUOMODO He's a very wilful gentleman at this time i'faith. He knows
as well what to do with it as I myself, iwis. There's no merchant in

town but will be greedy upon't and pay down money upo'th'nail;
they'll dispatch it over to Middleburgh presently and raise double   185
commodity by exchange.° If not, you know 'tis Term-time, and
Michaelmas Term too, the drapers' harvest° for footcloths, riding-
suits, walking-suits, chamber gowns, and hall gowns.°

EASY Nay, I'll say that, it comes in as fit a time as can be.

QUOMODO Nay, take me with you again° ere you go, sir; I offer him   190
no trash, tell him, but present money, say, where I know some
gentlemen in town ha' been glad, and are glad at this time, to take
up commodities in hawks' hoods and brown paper.°

EASY Oh horrible! Are there such fools in town?

QUOMODO I offer him no trash, tell him, upon my religion, you   195
may say.—[Aside] Now, my sweet Shortyard; now the hungry
fish begins to nibble; one end of the worm is in his mouth
i'faith.

THOMASINE [aside] Why stand I here—as late our graceless dames
That found no eyes—to see that gentleman°   200
Alive, in state and credit, executed,°
Help to rip up himself, does all he can?°
Why am I wife to him that is no man?°
I suffer in that gentleman's confusion.

EASY Nay, be persuaded in that, Master Blastfield; 'tis ready money   205
at the merchants'; beside, the winter season and all falls in as pat
as can be to help it.

SHORTYARD Well, Master Easy, none but you could have persuaded
me to that.—Come, would you would dispatch then, Master
Quomodo. Where's this cloth?   210

QUOMODO Full and whole within, [displaying a sample] all of this
piece, of my religion, Master Blastfield. Feel't, nay, feel't and spare
not, gentlemen; your fingers and your judgement.

SHORTYARD Cloth's good.

EASY By my troth, exceeding good cloth; a good wale 't'as.   215

QUOMODO Falselight!

        [Enter Falselight]

FALSELIGHT I'm ne'er out o'th'shop, sir.°

QUOMODO Go, call in a porter presently to carry away the cloth with
the star mark.°—Whither will you please to have it carried, Master
Blastfield?   220

SHORTYARD Faith, to Master Beggarland, he's the only merchant
now; or his brother,° Master Stilliard-down,° there's little difference.

QUOMODO Y'ave happened upon the money men, sir; they and
some of their brethren, I can tell you, will not stick to offer thirty

thousand pound to be cursed° still; great monied men, their stocks   225
lie in the poor's throats.° But you'll see me sufficiently discharged,°
Master Blastfield, ere you depart?

SHORTYARD You have always found me righteous in that.

QUOMODO Falselight.

FALSELIGHT Sir?   230

QUOMODO You may bring a scrivener along with you.

FALSELIGHT I'll remember that, sir.
        [*Exit Falselight*]

QUOMODO Have you sent for a citizen, Master Blastfield?

SHORTYARD No, faith, not yet.—Boy!

EASY What must you do with a citizen, sir?   235

SHORTYARD A custom they're bound to a-late by the default of evil
    debtors; no citizen must lend money without° two be bound in the
    bond; the second man enters but for custom sake.

EASY No? And must he needs be a citizen?

SHORTYARD By th'mass, stay, I'll learn that.—Master Quomodo.   240

QUOMODO Sir?

SHORTYARD Must the second party, that enters into bond only for
    fashion's sake, needs be a citizen? What say you to this gentleman
    for one?

QUOMODO Alas, sir, you know he's a mere stranger to me; I neither   245
    am sure of his going or abiding; he may inn here tonight and ride
    away tomorrow. Although I grant the chief burden lies upon you,
    yet we are bound to make choice of those we know, sir.

SHORTYARD Why, he's a gentleman of a pretty living, sir.

QUOMODO It may be so; yet, under both your pardons, I'd rather   250
    have a citizen.

EASY I hope you will not disparage me so. 'Tis well known I have
    three hundred pound° a year in Essex.

SHORTYARD Well said. To him thyself, take him up roundly.

EASY And how doubtfully soe'er° you account of me, I do not think   255
    but I might make my bond pass for a hundred pound i'th'city.

QUOMODO What, alone, sir?

EASY Alone, sir? Who says so? Perhaps I'd send down° for a tenant
    or two.

QUOMODO Ay, that's another case, sir.   260

EASY Another case let it be then!

QUOMODO Nay, grow not into anger, sir.

EASY Not take me into a bond? As good as you shall, goodman
    goosecap.

QUOMODO Well, Master Blastfield, because I will not disgrace the 265
    gentleman, I'm content for once; but we must not make a practice
    on't.
EASY No, sir, now you would, you shall not.
QUOMODO [aside] Cuds me, I'm undone; he's gone again.
SHORTYARD [aside] The net's broke.   270
THOMASINE [aside] Hold there,° dear gentleman.
EASY Deny me that small courtesy? 'Sfoot, a very Jew will not deny
    it me.
SHORTYARD [aside] Now must I catch him warily.
EASY A jest indeed! Not take me into a bond, quo'they.   275
SHORTYARD Master Easy. [Takes him to one side] Mark my words, if
    it stood not upon the eternal loss of thy credit against supper—
EASY Mass, that's true.
SHORTYARD The pawning of thy horse for his own victuals—
EASY Right i'faith.   280
SHORTYARD And thy utter dissolution amongst gentlemen forever—
EASY Pox on't!
SHORTYARD Quomodo should hang, rot, stink—
QUOMODO [aside] Sweet boy i'faith.
SHORTYARD Drop, damn.°   285
QUOMODO [aside] Excellent Shortyard!
EASY I forgot all this. What meant I to swagger before I had money
    in my purse?—How does Master Quomodo? Is the bond ready?
QUOMODO Oh, sir!
        Enter Dustbox, the scrivener
EASY Come, we must be friends; here's my hand.°   290
QUOMODO Give it the scrivener; here he comes.
DUSTBOX Good day, Master Quomodo. Good morrow, gentlemen.
QUOMODO We must require a little aid from your pen, good Master
    Dustbox.
        [The Scrivener begins to draw up the document]
DUSTBOX What be the gentlemen's names that are bound, sir?   295
QUOMODO Master John Blastfield, esquire, i'th'wild° of Kent, and—
    what do they call your bedfellow's name?
SHORTYARD Master Richard Easy; you may easily hit on't.
QUOMODO Master Richard Easy, of Essex, gentleman; both bound
    to Ephestian Quomodo, citizen and draper, of London; the sum,   300
    two hundred pound.—What time do you take, Master Blastfield,
    for the payment?
SHORTYARD I never pass my month, you know.

QUOMODO I know it, sir. October sixteenth today; sixteenth of
    November, say.   305

EASY Is it your custom to return° so soon, sir?

SHORTYARD I never miss you.

    Enter Falselight, like a porter, sweating

FALSELIGHT I am come for the rest of the same piece,° Master
    Quomodo.

QUOMODO Star mark, this is it. Are all the rest gone?   310

FALSELIGHT They're all at Master Stilliard-down's by this time.

EASY How the poor rascal's all in a froth!

SHORTYARD Push, they're ordained to sweat for gentlemen; porters'
    backs and women's bellies bear up the world.

    [*Exit Falselight with cloth*]

EASY 'Tis true i'faith; they bear men and money, and that's the   315
    world.

SHORTYARD Y'ave found it,° sir.

DUSTBOX I'm ready to° your hands,° gentlemen.

    [*He presents the bond*]

SHORTYARD Come, Master Easy.

    [*He invites Easy to sign first*]

EASY I beseech you, sir.   320

SHORTYARD It° shall be yours, I say.

EASY Nay, pray, Master Blastfield.

SHORTYARD I will not i'faith.

EASY What do you mean, sir?

SHORTYARD I should show little bringing up, to take the way of° a 325
    stranger.

EASY By my troth, you do yourself wrong though, Master Blastfield.

SHORTYARD Not a whit, sir.

EASY But to avoid strife, you shall have your will of me for once.

SHORTYARD Let it be so, I pray.   330

QUOMODO [*aside*] Now I begin to set one foot upon the land.
    Methinks I am felling of trees° already; we shall have some Essex
    logs yet to keep Christmas° with, and that's a comfort.

THOMASINE [*aside*] Now is he quart'ring out; the executioner°
    Strides over him; with his own blood he writes.°   335
    I am no dame that can endure such sights.

    Exit [*Thomasine above*]

SHORTYARD [*aside*] So his right wing is cut; he will not fly far
    Past the two city hazards, Poultry and Wood Street.

EASY How like you my Roman hand° i'faith?

DUSTBOX Exceeding well, sir, but that you rest too much upon your   340
 R's, and make your E's° too little.
EASY I'll mend that presently.
DUSTBOX Nay, 'tis done now, past mending.
        [*Shortyard signs*]
 You both deliver this to Master Quomodo as your deed?
SHORTYARD We do, sir.   345
QUOMODO I thank you, gentlemen.
        [*Exit Dustbox*]
SHORTYARD Would the coin° would come away now. We have
 deserved for't.
        Enter Falselight [dressed as a porter] with the cloth
FALSELIGHT By your leave a little,° gentlemen.
SHORTYARD How now? What's the matter? Speak!   350
FALSELIGHT As fast as I can, sir. All the cloth's come back again.
QUOMODO How?
SHORTYARD What's the news?
FALSELIGHT The passage° to Middleborrow is stopped,° and there-
 fore neither Master Stilliard-down nor Master Beggarland, nor any   355
 other merchant, will deliver present money upon't.
QUOMODO Why, what hard luck have you, gentlemen!
        [*Exit Falselight*]
EASY Why, Master Blastfield!
SHORTYARD Pish!
EASY You're so discontented too presently, a man cannot tell how to   360
 speak to you.
SHORTYARD Why, what would you say?
EASY We must make somewhat on't now, sir.
SHORTYARD Ay, where? How? The best is, it lies all upon my neck.
 —Master Quomodo, can you help me to any money for't? Speak.   365
QUOMODO Troth, Master Blastfield, since myself is so unfurnished,
 I know not the means how. There's one i'th'street, a new
 setter-up;° if any lay out money upon't, 'twill be he.
SHORTYARD His name?
QUOMODO Master Idem.° But you know we cannot give but greatly   370
 to your loss because we gain and live by't.°
SHORTYARD 'Sfoot, will he give anything?
EASY Ay, stand° upon that.
SHORTYARD Will he give anything? The brokers will give nothing,
 to no purpose.   375
QUOMODO Falselight!

[Enter Falselight above]

FALSELIGHT Over your head,° sir.

QUOMODO Desire Master Idem to come presently and look
upo'th'cloth.

FALSELIGHT I will, sir.   380

[Exit Falselight above]

SHORTYARD What if he should offer but a hundred pound?

EASY If he want twenty° on't, let's take it.

SHORTYARD Say you so?

EASY Master Quomodo will have four or five hundred pound for you
of his own within three or four days.   385

SHORTYARD 'Tis true, he said so indeed.

[Enter Thomasine]

EASY Is that your wife, Master Quomodo?

QUOMODO That's she, little Thomasine!

EASY Under your leave, sir, I'll show myself a gentleman.°

QUOMODO Do, and welcome, Master Easy.   390

EASY I have commission for what I do, lady, from your husband.

[Kisses her]

THOMASINE You may have a stronger commission for the next, an't
please you; that's from myself.

Enter Sim

EASY You teach me the best law, lady.

THOMASINE *[aside]* Beshrew my blood, a proper springall° and a   395
sweet gentleman.

QUOMODO My son, Sim Quomodo. Here's more work for you,
Master Easy; you must salute him too;—*[aside]* for he's like to be
heir of thy land, I can tell thee.

SIM *Vim, vitam, spemque salutem.*°   400

QUOMODO He shows you there° he was a Cambridge man, sir, but
now he's a Templar.° Has he not good grace to make a lawyer?

EASY A very good grace to make a lawyer.

SHORTYARD *[aside]* For, indeed, he has no grace° at all.

QUOMODO Some gave me counsel to make him a divine.   405

EASY Fie, fie!

QUOMODO But some of our Livery° think it an unfit thing that our
own sons should tell us of our vices; others, to make him a
physician, but then, being my heir, I'm afraid he would make me
away;° now, a lawyer, they're all willing to, because 'tis good for   410
our trade and increaseth the number of cloth gowns,° and indeed

'tis the fittest for a citizen's son, for our word is, 'What do ye lack?'
and their word is, 'What do you give'?

EASY Exceeding proper.

    Enter Falselight (for° Master Idem)

QUOMODO Master Idem, welcome.   415

FALSELIGHT I have seen the cloth, sir.

QUOMODO Very well.

FALSELIGHT I am but a young setter-up; the uttermost I dare
venture upon't is three-score pound.

SHORTYARD What?   420

FALSELIGHT If it be for me,° so, I am for it; if not, you have your
cloth and I have my money.

EASY Nay, pray, Master Blastfield, refuse not his kind offer.

SHORTYARD A bargain then, Master Idem, clap hands.—[*Aside*] He's
finely cheated.—Come, let's all to the next tavern and see the   425
money paid.

EASY A match!

QUOMODO I follow you, gentlemen; take my son along with you.

    Exeunt [all but Quomodo]

Now to my keys;° I'm Master Idem, he must fetch the money.
First have I caught him in a bond for two hundred pound, and   430
[now have I]° my two hundred pounds' worth o'cloth again for
three-score pound. Admire me, all you students at Inns of
Cozenage.°

    Exit

[3.1]

*Enter Lethe's pander, Hellgill, the Country Wench coming in
with a new fashion gown, dressed gentlewoman-like. The Tailor
points° it, and [Mistress Comings] a tirewoman,° busy about her
head*

HELLGILL You talk of an alteration; here's the thing itself.° What
base birth does not raiment make glorious? And what glorious
births do not rags make infamous? Why should not a woman
confess what she is now, since the finest are but deluding shadows
begot between tirewomen and tailors? For instance, behold their   5
parents.°

MISTRESS COMINGS Say what you will, this wire° becomes you
best.—How say you, tailor?

TAILOR I promise you, 'tis a wire would draw me from my work
seven days a week.   10

COUNTRY WENCH Why, do you work o'Sundays, tailor?

TAILOR Hardest of all o'Sundays, because we are most forbidden.

COUNTRY WENCH Troth, and so do most of us women; the better
day the better deed, we think.

MISTRESS COMINGS Excellent, exceeding i'faith. A narrow-eared°   15
wire sets out a cheek so fat and so full, and if you be ruled by me,
you shall wear your hair still like a mock-face behind; 'tis such an
Italian° world, many men know not before from behind.

TAILOR How like you the sitting of this gown now, Mistress
Comings?   20

MISTRESS COMINGS It sits at marvellous good ease and comely
discretion.

HELLGILL Who would think now this fine sophisticated squall came
out of the bosom of a barn and the loins of a hay-tosser?

COUNTRY WENCH Out, you saucy, pestiferous pander! I scorn that   25
i'faith.

HELLGILL Excellent; already the true phrase and style of a strumpet.
Stay, a little more of the red,° and then I take my leave of your
cheek for four and twenty hours. Do you not think it impossible
that her own father should know her now if he saw her?   30

COUNTRY WENCH Why, I think no less. How can he know me when
I scarce know myself?

HELLGILL 'Tis right.

COUNTRY WENCH But so well you lay wait for a man for me!°

HELLGILL I protest I have bestowed much labour about it; and in fit   35
  time, good news, I hope.

> Enter one [*a Servant*]° *bringing in her Father in disguise to*
> *serve her*

SERVANT I've found one yet at last, in whose preferment I hope to
  reap credit.

COUNTRY WENCH Is that the fellow?

SERVANT Lady, it is.   40

COUNTRY WENCH Art thou willing to serve me, fellow?

FATHER So please you, he that has not the heart to serve such a
  mistress as your beautiful self deserves to be honoured for a fool
  or knighted for a coward.

COUNTRY WENCH There's too many of them already.°   45

FATHER 'Twere sin then to raise the number.

COUNTRY WENCH Well, we'll try both our likings° for a month, and
  then either proceed or let fall the suit.

FATHER Be it as you have spoke; but 'tis my hope, a longer Term.

COUNTRY WENCH No, truly, our Term ends once a month;° we   50
  should get more than the lawyers, for they have but four Terms a
  year and we have twelve, and that makes 'em run so fast to us in
  the vacation.°

FATHER [*aside*] A mistress of a choice beauty! Amongst such imperfect creatures° I ha' not seen a perfecter; I should have reckoned   55
  the fortunes of my daughter amongst the happiest, had she lighted
  into such a service, whereas now I rest doubtful whom or where
  she serves.°

COUNTRY WENCH [*giving money*] There's for your bodily advice,
  Tailor; and there's for your head-counsel; and I discharge you both   60
  till tomorrow morning again.

TAILOR At which time our neatest attendance.

MISTRESS COMINGS I pray have an especial care, howsoever you
  stand or lie, that nothing fall upon your hair to batter your wire.

COUNTRY WENCH I warrant you for that.   65

> *Exeunt* [*Tailor and Mistress Comings*]

  Which gown becomes me best now, the purple satin or this?

HELLGILL If my opinion might rule over you—

> *Enter Lethe with Rearage and Salewood*

LETHE Come, gallants, I'll bring you to a beauty shall strike your
  eyes into your hearts; what you see you shall desire, yet never
  enjoy.   70

REARAGE And that's a villainous torment.

SALEWOOD And is she but your underput, Master Lethe?

LETHE No more, of my credit; and a gentlewoman of a great house, noble parentage, unmatchable education, my plain pung. I may grace her with the name of a courtesan, a backslider, a prostitution, 75 or such a toy; but when all comes to all,° 'tis but a plain pung. Look you, gentlemen, that's she; behold her.

COUNTRY WENCH Oh, my beloved strayer! I consume° in thy absence.

LETHE La you now! You shall not say I'll be proud to you, 80 gentlemen; I give you leave to salute° her.—[Aside] I'm afraid of nothing now but that she'll utterly disgrace 'em, turn tail to 'em, and place their kisses behind her. No, by my faith, she deceives me; by my troth, she's kissed 'em both with her lips. I thank you for that music, masters. 'Slid, they both court her at once, and see 85 if she ha' not the wit to stand still and let 'em. I think if two men were brewed into one, there is that woman would drink 'em up both.

REARAGE [to her] A coxcomb! He a courtier?

COUNTRY WENCH He says he has a place there.° 90

SALEWOOD So has the fool, a better place than he, and can come° where he dare not show his head.

LETHE Nay, hear you me, gentlemen—

SALEWOOD I protest you were the last man we spoke on.° We're a little busy yet; pray stay there awhile;° we'll come to you presently. 95

LETHE [aside] This is good i'faith; endure this, and be a slave forever! Since you neither savour of good breeding nor bringing up, I'll slice your hamstrings, but I'll make you show mannerly.—Pox on you, leave° courting! I ha' not the heart to hurt an Englishman, i'faith, or else— 100

SALEWOOD What else?

LETHE Prithee let's be merry; nothing else.—Here,° fetch some wine.

COUNTRY WENCH Let my servant go for't.

LETHE Yours? Which is he?

FATHER This, sir. 105
   [Aside] But I scarce like my mistress now; the loins
   Can ne'er be safe where the flies be so busy.°
   Wit, by experience bought, foils wit at school;
   Who proves a deeper knave than a spent fool?—°
   I am gone for your worship's wine, sir. 110
      [Exit Father]

HELLGILL [*taking Lethe aside*] Sir, you put up° too much indignity;
    bring company to cut your own throat. The fire is not yet so hot
    that you need two screens° before it; 'tis but new kindled yet. If
    'twere risse to a flame, I could not blame you then to put others
    before you; but, alas, all the heat yet is comfortable; a cherisher,   115
    not a defacer.°

LETHE Prithee let 'em alone; they'll be ashamed on't anon, I trow, if
    they have any grace in 'em.

HELLGILL [*aside*] I'd fain have him quarrel, fight, and be assuredly
    killed, that I might beg his place,° for there's ne'er a one void yet.   120
        [*Exit Hellgill.*] *Enter Shortyard* [*alias Blastfield*] *with
        Easy*

COUNTRY WENCH You'll make him° mad anon.

SALEWOOD 'Tis to that end.°

SHORTYARD Yet at last Master Quomodo is as firm as his
    promise.°

EASY Did I not tell you still he would?   125

SHORTYARD Let me see, I am seven hundred pound in bond now°
    to the rascal.

EASY Nay, y'are no less, Master Blastfield, look to't. By my troth, I
    must needs confess, sir, you ha' been uncommonly kind to me
    since I ha' been in town; but Master Alsup shall know on't.   130

SHORTYARD That's my ambition, sir.

EASY I beseech you, sir—stay, this is Lethe's haunt;° see, we have
    catched him.

LETHE Master Blastfield and Master Easy, y'are kind gentlemen both.

SHORTYARD Is that the beauty you famed° so?   135

LETHE The same.

SHORTYARD Who be those so industrious about her?

LETHE Rearage and Salewood. I'll tell you the unmannerliest trick of
    'em that ever you heard in your life.

SHORTYARD Prithee what's that?   140

LETHE I invited 'em hither to look upon her, brought 'em along
    with me, gave 'em leave to salute her in kindness; what do they
    but most saucily fall in love with her, very impudently court her
    for themselves, and, like two crafty attorneys finding a hole° in my
    lease, go about to defeat me of my right.°   145

SHORTYARD Ha' they so little conscience?

LETHE The most uncivil'st part° that you have seen! I know they'll
    be sorry for't when they have done, for there's no man but gives
    a sigh after his sin of women;° I know it by myself.°

SHORTYARD [*to Rearage and Salewood*] You parcel of a rude, saucy,   150
and unmannerly nation°—

LETHE [*aside*] One good thing in him, he'll tell 'em on't roundly.

SHORTYARD Cannot a gentleman purchase a little fire to thaw his
appetite by, but must you, that have been daily singed in the flame,
be as greedy to beguile him on't? How can it appear in you but   155
maliciously, and that you go about to engross hell to yourselves?
Heaven forbid that you should not suffer a stranger to come in;
the devil himself is not so unmannerly. I do not think but some of
them° rather will be wise enough to beg offices° there° before you
and keep you out;° marry, all the spite will be, they cannot sell   160
'em° again.

EASY Come, are you not to blame? Not to give place—to us,° I mean.

LETHE A worse and worse° disgrace!

COUNTRY WENCH Nay, gentlemen, you wrong us° both then. Stand
from me; I protest I'll draw my silver bodkin upon you.   165

SHORTYARD Clubs, clubs! Gentlemen, stand upon your guard.

COUNTRY WENCH A gentlewoman must swagger a little now and
then, I perceive; there would be no civility in her chamber else.
Though it may be hard fortune to have my keeper there a coward,
the thing that's kept is a gentlewoman born.   170

SHORTYARD And, to conclude, a coward, infallible of your side;°
why, do you think, i'faith, I took you to be a coward?° Do I think
you'll turn your back to any man living? You'll be whipped
first.°

EASY And then indeed she turns her back to some man living.   175

SHORTYARD But that man shows himself a knave, for he dares not
show his own face° when he does it; for some of the Common
Council° in Henry the VIII's days° thought it modesty at that time
that one vizard should look upon another.

EASY 'Twas honestly considered of 'em i'faith.   180

Enter Mother Gruel

SHORTYARD How now? What piece of stuff° comes here?

LETHE [*aside*] Now some good news yet to recover my repute and grace
me in this company.—Gentlemen, are we friends among ourselves?

SHORTYARD United.

[*Enter Father with wine*]

LETHE Then here comes Rhenish to confirm our amity.—   185
Wagtail, salute them all, they are friends.

COUNTRY WENCH Then, saving my quarrel, to you all.

[She toasts them and they her]

SHORTYARD To's all.

COUNTRY WENCH Now beshrew your hearts, an you do not.°

SHORTYARD To sweet Master Lethe.   190

LETHE Let it flow this way, dear Master Blastfield.—Gentlemen, to
you all.

SHORTYARD This Rhenish wine is like the scouring-stick to a gun,
it makes the barrel° clear; it has an excellent virtue, it keeps all the
sinks in man and woman's body sweet in June and July; and, to   195
say truth, if ditches were not cast° once a year, and drabs once a
month,° there would be no abiding i'th'city.

LETHE Gentlemen, I'll make you privy to° a letter I sent.

SHORTYARD A letter comes well after privy; it makes amends.

LETHE There's one Quomodo a draper's daughter in town,   200
Whom for her happy portion I wealthily affect.

REARAGE And not for love?
    [To Salewood]   This makes for me, his rival;°
Bear witness.

LETHE The father does elect me for the man,
The daughter says the same.

SHORTYARD   Are you not well?°   205

LETHE Yes, all but for the mother; she's my sickness.

SHORTYARD Byrlady, and the mother° is a pestilent, wilful, troublesome sickness, I can tell you, if she light upon you handsomely.

LETHE I find it so; she for a stranger pleads,
Whose name I ha' not learned.   210

REARAGE [to Salewood] And e'en now he called me by it.

LETHE Now, as my letter told her, since only her assent kept aloof
off, what might I think on't but that she merely doted upon me
herself?

SHORTYARD Very assuredly.   215

SALEWOOD [to Rearage] This makes still for you.

SHORTYARD Did you let it go so° i'faith?

LETHE You may believe it, sir. Now what says her answer?

SHORTYARD Ay, her answer.

MOTHER GRUEL She says you're a base, proud knave, and like your   220
worship.

LETHE How?

SHORTYARD Nay, hear out her answer, or there's no goodness in you.

MOTHER GRUEL You ha' forgot, she says, in what pickle your
worship came up, and brought two of your friends to give their   225
words for a suit of green kersey.

LETHE Drudge, peace, or—

SHORTYARD Show yourself a gentleman; she° had the patience to
read your letter, which was as bad as this can be. What will she
think on't? Not hear her answer!—Speak, good his drudge. 230

MOTHER GRUEL And as for her daughter, she hopes she'll be ruled
by her in time and not be carried away with a cast of manchets,°
a bottle of wine, and a custard, which once made her daughter sick,
because you came by it with a bad conscience.

LETHE Gentlemen, I'm all in a sweat. 235

SHORTYARD That's very wholesome for your body; nay, you must
keep in your arms.°

MOTHER GRUEL Then she demanded of me whether I was your
worship's aunt or no.

LETHE Out, out, out! 240

MOTHER GRUEL Alas, said I, I am a poor drudge of his.
Faith, an thou wert his mother, quoth she, he'd make thee his
drudge, I warrant him. Marry, out upon him, quoth I, an't like
your worship.

LETHE Horror, horror! I'm smothered; let me go; torment me not. 245
          Exit [Lethe]

SHORTYARD An you love me let's follow him, gentlemen.

REARAGE, SALEWOOD Agreed.
          Exeunt [Rearage and Salewood]

SHORTYARD I count a hundred pound well spent to pursue a good
jest, Master Easy.

EASY By my troth, I begin to bear that mind° too. 250

SHORTYARD Well said i'faith; hang money! Good jests are worth
silver at all times.

EASY They're worth gold, Master Blastfield.
          Exeunt [all but Country Wench and her Father]

COUNTRY WENCH Do you deceive me so? Are you toward° marriage, i'faith, Master Lethe? It shall go hard but I'll forbid the 255
banns; I'll send a messenger into your bones,° another into your
purse,° but I'll do't.
          Exit [Country Wench]

FATHER Thou fair and wicked creature, steeped in art,
Beauteous and fresh, the soul the foulest part!
A common filth is like a house possessed,° 260
Where, if not spoiled, you'll come out 'fraid at least.°
This service likes not me; though I rest poor,°
I hate the basest use, to screen a whore.°

The human stroke ne'er made him; he that can
Be bawd to woman never leapt from man;°   265
Some monster won his mother.
I wished my poor child hither, doubled wrong!°
A month and such a mistress were too long;
Yet here awhile in others' lives I'll see
How former follies did appear in me.   270
    Exit

[3.2]

    Enter Easy with Shortyard's Boy

EASY Boy!

BOY Anon, sir.

EASY Where left you Master Blastfield, your master, say you?

BOY An hour since I left him in Paul's,° sir.—[*Aside*] But you'll not
find him the same man again next time you meet him.   5

EASY Methinks I have no being without his company; 'tis so full of
kindness and delight, I hold him to be the only companion in
earth.

BOY [*aside*] Ay, as companions go nowadays, that help to spend a
man's money.   10

EASY So full of nimble wit, various discourse, pregnant apprehension, and uncommon entertainment! He might keep company with
any lord for his grace.

BOY [*aside*] Ay, with any lord that were past it.°

EASY And such a good, free-hearted, honest, affable kind of gentle-   15
man. Come, boy, a heaviness will possess me till I see him.
    [*Exit Easy*]

BOY But you'll find yourself heavier then by a seven hundred pound
weight. Alas, poor birds that cannot keep the sweet country where
they fly at pleasure, but must needs come to London to have their
wings clipped and are fain to go hopping home again.   20
    Exit

[3.3]

Enter Shortyard and Falselight, like a Sergeant and a
Yeoman, to arrest Easy

SHORTYARD So, no man is so impudent to deny that. Spirits can
change their shapes,° and soonest of all into sergeants because they
are cousin-germans to spirits; for there's but two kinds of arrests
till doomsday: the devil for the soul, the sergeant for the body. But
afterward the devil arrests body and soul, sergeant and all, if they   5
be knaves still and deserve it. Now, my Yeoman Falselight.

FALSELIGHT I attend you, good Sergeant Shortyard.

SHORTYARD No more Master Blastfield now. Poor Easy, hardly
beset.

FALSELIGHT But how if he should go to prison? We're in a mad   10
state° then, being not sergeants.

SHORTYARD Never let it come near thy belief that he'll take prison,
or stand out in law,° knowing the debt to be due, but still expect
the presence of Master Blastfield, kind Master Blastfield, worshipful Master Blastfield, and at the last—   15

BOY [*within*]° Master Shortyard, Master Falselight!

SHORTYARD The boy, a warning-piece. See where he comes.

Enter Easy with the Boy

EASY Is not in Paul's.°

BOY He is not far off, sure, sir.

EASY When was his hour,° say'st thou?   20

BOY Two, sir.

EASY Why, two has struck.

BOY No, sir, they are now a-striking.°

SHORTYARD Master Richard Easy of Essex, we arrest you.

EASY Hah?   25

BOY Alas, a surgeon! He's hurt i'th'shoulder.

Exit [Boy]

SHORTYARD Deliver your weapons quietly, sir.

EASY Why, what's the matter?

SHORTYARD Y'are arrested at the suit of Master Quomodo.

EASY Master Quomodo?   30

SHORTYARD How strange you make it. You're a landed gentleman,
sir; I know° 'tis but a trifle, a bond of seven hundred pound.

EASY La, I knew you had mistook; you should arrest one Master
Blastfield, 'tis his bond, his debt.

SHORTYARD Is not your name there?   35
EASY True, for fashion's sake.
SHORTYARD Why, and 'tis for fashion's sake that we arrest you.
EASY Nay, an it be no more, I yield to that. I know Master Blastfield
     will see me take no injury, as long as I'm in town, for Master
     Alsup's sake.   40
SHORTYARD Who's that, sir?
EASY An honest gentleman in Essex.
SHORTYARD Oh, in Essex! I thought you had been in° London,
     where now your business lies; honesty from Essex will be a great
     while a-coming, sir; you should look out an honest pair of   45
     citizens.°
EASY Alas, sir, I know not where to find 'em.
SHORTYARD No? There's enow in town.
EASY I know not one, by my troth; I am a mere stranger for these
     parts; Master Quomodo is all, and the honestest that I know.   50
SHORTYARD To him, then, let's set forward.—Yeoman Spiderman,
     cast an eye about for Master Blastfield.
EASY Boy!—Alas, the poor boy was frighted away at first.
SHORTYARD Can you blame him, sir? We that daily fray away
     knights may fright away boys, I hope.   55
          Exeunt

[3.4]

Enter Quomodo with the Boy, [Thomasine watching above]

QUOMODO Hah! Have they him say'st thou?
BOY   As sure as—
QUOMODO The land's mine; that's sure enough, boy.
     Let me advance thee, knave, and give thee a kiss;
     My plot's so firm, I dare it now to miss.
     Now shall I be divulged a landed man   5
     Throughout the Livery; one points, another whispers,°
     A third frets inwardly; let him fret and hang!
     Especially his envy I shall have
     That would be fain, yet cannot be, a knave,
     Like an old lecher, girt in a furred gown,°   10
     Whose mind stands stiff, but his performance down.°
     Now come my golden days in.

—Whither is the worshipful Master Quomodo and his fair bedfellow rid forth?—To his land in Essex!—Whence comes those
goodly load of logs?—From his land in Essex!—Where grows this   15
pleasant fruit? says one citizen's wife in the Row.°—At Master
Quomodo's orchard in Essex.—Oh, oh, does it so? I thank you for
that good news i'faith.

BOY Here they come with him, sir.
    [*Exit Boy*]

QUOMODO Grant me patience in my joys, that, being so great, I run   20
not mad with 'em.
    [*Enter Shortyard and Falselight, disguised as a Sergeant and a
    Yeoman, bringing in Easy*]

SHORTYARD Bless Master Quomodo.

QUOMODO How now, sergeants? Who ha' you brought me here?—
Master Easy!

EASY Why, la you now, sergeants, did I not tell you you mistook?   25

QUOMODO Did you not hear me say I had rather ha' had Master
Blastfield, the more sufficient man, a great deal?

SHORTYARD Very true, sir, but this gentleman lighting into our
hands first—

QUOMODO Why,° did you so, sir?   30

SHORTYARD We thought to make good use of that opportunity and
hold him fast.

QUOMODO You did well in that, I must needs say, for your own
securities. But 'twas not in my mind, Master Easy, to have you
first, you must needs think so.   35

EASY I dare swear that, Master Quomodo.

QUOMODO But since you are come to me, I have no reason to refuse
you; I should show little manners in that, sir.

EASY But I hope you spake not in that sense, sir, to impose the bond
upon me.   40

QUOMODO By my troth, that's my meaning, sir; you shall find me
an honest man; you see I mean what I say. Is not the day past, the
money untendered? You'd ha' me live uprightly, Master Easy?

EASY Why, sir, you know Master Blastfield is the man.

QUOMODO Why, sir, I know Master Blastfield is the man; but is he   45
any more than one man? Two entered into bond to me, or I'm
foully cozened.

EASY You know my entrance was but for fashion sake.

QUOMODO Why, I'll agree to you; you'll grant 'tis the fashion
likewise, when the bond's due, to have the money paid again.   50

SHORTYARD So we have told him, sir, and that it lay in your worship's courtesy° to arrest which you please.

QUOMODO Marry, does it, sir; these fellows know the law. Beside, you offered yourself into bond to me, you know, when I had no stomach to you; now beshrew your heart for your labour! I might ha' had a good° substantial citizen, that would ha' paid the sum roundly, although I think you sufficient enough for seven hundred pound; beside the forfeiture, I would be loath to disgrace you so much before sergeants. 55

EASY If you would ha' the patience, sir, I do not think but Master Blastfield is at carrier's° to receive the money. 60

QUOMODO He will prove the honester man, then, and you the better discharged. I wonder he should break with me; 'twas never his practice. You must not be angry with me now, though you were somewhat hot when you entered into bond; you may easily go in angrily, but you cannot come out so. 65

EASY No, the devil's in't for that.

SHORTYARD Do you hear, sir? [*Taking him aside*] O'my troth, we pity you; ha' you any store of crowns about you?

EASY Faith, a poor store, yet they shall be at their service that will strive to do me good. We were both drunk last night and ne'er thought upon the bond. 70

SHORTYARD I must tell you this, you have fell into the hands of a most merciless devourer, the very gull° o'the city; should you offer him money, goods, or lands now, he'd rather have your body in prison, he's o'such a nature. 75

EASY Prison? W'are undone then!

SHORTYARD He's o'such a nature, look! Let him owe any man a spite, what's his course? He will lend him money today o'purpose to 'rest him tomorrow. 80

EASY Defend me!°

SHORTYARD H'as at least sixteen at this instant proceeded° in both the Counters: some bach'lors, some masters, some doctors of captivity of twenty years' standing;° and he desires nothing more than imprisonment. 85

EASY Would Master Blastfield would come away!

SHORTYARD Ay, then things would not be as they are. What will you say to us, if we procure you two substantial subsidy° citizens to bail you, spite on's heart,° and set you at liberty to find out Master Blastfield?

EASY Sergeant, here, take all!° I'll be dear to you, do but perform it. 90

SHORTYARD [*aside to Falselight*] Much!°

FALSELIGHT [*aside to Shortyard*] Enough, sweet sergeant, I hope I
    understand thee.

SHORTYARD I love to prevent the malice of such a rascal; perhaps
    you might find Master Blastfield tonight.   95

EASY Why, we lie together, man, there's the jest on't.

SHORTYARD Fie! And you'll seek to secure your bail?
    Because they will be two citizens of good account;° you must do
    that for your credit sake.

EASY I'll be bound to save them harmless.°   100

SHORTYARD A pox on him, you cut his throat then. No words!°

EASY What's it you require me, Master Quomodo?

QUOMODO You know that before this time, I hope, sir; present
    money or present imprisonment.

SHORTYARD [*to Easy*] I told you so.   105

EASY We ne'er had money of you.

QUOMODO You had commodities, an't please you.

EASY Well, may I not crave so much liberty upon my word° to seek
    out Master Blastfield?

QUOMODO Yes, an you would not laugh at me. We are sometimes   110
    gulls to gentlemen, I thank 'em; but gentlemen are never gulls to
    us, I commend 'em.

SHORTYARD Under your leave, Master Quomodo, the gentleman
    craves the furtherance of an hour; and it sorts well with our
    occasion at this time, having a little urgent business at Guildhall;   115
    at which minute we'll return and see what agreement is made.

QUOMODO Nay, take him along with you, sergeant.

EASY [*aside*] I'm undone then.

SHORTYARD He's your prisoner, and being safe in your house at
    your own disposing, you cannot deny him such a request; beside,   120
    he hath a little faith in Master Blastfield's coming, sir.

QUOMODO Let me not be too long delayed, I charge you.

EASY Not an hour i'faith, sir.
        Exeunt [*Shortyard and Falselight*]

QUOMODO Oh, Master Easy, of all men living I never dreamt° you
    would ha' done me this injury: make me wound my credit, fail in   125
    my commodities, bring° my state° into suspicion. For the breaking
    of your day° to me has broken my day to others.

EASY You tell me of that still which is no fault of mine, Master
    Quomodo.

QUOMODO Oh, what's a man but his honesty, Master Easy? And   130
    that's° a fault amongst most of us all. Mark but this note;° I'll give

you good counsel now. As often as you give your name to a bond,
you must think you christen a child and take the charge° on't too;
for as the one, the bigger it grows the more cost it requires, so
the other, the longer it lies the more charges it puts you to. Only   135
here's the difference: a child must be broke° and a bond must not;
the more you break children, the more you keep 'em under, but the
more you break bonds, the more they'll leap in your face; and
therefore, to conclude, I would never undertake to be gossip to that
bond which I would not see well brought up.   140

EASY Say you so, sir? I'll think upon your counsel hereafter for't.

QUOMODO [aside] Ah, fool, thou shouldst ne'er ha' tasted such wit,
but that I know 'tis too late.

THOMASINE [aside] The more I grieve.

QUOMODO To put all this into the compass of a little hoop ring:°   145
    'Make this account, come better days or worse,
    So many bonds abroad, so many boys at nurse.'°

EASY A good medicine° for a short memory. But since you have
entered° so far, whose children are desperate debts, I pray?

QUOMODO Faith, they are like the offsprings of stolen lust, put to   150
the hospital; their fathers are not to be found; they are either too
far abroad or too close within.° And thus for your memory's sake:
    'The desperate debtor hence derives his name,
    One that has neither money, land, nor fame;
    All that he makes proves bastards and not bands,°   155
    But such as yours, at first are born to lands.'°

EASY But all that I beget hereafter I'll soon disinherit,° Master
Quomodo.

QUOMODO [aside] In the meantime here's a shrewd knave will
disinherit you.   160

EASY Well, to put you out of all doubt, Master Quomodo, I'll not
trust to your courtesy; I ha' sent for bail.

QUOMODO How? Y'ave cozened me there i'faith.

EASY Since the worst comes to the worst, I have those friends
i'th'city, I hope, that will not suffer me to lie° for seven hundred   165
pound.

QUOMODO And you told me that you had no friends here at all; how
should a man trust you now?

EASY That was but to try your courtesy, Master Quomodo.

QUOMODO [aside] How unconscionably he gulls himself.—They must   170
be wealthy subsidy-men,° sir, at least forty pounds° i'th'King's
Books, I can tell you, that do such a feat for you.

Enter Shortyard and Falselight, like wealthy citizens in satin suits

EASY Here they come, whatso'er they are.

QUOMODO Byrlady, alderman's deputies!° I am very sorry for you, sir; I cannot refuse such men.   175

SHORTYARD Are you the gentleman in distress?

EASY None more than myself, sir.

QUOMODO [*aside*] He speaks truer than he thinks, for if he knew
The hearts that owe those faces! A dark shop's good°
For somewhat.   180

EASY That was all, sir.°

SHORTYARD And that's enough, for by that means you have made yourself liable to the bond as well as that Basefield.

EASY Blastfield, sir.

SHORTYARD Oh, cry you mercy, 'tis Blastfield indeed.   185

EASY But, under both your worships' favours, I know where to find him presently.

SHORTYARD That's all your refuge.°
      [*Enter Boy*]

BOY News, good news, Master Easy!

EASY What, boy?   190

BOY Master Blastfield, my master, has received a thousand pound and will be at his lodging at supper.

EASY Happy news! Hear you that, Master Quomodo?

QUOMODO 'Tis enough for you to hear that; y'are the fortunate man, sir.   195

EASY Not now,° I beseech your good worships.

SHORTYARD Gentleman, what's your t'other° name?

EASY Easy.

SHORTYARD Oh, Master Easy. I would we could rather pleasure you otherwise,° Master Easy; you should soon perceive it. I'll speak a   200
proud word: we have pitied more gentlemen in distress than any two citizens within the freedom. But to be bail to seven hundred pound action is a matter of shrewd weight.

EASY I'll be bound to secure you.

SHORTYARD Tut, what's your bond, sir?   205

EASY Body, goods, and lands, immediately before Master Quomodo.°

SHORTYARD Shall we venture once again that have been so often undone by gentlemen?

FALSELIGHT I have no great stomach to't; it will appear in us more pity than wisdom.   210

EASY Why should you say so, sir?

SHORTYARD I like the gentleman's face well; he does not look as if he would deceive us.

EASY Oh, not I, sir.

SHORTYARD Come, we'll make a desperate voyage once again; we'll try his honesty, and take his single bond, of body, goods, and lands.

EASY I dearly thank you, sir.

SHORTYARD Master Quomodo!

QUOMODO Your worships.

SHORTYARD We have took a course to set your prisoner free.

QUOMODO Your worships are good bail; you content me.

SHORTYARD Come, then, and be a witness to a recullisance.°

QUOMODO With all my heart, sir.

SHORTYARD Master Easy, you must have an especial care now to find out that Blastfield.

EASY I shall have him at my lodging, sir.

SHORTYARD The suit will be followed against you else; Master Quomodo will come upon us and forsake you.°

EASY I know that, sir.

SHORTYARD Well, since I see you have such a good mind to be honest, I'll leave some greater affairs and sweat with you to find him myself.

EASY Here, then, my misery ends:
    A stranger's kindness oft exceeds a friend's.
        Exeunt [all but Thomasine above]

THOMASINE Thou art deceived, thy misery but begins;
    'To beguile goodness is the core of sins.'°
    My love is such unto thee that I die
    As often as thou drink'st up injury,°
    Yet have no means to warn thee from't; for 'he
    That sows in craft does rape in jealousy.'°
        [Exit]

[3.5]

[Enter Rearage and Salewood]

REARAGE Now the letter's made up° and all; it wants but the print of a seal, and away it goes to Master Quomodo. Andrew Lethe is well whipped in't; his name stands in a white sheet° here and does penance for him.

SALEWOOD You have shame° enough against him, if that be good.   5

REARAGE First, as a contempt of that reverend ceremony he has in hand, to wit, marriage.

SALEWOOD Why do you say, 'to wit, marriage', when you know there's none will marry that's wise?

REARAGE Had it not more need, then, to have wit to put to't if it be   10
grown to a folly?

SALEWOOD Y'ave won, I'll give't you.°

REARAGE 'Tis no thanks now.° But, as I was saying, as a foul contempt to that sacred ceremony, he most audaciously keeps a drab in town; and, to be free from the interruption of blue beadles   15
and other bawdy° officers, he most politicly lodges her in a constable's house.

SALEWOOD That's a pretty point i'faith.

REARAGE And so the watch, that should fetch her out,° are her chiefest guard to keep her in.   20

SALEWOOD It must needs be, for look how° the constable plays his conscience, the watchmen will follow the suit.°

REARAGE Why, well then.

Enter Easy with Shortyard, like a citizen

EASY All night from me? He's hurt, he's made away.°

SHORTYARD Where shall we seek him now? You lead me fair   25
jaunts,° sir.

EASY Pray, keep a little patience, sir; I shall find him at last, you shall see.

SHORTYARD A citizen of my ease and substance to walk so long afoot!   30

EASY You should ha' had my horse, but that he has eaten out his head,° sir.

SHORTYARD How? Would you had me hold him by the tail, sir, then?

EASY Manners forbid! 'Tis no part of my meaning,° sir. Oh, here's   35
Master Rearage and Master Salewood; now we shall hear of him presently.—Gentlemen both.

SALEWOOD Master Easy, how fare you, sir?

EASY Very well in health. Did you see Master Blastfield this morning?   40

SALEWOOD I was about to move it to you.°

REARAGE We were all three in a mind° then.

SALEWOOD I ha' not set eye on him these two days.

REARAGE I wonder he keeps so long from us i'faith.

EASY I begin to be sick.   45
SALEWOOD Why, what's the matter?
EASY Nothing, in troth, but a great desire I had to have seen him.
REARAGE I wonder you should miss on't lately; you're his bedfellow.
EASY I lay alone tonight i'faith; I do not know how.—Oh, here comes
    Master Lethe, he can dispatch me.   50
      [Enter Lethe]
    Master Lethe!
LETHE What's your name, sir? Oh, cry you mercy, Master Easy.
EASY When parted you from Master Blastfield, sir?
LETHE Blastfield's an ass; I have sought him these two days to beat
    him.   55
EASY Yourself all alone, sir?
LETHE I° and three more.
     Exit Lethe
SHORTYARD *[aside]* I am glad I am where I am then;° I perceive
    'twas time of all hands.°
REARAGE *[to Salewood]* Content,° i'faith, let's trace him.°   60
    Exeunt [Rearage and Salewood] after Lethe
SHORTYARD What, have you found him yet? Neither? What's to be
    done now? I'll venture my body no further for any gentleman's
    pleasure; I know not how soon I may be called upon,° and now to
    overheat myself—
EASY I'm undone!   65
SHORTYARD This is you that slept with him. You can make fools of
    us, but I'll turn you over to Quomodo for't.
EASY Good sir—
SHORTYARD I'll prevent mine own danger.
EASY I beseech you, sir—   70
SHORTYARD Though I love gentlemen well, I do not mean to be
    undone for 'em.
EASY Pray, sir, let me request you, sir; sweet sir, I beseech you, sir—
    Exeunt. Music

[4.1]

*Enter Quomodo, his disguised spirits [Shortyard and
Falselight dressed as wealthy citizens], after whom Easy
follows hard*

SHORTYARD Made fools of us! Not to be found!

QUOMODO What, what?

EASY Do not undo me quite,° though, Master Quomodo.

QUOMODO Y'are very welcome, Master Easy, I ha' nothing to say to
you; I'll not touch you, you may go when you please. I have good   5
bail here, I thank their worships.

EASY What shall I say, or whom shall I beseech?

SHORTYARD Gentlemen! 'Slid, they were born to undo us, I think;
but, for my part, I'll make an oath before Master Quomodo here,
ne'er to do gentlemen good while I live.   10

FALSELIGHT I'll not be long behind you.

SHORTYARD Away! If you had any grace in you, you would be
ashamed to look us i'th'face, iwis! I wonder with what brow
you can come amongst us. I should seek my fortunes far° enough,
if I were you, and neither return to Essex to be a shame to   15
my predecessors, nor to remain about London to be a mock to my
successors.

QUOMODO [aside] Subtle Shortyard!

SHORTYARD Here are his lands forfeited to us, Master Quomodo;
and to avoid the inconscionable trouble of law, all the assurance°   20
he made to us we willingly resign to you.

QUOMODO What shall I do with rubbish? Give me money. 'Tis for
your worships to have land, that keep great houses; I should be
hoisted.°

SHORTYARD But, Master Quomodo, if you would but conceive it   25
aright, the land would fall fitter to you than to us.

EASY [aside] Curts'ing° about my land!

SHORTYARD You have a towardly son and heir, as we hear.

QUOMODO I must needs say he is a Templar° indeed.

SHORTYARD We have neither posterity in town nor hope for any   30
abroad;° we have wives, but the marks° have been out of their mouths
these twenty years, and, as it appears, they did little good when
they were in.° We could not stand about° it, sir; to get riches and
children too, 'tis more than one man can do. And I am of those

citizen's minds that say, let our wives make shift for children, an   35
they will,° they get none of us; and I cannot think but he that has
both much wealth and many children has had more helps coming
in than himself.

QUOMODO I am not a bow wide° of your mind, sir. And for the thrifty
and covetous hopes I have in my son and heir, Sim Quomodo,   40
that he will never trust his land in wax and parchment,° as many
gentlemen have done before him—

EASY [aside] A by-blow for me.

QUOMODO I will honestly discharge you, and receive it in due form
and order of law to strengthen it forever to my son and heir, that   45
he may undoubtedly enter upon't without the let or molestation of
any man at his or our pleasure whensoever.

SHORTYARD 'Tis so assured unto you.

QUOMODO Why, then Master Easy, y'are a free man, sir; you may
deal in what you please and go whither you will.   50

        [Enter Thomasine]°

Why, Thomasine, Master Easy is come from Essex; bid him
welcome in a cup of small beer.

THOMASINE [aside] Not only vile, but in it tyrannous.

QUOMODO If it please you, sir, you know the house;° you may visit
us often and dine with us once a quarter.   55

EASY Confusion light on you, your wealth and heir;
    Worm gnaw your conscience, as the moth your ware.°
    I am not the first heir that robbed or begged.°

        Exit [with Thomasine]°

QUOMODO Excellent, excellent, sweet spirits!

SHORTYARD Landed Master Quomodo!   60

QUOMODO Delicate Shortyard, commodious Falselight,
    Hug and away, shift, shift;
    'Tis sleight, not strength, that gives the greatest lift.°

        [Exeunt Shortyard and Falselight]

    Now my desires are full for this time.
    Men may have cormorant wishes, but, alas,   65
    A little thing, three hundred pound a year,
    Suffices nature, keeps life and soul together.
    I'll have 'em lopped immediately; I long°
    To warm myself by th'wood.
    A fine journey in the Whitsun holidays, i'faith, to ride down with   70
    a number of citizens and their wives, some upon pillions, some
    upon sidesaddles, I° and little Thomasine i'th'middle, our son and

heir, Sim Quomodo, in a peach-colour taffeta jacket, some horse-
length or a long yard before us; there will be a fine show on's, I
can tell you; where we citizens will laugh and lie down,° get all our   75
wives with child against a bank and get up again.

Stay, hah! hast thou that wit i'faith? 'Twill be admirable. To
see how the very thought of green fields puts a man into sweet
inventions. I will presently possess Sim Quomodo of all the land;
I have a toy, and I'll do't. And because I see before mine eyes that   80
most of our heirs prove notorious rioters after our deaths, and
that cozenage in the father wheels about to folly in the son, our
posterity commonly foiled at the same weapon° at which we played
rarely; and being the world's beaten word,° what's got over the
devil's back (that's by knavery) must be spent under his belly°   85
(that's by lechery); being awake in these knowings, why should not
I oppose 'em now and break destiny of her custom, preventing
that by policy, which without it must needs be destiny? And I have
took the course;° I will forthwith sicken, call for my keys,° make
my will and dispose of all; give my son this blessing, that he trust   90
no man, keep his hand from a quean and a scrivener,° live in his
father's faith, and do good to nobody. Then will I begin to rave
like a fellow of a wide° conscience, and, for all the world, counterfeit
to the life that which I know I shall do when I die: take on for my
gold, my lands, and my writings, grow worse and worse, call upon   95
the devil, and so make an end.

By this time I have indented with a couple of searchers,° who, to
uphold my device, shall fray them out o'th'chamber with report
of sickness,° and so, la, I start up and recover again. For in this
business I will trust, no, not my spirits, Falselight and Shortyard,   100
but in disguise note the condition of all: how pitiful my wife takes
my death, which will appear by November in her eye° and the fall
of the leaf in her body,° but especially by the cost she bestows upon
my funeral, there shall I try her love and regard; my daughter's
marrying to my will and liking; and my son's affection after my   105
disposing;° for, to conclude, I am as jealous of this land as of
my wife, to know what would become of it after my decease.

    Exit

[4.2]

Enter Courtesan [Country Wench] with her disguised Father

FATHER Though I be poor, 'tis my glory to live honest.

COUNTRY WENCH I prithee do not leave me.

FATHER   To be bawd!
Hell has not such an office.
I thought at first your mind had been preserved
In virtue and in modesty of blood,   5
That such a face had not been made to please
The unsettled appetites of several men,
Those eyes turned up through prayer, not through lust;
But you are wicked, and my thoughts unjust.°

COUNTRY WENCH Why, thou art an unreasonable fellow i'faith. Do   10
not all trades live by their ware° and yet called honest livers?
Do they not thrive best when they utter most and make it away
by the great?° Is not wholesale° the chiefest merchandise? Do you
think some merchants could keep their wives so brave, but for
their wholesale? You're foully deceived, an you think so.   15

FATHER You are so glued to punishment and shame,
Your words e'en deserve whipping.
To bear the habit of a gentlewoman
And be in mind so distant!°

COUNTRY WENCH Why, you fool you, are not gentlewomen sinners?   20
And there's no courageous sinner amongst us but was a gentlewoman by her mother's side,° I warrant you. Besides, we are not
always bound to think those our fathers that marry our mothers,
but those that lie with our mothers, and they may be gentlemen
born and born again for aught we know, you know.   25

FATHER True, corruption may well be generation's first;°
'We're bad by nature, but by custom worst.'

> *Exeunt*

[4.3]

A bell tolls; a confused cry within

THOMASINE [*within*] Oh, my husband!

SIM [*within*] My father, oh, my father!

FALSELIGHT [*within*] My sweet master, dead!
    Enter Shortyard and the Boy
SHORTYARD Run, boy, bid 'em ring out; he's dead, he's gone.
BOY Then is as arrant a knave gone as e'er was called upon.°   5
    [*Exit Boy*]
SHORTYARD The happiest good that ever Shortyard felt!
  I want to be expressed, my mirth is such;°
  To be struck now, e'en when his joys were high!
  Men only kiss their knaveries and so die,°
  I've often marked it.   10
  He was a famous cozener while he lived,
  And now his son shall reap it; I'll ha' the lands,
  Let him study law after; 'tis no labour
  To undo him forever. But for Easy,
  Only good confidence did make him foolish,°   15
  And not the lack of sense—that was not it;
  'Tis worldly craft beats down a scholar's wit.
  For this our son and heir now, he°
  From his conception was entailed an ass,°
  And he has kept it well, twenty-five years now;°   20
  Then the slightest art will do't; the lands lie fair;
  'No sin to beggar a deceiver's heir.'
    Exit [Shortyard.] Enter Thomasine with Winnifred, her maid,
    in haste
THOMASINE Here, Winnifred, here, here, here; I have always found
  thee secret.
WINNIFRED You shall always find me so, mistress.   25
THOMASINE Take this letter and this ring.
WINNIFRED Yes forsooth.
THOMASINE Oh, how all the parts about me shake! Inquire for one
  Master Easy at his old lodging i'th'Blackfriars.
WINNIFRED I will indeed forsooth.   30
THOMASINE Tell him the party that sent him a hundred pound
  t'other day to comfort his heart has likewise sent him this letter
  and this ring, which has that virtue to recover him again forever,
  say. Name nobody, Winnifred.
WINNIFRED Not so much as you forsooth.   35
THOMASINE Good girl. Thou shalt have a mourning gown at the
  burial,° of mine honesty.
WINNIFRED And I'll effect your will, o'my fidelity.
    Exit [Winnifred]

THOMASINE I do account myself the happiest widow that ever   40
counterfeited weeping, in that I have the leisure now both to do
that gentleman good and do myself a pleasure; but I must seem
like a hanging moon,° a little waterish awhile.
    Enter Rearage, Courtesan's Father following
REARAGE I entertain both thee and thy device;
    'Twill put 'em both to shame.
FATHER   That is my hope, sir,°
    Especially that strumpet.
    [*Exit Father*]
REARAGE   Save you, sweet widow!   45
    I suffer for your heaviness.
THOMASINE Oh, Master Rearage, I have lost the dearest husband
    that ever a woman did enjoy.
REARAGE You must have patience yet.
THOMASINE Oh, talk not to me of patience, an you love me, good   50
    Master Rearage.
REARAGE Yet if all tongues go right,° he did not use you so well as
    a man mought.
THOMASINE Nay, that's true indeed, Master Rearage; he ne'er used
    me so well as a woman might have been used, that's certain; in   55
    troth, 't'as° been our greatest falling out, sir; and though it be the
    part of a widow to show herself a woman° for her husband's
    death, yet when I remember all his unkindness, I cannot weep a
    stroke,° i'faith, Master Rearage. And therefore wisely did a great
    widow in this land comfort up another: 'Go to, lady', quoth she,   60
    'leave blubbering; thou thinkest upon thy husband's good parts
    when thou sheddest tears; do but remember how often he has lain
    from thee, and how many naughty slippery turns he has done thee,
    and thou wilt ne'er weep for him, I warrant thee'. You would not
    think how that counsel has wrought with me, Master Rearage; I   65
    could not dispend another tear now, an you would give me ne'er
    so much.
REARAGE Why, I count you the wiser widow; it shows you have
    wisdom when you can check your passion. For mine own part, I
    have no sense to sorrow for his death, whose life was the only rub   70
    to my affection.
THOMASINE Troth, and so it was to mine; but take courage now;
    you're a landed gentleman, and my daughter is seven hundred
    pound° strong to join with you.
REARAGE But Lethe lies i'th'way.

THOMASINE   Let him lie still;   75
  You shall tread o'er him, or I'll fail in will.°
REARAGE Sweet widow!
        Exeunt

[4.4]

        Enter Quomodo like a Beadle°

QUOMODO What a beloved man did I live!° My servants gall their
  fingers with wringing,° my wife's cheeks smart with weeping, tears
  stand in every corner; you may take water° in my house. But am
  not I a wise fool now? What if my wife should take my death so
  to heart that she should sicken upon't, nay, swoon, nay, die? When   5
  did I hear of a woman do so? Let me see. Now I remember me, I
  think 'twas before my time; yes, I have heard of those wives that
  have wept, and sobbed, and swooned; marry, I never heard but
  they recovered again; that's a comfort, la, that's a comfort, and I
  hope so will mine. Peace, 'tis near upon the time,° I see; here   10
  comes the worshipful Livery;° I have the Hospital Boys;° I perceive
  little Thomasine will bestow cost of me.°
  I'll listen to the common censure now,
  How the world tongues me when my ear lies low.
        Enter the Livery [and the Hospital Boys]
FIRST LIVERYMAN Who, Quomodo? Merely enriched by shifts   15
  And cozenages, believe it.
QUOMODO [*aside*] I see the world is very loath to praise me,
  'Tis rawly friends with me; I cannot blame it,
  For what I have done has been to vex and shame it.
  Here comes my son, the hope, the landed heir,   20
  One whose rare thrift will say, 'Men's tongues, you lie;
  I'll keep by law what was got craftily.'
        [*Enter Sim*]
  Methinks I hear him say so.
  He does salute the Livery with good grace
  And solemn gesture.   25
  [*To him*] Oh, my young worshipful master, you have parted from
  a dear father, a wise and provident father.
SIM Art thou grown an ass now?
QUOMODO Such an honest father—

SIM   Prithee, beadle, leave thy lying; I am scarce able to endure thee   30
    i'faith; what honesty didst thou e'er know by my father? Speak!
    Rule your tongue, beadle, lest I make you prove it, and then I
    know what will become of you; 'tis the scurviest thing i'th'earth to
    belie the dead so, and he's a beastly son and heir that will stand
    by and hear his father belied to his face; he will ne'er prosper, I   35
    warrant him. Troth, if I be not ashamed to go to church with
    him, I would I might be hanged; I hear° such filthy tales go on
    him. Oh, if I had known he had been such a lewd fellow in his life,
    he should ne'er have kept me company.

QUOMODO [*aside*] Oh, oh, oh!   40

SIM   But I am glad he's gone, though 'twere long first;° Shortyard and
    I will revel it i'faith; I have made him my rentgatherer already.

QUOMODO [*aside*] He shall be speedily disinherited; he gets not a
    foot,° not the crown of a molehill. I'll sooner make a courtier my
    heir, for teaching my wife tricks,° than thee, my most neglectful   45
    son! Oh, now the corse, I shall observe yet farther.
        A counterfeit corpse brought in, [followed by] Thomasine and all
        the Mourners (equally counterfeit)
    Oh, my most modest, virtuous, and remembering wife,
    She shall have all when I die, she shall have all.
        Enter Easy

THOMASINE [*aside*] Master Easy? 'Tis. Oh, what shift shall I make
    now?—Oh!   50
        Falls down in a feigned swoon

QUOMODO [*aside*] Sweet wife, she swoons; I'll let her alone; I'll have
    no mercy at this time; I'll not see her, I'll follow the corpse.
        Exit [Quomodo following the funeral procession]

EASY [*to corpse*] The devil grind thy bones, thou cozening rascal!

[OLD WOMAN]° Give her a little more air; tilt up her head.—
    Comfort thyself, good widow; do not fall like a beast for a hus-   55
    band; there's more than we can well tell where to put 'em, good
    soul.

THOMASINE Oh, I shall be well anon.

[OLD WOMAN] Fie, you have no patience i'faith. I have buried four
    husbands and never offered 'em° such abuse.   60

THOMASINE [*to Easy*] Cousin, how do you?

EASY   Sorry to see you ill, coz.

THOMASINE (*pointing after the coffin*) The worst is past I hope.

EASY   I hope so too.

THOMASINE Lend me your hand, sweet coz, I have troubled you.°

[OLD WOMAN] No trouble indeed forsooth. [*To Easy*] Good cousin,
    have a care of her; comfort her up as much as you can, and all little   65
    enough, I warrant ye.
                Exit [*Old Woman*]
THOMASINE My most sweet love!
EASY   My life is not so dear.
THOMASINE I have always pitied you.
EASY   Y'ave shown it here
    And given the desperate hope!
THOMASINE   Delay not now,
    Y'ave understood my love; I have a priest ready;   70
    This is the fittest season, no eye offends us,°
    Let this kiss
    Restore thee to more wealth, me to more bliss.
EASY The angels have provided for me.
            [*Exeunt*]

[5.1]

Enter Shortyard with writings,° having cozened Sim
Quomodo

SHORTYARD I have not scope enough within my breast
　To keep my joys contained; I'm Quomodo's heir,
　The lands, assurances, and all are mine;
　I have tripped his son's heels up above the ground
　His father left him. Had I not encouragement?　　　　　　　5
　Do not I know, what proves the father's prey,
　The son ne'er looks on't, but it melts away?°
　Do not I know, the wealth that's got by fraud,
　Slaves share it like the riches of a bawd?
　Why, 'tis a curse unquenchable, ne'er cools.　　　　　　　10
　Knaves still commit their consciences to fools,
　And they betray who owed 'em. Here's all the bonds,°
　All Easy's writings; let me see.
　　　Enter Quomodo's wife [*Thomasine*] *married to Easy*
THOMASINE Now my desires wear crowns.
EASY　　　　　　　　　　　　　　My joys exceed;
　Man is ne'er healthful till his follies bleed.°　　　　　　　15
THOMASINE Oh, behold the villain who in all those shapes°
　Confounded your estate.
EASY　　　　　　　　That slave! That villain!
SHORTYARD [*reading*] 'So many acres of good meadow—'
EASY　　　　　　　　　　　　　　　　　Rascal!
SHORTYARD I hear you, sir.
EASY Rogue, Shortyard, Blastfield, sergeant, deputy,° cozener!　　20
SHORTYARD Hold, hold.
EASY I thirst the execution of his ears.°
THOMASINE Hate you that office.°
EASY I'll strip him bare for punishment and shame.
SHORTYARD Why, do but hear me, sir; you will not think　　　25
　What I have done for you.
EASY　　　　　　　　Given his son my lands!
SHORTYARD Why, look you, 'tis not so, you're not told true;
　I have cozened him again merely for you,
　Merely for you, sir; 'twas my meaning then
　That you should wed her and have all again.　　　　　　　30

O'my troth, it's true, sir; look you then here, sir.
> [*He gives Easy the writings*]

You shall not miss a little scroll, sir. Pray, sir,°
Let not the city know me for a knave;
There be richer men would envy my preferment,
If I should be known before 'em.°   35

EASY Villain, my hate to more revenge is drawn;
When slaves are found,° 'tis their base art to fawn.—
Within there!
> [*Enter Officers*]

SHORTYARD How now? Fresh warders!°

EASY This is the other,° bind him fast.—Have I found you,   40
Master Blastfield?

SHORTYARD   This is the fruit of craft.
Like him that shoots up high, looks for the shaft,
And finds it in his forehead, so does hit
The arrow of our fate; wit destroys wit;
The head the body's bane and his own bears.—°   45
You ha' corn enough, you need not reap mine ears.°

EASY Sweet Master Blastfield!—I loathe his voice; away!°
> *Exit [Shortyard with Officers]*

THOMASINE What happiness was here! But are you sure you have all?

EASY I hope so, my sweet wife.

THOMASINE What difference there is in husbands, not only in one   50
thing° but in all.

EASY Here's good deeds and bad deeds, the writings that keep my
lands to me, and the bonds that gave it away from me.
These, my good deeds, shall to more safety turn,
And these, my bad, have their deserts and burn.   55
I'll see thee again presently; read there.°
> [*Exit Easy*]

THOMASINE Did he want all, who would not love his care?°
> *Enter Quomodo [disguised as a Beadle]*

QUOMODO [*aside*] What a wife hast thou, Ephestian Quomodo! So
loving, so mindful of her duty, not only seen to weep, but known to
swoon. I knew a widow about Saint Antholin's° so forgetful of her   60
first husband that she married again within the twelvemonth; nay,
some, byrlady, within the month; there were sights to be seen! Had
they my wife's true sorrows, seven months° nor seven years would
draw 'em to the stake. I would most tradesmen had such a wife as I;
they hope they have, we must all hope the best. Thus in her honour: 65

> A modest wife is such a jewel,
> Every goldsmith cannot show it;°
> He that's honest and not cruel
> Is the likeliest man to owe it.°

And that's I; I made it by myself; and coming to her as a beadle   70
for my reward this morning, I'll see how she takes my death next
her heart.

THOMASINE Now, beadle.

QUOMODO Bless your mistress-ship's eyes from too many tears,
Although you have lost a wise and worshipful gentleman.   75

THOMASINE You come for your due, beadle, here i'th'house?°

QUOMODO Most certain; the Hospital money° and mine own° poor
forty pence.

THOMASINE I must crave a discharge from you, beadle.

QUOMODO Call your man; I'll heartily set my hand to a memoran-   80
dum.

THOMASINE You deal the trulier.

QUOMODO [aside] Good wench still.

THOMASINE George!

> [Enter Servant]

Here is the beadle come for his money; draw a memorandum that   85
he has received all his due he can claim here i'th'house after this
funeral.

> [The Servant writes]

QUOMODO [aside] What politic directions she gives him, all to secure
herself. 'Tis time, i'faith, now to pity her; I'll discover myself to
her ere I go; but came it off with some lively jest now, that were   90
admirable. I have it! After the memorandum is written and all, I'll
set my own name to't, Ephestian Quomodo; she'll start, she'll
wonder how Ephestian Quomodo came thither° that was buried
yesterday. Y'are beset, little Quomodo.°

THOMASINE [counting out money] Nineteen, twenty, five pound; one,   95
two, three, and fourpence.°

> [Quomodo signs]

QUOMODO [aside] So, we shall have good sport when 'tis read.

> [Exit Servant.] [Enter Easy]

EASY How now, lady, paying away money so fast?

THOMASINE The beadle's due here, sir.

QUOMODO [aside] Who? 'Tis Easy!° What makes Easy in my   100
house?
He is not my wife's overseer, I hope.

EASY What's here?

QUOMODO [*aside*] He makes me sweat.

EASY [*reading*] 'Memorandum: that I have received of Richard Easy   105
all my due I can claim here i'th'house or any° hereafter for me. In
witness whereof I have set to mine own hand: *Ephestian Quomodo*.'

QUOMODO [*aside*] What have I done? Was I mad?

EASY Ephestian Quomodo?

QUOMODO Ay, well, what then, sir? Get you out of my house   110
First, you Master Prodigal Had-land. Away!°

THOMASINE What, is the beadle drunk or mad?
Where are my men to thrust him out o'doors?

QUOMODO Not so, good Thomasine, not so.

THOMASINE This fellow must be whipped.

QUOMODO   Thank you, good wife.   115

EASY I can no longer bear him.

THOMASINE   Nay, sweet husband.

QUOMODO [*aside*] Husband? I'm undone, beggared, cozened, confounded forever! Married already?—Will it please you know me
now, Mistress Harlot and Master Horner?° Who am I now?
        [*Discovers himself*]

THOMASINE Oh, he's as like my t'other husband as can be.   120

QUOMODO I'll have judgement; I'll bring you before a judge; you
shall feel, wife, whether my flesh be dead or no; I'll tickle you
i'faith, i'faith.
        Exit [*Quomodo*]

THOMASINE The judge that he'll solicit knows me well.

EASY Let's on then and our grievances first tell.   125
        Exeunt

[5.2]

Enter Lethe with Officers, taken with his Harlot, [Rearage and
Susan looking on]

REARAGE Here they come.

SUSAN   Oh where?

LETHE   Heart of shame!
Upon my wedding morning, so disgraced!
Have you so little conscience, officers,

You will not take a bribe?°

COUNTRY WENCH Master Lethe, we may lie together lawfully   5
hereafter, for we are coupled together before people enow i'faith.

    [*Exeunt officers with Lethe and his Harlot*]

REARAGE There goes the strumpet.

SUSAN Pardon my wilful blindness, and enjoy me;°
For now the difference appears too plain
Betwixt a base slave and a true gentleman.   10

REARAGE I do embrace thee in the best of love.

    [*Aside*] How soon affections fail, how soon they prove.°

      [*Exeunt*]

[5.3]

*Enter Judge, Easy and Thomasine in talk with him, [Shortyard
and Falselight in the custody of officers]*

JUDGE His cozenages are odious; he the plaintiff!
Not only framed deceitful in his life,
But so to mock his funeral.

EASY   Most just.°
The Livery all assembled, mourning weeds
Throughout his house e'en down to his last servant,   5
The herald richly hired to lend him arms°
Feigned from his ancestors, which I dare swear knew°
No other arms but those they laboured with,
All preparations furnished, nothing wanted
Save that which was the cause of all: his death.   10
If he be living!

JUDGE   'Twas an impious part.

EASY We are not certain yet it is himself,
But some false spirit that assumes his shape
And seeks still to deceive me.

    [*Enter Quomodo*]

QUOMODO   Oh, are you come?—
My lord!—They're here. Good morrow, Thomasine.   15

JUDGE Now, what are you?

QUOMODO I am Quomodo, my lord, and this my wife;
Those my two men that are bound wrongfully.

JUDGE How are we sure y'are he?

QUOMODO Oh, you cannot miss, my lord.

JUDGE   I'll try you.   20
  Are you the man that lived the famous cozener?

QUOMODO Oh no, my lord.

JUDGE Did you deceive this gentleman of his right
  And laid nets o'er his land?

QUOMODO   Not I, my lord.

JUDGE Then y'are not Quomodo but a counterfeit.   25
  [*To Officers*] Lay hands on him and bear him to the whip.

QUOMODO Stay, stay a little, I pray;
  Now I remember me, my lord,
  I cozened him indeed, 'tis wondrous true.

JUDGE Then I dare swear this is no counterfeit.   30
  Let all doubts cease; this man is Quomodo.

QUOMODO Why, la you now, you would not believe this?
  I am found what I am.°

JUDGE But setting these thy odious shifts° apart,
  Why did that thought profane enter thy breast   35
  To mock the world with thy supposèd death?

QUOMODO Conceive you not that, my lord? A policy.

JUDGE So.

QUOMODO For, having gotten the lands, I thirsted still
  To know what fate would follow 'em.   40

JUDGE Being ill got.

QUOMODO   Your lordship apprehends me.°

JUDGE I think I shall anon.

QUOMODO   And thereupon°
  I, out of policy, possessed my son,
  Which since I have found lewd and now intend
  To disinherit him forever.   45
  Not only this was in my death set down,°
  But thereby a firm trial of my wife,
  Her constant sorrows, her rememb'ring virtues;
  All which are dews; the shine of a next morning°
  Dries 'em up all, I see't.   50

JUDGE Did you profess wise cozenage and would dare
  To put a woman to her two days' choice,
  When oft a minute does it?

QUOMODO   Less, a moment.
  The twinkling of an eye, a glimpse, scarce something does it.
  Your lordship yet will grant she is my wife?   55

THOMASINE Oh heaven!

JUDGE After some penance, and the dues of law,
  I must acknowledge that.

QUOMODO   I scarce like
  Those dues of law.

EASY   My lord,
  Although the law too gently 'lot his wife,   60
  The wealth he left behind he cannot challenge.

QUOMODO How?

EASY Behold his hand against it.
     [*Showing memorandum*]

QUOMODO [*aside*] He does devise all means to make me mad,
  That I may no more lie with my wife   65
  In perfect memory; I know't, but yet°
  The lands will maintain me in my wits;
  The land will do so much for me.

JUDGE [*reading*] 'In witness whereof I have set to mine own hand:
  Ephestian Quomodo'. 'Tis firm enough your own, sir.   70

QUOMODO A jest, my lord; I did I knew not what.

JUDGE It should seem so; deceit is her own foe,
  Craftily gets, and childishly lets go.
  But yet the lands are his.

QUOMODO   I warrant ye.

EASY No, my good lord, the lands know the right heir;°   75
  I am their master once more.

QUOMODO   Have you the lands?

EASY Yes, truly, I praise heaven.

QUOMODO   Is this good dealing?
  Are there such consciences abroad? How?
  Which way could he come by 'em?

SHORTYARD   My lord,
  I'll quickly resolve you that, it comes to me.°   80
  This cozener, whom too long I called my patron,
  To my thought dying, and the fool, his son,°
  Possessed of all, which my brain partly sweat for,
  I held it my best virtue by a plot
  To get from him what for him was ill got—   85

QUOMODO Oh, beastly Shortyard!

SHORTYARD   When no sooner mine,
  But I was glad more quickly to resign.

JUDGE Craft, once discovered, shows her abject line.°

QUOMODO [*aside*] He hits me everywhere, for craft, once known,
  Does teach fools wit, leaves the deceiver none.   90
  My deeds have cleft me, cleft me!
        Enter Officers with Lethe and the Harlot [followed by Rearage,
        Salewood, Hellgill, Mother Gruel, and Susan]
FIRST OFFCER Room there!
QUOMODO [*aside*] A little yet to raise my spirit;
  Here Master Lethe comes to wed my daughter;
  That's all the joy is left me.—Hah! Who's this?   95
JUDGE What crimes have those brought forth?
SALEWOOD   The shame of lust;°
  Most viciously on this, his wedding morning,
  This man was seized in shame with that bold strumpet.
JUDGE Why, 'tis she he means to marry.
LETHE   No, in truth.
JUDGE In truth, you do;   100
  Who, for his wife, his harlot doth prefer,°
  Good reason 'tis that he should marry her.
COUNTRY WENCH I crave it on my knees; such was his vow at first.
HELLGILL [*aside*] I'll say so too and work out mine own safety.
  —Such was his vow at first, indeed, my lord.°   105
  Howe'er his mood has changed him!
LETHE   Oh, vile slave!
COUNTRY WENCH He says it true, my lord.
JUDGE   Rest content,
  He shall both marry and taste punishment.
LETHE Oh intolerable! I beseech your good lordship, if I must
  have an outward punishment, let me not marry an inward, whose   110
  lashes will ne'er out,° but grow worse and worse. I have a wife
  stays for me this morning with seven hundred pound in her
  purse; let me be speedily whipped and be gone, I beseech your
  lordship.
SALEWOOD He speaks no truth, my lord; behold the virgin,°   115
  Wife to a well-esteemèd gentleman,
  Loathing the sin he follows.°
LETHE I was betrayed, yes, faith.
REARAGE . . . His own mother, my lord,°
  Which he confessed, through ignorance and disdain,   120
  His name so changed to abuse the world and her.
LETHE [*aside*] Marry a harlot, why not? 'Tis an honest man's fortune.
  I pray, did not one of my countrymen marry my sister? Why, well

then, if none should be married but those that are honest, where
should a man seek a wife after Christmas?° I pity that gentleman   125
that has nine daughters to bestow, and seven of 'em seeded already;
they will be good stuff by that time.—
I do beseech your lordship to remove
The punishment; I am content to marry her.

JUDGE There's no removing of your punishment—   130

LETHE Oh, good my lord!

JUDGE   Unless one here assembled,
Whom you have most unnaturally abused,
Beget your pardon.

LETHE [aside]   Who should that be?
Or who would do't that has been so abused?
A troublesome penance. [To Quomodo] Sir—   135

QUOMODO Knave in your face! Leave your mocking, Andrew;
Marry your quean and be quiet.

LETHE   Master Easy—

EASY I'm sorry you take such a bad course, sir.

LETHE Mistress Quomodo—

THOMASINE   Inquire my right name
Again next time; now go your ways like an ass°   140
As you came.

LETHE [aside] Mass, I forget my mother all this while;
I'll make her do't at first.—[kneeling] Pray, mother,
Your blessing for once.

MOTHER GRUEL   Call'st me mother? Out,
I defy thee, slave!

LETHE   Call me slave   145
As much you will, but do not shame me now;
Let the world know you are my mother.

MOTHER GRUEL Let me not have this villain put upon me,
I beseech your lordship.

JUDGE He's justly cursed; she loathes to know him now,   150
Whom he before did as much loathe to know.
Wilt thou believe me, woman?

MOTHER GRUEL   That's soon done.

JUDGE Then know him for a villain; 'tis thy son.°

MOTHER GRUEL Art thou Andrew, my wicked son Andrew?

LETHE You would not believe me, mother.

MOTHER GRUEL   How art thou changed!   155
Is this suit fit for thee, a tooth-drawer's son?

This country has e'en spoiled thee since thou cam'st hither;
Thy manners . . . better than thy clothes,°
But now whole clothes, and ragged manners.
It may well be said that truth goes naked,   160
For when thou hadst scarce a shirt thou hadst
More truth about thee.

JUDGE Thou art thine own affliction, Quomodo.
    Shortyard we banish; 'tis our pleasure.

SHORTYARD Henceforth no woman shall complain for measure.   165

JUDGE And that all error from our works may stand,
    We banish Falselight evermore the land.

        [*Exeunt*]

A TRICK TO CATCH
THE OLD ONE

THE ACTORS IN THE COMEDY

Theodorus° Witgood
Pecunius° Lucre, his uncle
Walkadine° Hoard
Onesiphorus° Hoard,° his brother
Limber° ⎱
Kix° ⎰ Lucre's friends   5
Sir Tristram° Lamprey°
Spitchcock° ⎱
Harry Dampit° ⎰ Hoard's friends
Gulf° ⎱ Usurers°   10
Sam Freedom, Lucre's wife's son
Moneylove
Host
Sir Lancelot°
George, Lucre's servant   15
Arthur, Walkadine Hoard's servant
Creditors, Gentlemen,° Drawer, Vintner, Boy, Scrivener, etc.
Courtesan°
Mistress Lucre
Joyce, niece to Hoard   20
Lady Foxstone°
Audrey, Dampit's servant

[1.1]

Enter Witgood, a gentleman, solus

WITGOOD All's gone! Still thou'rt a gentleman, that's all;° but a poor
one, that's nothing. What milk brings thy meadows° forth now?
Where are thy goodly uplands and thy downlands?° All sunk into
that little pit,° lechery. Why should a gallant pay but two shillings
for his ordinary that nourishes him, and twenty times two for his   5
brothel that consumes° him? But where's Long-acre?° In my uncle's
conscience, which is three years' voyage about;° he that sets out
upon his conscience° ne'er finds the way home again; he is either
swallowed in the quicksands of law-quillets or splits upon the piles
of a *praemunire*. Yet these old fox-brained and ox-browed uncles   10
have still defences for their avarice, and apologies for their
practices, and will thus greet our follies:

> He that doth his youth expose
> To brothel, drink, and danger,
> Let him that is his nearest kin   15
> Cheat him before a stranger.°

And that's his uncle, 'tis a principle in usury. I dare not visit the
city; there I should be too soon visited by that horrible plague,
my debts, and by that means I lose a virgin's love, her portion,
and her virtues. Well, how should a man live now that has no   20
living? Hum. Why, are there not a million of men in the world
that only sojourn upon their brain and make their wits their
mercers;° and am I but one amongst that million and cannot thrive
upon't? Any trick, out of the compass of law° now, would come
happily to me.   25

Enter Courtesan

COURTESAN My love.

WITGOOD My loathing! Hast thou been the secret consumption of
my purse, and now com'st to undo my last means, my wits? Wilt
leave no virtue in me, and yet thou ne'er the better?

> Hence, courtesan, round-webbed tarantula,°   30
> That dryest the roses in the cheeks of youth!°

COURTESAN I have been true unto your pleasure; and all your lands
thrice racked was never worth the jewel which I prodigally gave
you, my virginity;

> Lands mortgaged may return, and more esteemed,   35

But honesty, once pawned, is ne'er redeemed.

WITGOOD   Forgive; I do thee wrong
To make thee sin and then to chide thee for't.

COURTESAN   I know I am your loathing now. Farewell.

WITGOOD   Stay, best invention,° stay.   40

COURTESAN   I that have been the secret consumption of your purse,
shall I stay now to undo your last means, your wits? Hence,
courtesan, away!

WITGOOD   I prithee make me not mad at my own weapon.° Stay° (a
thing few women can do, I know that, and therefore they had need   45
wear stays); be not contrary. Dost love me? Fate has so cast it that
all my means I must derive from thee.

COURTESAN   From me! Be happy then;
What lies within the power of my performance
Shall be commanded of thee.   50

WITGOOD   Spoke like an honest drab i'faith; it may prove something.° What trick is not an embryon at first until a perfect° shape
come over it?

COURTESAN   Come, I must help you; whereabouts left you?
I'll proceed.   55
Though you beget, 'tis I must help to breed.
Speak, what is't? I'd fain conceive it.

WITGOOD   So, so, so; thou shall presently take the name and form
upon thee of a rich country widow, four hundred a year valiant,
in woods, in bullocks, in barns, and in rye-stacks. We'll to London 60
and to my covetous uncle.

COURTESAN   I begin to applaud thee; our states being both desperate,
they are soon resolute.° But how for horses?

WITGOOD   Mass, that's true; the jest will be of some continuance. Let
me see; horses now, a bots° on 'em! Stay, I have acquaintance with   65
a mad host,° never yet bawd° to thee. I have rinsed the whoreson's
gums in mull-sack many a time and often; put but a good tale into
his ear now, so it come off cleanly, and there's horse and man for
us, I dare warrant thee.

COURTESAN   Arm your wits then   70
Speedily; there shall want nothing in me,
Either in behaviour, discourse, or fashion,
That shall discredit your intended purpose.
I will so artfully disguise my wants,°
And set so good a courage on my state,°   75
That I will be believed.

WITGOOD Why, then, all's furnished. I shall go nigh° to catch that
old fox, mine uncle. Though he make but some amends for my
undoing, yet there's some comfort in't—he cannot otherwise choose
(though it be but in hope to cozen me again) but supply any   80
hasty° want that I bring to town with me. The device well and
cunningly carried, the name of a rich widow and four hundred a
year in good earth, will so conjure up a kind of usurer's love in
him to me, that he will not only desire my presence, which at
first shall scarce be granted him—I'll keep off o'purpose—but I   85
shall find him so officious to deserve,° so ready to supply. I know
the state of an old man's affection so well; if his nephew be poor
indeed, why, he lets God alone with him;° but if he be once rich,
then he'll be the first man that helps him.

COURTESAN 'Tis right the world;° for in these days an old man's   90
love to his kindred is like his kindness to his wife, 'tis always done
before he comes at it.°

WITGOOD I owe thee for that jest. Begone; here's all my wealth.
[*Gives money*] Prepare thyself, away! I'll to mine host with all
possible haste, and with the best art and most profitable form pour 95
the sweet circumstance into his ear, which shall have the gift° to
turn all the wax to honey.
   [*Exit Courtesan*]
How now? Oh, the right worshipful seniors of our country!
   [*Enter Onesiphorus Hoard, Limber, and Kix*]°

ONESIPHORUS Who's that?

[LIMBER] Oh, the common rioter,° take no note of him.   100

WITGOOD [*aside*] You will not see me now; the comfort is, ere it be
long you will scarce see yourselves.°
   [*Exit Witgood*]

ONESIPHORUS I wonder how he breathes; h'as consumed all upon
that courtesan!

[LIMBER] We have heard so much.   105

ONESIPHORUS You have heard all truth. His uncle and my
brother° have been these three years mortal adversaries. Two old
tough spirits, they seldom meet but fight, or quarrel when 'tis
calmest;
I think their anger be the very fire   110
That keeps their age alive.

[LIMBER] What was the quarrel, sir?

ONESIPHORUS Faith, about a purchase, fetching over a young heir;
Master Hoard, my brother, having wasted much time in beating

141

the bargain,° what did me old Lucre, but as his conscience moved   115
him, knowing the poor gentleman, stepped in between 'em and
cozened him himself.

[LIMBER] And was this all, sir?

ONESIPHORUS This was e'en it, sir; yet for all this, I know no reason
but the match might go forward betwixt his wife's son and my niece.°   120
What though there be a dissension between the two old men, I see
no reason it should put a difference between the two younger; 'tis
as natural for old folks to fall out as for young to fall in.° A scholar°
comes a-wooing to my niece; well, he's wise, but he's poor; her son
comes a-wooing to my niece; well, he's a fool, but he's rich.   125

[LIMBER] Ay, marry, sir?

ONESIPHORUS Pray, now, is not a rich fool better than a poor
philosopher?

[LIMBER] One would think so i'faith!

ONESIPHORUS She now remains at London with my brother, her   130
second uncle, to learn fashions, practise music; the voice between
her lips, and the viol° between her legs; she'll be fit for a consort°
very speedily. A thousand good pound is her portion; if she marry,
we'll ride up and be merry.

[KIX] A match, if it be a match.°   135

    Exeunt

[1.2]

Enter at one door, Witgood, at the other, Host

WITGOOD Mine host!

HOST Young Master Witgood.

WITGOOD I have been laying° all the town for thee.

HOST Why, what's the news, bully Hadland?°

WITGOOD What geldings are in the house of thine own?°   5
Answer me to that first.

HOST Why, man, why?

WITGOOD Mark me what I say; I'll tell thee such a tale in thine ear
that thou shalt trust me in spite of thy teeth,° furnish me with
some money, willy-nilly, and ride up with me thyself *contra volun-*   10
tatem et professionem.°

HOST How? Let me see this trick, and I'll say thou hast more art than
a conjuror.

WITGOOD Dost thou joy in my advancement?

HOST Do I love sack and ginger?°   15

WITGOOD Comes my prosperity desiredly to thee?

HOST Come forfeitures to a usurer, fees to an officer, punks to an host, and pigs to a parson° desiredly? Why, then, la.

WITGOOD Will the report of a widow of four hundred a year, boy, make thee leap, and sing, and dance, and come to thy place again?°   20

HOST Wilt thou command me now? I am thy spirit; conjure me into any shape.

WITGOOD I ha' brought her from her friends, turned back the horses by a sleight; not so much as one amongst her six men, goodly large yeomanly fellows, will she trust with this her purpose. By   25
this light, all unmanned,° regardless of her state, neglectful of vainglorious ceremony, all for my love; oh, 'tis a fine little voluble tongue, mine host, that wins a widow.

HOST No, 'tis a tongue with a great T,° my boy, that wins a widow.

WITGOOD Now, sir, the case stands thus: good mine host, if thou   30
lov'st my happiness, assist me.

HOST Command all my beasts i'th'house.

WITGOOD Nay, that's not all neither; prithee take truce with thy joy and listen to me. Thou know'st I have a wealthy uncle i'th'city, somewhat the wealthier by my follies; the report of this fortune,   35
well and cunningly carried, might be a means to draw some goodness from the usuring rascal; for I have put her in hope already of some estate that I have either in land or money. Now if I be found true in neither, what may I expect but a sudden breach of our love, utter dissolution of the match, and confusion of my   40
fortunes for ever?

HOST Wilt thou but trust the managing of thy business with me?

WITGOOD With thee? Why, will I desire to thrive in my purpose? Will I hug four hundred a year, I that know the misery of nothing? Will that man wish a rich widow that has never a hole to   45
put his head in?° With thee, mine host? Why, believe it, sooner with thee than with a covey of counsellors!

HOST Thank you for your good report, i'faith, sir, and if I stand you not in stead, why then let an host come off *hic et haec hostis*,° a deadly enemy to dice, drink, and venery. Come, where's this widow?   50

WITGOOD Hard at Park End.°

HOST I'll be her servingman for once.

WITGOOD Why, there we let off° together, keep full time;° my thoughts were striking then just the same number.

HOST I knew't. Shall we then see our merry days again?   55
WITGOOD Our merry nights—which ne'er shall be more seen.°
          Exeunt

[1.3]

Enter at several doors, old Lucre, and old Hoard, Gentlemen
[*Lamprey, Spitchcock, Sam Freedom and Moneylove*] *coming
between them, to pacify 'em*

LAMPREY Nay, good Master Lucre, and you, Master Hoard, anger
   is the wind which you're both too much troubled withal.
HOARD Shall my adversary thus daily affront me, ripping up the old
   wound of our malice, which three summers could not close up?
   Into which wound the very sight of him drops scalding lead instead   5
   of balsamum.
LUCRE Why, Hoard, Hoard, Hoard, Hoard, Hoard; may I not pass
   in the state of quietness to mine own house? Answer me to
   that, before witness,° and why? I'll refer the cause to honest,
   even-minded gentlemen, or require the mere indifferences of   10
   the law to decide this matter. I got the purchase, true; was't
   not any man's case?° Yes. Will a wise man stand as a bawd,°
   whilst another wipes his nose° of the bargain? No, I answer no in
   that case.
LAMPREY Nay, sweet Master Lucre.   15
HOARD Was it the part of a friend? No, rather of a Jew.° Mark what
   I say. When I had beaten the bush to the last bird,° or, as I may
   term it, the price to a pound, then like a cunning usurer to come
   in the evening° of the bargain and glean all my hopes in a minute.
   To enter, as it were, at the back door of the purchase. For thou   20
   ne'er cam'st the right way by it.
LUCRE Hast thou the conscience to tell me so without any impeachment to thyself?
HOARD Thou that canst defeat° thy own nephew, Lucre, lap° his
   lands into bonds, and take the extremity of thy kindred's for-   25
   feitures because he's a rioter, a wastethrift, a brothel-master, and
   so forth—what may a stranger expect from thee, but *vulnera dilacerata*,° as the poet says, dilacerate dealing?
LUCRE Upbraid'st thou me with nephew? Is all imputation laid upon
   me? What acquaintance have I with his follies? If he riot, 'tis he   30

must want it;° if he surfeit, 'tis he must feel it; if he drab it, 'tis
he must lie by't.° What's this to me?

HOARD What's all to thee? Nothing, nothing; such is the gulf of thy
desire and the wolf of thy conscience; but be assured, old Pecunius
Lucre, if ever fortune so bless me that I may be at leisure to vex   35
thee, or any means so favour me that I may have opportunity to
mad thee, I will pursue it with that flame of hate, that spirit of
malice, unrepressed wrath, that I will blast thy comforts.

LUCRE Ha, ha, ha!

LAMPREY Nay, Master Hoard, you're a wise gentleman.   40

HOARD I will so cross thee.

LUCRE And I thee.

HOARD So without mercy fret thee.

LUCRE So monstrously oppose thee!

HOARD Dost scoff at my just anger? Oh, that I had as much power   45
as usury has over thee!

LUCRE Then thou wouldst have as much power as the devil has over
thee.

HOARD Toad!

LUCRE Aspic!   50

HOARD Serpent!

LUCRE Viper!

SPITCHCOCK Nay, gentlemen, then we must divide you perforce.

LAMPREY When the fire grows too unreasonable hot, there's no
better way than to take off the wood.   55

> *Exeunt [Hoard, Lucre, Lamprey, and Spitchcock,] leaving Sam
> [Freedom] and Moneylove*

SAM A word, good signior.

MONEYLOVE How now, what's the news?

SAM 'Tis given me to understand that you are a rival of mine in the
love of Mistress Joyce, Master Hoard's niece: say me ay, say me
no.   60

MONEYLOVE Yes, 'tis so.

SAM Then look to yourself; you cannot live long. I'm practising every
morning; a month hence I'll challenge you.

MONEYLOVE Give me your hand upon't; there's my pledge I'll meet
you!   65

> *Strikes him. Exit [Moneylove]*

SAM Oh, oh! What reason had you for that, sir, to strike before the
month?° You knew I was not ready for you, and that made you so
crank. I am not such a coward to strike again,° I warrant you. My

ear has the law of° her side, for it burns horribly. I will teach him
to strike a naked° face, the longest day of his life.° 'Slid, it shall   70
cost me some money, but I'll bring this box° into the Chancery.

Exit

[1.4]

Enter Witgood and the Host

HOST Fear you nothing, sir; I have lodged her in a house of credit,
I warrant you.

WITGOOD Hast thou the writings?°

HOST Firm, sir.

[*Enter Dampit and Gulf, who talk apart*]

WITGOOD Prithee stay and behold two the most prodigious rascals   5
that ever slipped into the shape of men: Dampit, sirrah, and young
Gulf, his fellow caterpillar.

HOST Dampit? Sure I have heard of that Dampit.

WITGOOD Heard of him? Why, man, he that has lost both his ears°
may hear of him: a famous infamous trampler of time,° his own   10
phrase. Note him well: that Dampit, sirrah, he in the uneven beard
and the serge cloak° is the most notorious, usuring, blasphemous,
atheistical, brothel-vomiting° rascal that we have in these latter times
now extant,° whose first beginning was the stealing of a masty dog
from a farmer's house.°   15

HOST He looked as if he would obey the commandment well, when
he began first with stealing.°

WITGOOD True. The next town he came at he set the dogs together
by th'ears.°

HOST A sign he should follow the law, by my faith.   20

WITGOOD So it followed indeed; and being destitute of all fortunes,
staked his masty° against a noble, and by great fortune his dog had
the day. How he made it up ten shillings I know not, but his own
boast is that he came to town but with ten shillings in his purse,
and now is credibly worth ten thousand pound!   25

HOST How the devil came he by it?

WITGOOD How the devil came he not by it? If you put in the devil
once,° riches come with a vengeance. H'as been a trampler of
the law, sir, and the devil has a care of his footmen.° The rogue
has spied me now; he nibbled me finely once too; a pox search   30

you—oh, Master Dampit!—[*aside*] the very loins of thee!°—[*to Gulf*] cry you mercy, Master Gulf, you walk so low,° I promise you I saw you not, sir!

GULF He that walks low walks safe, the poets tell us.°

WITGOOD [*aside*] And nigher hell by a foot and a half than the rest   35
  of his fellows. [*To Dampit*] But my old Harry!

DAMPIT My sweet Theodorus!

WITGOOD 'Twas a merry world when thou cam'st to town with ten
  shillings in thy purse.

DAMPIT And now worth ten thousand pound, my boy. Report it,   40
  Harry Dampit, a trampler of time: say, he would be up in a
  morning, and be here with his serge gown, dashed up to the hams
  in a cause; have his feet stink about Westminster Hall, and come
  home again; see the galleons, the galleasses, the great armadas of
  the law; then there be hoys and petty vessels, oars and scullers   45
  of the time; there be picklocks° of the time too. Then I would be
  here, I would trample up and down like a mule; now to the judges,
  'May it please your reverend-honourable fatherhoods'; then to
  my counsellor, 'May it please your worshipful patience'; then to
  the examiner's office,° 'May it please your mastership's gentleness';   50
  then to one of the clerks, 'May it please your worshipful lousiness',
  for I find him scrubbing in his codpiece; then to the Hall again,
  then to the chamber again—

WITGOOD And when to the cellar° again?

DAMPIT E'en when thou wilt again. Tramplers of time, motions of   55
  Fleet Street, and visions of Holborn;° here I have fees of one, there
  I have fees of another; my clients come about me, the fooliaminy
  and coxcombry of the country; I still trashed and trotted for other
  men's causes. Thus was poor Harry Dampit made rich by others'
  laziness, who, though they would not follow their own suits, I   60
  made 'em follow me with their purses.

WITGOOD Didst thou so, old Harry?

DAMPIT Ay, and I soused° 'em with bills of charges i'faith; twenty
  pound a year have I brought in for boat-hire, and I ne'er stepped
  into boat in my life.   65

WITGOOD Tramplers of time!

DAMPIT Ay, tramplers of time, rascals of time, bull-beggars!

WITGOOD Ah, thou'rt a mad old Harry! Kind Master Gulf, I am
  bold to renew my acquaintance.

GULF I embrace it, sir.   70

  Music. Exeunt

147

[2.1]

Enter Lucre

LUCRE My adversary evermore twits me with my nephew, forsooth,
my nephew. Why may not a virtuous uncle have a dissolute
nephew? What though he be a brotheller, a wastethrift, a common
surfeiter, and, to conclude, a beggar; must sin in him call up shame
in me? Since we have no part in their follies, why should we have   5
part in their infamies? For my strict hand toward his mortgage,
that I deny not, I confess I had an uncle's pen'worth:° let me
see, half in half,° true. I saw neither hope of his reclaiming° nor
comfort in his being, and was it not then better bestowed upon
his uncle than upon one of his aunts? I need not say bawd, for   10
everyone knows what 'aunt' stands for in the last translation.°

   [Enter Servant]

Now, sir?

SERVANT There's a country serving-man, sir, attends to speak with
your worship.

LUCRE I'm at best leisure now; send him in to me.   15

   [Exit Servant.] Enter Host like a serving-man

HOST Bless your venerable worship.

LUCRE Welcome, good fellow.

HOST *[aside]* He calls me thief at first sight, yet he little thinks I am
an host!

LUCRE What's thy business with me?   20

HOST Faith, sir, I am sent from my mistress to any sufficient
gentleman indeed, to ask advice upon a doubtful point; 'tis
indifferent, sir, to whom I come, for I know none, nor did my
mistress direct me to any particular man, for she's as mere a
stranger here as myself; only I found your worship within, and 'tis   25
a thing I ever loved, sir, to be dispatched as soon as I can.

LUCRE *[aside]* A good blunt honesty, I like him well.—What is thy
mistress?

HOST Faith, a country gentlewoman and a widow, sir. Yesterday was
the first flight of us,° but now she intends to stay till a little term   30
business° be ended.

LUCRE Her name, I prithee?

HOST It runs there in the writings,° sir, among her lands: Widow Medler.°

LUCRE Medler? Mass, have I ne'er heard of that widow? 35

HOST Yes, I warrant you, have you, sir; not the rich widow in Staffordshire?

LUCRE Cuds me, there 'tis indeed; thou hast put me into memory; there's a widow indeed; ah, that I were a bachelor again.

HOST No doubt your worship might do much then, but she's fairly 40 promised to a bachelor already.

LUCRE Ah, what is he, I prithee?

HOST A country gentleman too, one whom your worship knows not, I'm sure; he's spent some few follies in his youth, but marriage, by my faith, begins to call him home; my mistress loves him, sir, 45 and love covers faults,° you know: one Master Witgood, if ever you have heard of the gentleman.

LUCRE Ha? Witgood, say'st thou?

HOST That's his name indeed, sir; my mistress is like to bring him to a goodly seat° yonder—four hundred a year, by my faith. 50

LUCRE But, I pray, take me with you.°

HOST Ay, sir?

LUCRE What countryman might this young Witgood be?

HOST A Leicestershire gentleman, sir.

LUCRE [aside] My nephew, by th'mass, my nephew! I'll fetch out 55 more of this i'faith; a simple country fellow, I'll work't out of him.—And is that gentleman, say'st thou, presently to marry her?

HOST Faith, he brought her up to town, sir; h'as the best card in all the bunch for't, her heart; and I know my mistress will be married 60 ere she go down;° nay I'll swear that, for she's none of those widows that will go down first and be married after; she hates that, I can tell you, sir.

LUCRE By my faith, sir, she is like to have a proper gentleman and a comely; I'll give her that gift!° 65

HOST Why, does your worship know him, sir?

LUCRE I know him! Does not all the world know him? Can a man of such exquisite qualities be hid under a bushel?

HOST Then your worship may save me a labour, for I had charge given me to enquire after him. 70

LUCRE Enquire of him? If I might counsel thee, thou shouldst ne'er trouble thyself further; enquire of him of no more but of me; I'll fit thee!° I grant he has been youthful, but is he not now reclaimed?

Mark you that, sir; has not your mistress, think you, been wanton
in her youth? If men be wags, are there not women wagtails?   75

HOST No doubt, sir.

LUCRE Does not he return wisest that comes home whipped with his
own follies?

HOST Why, very true, sir.

LUCRE The worst report you can hear of him, I can tell you, is that   80
he has been a kind gentleman, a liberal, and a worthy; who but
lusty Witgood, thrice noble Witgood!

HOST Since your worship has so much knowledge in him, can you
resolve° me, sir, what his living might be? My duty binds me, sir,
to have a care of my mistress's estate; she has been ever a good   85
mistress to me, though I say it. Many wealthy suitors has she
non-suited° for his sake; yet though her love be so fixed, a man
cannot tell whether his non-performance° may help to remove it,
sir; he makes us believe he has lands and living.

LUCRE Who, young Master Witgood? Why, believe it, he has as   90
goodly a fine living out yonder—what do you call the place?

HOST Nay, I know not, i'faith.

LUCRE Hum—see, like a beast, if I have not forgot the name—puh!
And out yonder again, goodly grown woods and fair meadows; pax
on't! I can ne'er hit of that place neither.—He? Why, he's Witgood   95
of Witgood Hall, he an unknown thing!

HOST Is he so, sir? To see how rumour will alter! Trust me, sir, we
heard once he had no lands, but all lay mortgaged to an uncle he
has in town here.

LUCRE Push! 'Tis a tale, 'tis a tale.   100

HOST I can assure you, sir, 'twas credibly reported to my mistress.

LUCRE Why, do you think, i'faith, he was ever so simple to mortgage
his lands to his uncle, or his uncle so unnatural to take the extremity
of such a mortgage?

HOST That was my saying still,° sir.   105

LUCRE Puh, ne'er think it.

HOST Yet that report goes current.°

LUCRE Nay, then you urge me: cannot I tell that best that am his uncle?

HOST How, sir? What have I done!

LUCRE Why, how now, in a swoon, man?   110

HOST Is your worship his uncle, sir?

LUCRE Can that be any harm to you, sir?

HOST I do beseech you, sir, do me the favour to conceal it. What a
beast was I to utter so much! Pray, sir, do me the kindness to keep

it in; I shall have my coat pulled o'er my ears,° an't should be   115
known; for the truth is, an't please your worship, to prevent much°
rumour and many suitors, they intend to be married very suddenly
and privately.

LUCRE And dost thou think it stands with my judgement to do them
injury? Must I needs say the knowledge of this marriage comes   120
from thee? Am I a fool at fifty-four? Do I lack subtlety now, that
have got all my wealth by it? There's a leash of angels for thee:
come, let me woo thee; speak, where lie° they?

HOST So I might have no anger, sir—

LUCRE Passion of me, not a jot; prithee come.   125

HOST I would not have it known it came by my means.

LUCRE Why, am I a man of wisdom?

HOST I dare trust your worship, sir, but I'm a stranger to your house;
and to avoid all intelligencers, I desire your worship's ear.

LUCRE [aside] This fellow's worth a matter of trust.—Come, sir.   130
      [Host whispers to him]
Why, now, thou'rt an honest lad.—Ah, sirrah nephew!

HOST Please you, sir, now I have begun with your worship, when
shall I attend for your advice upon that doubtful point?° I must
come warily now.

LUCRE Tut, fear thou nothing; tomorrow's evening shall resolve the   135
doubt.

HOST The time shall cause my attendance.

LUCRE Fare thee well.
      Exit [Host]
There's more true honesty in such a country serving-man than in
a hundred of our cloak companions:° I may well call 'em compan-   140
ions, for since blue coats have been turned into cloaks,° we can
scarce know the man from the master.—George!
      [Enter George]

GEORGE Anon, sir.

LUCRE List hither: [whispers]—keep the place secret. Commend me
to my nephew; I know no cause, tell him, but he might see his   145
uncle.

GEORGE I will, sir.

LUCRE And do you hear, sir, take heed you use him with respect and
duty.

GEORGE [aside] Here's a strange alteration: one day he must be turned   150
out like a beggar, and now he must be called in like a knight!
      Exit [George]

LUCRE Ah, sirrah, that rich widow! Four hundred a year! Beside, I
hear she lays claim to a title of a hundred more. This falls un-
happily that he should bear a grudge to me now, being likely to
prove so rich. What is't, trow, that he makes me a stranger for?   155
Hum, I hope he has not so much wit to apprehend that I cozened
him: he deceives me then.° Good heaven, who would have thought
it would ever have come to this pass! Yet he's a proper gentleman,
i'faith, give him his due—marry, that's his mortgage; but that I
ne'er mean to give him. I'll make him rich enough in words if that   160
be good; and if it come to a piece of money, I will not greatly stick
for't; there may be hope some of the widow's lands, too, may one
day fall upon me, if things be carried wisely.
        [*Enter George*]
    Now, sir, where is he?
GEORGE He desires your worship to hold him excused; he has such   165
weighty business, it commands him wholly from all men.
LUCRE Were those my nephew's words?
GEORGE Yes, indeed, sir.
LUCRE [*aside*] When men grow rich, they grow proud too, I perceive
that. He would not have sent me such an answer once within this   170
twelvemonth; see what 'tis when a man's come to his lands.—
Return to him again, sir; tell him his uncle desires his company
for an hour; I'll trouble him but an hour, say; 'tis for his own
good, tell him; and, do you hear, sir, put 'worship' upon him.° Go
to, do as I bid you; he's like to be a gentleman of worship very   175
shortly.
GEORGE [*aside*] This is good sport i'faith.
        Exit [*George*]
LUCRE Troth, he uses his uncle discourteously now. Can he tell what
I may do for him? Goodness may come from me in a minute that
comes not in seven year again. He knows my humour; I am not   180
so usually good; 'tis no small thing that draws kindness from me,
he may know that an he will. The chief cause that invites me
to do him most good is the sudden astonishing of old Hoard, my
adversary. How pale his malice will look at my nephew's advancement. With what a dejected spirit he will behold his fortunes,   185
whom but last day he proclaimed rioter, penurious makeshift,
despised brothel-master. Ha, ha! 'Twill do me more secret joy than
my last purchase, more precious comfort than all these widows'
revenues.
        [*Enter George*]

Now, sir.   190

GEORGE With much entreaty he's at length come, sir.
        [*Exit George*]
        Enter Witgood

LUCRE Oh, nephew, let me salute you, sir. You're welcome, nephew.

WITGOOD Uncle, I thank you.

LUCRE Y'ave a fault, nephew; you're a stranger here. Well, heaven
       give you joy.   195

WITGOOD Of what, sir?

LUCRE Hah, we can hear! You might have known your uncle's house
       i'faith, you and your widow; go to, you were too blame, if I may
       tell you so without offence.

WITGOOD How could you hear of that, sir?   200

LUCRE Oh, pardon me, it was your will to have it kept° from me, I
       perceive now.

WITGOOD Not for any defect of love, I protest, uncle.

LUCRE Oh, 'twas unkindness, nephew. Fie, fie, fie.

WITGOOD I am sorry you take it in that sense, sir.   205

LUCRE Puh, you cannot colour it, i'faith, nephew.

WITGOOD Will you but hear what I can say in my just excuse, sir?

LUCRE Yes, faith, will I, and welcome.

WITGOOD You that know my danger i'th'city, sir, so well, how great
         my debts are and how extreme my creditors, could not out of your 210
         pure judgement, sir, have wished us hither.

LUCRE Mass, a firm reason indeed.

WITGOOD Else, my uncle's house, why, 't'ad been the only make-
         match.

LUCRE Nay, and thy credit.   215

WITGOOD My credit? Nay, my countenance.° Push, nay, I know,
         uncle, you would have wrought it so by your wit; you would have
         made her believe in time the whole house had been mine.

LUCRE Ay, and most of the goods too.

WITGOOD La you there; well, let 'em all prate what they will, there's 220
         nothing like the bringing of a widow to one's uncle's house.°

LUCRE Nay, let nephews be ruled as they list, they shall find their
       uncle's house the most natural place when all's done.

WITGOOD There they may be bold.

LUCRE Life, they may do anything there, man, and fear neither   225
       beadle nor summoner. An uncle's house! A very Cole Harbour!°
       Sirrah, I'll touch thee near now: hast thou so much interest in° thy
       widow that by a token thou couldst presently send for her?

WITGOOD Troth, I think I can, uncle.

LUCRE Go to, let me see that!   230

WITGOOD Pray command one of your men hither, uncle.

LUCRE George!

    [*Enter George*]

GEORGE Here, sir.

LUCRE Attend my nephew!

    [*Witgood whispers to George, who then goes out*]

    [*Aside*] I love a'life to prattle with a rich widow; 'tis pretty   235
methinks when our tongues go together;° and then to promise
much and perform little; I love that sport a'life i'faith. Yet I am in
the mood now to do my nephew some good if he take me
handsomely.°—What, have you dispatched?

WITGOOD I ha' sent, sir.   240

LUCRE Yet I must condemn you of unkindness, nephew.

WITGOOD Heaven forbid, uncle!

LUCRE Yes, faith, must I; say your debts be many, your creditors
importunate, yet the kindness of a thing is all, nephew; you might
have sent me close word on't without the least danger or prejudice   245
to your fortunes.

WITGOOD Troth, I confess it, uncle, I was too blame there; but
indeed my intent was to have clapped it up suddenly,° and so have
broke forth like a joy to my friends and a wonder to the world.
Beside, there's a trifle of a forty pound matter toward the setting   250
of me forth;° my friends should ne'er have known on't; I meant to
make shift for that myself.

LUCRE How, nephew? Let me not hear such a word again, I beseech
you—shall I be beholding to you?

WITGOOD To me? Alas, what do you mean, uncle?   255

LUCRE I charge you upon my love: you trouble nobody but myself.

WITGOOD Y'ave no reason for that, uncle.

LUCRE Troth, I'll ne'er be friends with you while you live, and
you do.

WITGOOD Nay, an you say so, uncle, here's my hand, I will not do't. 260

LUCRE Why, well said. There's some hope in thee, when thou wilt
be ruled; I'll make it up fifty, faith, because I see thee so reclaimed.
Peace, here comes my wife with Sam, her t'other husband's son.

    [*Enter Mistress Lucre and Sam*]

WITGOOD Good aunt—

SAM Cousin Witgood! I rejoice in my salute: you're most welcome to 265
this noble city governed with the sword in the scabbard.°

WITGOOD [*aside*] And the wit in the pommel°—good Master Sam Freedom, I return the salute.

LUCRE By the mass, she's coming; wife, let me see now how thou wilt entertain her.   270

MISTRESS LUCRE I hope I am not to learn, sir, to entertain a widow; 'tis not so long ago since I was one myself.

    [*Enter Courtesan*]

WITGOOD Uncle.

LUCRE She's come indeed!

WITGOOD My uncle was desirous to see you, widow, and I presumed   275
to invite you.

COURTESAN The presumption was nothing, Master Witgood: is this your uncle, sir?

LUCRE Marry am I, sweet widow, and his good uncle he shall find me; [*kisses her*] ay, by this smack that I give thee thou'rt wel-   280
come.—Wife, bid the widow welcome the same way again.

    [*She kisses the Courtesan*]

SAM [*aside*] I am a gentleman now too, by my father's° occupation, and I see no reason but I may kiss a widow by my father's copy;° truly, I think the charter° is not against it; surely these are the words: 'The son, once a gentleman, may revel it, though his   285
father were a dauber'; 'tis about the fifteenth page. I'll to her.

    [*Offers to kiss the Courtesan, who repulses him*]

LUCRE Y'are not very busy° now; a word with thee, sweet widow—

SAM [*aside*] Coad's nigs! I was never so disgraced since the hour my mother whipped me.

LUCRE Beside, I have no child of mine own to care for; she's my   290
second wife, old, past bearing; clap sure to him, widow; he's like to be my heir, I can tell you.

COURTESAN Is he so, sir?

LUCRE He knows it already, and the knave's proud on't; jolly rich widows have been offered him here i'th'city, great merchants'   295
wives, and do you think he would once look upon 'em? Forsooth, he'll none. You are beholding to him i'th'country, then, ere we could be; nay, I'll hold a wager, widow, if he were once known to be in town he would be presently sought after; nay, and happy were they that could catch him first.   300

COURTESAN I think so.

LUCRE Oh, there would be such running to and fro, widow, he should not pass the streets for 'em; he'd be took up in one great house or other presently. Fah! They know he has it, and must have

it.° You see this house here, widow; this house and all comes to   305
him, goodly rooms, ready furnished, ceiled with plaster of Paris,
and all hung about° with cloth of arras.—Nephew!

WITGOOD Sir.

LUCRE Show the widow your house; carry her into all the rooms,
and bid her welcome.—You shall see, widow.—[*Aside to Witgood*]   310
Nephew, strike° all sure above,° an thou beest a good boy—ah!

WITGOOD Alas, sir, I know not how she would take it.

LUCRE The right way, I warrant 'ee. A pox, art an ass? Would I were
in thy stead! Get you up; I am ashamed of you.

     [*Exeunt Witgood and Courtesan*]

So, let 'em agree as they will now; many a match has been struck   315
up in my house a'this fashion: let 'em try all manner of ways, still
there's nothing like an uncle's house to strike the stroke in. I'll
hold my wife in talk a little.—Now, Jinny, your son there goes
a-wooing to a poor gentlewoman but of a thousand° portion; see
my nephew, a lad of less hope, strikes at four hundred a year in   320
good rubbish.

MISTRESS LUCRE Well, we must do as we may, sir.

LUCRE I'll have his money ready told for him again° he come down.
Let me see too; by th'mass, I must present the widow with some
jewel, a good piece o'plate or such a device; 'twill hearten her on   325
well. I have a very fair standing cup,° and a good high standing
cup will please a widow above all other pieces.

     Exit [*Lucre*]

MISTRESS LUCRE Do you mock us with your nephew?—I have a plot
in my head, son; i'faith, husband, to cross you.

SAM Is it a tragedy plot or a comedy plot, good mother?   330

MISTRESS LUCRE 'Tis a plot shall vex him. I charge you, of my
blessing, son Sam, that you presently withdraw the action of your
love from Master Hoard's niece.

SAM How, mother!

MISTRESS LUCRE Nay, I have a plot in my head i'faith. Here, take   335
this chain of gold and this fair diamond; dog me the widow
home to her lodging, and at thy best opportunity fasten 'em both
upon her—nay, I have a reach; I can tell you thou art known
what thou art, son, among the right worshipful, all the twelve
companies.°   340

SAM Truly I thank 'em for it.

MISTRESS LUCRE He?° He's a scab to° thee; and so certify her thou
hast two hundred a year of thyself, beside thy good parts—a proper

person and a lovely. If I were a widow, I could find in my heart
to have thee myself, son; ay, from 'em all.   345

SAM Thank you for your good will,° mother, but indeed I had rather
have a stranger; and if I woo her not in that violent° fashion, that
I will make her be glad to take these gifts ere I leave her, let me
never be called the heir° of your body.

MISTRESS LUCRE Nay, I know there's enough in you,° son, if you   350
once come to put it forth.

SAM I'll quickly make a bolt or a shaft on't.°

    Exeunt

[2.2]

Enter Hoard and Moneylove

MONEYLOVE Faith, Master Hoard, I have bestowed many months in
the suit of your niece, such was the dear love I ever bore to her
virtues; but since she hath so extremely denied me, I am to lay out
for my fortunes elsewhere.

HOARD Heaven forbid but you should, sir. I ever told you my niece   5
stood otherwise affected.°

MONEYLOVE I must confess you did, sir; yet in regard of my great
loss of time, and the zeal with which I sought your niece, shall I
desire one favour of your worship?

HOARD In regard of those two 'tis hard but you shall, sir.   10

MONEYLOVE I shall rest grateful. 'Tis not full three hours, sir, since
the happy rumour of a rich country widow came to my hearing.

HOARD How? A rich country widow?

MONEYLOVE Four hundred a year landed.

HOARD Yea?   15

MONEYLOVE Most firm, sir, and I have learned her lodging; here
my suit begins, sir: if I might but entreat your worship to be a
countenance° for me and speak a good word—for your words
will pass°—I nothing doubt but I might set fair for the widow;
nor shall your labour, sir, end altogether in thanks, two hundred   20
angels—

HOARD So, so, what suitors has she?

MONEYLOVE There lies the comfort, sir; the report of her is yet but
a whisper, and only solicited by young riotous Witgood, nephew
to your mortal adversary.   25

HOARD Ha! Art certain he's her suitor?

MONEYLOVE Most certain, sir, and his uncle very industrious to beguile the widow and make up the match!

HOARD So? Very good!

MONEYLOVE Now, sir, you know this young Witgood is a spend-   30
thrift, dissolute fellow.

HOARD A very rascal.

MONEYLOVE A midnight surfeiter.

HOARD The spume of a brothel-house.

MONEYLOVE True, sir! Which being well told in your worship's   35
phrase,° may both heave him out of her mind and drive a fair way
for me to the widow's affections.

HOARD Attend me about five.

MONEYLOVE With my best care, sir.

            Exit [*Moneylove*]

HOARD Fool, thou hast left thy treasure with a thief; to trust a   40
widower with a suit in love! Happy revenge, I hug thee. I have not
only the means laid before me extremely to cross my adversary and
confound the last hopes of his nephew, but thereby to enrich my
state, augment my revenues, and build mine own fortunes greater.
Ha, ha!   45
I'll mar your phrase, o'erturn your flatteries,°
Undo your windings, policies, and plots,
Fall like a secret and dispatchful plague
On your secured comforts. Why, I am able
To buy three of Lucre, thrice outbid him,   50
Let my out-monies be reckoned and all.

            Enter three Creditors

FIRST CREDITOR I am glad of this news.

SECOND CREDITOR So are we, by my faith.

THIRD CREDITOR Young Witgood will be a gallant again now.

HOARD [*listening*] Peace!   55

FIRST CREDITOR I promise you, Master Cockpit, she's a mighty rich
widow.

SECOND CREDITOR Why, have you ever heard of her?

FIRST CREDITOR Who? Widow Medler? She lies open° to much
rumour.   60

THIRD CREDITOR Four hundred a year, they say, in very good land.

FIRST CREDITOR Nay, take't of my word, if you believe that, you
believe the least.

SECOND CREDITOR And to see how close he° keeps it!

FIRST CREDITOR Oh, sir, there's policy in that, to prevent better   65
suitors.

THIRD CREDITOR He owes me a hundred pound, and I protest I
never looked for a penny.

FIRST CREDITOR He little dreams of our coming; he'll wonder to see
his creditors upon him.   70
    Exeunt [Creditors]

HOARD Good, his creditors; I'll follow. This makes for me:° all know
the widow's wealth; and 'tis well known I can estate her fairly, ay,
and will.
    In this one chance shines a twice happy fate:
    I both deject my foe and raise my state.   75
        Music. Exit

[3.1]

[Enter] Witgood with his Creditors

WITGOOD Why, alas, my creditors, could you find no other time to undo me but now? Rather your malice appears in this than the justness of the debt.

FIRST CREDITOR Master Witgood, I have forborne my money long.

WITGOOD I pray speak low, sir. What do you mean?   5

SECOND CREDITOR We hear you are to be married suddenly to a rich country widow.

WITGOOD What can be kept so close but you creditors hear on't? Well, 'tis a lamentable state that our chiefest afflictors should first hear of our fortunes. Why, this is no good course i'faith, sirs; if   10 ever you have hope to be satisfied, why do you seek to confound the means that should work it? There's neither piety, no, nor policy in that. Shine favourably now; why, I may rise and spread again to your great comforts.

FIRST CREDITOR He says true i'faith.   15

WITGOOD Remove me now and I consume for ever.

SECOND CREDITOR Sweet gentleman!

WITGOOD How can it thrive which from the sun you sever?

THIRD CREDITOR It cannot indeed!

WITGOOD Oh, then show patience. I shall have enough to satisfy you all. 20

FIRST CREDITOR Ay, if we could be content,° a shame take us.°

WITGOOD For, look you, I am but newly sure° yet to the widow, and what a rend might this discredit make. Within these three days will I bind you lands for your securities.

FIRST CREDITOR No, good Master Witgood,   25
Would 'twere as much as we dare trust you with!°

WITGOOD I know you have been kind; however, now,
Either by wrong report or false incitement,
Your gentleness is injured. In such
A state as this a man cannot want foes.   30
If on the sudden he begin to rise,
No man that lives can count his enemies.
You had some intelligence, I warrant ye,
From an ill-willer.

SECOND CREDITOR Faith, we heard you brought up a rich widow,   35
sir, and were suddenly to marry her.

WITGOOD Ay, why, there it was, I knew 'twas so; but since you
are so well resolved of my faith toward you, let me be so much
favoured of you, I beseech you all—

ALL Oh, it shall not need, i'faith, sir—   40

WITGOOD As to lie still awhile and bury my debts in silence till I be
fully possessed of the widow; for the truth is—I may tell you as
my friends—

ALL Oh, oh, oh!

WITGOOD I am to raise a little money in the city toward the setting   45
forth of myself for mine own credit and your comfort. Now if my
former debts should be divulged, all hope of my proceedings were
quite extinguished!

FIRST CREDITOR [aside to Witgood] Do you hear, sir? I may deserve
your custom hereafter; pray let my money be accepted before a   50
stranger's. Here's forty pound I received as I came to you; if that
may stand you in any stead, make use on't; nay, pray sir, 'tis at
your service.

WITGOOD [aside to First Creditor] You do so ravish me with kindness,
that I'm constrained to play the maid and take it!°   55

FIRST CREDITOR [aside to Witgood] Let none of them see it, I
beseech you.

WITGOOD [aside] Fah!

FIRST CREDITOR [aside to Witgood] I hope I shall be first in your
remembrance after the marriage rites.   60

WITGOOD [aside to First Creditor] Believe it firmly.

FIRST CREDITOR So.—What, do you walk, sirs?

SECOND CREDITOR I go.—[Aside to Witgood] Take no care, sir, for
money to furnish you; within this hour I'll send you sufficient.—
Come Master Cockpit, we both stay for you.   65

THIRD CREDITOR I ha' lost a ring i'faith; I'll follow you presently.

    [Exeunt First and Second Creditors]

But you shall find it, sir; I know your youth and expenses have
disfurnished you of all jewels; there's a ruby of twenty pound
price, sir; bestow it upon your widow. What, man, 'twill call up   70
her blood to you; beside, if I might so much work with you, I
would not have you beholding to those blood-suckers for any
money.

WITGOOD Not I, believe it.

THIRD CREDITOR They're a brace of cut-throats!   75

WITGOOD I know 'em.

THIRD CREDITOR Send a note of all your wants to my shop, and I'll
    supply you instantly.

WITGOOD Say you so? Why, here's my hand then, no man living
    shall do't but thyself.   80

THIRD CREDITOR Shall I carry it away from 'em both then?

WITGOOD I'faith, shalt thou!

THIRD CREDITOR Troth, then I thank you, sir.

WITGOOD Welcome, good Master Cockpit!

        Exit [*Third Creditor*]

    Ha, ha, ha! Why, is not this better now than lying a-bed? I perceive   85
    there's nothing conjures up wit sooner than poverty, and nothing
    lays it down sooner than wealth and lechery. This has some
    savour yet. Oh, that I had the mortgage from mine uncle as sure
    in possession as these trifles. I would forswear brothel at noonday
    and muscadine and eggs at midnight.   90

        Enter Courtesan

COURTESAN Master Witgood? Where are you?

WITGOOD Holla!

COURTESAN Rich news!

WITGOOD Would 'twere all in plate.

COURTESAN There's some in chains and jewels. I am so haunted   95
    with suitors, Master Witgood, I know not which to dispatch first.

WITGOOD You have the better Term,° by my faith.

COURTESAN Among the number, one Master Hoard, an ancient
    gentleman.

WITGOOD Upon my life, my uncle's adversary.   100

COURTESAN It may well hold so, for he rails on you,
    Speaks shamefully of him.

WITGOOD   As I could wish it.°

COURTESAN I first denied him, but so cunningly
    It rather promised him assurèd hopes
    Than any loss of labour.

WITGOOD   Excellent.   105

COURTESAN I expect him every hour with gentlemen,
    With whom he labours to make good his words
    To approve you riotous, your state consumed,
    Your uncle—

WITGOOD Wench, make up thy own fortunes now, do thyself a good   110
    turn once in thy days. He's rich in money, moveables, and lands;
    marry him, he's an old doting fool, and that's worth all; marry him,
    'twould be a great comfort to me to see thee do well i'faith; marry

him, 'twould ease my conscience well to see thee well bestowed; I
have a care of thee i'faith.   115

COURTESAN Thanks, sweet Master Witgood.

WITGOOD I reach at farther happiness:° first, I am sure it can be
no harm to thee, and there may happen goodness to me by it.
Prosecute it well; let's send up for our wits, now we require their
best and most pregnant assistance.   120

COURTESAN Step in, I think I hear 'em.

> *Exit [Courtesan with Witgood.] Enter Hoard and Gentle-*
> *men [Lamprey and Spitchcock] with the Host [as] serving-*
> *man*

HOARD Art thou the widow's man? By my faith, sh'as a company of
proper men then.

HOST I am the worst of six, sir; good enough for blue-coats.°

HOARD Hark hither. I hear say thou art in most credit with her.   125

HOST Not so, sir.

HOARD Come, come, thou'rt modest. There's a brace of royals;
prithee help me to th'speech of° her.

HOST I'll do what I may, sir, always saving myself harmless.°

HOARD Go to, do't, I say; thou shalt hear better from me.°   130

HOST [aside] Is not this a better place than five mark a year standing wages? Say a man had but three such clients in a day, methinks
he might make a poor° living on't; beside, I was never brought up
with so little honesty to refuse any man's money, never. What gulls
there are o'this side the world! Now know I the widow's mind,   135
none but my young master comes in her clutches.° Ha, ha, ha!

> *Exit [Host]*

HOARD Now my dear gentlemen, stand firmly to me; you know
his° follies and my worth.

[LAMPREY] We do, sir.

[SPITCHCOCK] But, Master Hoard, are you sure he is not i'th'house   140
now?

HOARD Upon my honesty I chose this time
O'purpose fit; the spendthrift is abroad.
Assist me; here she comes.

> *[Enter Courtesan]*

> Now, my sweet widow.

COURTESAN Y'are welcome, Master Hoard.   145

HOARD [aside] Dispatch, sweet gentlemen, dispatch.
—I am come, widow, to prove those my words
Neither of envy sprung nor of false tongues,

But such as their deserts and actions°
Do merit and bring forth, all which these gentlemen,   150
Well known and better reputed, will confess.

COURTESAN   I cannot tell
How my affections may dispose of me,
But surely if they find him so desertless,
They'll have that reason to withdraw themselves.   155
And therefore, gentlemen, I do entreat you,
As you are fair in reputation
And in appearing form, so shine in truth.
I am a widow, and, alas, you know,
Soon overthrown; 'tis a very small thing°   160
That we withstand, our weakness is so great.°
Be partial unto neither, but deliver°
Without affection your opinion.°

HOARD   And that will drive it home.°

COURTESAN   Nay, I beseech your silence, Master Hoard;   165
You are a party.

HOARD   Widow, not a word!°

[LAMPREY] The better first to work you to belief,
Know neither of us owe him flattery,°
Nor t'other malice, but unbribed censure,°
So help us our best fortunes.

COURTESAN   It suffices.   170

[LAMPREY] That Witgood is a riotous, undone man,
Imperfect both in fame and in estate,
His debts wealthier than he, and executions
In wait for his due body, we'll maintain°
With our best credit and our dearest blood.   175

COURTESAN   Nor land nor living, say you? Pray, take heed
You do not wrong the gentleman!

[LAMPREY]   What we speak
Our lives and means are ready to make good.

COURTESAN   Alas, how soon are we poor souls beguiled!

[SPITCHCOCK] And for his uncle—

HOARD   Let that come to me.   180
His uncle, a severe extortioner;
A tyrant at a forfeiture; greedy of others'
Miseries; one that would undo his brother,
Nay, swallow up his father, if he can,
Within the fathoms of his conscience.°   185

[LAMPREY] Nay, believe it, widow,
 You had not only matched yourself to wants,
 But in an evil and unnatural stock.
HOARD [aside] Follow hard, gentlemen, follow hard!
COURTESAN Is my love so deceived? Before you all   190
 I do renounce him; on my knees I vow
 He ne'er shall marry me.
WITGOOD [looking in] Heaven knows he never meant it!
HOARD [aside to Lamprey and Spitchcock] There, take her at the
 bound.°
[LAMPREY] Then with a new and pure affection,   195
 Behold yon gentleman, grave, kind, and rich,
 A match worthy yourself; esteeming him,
 You do regard your state.
HOARD [aside to Lamprey and Spitchcock] I'll make her a jointure,
 say.
[LAMPREY] He can join land to land, and will possess you°   200
 Of what you can desire.
[SPITCHCOCK]   Come, widow, come.
COURTESAN The world is so deceitful!
[LAMPREY]   There 'tis deceitful,°
 Where flattery, want, and imperfection lies;
 But none of these in him; push!
COURTESAN   Pray, sir—°
[LAMPREY] Come, you widows are ever most backward when you   205
 should do yourselves most good; but were it to marry a chin not
 worth a hair° now, then you would be forward enough! Come, clap
 hands, a match.
HOARD With all my heart, widow.—Thanks gentlemen,
 I will deserve your labour—[to Courtesan] and thy love.°   210
COURTESAN Alas, you love not widows but for wealth!
 I promise you I ha' nothing, sir.
HOARD   Well said, widow,
 Well said. Thy love is all I seek, before
 These gentlemen.
COURTESAN   Now I must hope the best.
HOARD My joys are such they want to be expressed.°   215
COURTESAN But, Master Hoard, one thing I must remember° you of
 before these gentlemen, your friends. How shall I suddenly° avoid
 the loathed soliciting of that perjured Witgood, and his tedious,
 dissembling uncle, who this very day hath appointed a meeting for

the same purpose° too, where, had not the truth come forth, I had   220
been undone, utterly undone.

HOARD   What think you of that, gentlemen?

[LAMPREY]   'Twas well devised.

HOARD   Hark thee, widow: train out young Witgood single;° hasten
him thither with thee somewhat before the hour, where, at the   225
place appointed, these gentlemen and my self will wait the opportunity, when, by some sleight removing him from thee, we'll
suddenly enter and surprise thee, carry thee away by boat to Cole
Harbour,° have a priest ready, and there clap it up instantly. How
lik'st it, widow?   230

COURTESAN   In that it pleaseth you, it likes me well.

HOARD   I'll kiss thee for those words.—Come, gentlemen;
Still must I live a suitor to your favours,
Still to your aid beholding.

[LAMPREY]   We're engaged, sir;
'Tis for our credits now to see't well ended.   235

HOARD   'Tis for your honours, gentlemen; nay, look to't;
Not only in joy but I in wealth excel.—
No more sweet widow but sweet wife, farewell.

COURTESAN   Farewell, sir.
         *Exeunt [Hoard with Lamprey and Spitchcock.] Enter Wit-
         good*

WITGOOD   Oh, for more scope! I could laugh eternally. Give you joy,   240
Mistress Hoard; I promise your fortune was good forsooth; y'ave
fell upon wealth enough, and there's young gentlemen enow can
help you to the rest.° Now it requires our wits; carry thyself but
heedfully now, and we are both—
         [Enter Host]

HOST   Master Witgood, your uncle.   245

WITGOOD   *[aside to Courtesan]* Cuds me! Remove thyself a while. I'll
serve for° him.
         [Exeunt Courtesan and Host.] Enter Lucre

LUCRE   Nephew, good morrow, nephew.

WITGOOD   The same to you, kind uncle.

LUCRE   How fares the widow? Does the meeting hold?   250

WITGOOD   Oh, no question of that, sir.

LUCRE   I'll strike the stroke then for thee; no more days.°

WITGOOD   The sooner the better, uncle. Oh, she's mightily followed!°

LUCRE   And yet so little rumoured.   255

WITGOOD Mightily! Here comes one old gentleman, and he'll make her a jointure of three hundred a year forsooth; another wealthy suitor will estate his son in his lifetime, and make him weigh down° the widow; here a merchant's son will possess her with no less than three goodly lordships at once, which were all pawns to his father.   260

LUCRE Peace, nephew, let me hear no more of 'em; it mads me. Thou shalt prevent 'em all. No words to the widow of my coming hither. Let me see—'tis now upon nine; before twelve, nephew, we will have the bargain struck, we will, i'faith, boy.   265

WITGOOD Oh, my precious uncle!

    [*Exeunt*]

[3.2]

    [*Enter*] *Hoard and his Niece*

HOARD Niece, sweet niece, prithee have a care to my house; I leave all to thy discretion. Be content to dream awhile; I'll have a husband for thee shortly; put that care upon me, wench, for in choosing wives and husbands I am only fortunate. I have that gift given me.

    Exit [*Hoard*]

NIECE But it is not likely you should choose for me,   5
    Since nephew to your chiefest enemy
    Is he whom I affect; but oh forgetful!
    Why dost thou flatter thy affections so
    With name of him, that for a widow's bed
    Neglects thy purer love? Can it be so,   10
    Or does report dissemble?

    [*Enter George*]

                    How now, sir?

GEORGE A letter with which came a private charge.°

NIECE Therein I thank your care.

    [*Exit George*]

    I know this hand. (*Reads*) 'Dearer than sight, what the world reports of me yet believe not; rumour will alter shortly. Be thou   15 constant; I am still the same that I was in love, and I hope to be the same in fortunes.

                           Theodorus Witgood.'

I am resolved; no more shall fear or doubt
Raise their pale powers to keep affection out.   20
    Exit

[3.3]

Enter, with a Drawer, Hoard and two Gentlemen [Lamprey
and Spitchcock]

DRAWER You're very welcome, gentlemen.—Dick,° show those
    gentlemen the Pomegranate° there.
HOARD Hist!
DRAWER Up those stairs, gentlemen.
HOARD Pist! Drawer—   5
DRAWER Anon, sir.
HOARD Prithee ask at the bar if a gentlewoman came not in lately.
DRAWER William at the bar, did you see any gentlewoman came in
    lately? Speak you ay, speak you no.
WILLIAM (*within*) No, none came in yet but Mistress Florence.   10
DRAWER He says none came in yet, sir, but one Mistress Florence.
HOARD What is that Florence? A widow?
DRAWER Yes, a Dutch widow.
HOARD How?
DRAWER That's an English drab, sir. Give your worship good   15
    morrow.
    [*Exit Drawer*]
HOARD A merry knave i'faith. I shall remember a Dutch widow the
    longest day of my life.
[LAMPREY] Did not I use most art to win the widow?
[SPITCHCOCK] You shall pardon me for that, sir; Master Hoard   20
    knows I took her at best 'vantage.
HOARD What's that, sweet gentlemen, what's that?
[SPITCHCOCK] He will needs bear me down° that his art only
    wrought with the widow most.
HOARD Oh, you did both well, gentlemen, you did both well, I thank   25
    you.
[LAMPREY] I was the first that moved her.
HOARD You were i'faith.
[SPITCHCOCK] But it was I that took her at the bound.°
HOARD Ay, that was you; faith, gentlemen, 'tis right.   30

[LAMPREY] I boasted least, but 'twas I joined their hands.

HOARD By th'mass, I think he did. You did all well, gentlemen, you
did all well; contend no more.

[LAMPREY] Come, yon room's fittest.

HOARD True, 'tis next the door.°   35

    Exit [Hoard with Lamprey and Spitchcock.] Enter Witgood,
    Courtesan, [Drawer] and Host

DRAWER You're very welcome; please you to walk upstairs, cloth's
laid, sir.

COURTESAN Upstairs! Troth, I am weary, Master Witgood.

WITGOOD Rest yourself here awhile, widow; we'll have a cup of
muscadine in this little room.   40

DRAWER A cup of muscadine? You shall have the best, sir.

WITGOOD But do you hear, sirrah?

DRAWER Do you call? Anon, sir.

WITGOOD What is there provided for dinner?

DRAWER I cannot readily tell you, sir; if you please, you may go into   45
the kitchen and see yourself, sir; many gentlemen of worship do
use to do it, I assure you, sir.

    [Exit Drawer]

HOST A pretty familiar prigging rascal; he has his part without book!

WITGOOD Against° you are ready to drink to me, widow, I'll be
present to pledge you.   50

COURTESAN Nay, I commend your care, 'tis done well of you.

    [Exit Witgood]

'Las,° what have I forgot!

HOST What, mistress?

COURTESAN I slipped my wedding ring off when I washed and left
it at my lodging; prithee run, I shall be sad without it.   55

    [Exit Host]

So, he's gone!—Boy!

    [Enter Boy]

BOY Anon forsooth.

COURTESAN Come hither, sirrah: learn secretly if one Master Hoard,
an ancient gentleman, be about house.

BOY I heard such a one named.   60

COURTESAN Commend me to him.

    Enter Hoard with Gentlemen [Lamprey and Spitchcock]

HOARD I'll do thy° commendations!

COURTESAN Oh, you come well: away, to boat, begone.

HOARD Thus wise men are revenged, give two for one.

Exeunt [Courtesan, Hoard, Lamprey and Spitchcock.] Enter
Witgood and Vintner

WITGOOD I must request you, sir, to show extraordinary care; my   65
uncle comes with gentlemen, his friends, and 'tis upon a making.°

VINTNER Is it so? I'll give a special charge, good Master Witgood.
May I be bold to see her?

WITGOOD Who, the widow? With all my heart, i'faith, I'll bring you
to her.   70

VINTNER If she be a Staffordshire gentlewoman, 'tis much if° I know
her not.

WITGOOD How now? Boy, drawer!

VINTNER Hie!

BOY [*coming forward*] Do you call, sir?   75

WITGOOD Went the gentlewoman up that was here?

BOY Up, sir? She went out, sir.

WITGOOD Out, sir?

BOY Out, sir. One Master Hoard with a guard of gentlemen carried
her out at back door a pretty while since, sir.   80

WITGOOD Hoard? Death and darkness! Hoard?

Enter Host

HOST The devil of ring I can find!

WITGOOD How now, what news? Where's the widow?

HOST My mistress? Is she not here, sir?

WITGOOD More madness yet.   85

HOST She sent me for a ring.

WITGOOD A plot, a plot! To boat!° She's stole away!

HOST What?

Enter Lucre with Gentlemen [Limber and Kix]

WITGOOD Follow, enquire old Hoard, my uncle's adversary—
[*Exit Host*]

LUCRE Nephew, what's that?   90

WITGOOD Thrice miserable wretch!

LUCRE Why, what's the matter?

VINTNER The widow's borne away, sir.

LUCRE Ha? Passion of me!—A heavy welcome, gentlemen.

[LIMBER] The widow gone?   95

LUCRE Who durst attempt it?

WITGOOD Who but old Hoard, my uncle's adversary!

LUCRE How!

WITGOOD With his confederates.

LUCRE Hoard, my deadly enemy! Gentlemen, stand to me,   100

I will not bear it, 'tis in hate of me;
That villain seeks my shame, nay thirsts my blood;°
He owes me mortal malice.
I'll spend my wealth on this despiteful plot°
Ere he shall cross me and my nephew thus.   105
WITGOOD So maliciously.

   Enter Host

LUCRE How now, you treacherous rascal?
HOST That's none of my name, sir.
WITGOOD Poor soul, he knew not on't.
LUCRE I'm sorry. I see then 'twas a mere plot.°   110
HOST I traced 'em nearly—
LUCRE   Well?
HOST   And hear for certain°
 They have took Cole Harbour.
LUCRE   The devil's sanctuary!°
 They shall not rest, I'll pluck her from his arms.
 Kind and dear gentlemen,
 If ever I had seat within your breasts—   115
[LIMBER] No more, good sir, it is a wrong to us
 To see you injured in a cause so just;
 We'll spend our lives, but we will right our friends.
LUCRE Honest and kind. Come, we have delayed too long:
 Nephew take comfort, a just cause is strong.   120
WITGOOD That's all my comfort, uncle.

   Exeunt [Lucre, Limber, Kix, Vintner, Host and Boy]
          Ha, ha, ha!
Now may events fall luckily and well:
He that ne'er strives, says wit, shall ne'er excel.

   Exit

[3.4]

   Enter Dampit, the Usurer, drunk

DAMPIT When did I say my prayers? In anno '88 when the great
 armada was coming; and in anno '99° when the great thunder and
 lightning was. I prayed heartily then, i'faith, to overthrow Poovies'
 new buildings;° I kneeled by my great iron chest, I remember.

   [*Enter Audrey*]

AUDREY Master Dampit, one may hear you before they see you; you   5
keep sweet hours, Master Dampit; we were all abed three hours ago.

DAMPIT Audrey?

AUDREY Oh, y'are a fine gentleman!

DAMPIT So I am, i'faith, and a fine scholar. Do you use to go to bed
so early, Audrey?   10

AUDREY Call you this early, Master Dampit?

DAMPIT Why, is't not one of clock i'th'morning? Is not that early
enough? Fetch me a glass of fresh beer.

AUDREY Here, I have warmed your nightcap for you, Master
Dampit.   15

DAMPIT Draw it on then. I am very weak, truly; I have not eaten so
much as the bulk of an egg these three days.

AUDREY You have drunk the more, Master Dampit.

DAMPIT What's that?

AUDREY You mought an you would, Master Dampit.   20

DAMPIT I answer you I cannot. Hold your prating; you prate too
much and understand too little. Are you answered? Give me a glass
of beer.

AUDREY May I ask how you do, Master Dampit?

DAMPIT How do I? I'faith, naught.   25

AUDREY I ne'er knew you do otherwise.

DAMPIT I eat not one penn'ort' of bread these two years. Give me a
glass of fresh beer. I am not sick, nor I am not well.

AUDREY Take this warm napkin about your neck, sir, whilst I help
to make you unready.°   30

DAMPIT How now, Audrey-prater,° with your scurvy devices, what
say you now?

AUDREY What say I, Master Dampit? I say nothing but that you are
very weak.

DAMPIT Faith, thou hast more cony-catching° devices than all   35
London!

AUDREY Why, Master Dampit, I never deceived you in all my life!

DAMPIT Why was that? Because I never did trust thee.

AUDREY I care not what you say, Master Dampit!

DAMPIT Hold thy prating. I answer thee, thou art a beggar, a quean,   40
and a bawd. Are you answered?

AUDREY Fie, Master Dampit! A gentleman, and have such words.

DAMPIT Why, thou base drudge of infortunity, thou kitchen-stuff
drab of beggary, roguery and coxcombry, thou cavern-fed° quean

of foolery, knavery and bawdreaminy,° I'll tell thee what, I will not 45
give a louse for thy fortunes.

AUDREY No, Master Dampit? And there's a gentleman comes a-
wooing to me, and he doubts nothing, but that you will get me
from him.

DAMPIT I? If I would either have thee or lie with thee for two 50
thousand pound, would I might be damned! Why, thou base,
impudent quean of foolery, flattery and coxcombry, are you
answered?

AUDREY Come, will you rise and go to bed, sir?

DAMPIT Rise and go to bed too, Audrey? How does Mistress 55
Proserpine?°

AUDREY Fooh—

DAMPIT She's as fine a philosopher of a stinkard's wife as any within
the liberties—fah, fah, Audrey!

AUDREY How now, Master Dampit? 60

DAMPIT Fie upon't, what a choice of stinks is here.° What hast thou
done, Audrey? Fie upon't, here's a choice of stinks indeed. Give
me a fresh glass of beer, and then I will to bed.

AUDREY It waits for you above, sir.

DAMPIT Foh! I think they burn horns° in Barnard's Inn; if ever I 65
smelt such an abominable stink, usury forsake me.

[*Exit Dampit*]

AUDREY They be the stinking nails of his trampling feet, and he talks
of burning of horns.

Exit

[4.1]

Enter at Cole Harbour, Hoard, the Widow, and Gentlemen
[Lamprey and Spitchcock], he° married now

[LAMPREY] Join hearts, join hands,
   In wedlock's bands,
   Never to part
   Till death cleave your heart;
   You shall forsake all other women,   5
   You lords, knights, gentlemen and yeomen.
   What my tongue slips°
   Make up with your lips.

HOARD [*kissing her*] Give you joy, Mistress Hoard; let the kiss come
  about.   10
       [*The Gentlemen kiss the Courtesan. Knocking within*]
  Who knocks? Convey my little pig-eater out.

LUCRE [*within*] Hoard?

HOARD Upon my life, my adversary, gentlemen.

LUCRE Hoard, open the door, or we will force it ope:
  Give us the widow.

HOARD   Gentlemen, keep 'em out.   15

LAMPREY He comes upon his death that enters here.

LUCRE [*within*] My friends assist me.

HOARD   He has assistants, gentlemen.

LAMPREY Tut, nor him, nor them, we in this action fear.

LUCRE [*within*] Shall I, in peace, speak one word with the widow?

COURTESAN Husband and gentleman, hear me but a word.   20

HOARD Freely, sweet wife.

COURTESAN   Let him in peaceably;
  You know we're sure from any act of his.°

HOARD Most true.

COURTESAN You may stand by and smile at his old weakness;
  Let me alone to answer him.

HOARD   Content,   25
  'Twill be good mirth i'faith; how think you, gentlemen?

LAMPREY Good gullery!

HOARD   Upon calm conditions let him in.°

LUCRE [*within*] All spite and malice—

LAMPREY   Hear me, Master Lucre.

So you will vow a peaceful entrance°
With those your friends, and only exercise   30
Calm conference with the widow without fury,
The passage shall receive you.
LUCRE [*within*]   I do vow it.
LAMPREY Then enter and talk freely; here she stands.
        Enter Lucre, [Limber, Kix and Host]
LUCRE Oh, Master Hoard, your spite has watched the hour.°
    You're excellent at vengeance, Master Hoard.   35
HOARD Ha, ha, ha!
LUCRE   I am the fool you laugh at:
    You are wise, sir, and know the seasons well.
    Come hither, widow; why is it thus?
    Oh, you have done me infinite disgrace
    And your own credit no small injury.   40
    Suffer mine enemy so despitefully
    To bear you from my nephew! Oh, I had
    Rather half my substance had been forfeit
    And begged by some starved rascal.
COURTESAN Why, what would you wish me do, sir?   45
    I must not overthrow my state for love,
    We have too many precedents for that;
    From thousands of our wealthy undone widows
    One may derive some wit. I do confess
    I loved your nephew; nay, I did affect him   50
    Against the mind and liking of my friends;°
    Believed his promises, lay here in hope
    Of flattered living and the boast of lands.°
    Coming to touch his wealth and state indeed,°
    It appears dross; I find him not the man,   55
    Imperfect, mean, scarce furnished of his needs;°
    In words, fair lordships, in performance, hovels.
    Can any woman love the thing that is not?
LUCRE Broke you for this?
COURTESAN   Was it not cause too much?
    Send to enquire his state: most part of it   60
    Lay two years mortgaged in his uncle's hands.
LUCRE Why, say it did, you might have known my mind;
    I could have soon restored it.
COURTESAN Ay, had I but seen any such thing performed,
    Why, 'twould have tied my affection, and contained   65

Me in my first desires. Do you think, i'faith,
That I could twine such a dry oak as this,°
Had promise in your nephew took effect?

LUCRE Why, and there's no time past; and rather than
My adversary should thus thwart my hopes,   70
I would—

COURTESAN Tut, y'ave been ever full of golden speech.
If words were lands your nephew would be rich.

LUCRE Widow, believe it; I vow by my best bliss,
Before these gentlemen, I will give in   75
The mortgage to my nephew instantly,
Before I sleep or eat.

[LIMBER]°   We'll pawn our credits,
Widow; what he speaks shall be performed
In fullness.

LUCRE   Nay, more: I will estate him
In farther blessings; he shall be my heir.   80
I have no son;
I'll bind myself to that condition.

COURTESAN When I shall hear this done, I shall soon yield
To reasonable terms.

LUCRE   In the mean season,
Will you protest, before these gentlemen,   85
To keep yourself as you are now at this present?°

COURTESAN I do protest before these gentlemen,
I will be as clear then as I am now.

LUCRE I do believe you. Here's your own honest servant,
I'll take him along with me.

COURTESAN   Ay, with all my heart.   90

LUCRE He shall see all performed and bring you word.

COURTESAN That's all I wait for.

HOARD What, have you finished, Master Lucre? Ha, ha, ha, ha!

LUCRE So laugh, Hoard, laugh at your poor enemy, do;
The wind may turn, you may be laughed at too.   95
Yes, marry, may you, sir. Ha, ha, ha!
        Exeunt [Lucre, Limber, Kix and Host]

HOARD Ha, ha, ha! If every man that swells in malice
Could be revenged as happily as I,
He would choose hate and forswear amity.
What did he say, wife, prithee?   100

COURTESAN Faith, spoke to ease his mind.

HOARD Oh—oh—oh!

COURTESAN You know now, little to any purpose.

HOARD True, true, true.

COURTESAN He would do mountains now.°   105

HOARD Ay, ay, ay, ay.

LAMPREY Y'ave struck him dead, Master Hoard.

SPITCHCOCK Ay, and his nephew desperate.

HOARD I know't, sirs, I.

    Never did man so crush his enemy!   110
        Exeunt

[4.2]

    Enter Lucre with Gentlemen [Limber, Kix and Host] meeting
    Sam Freedom

LUCRE My son-in-law,° Sam Freedom. Where's my nephew?

SAM Oh man in lamentation,° father!

LUCRE How!

SAM He thumps his breast like a gallant dicer that has lost his doublet
    and stands in's shirt to do penance.   5

LUCRE Alas, poor gentleman.

SAM I warrant you may hear him sigh in a still evening to your house
    at Highgate.°

LUCRE I prithee send him in.

SAM Were it to do a greater matter, I will not stick with you, sir, in   10
    regard you married my mother.
        [Exit Sam]

LUCRE Sweet gentlemen, cheer him up. I will but fetch the mortgage
    and return to you instantly.

[LIMBER] We'll do our best, sir.
        Exit [Lucre]
                See where he comes

    E'en joyless and regardless of all form.°   15
        [Enter Witgood]

[KIX] Why, how now,° Master Witgood? Fie, you a firm° scholar
    and an understanding gentleman, and give your best parts to
    passion?

[LIMBER] Come, fie!

WITGOOD Oh, gentlemen!   20

[LIMBER] Sorrow of me, what a sigh was there, sir!
   Nine such widows are not worth it.

WITGOOD To be borne from me by that lecher Hoard!

[LIMBER] That vengeance is your uncle's, being done
   More in despite to him than wrong to you.   25
   But we bring comfort now.

WITGOOD   I beseech you, gentlemen.

[KIX] Cheer thyself, man, there's hope of her i'faith!

WITGOOD Too gladsome to be true.

      Enter Lucre

LUCRE   Nephew, what cheer?
   Alas, poor gentleman, how art thou changed!
   Call thy fresh blood into thy cheeks again: 30
   She comes.

WITGOOD   Nothing afflicts me so much
   But that it is your adversary, uncle,
   And merely plotted in despite of you.°

LUCRE Ay, that's it mads me, spites me! I'll spend my wealth ere he
   shall carry° her so because I know 'tis only to spite me. Ay, this is   35
   it. Here, nephew [*giving a paper*], before these kind gentlemen I
   deliver in your mortgage, my promise to the widow; see, 'tis done.
   Be wise, you're once more master of your own. The widow shall
   perceive now you are not altogether such a beggar as the world
   reputes you; you can make shift to bring her to three hundred a   40
   year, sir.

[LIMBER] Byrlady, and that's no toy, sir.

LUCRE A word, nephew.

[LIMBER] [*to Host*] Now you may certify the widow.

LUCRE You must conceive it aright, nephew, now; to do you good I   45
   am content to do this.

WITGOOD I know it, sir.

LUCRE But your own conscience can tell I had it dearly enough of
   you.

WITGOOD Ay, that's most certain.   50

LUCRE Much money laid out, beside many a journey to fetch the
   rent. I hope you'll think on't, nephew.

WITGOOD I were worse than a beast else i'faith.

LUCRE Although to blind the widow and the world I out of policy
   do't, yet there's a conscience, nephew.   55

WITGOOD Heaven forbid else!

LUCRE When you are full possessed, 'tis nothing to return it.

WITGOOD Alas, a thing quickly done, uncle.

LUCRE Well said! You know I give it you but in trust.

WITGOOD Pray let me understand you rightly, uncle: you give it me   60
  but in trust?

LUCRE No.°

WITGOOD That is, you trust me with it.

LUCRE True, true.

WITGOOD [aside] But if ever I trust you with it again, would I might   65
  be trussed up for my labour.

LUCRE You can all witness, gentlemen, and you, sir yeoman?

HOST My life for yours, sir, now I know my mistress's mind so well°
  toward your nephew; let things be in preparation, and I'll train her
  hither in most excellent fashion.   70
        Exit [*Host*]

LUCRE A good old boy. Wife! Jinny!
        Enter Wife [*Mistress Lucre*]

MISTRESS LUCRE What's the news, sir?

LUCRE The wedding day's at hand. Prithee, sweet wife, express
  thy housewifery; thou'rt a fine cook, I know't; thy first husband
  married thee out of an alderman's kitchen. Go to!° He raised thee   75
  for raising of paste.° What, here's none but friends; most of our
  beginnings must be winked at. Gentlemen, I invite you all to my
  nephew's wedding against Thursday morning.

[LIMBER] With all our hearts, and we shall joy to see your enemy so
  mocked.   80

LUCRE He laughed at me, gentlemen; ha, ha, ha!
        Exeunt [*all but Witgood*]

WITGOOD He has no conscience, faith,
  Would laugh at them; they laugh at one another!°
  Who then can be so cruel? Troth, not I;
  I rather pity now than aught envy.°   85
  I do conceive such joy in mine own happiness,
  I have no leisure yet to laugh at their follies.
  [*To the mortgage*] Thou soul of my estate, I kiss thee,
  I miss life's comfort when I miss thee.
  Oh, never will we part again,   90
  Until I leave the sight of men.
  We'll ne'er trust conscience of our kin,
  Since cozenage brings that title in.°
        [*Exit*]

[4.3]

Enter three Creditors

FIRST CREDITOR I'll wait these seven hours but I'll see him caught.

SECOND CREDITOR Faith, so will I.

THIRD CREDITOR Hang him, prodigal, he's stripped of the widow.

FIRST CREDITOR O'my troth, she's the wiser; she has made the happier choice; and I wonder of what stuff those widows' hearts 5 are made of, that will marry unfledged boys before comely thrum-chinned gentlemen.

Enter a Boy

BOY News, news, news!

FIRST CREDITOR What, boy?

BOY The rioter is caught. 10

FIRST CREDITOR So, so, so, so! It warms me at the heart; I love a'life to see dogs upon men. Oh, here he comes.

Enter Witgood with Sergeants

WITGOOD My last joy was so great it took away the sense of all future afflictions. What a day is here o'ercast! How soon a black tempest rises! 15

FIRST CREDITOR Oh, we may speak with you now, sir! What's become of your rich widow? I think you may cast your cap at° the widow, may you not, sir?

SECOND CREDITOR He a rich widow? Who, a prodigal, a daily rioter, and a nightly vomiter? He a widow of account? He a hole 20 i'th'Counter!

WITGOOD You do well, my masters, to tyrannize over misery, to afflict the afflicted; 'tis a custom you have here amongst you; I would wish you never leave it, and I hope you'll do as I bid you.

FIRST CREDITOR Come, come, sir, what say you extempore now to 25 your bill of a hundred pound? A sweet debt for frotting your doublets.

SECOND CREDITOR Here's mine of forty.

THIRD CREDITOR Here's mine of fifty.

WITGOOD Pray, sirs, you'll give me breath?

FIRST CREDITOR No, sir, we'll keep you out of breath still, then we 30 shall be sure you will not run away from us.

WITGOOD Will you but hear me speak?

SECOND CREDITOR You shall pardon us for that, sir; we know you have too fair a tongue of your own: you overcame us too lately, a shame take you! We are like to lose all that for want of witnesses; 35

we dealt in policy then. Always when we strive to be most
politic, we prove most coxcombs; *non plus ultra*.° I perceive by us
we're not ordained to thrive by wisdom, and therefore we must be
content to be tradesmen.

WITGOOD Give me but reasonable time, and I protest I'll make you   40
ample satisfaction.

FIRST CREDITOR Do you talk of reasonable time to us?

WITGOOD 'Tis true, beasts know no reasonable time.

SECOND CREDITOR We must have either money or carcass.

WITGOOD Alas, what good will my carcass do you?   45

THIRD CREDITOR Oh, 'tis a secret delight we have amongst us! We
that are used to keep birds in cages have the heart to keep men in
prison, I warrant you.

WITGOOD [*aside*] I perceive I must crave a little more aid from my
wits: do but make shift for me this once and I'll forswear ever to   50
trouble you in the like fashion hereafter; I'll have better employment for you, an I live.—You'll give me leave, my masters, to
make trial of my friends and raise all means I can?

FIRST CREDITOR That's our desires, sir.

Enter Host

HOST Master Witgood.   55

WITGOOD Oh, art thou come?

HOST May I speak one word with you in private, sir?°

WITGOOD No, by my faith, canst thou. I am in hell here, and the
devils will not let me come to thee.

CREDITORS Do you call us devils? You shall find us Puritans.°—Bear   60
him away; let 'em talk as they go; we'll not stand to hear 'em.—
Ah, sir, am I a devil? I shall think the better of myself as long as
I live. A devil i'faith!°

Exeunt

[4.4]

Enter Hoard

HOARD What a sweet blessing hast thou, Master Hoard, above a
multitude! Wilt thou never be thankful? How dost thou think to
be blest another time? Or dost thou count this the full measure of
thy happiness? By my troth, I think thou dost: not only a wife large
in possessions, but spacious in content:° she's rich, she's young,   5

she's fair, she's wise;° when I wake I think of her lands—that revives
me; when I go to bed, I dream of her beauty—and that's enough for
me.° She's worth four hundred a year in her very smock, if a man
knew how to use it.° But the journey will be all, in troth, into the
country; to ride to her lands in state and order following—my brother   10
and other worshipful gentlemen, whose companies I ha' sent down
for already to ride along with us in their goodly decorum beards, their
broad velvet cassocks, and chains of gold twice or thrice double;
against which time I'll entertain some ten men of mine own into
liveries, all of occupations or qualities.° I will not keep an idle man   15
about me, the sight of which will so vex my adversary, Lucre—for
we'll pass by his door of purpose, make a little stand for nonce,° and
have our horses curvet before the window—certainly, he will never
endure it, but run up and hang himself° presently!

    [Enter Servant]

How now, sirrah, what news? Any that offer their service to me yet?   20
SERVANT Yes, sir, there are some i'th'hall that wait for your wor-
    ship's liking and desire to be entertained.
HOARD Are they of occupation?°
SERVANT They are men fit for your worship, sir.
HOARD Say'st so? Send 'em all in!   25

    [Exit Servant]

To see ten men ride after me in watchet liveries with orange-tawny
capes, 'twill cut his comb° i'faith.

    Enter All [Tailor, Barber, Perfumer, Falconer, and Huntsman]

How now? Of what occupation are you, sir?
TAILOR A tailor, an't please your worship.
HOARD A tailor? Oh, very good. You shall serve to make all the   30
    liveries.—What are you, sir?
BARBER A barber, sir.
HOARD A barber? Very needful: you shall shave all the house, and,
    if need require, stand for a reaper i'th'summer time.—You, sir?
PERFUMER A perfumer.   35
HOARD I smelt you before. Perfumers, of all men, had need carry
    themselves uprightly, for if they were once knaves they would be
    smelt out quickly.—To you, sir?
FALCONER A falconer, an't please your worship.
HOARD Sa ho, sa ho, sa ho!—And you, sir?   40
HUNTSMAN A huntsman, sir.
HOARD There, boy,° there, boy, there, boy! I am not so old but I
    have pleasant days to come. I promise you, my masters, I take

such a good liking to you that I entertain you all. I put you
already into my countenance,° and you shall be shortly in   45
my livery; but especially you two, my jolly falconer and my
bonny huntsman, we shall have most need of you at my wife's
manor houses i'th'country; there's goodly parks and champion
grounds for you; we shall have all our sports within ourselves;° all
the gentlemen o'th'country shall be beholding to us and our   50
pastimes.

FALCONER And we'll make your° worship admire, sir.

HOARD Say'st thou so? Do but make me admire, and thou shalt want
for nothing.—My tailor!

TAILOR Anon, sir.   55

HOARD Go presently in hand with° the liveries.

TAILOR I will, sir.

HOARD My barber.

BARBER Here, sir.

HOARD Make 'em all trim fellows, louse 'em well, especially my   60
huntsman, and cut all their beards of the Polonian fashion.°—My
perfumer.

PERFUMER Under your nose, sir.

HOARD Cast a better savour upon the knaves to take away the scent
of my tailor's feet and my barber's lotium-water.   65

PERFUMER It shall be carefully performed, sir.

HOARD But you, my falconer and huntsman, the welcom'st men alive
i'faith.

HUNTSMAN And we'll show you that, sir, shall deserve your worship's favour.   70

HOARD I prithee show me that. Go, you knaves all, and wash your
lungs i'th'buttery, go.
        [*Exeunt Tailor, Barber, Perfumer, Falconer, and Huntsman*]
By th'mass, and well remembered, I'll ask my wife that question.
Wife! Mistress Jane Hoard!
        Enter Courtesan altered in apparel

COURTESAN Sir, would you with me?   75

HOARD I would but know, sweet wife, which might stand best to thy
liking, to have the wedding dinner kept here or i'th'country?

COURTESAN Hum! Faith, sir, 'twould like me better here; here you
were married, here let all rites be ended.

HOARD Could a marquess give a better answer? Hoard, bear thy head   80
aloft, thou'st a wife will advance it.°
        [*Enter Host with a letter*]

What haste comes here now? Yea, a letter? Some dreg of my adversary's malice. Come hither; what's the news?

HOST A thing that concerns my mistress, sir.
        [*Gives letter to Courtesan*]

HOARD Why, then it concerns me, knave!   85

HOST Ay, and you, knave, too, cry your worship mercy: you are both like to come into trouble, I promise you, sir: a precontract.°

HOARD How? A precontract, say'st thou?

HOST I fear they have too much proof on't, sir. Old Lucre, he runs mad up and down and will to law as fast as he can; young Witgood laid   90
      hold on by his creditors, he exclaims upon you o't'other side, says you have wrought his undoing by the injurious detaining of his contract.

HOARD Body o'me!

HOST He will have utmost satisfaction;
      The law shall give him recompense, he says.   95

COURTESAN [*aside*] Alas, his creditors so merciless! My state being yet uncertain, I deem it not unconscionable to further him.

HOST True, sir,—

HOARD Wife, what says that letter? Let me construe it.

COURTESAN Cursed be my rash and unadvisèd words!   100
        [*Tears up the letter and stamps on it*]
      I'll set my foot upon my tongue
      And tread my inconsiderate grant to dust.°

HOARD Wife—

HOST [*aside*] A pretty shift i'faith. I commend a woman when she can make away a letter from her husband handsomely, and this was   105
      cleanly done, by my troth.

COURTESAN I did, sir!
      Some foolish words I must confess did pass,
      Which now litigiously he fastens on me.

HOARD Of what force? Let me examine 'em.   110

COURTESAN Too strong, I fear: would I were well freed of him!

HOARD Shall I compound?°

COURTESAN No, sir, I'd have it done some nobler way
      Of your side; I'd have you come off with honour;
      Let baseness keep with them. Why, have you not   115
      The means, sir? The occasion's offered you.

HOARD Where? How, dear wife?

COURTESAN He is now caught by his creditors; the slave's needy, his debts petty; he'll rather bind himself to all inconveniences° than rot in prison; by this only means° you may get a release from him.   120

'Tis not yet come to his uncle's hearing; send speedily for the
creditors; by this time he's desperate, he'll set his hand to
anything; take order for his debts, or discharge 'em quite. A pax
on him, let's be rid of a rascal.

HOARD Excellent! Thou dost astonish me.—Go, run, make haste;   125
bring both the creditors and Witgood hither.

HOST [aside] This will be some revenge° yet.
        [Exit Host]

HOARD In the mean space I'll have a release° drawn.—Within there!
        [Enter Servant]

SERVANT Sir?

HOARD Sirrah, come take directions; go to my scrivener.°   130

COURTESAN [aside] I'm yet like those whose riches lie in dreams;
        If I be waked, they're false; such is my fate
        Who ventures deeper than the desperate state.°
        Though I have sinned, yet could I become new,
        For, where I once vow, I am ever true.   135

HOARD Away, dispatch; on my displeasure, quickly.
        [Exit Servant]
        Happy occasion! Pray heaven he° be in the right vein now to set
        his hand to't, that nothing alter him. Grant that all his follies may
        meet in him at once to besot him enough. I pray for him i'faith,
        and here he comes.   140
        [Enter Witgood and Creditors]

WITGOOD What would you with me now, my uncle's spiteful
adversary?

HOARD Nay, I am friends.

WITGOOD   Ay, when your mischief's spent.

HOARD I heard you were arrested.

WITGOOD   Well, what then?
        You will pay none of my debts, I am sure.   145

HOARD A wise man cannot tell;
        There may be those conditions 'greed upon
        May move me to do much.

WITGOOD   Ay, when!—
        'Tis thou, perjured woman—Oh, no name
        Is vile enough to match thy treachery!—   150
        That art the cause of my confusion.

COURTESAN Out, you penurious slave!

HOARD Nay, wife, you are too froward;
        Let him alone; give losers leave to talk.°

WITGOOD Shall I remember thee of another promise   155
Far stronger than the first?

COURTESAN   I'd fain know that.

WITGOOD 'Twould call shame to thy cheeks.

COURTESAN   Shame!

WITGOOD   Hark in your ear.
[*Takes Courtesan aside*]
Will he come off, think'st thou, and pay my debts roundly?

COURTESAN Doubt nothing; there's a release a-drawing and all, to
which you must set your hand.   160

WITGOOD Excellent.

COURTESAN But methinks, i'faith, you might have made some shift
to discharge this yourself, having in the mortgage, and never have
burdened my conscience with it.

WITGOOD O'my troth, I could not, for my creditors' cruelties extend   165
to the present.

COURTESAN No more.—Why, do your worst for that, I defy you.

WITGOOD Y'are impudent. I'll call up witnesses.

COURTESAN Call up thy wits, for thou hast been devoted to follies a
long time.   170

HOARD Wife, y'are too bitter.—Master Witgood, and you, my masters,
you shall hear a mild speech come from me now, and this it is: 't'as
been my fortune, gentlemen, to have an extraordinary blessing poured
upon me o'late, and here she stands; I have wedded her and bedded
her, and yet she is little the worse. Some foolish words she hath   175
passed to you in the country, and some peevish debts you owe here
in the city; set the hare's head to the goose-giblet;° release you her of
her words, and I'll release you of your debts, sir.

WITGOOD Would you so? I thank you for that, sir; I cannot blame
you i'faith.   180

HOARD Why, are not debts better than words,° sir?

WITGOOD Are not words promises, and are not promises debts, sir?

HOARD He plays at back-racket° with me.

FIRST CREDITOR Come hither, Master Witgood, come hither; be
ruled by fools once.   185
[*Creditors take Witgood aside*]

SECOND CREDITOR We are citizens and know what belong to't.

FIRST CREDITOR Take hold of his offer; pax on her, let her go. If
your debts were once discharged, I would help you to a widow
myself worth ten of her.

THIRD CREDITOR Mass, partner, and now you remember me on't,   190 there's Master Mulligrub's sister° newly fallen a widow.

FIRST CREDITOR Cuds me, as pat as can be! There's a widow left for
you, ten thousand in money, beside plate, jewels, *et cetera*; I
warrant it a match; we can do all in all° with her. Prithee dispatch;
we'll carry thee to her presently.   195

WITGOOD My uncle will ne'er endure me when he shall hear I set
my hand to a release.

SECOND CREDITOR Hark, I'll tell thee a trick for that. I have spent
five hundred pound in suits in my time; I should be wise. Thou'rt
now a prisoner; make a release; take't of my word, whatsoever a   200
man makes as long as he is in durance,° 'tis nothing in law, not
thus much.

    [*Snaps his fingers*]

WITGOOD Say you so, sir?

THIRD CREDITOR I have paid for't, I know't.

WITGOOD Proceed then, I consent.   205

THIRD CREDITOR Why, well said.

HOARD How now, my masters, what have you done with him?

FIRST CREDITOR With much ado, sir, we have got him to consent.

HOARD Ah-a-a! And what came his debts to now?

FIRST CREDITOR Some eight score odd pounds, sir.   210

HOARD Naw, naw, naw, naw, naw! Tell me° the second time; give
me a lighter sum. They are but desperate debts,° you know, ne'er
called in but upon such an accident;° a poor, needy knave, he
would starve and rot in prison. Come, come, you shall have ten
shillings in the pound and the sum down roundly.   215

FIRST CREDITOR You must make it a mark, sir.

HOARD Go to, then; tell your money in the mean time, you shall find
little less there.—Come, Master Witgood, you are so unwilling to
do yourself good now.

    [*Enter Scrivener*]

Welcome, honest scrivener.—Now you shall hear the release read.   220

SCRIVENER [*reads*] 'Be it known to all men by these presents° that I,
Theodorus Witgood, gentleman, sole nephew to Pecunius Lucre,
having unjustly made title and claim to one Jane Medler, late
widow of Anthony Medler, and now wife to Walkadine Hoard, in
consideration of a competent sum of money to discharge my debts,   225
do forever hereafter disclaim any title, right, estate, or interest in
or to the said widow, late in the occupation of° the said Anthony
Medler, and now in the occupation of Walkadine Hoard; as also
neither to lay claim by virtue of any former contract, grant,

promise, or demise, to any of her manors,° manor houses, parks,   230
groves, meadow-grounds, arable lands, barns, stacks, stables, dove-
holes, and coney-burrows; together with all her cattle, money,
plate, jewels, borders, chains, bracelets, furnitures, hangings,
movables, or immovables. In witness whereof I, the said Theodorus Witgood, have interchangeably° set to my hand and seal   235
before these presents,° the day and date above written.'
WITGOOD What a precious fortune hast thou slipped° here, like a
  beast as thou art!
HOARD Come, unwilling heart, come.
WITGOOD Well, Master Hoard, give me the pen; I see   240
  'Tis vain to quarrel with our destiny.
       [Signs]
HOARD Oh, as vain a thing as can be; you cannot commit a greater
  absurdity, sir. So, so; give me that hand now: before all these
  presents, I am friends forever with thee.
WITGOOD Troth, and it were pity of my heart now if I should bear   245
  you any grudge i'faith.
HOARD Content. I'll send for thy uncle against the wedding dinner;
  we will be friends once again.
WITGOOD I hope to bring it to pass myself, sir.
HOARD How now? Is't right, my masters?   250
FIRST CREDITOR 'Tis something wanting,° sir; yet it shall be sufficient.
HOARD Why, well said; a good conscience makes a fine show
  nowadays. Come, my masters, you shall all taste of my wine ere
  you depart.
ALL We follow you, sir.   255
       [Exeunt Hoard, Courtesan, and Scrivener]
WITGOOD [aside] I'll try these fellows now.—A word, sir; what, will
  you carry me to that rich widow now?
FIRST CREDITOR Why, do you think we were in earnest i'faith?
  Carry you to a rich widow? We should get much credit by that: a
  noted rioter! a contemptible prodigal! 'Twas a trick we have   260
  amongst us to get in our money. Fare you well, sir.
       Exeunt [Creditors]
WITGOOD Farewell and be hanged, you short, pig-haired,° ram-
  headed° rascals. He that believes in you shall ne'er be saved, I
  warrant him. By this new league° I shall have some access unto my
  love.   265
       She [Joyce, Hoard's niece] is above
NIECE Master Witgood!

WITGOOD My life!

NIECE Meet me presently; that note directs you [*throwing it down*]; I
would not be suspected. Our happiness attends us. Farewell!

WITGOOD A word's enough.   270

      Exeunt

[4.5]

   Dampit, the usurer, in his bed;° Audrey spinning by; [Boy].

[SONG]

      ([*sung by*] *Audrey*)

   Let the usurer cram him, in interest that excel,
   There's pits enow to damn him before he comes to hell;°
   In Holborn some, in Fleet Street some,
   Where'er he come, there's some, there's some.°

DAMPIT *Trahe, trahito,°* draw the curtain, give me a sip of sack more.   5
     Enter Gentlemen° [*Lamprey and Spitchcock*]

LAMPREY Look you, did not I tell you he lay like the devil in chains
when he was bound for a thousand year?°

SPITCHCOCK But I think the devil had no steel bedstaffs;° he goes
beyond him for that.

LAMPREY Nay, do but mark the conceit° of his drinking; one must   10
wipe his mouth for him with a muckinder, do you see, sir?

SPITCHCOCK Is this the sick trampler?° Why, he is only bed-rid with
drinking.

LAMPREY True, sir. He spies us.

DAMPIT What? Sir Tristram? You come and see a weak man here, a   15
very weak man.

LAMPREY If you be weak in body you should be strong in prayer,
sir.

DAMPIT Oh, I have prayed too much, poor man.

LAMPREY There's a taste of his soul for you.   20

SPITCHCOCK Fah, loathsome!

LAMPREY I come to borrow a hundred pound of you, sir.

DAMPIT Alas, you come at an ill time; I cannot spare it i'faith; I
ha' but two thousand i'th'house.

AUDREY Ha, ha, ha!   25

DAMPIT Out, you gernative quean, the mullipood° of villainy, the
spinner of concupiscency!

Enter [an]other Gentleman [Sir Lancelot]

LANCELOT Yea, gentlemen, are you here before us? How is he now?

LAMPREY Faith, the same man still; the tavern bitch has bit him
i'th'head.°   30

LANCELOT We shall have the better sport with him; peace.—And
how cheers Master Dampit now?

DAMPIT Oh, my bosom Sir Lancelot, how cheer I? Thy presence is
restorative.

LANCELOT But I hear a great complaint of you, Master Dampit,   35
among gallants.

DAMPIT I am glad of that i'faith; prithee what?

LANCELOT They say you are waxed proud o'late, and if a friend visit
you in the afternoon you'll scarce know him.

DAMPIT Fie, fie! Proud? I cannot remember any such thing; sure I   40
was drunk then.

LANCELOT Think you so, sir?

DAMPIT There 'twas, i'faith, nothing but the pride of the sack, and
so certify 'em.—Fetch sack, sirrah!

BOY A vengeance sack you once.   45

[Exit Boy and returns with sack]

AUDREY Why, Master Dampit, if you hold on as you begin and lie
a little longer, you need not take care how to dispose your wealth,
you'll make the vintner your heir.

DAMPIT Out, you babliaminy, you unfeathered,° cremitoried quean,
you cullisance° of scabiosity!   50

AUDREY Good words, Master Dampit, to speak before a maid and a
virgin.

DAMPIT Hang thy virginity upon the pole of carnality!°

AUDREY Sweet terms! My mistress° shall know 'em.

LAMPREY Note but the misery of this usuring slave: here he lies like   55
a noisome dunghill full of the poison of his drunken blasphemies,
and they, to whom he bequeaths all, grudge him the very meat that
feeds him, the very pillow that eases him. Here may a usurer
behold his end. What profits it to be a slave in this world and a
devil i'th'next?   60

DAMPIT Sir Lancelot, let me buss thee, Sir Lancelot; thou art the
only friend that I honour and respect.

LANCELOT I thank you for that, Master Dampit.

DAMPIT Farewell, my bosom Sir Lancelot.

LANCELOT Gentlemen, an you love me, let me step behind you, and   65
one of you fall a-talking of me to him.

LAMPREY Content.—Master Dampit.

DAMPIT So, sir.

LAMPREY Here came Sir Lancelot to see you e'en now.

DAMPIT Hang him, rascal!   70

LAMPREY Who, Sir Lancelot?

DAMPIT Pythagorical° rascal!

LAMPREY Pythagorical?

DAMPIT Ay, he changes his cloak° when he meets a sergeant.

LANCELOT What a rogue's this!   75

LAMPREY I wonder you can rail at him, sir; he comes in love to see
you.

DAMPIT A louse for his love! His father was a comb-maker; I have
no need of his crawling° love. He comes to have longer day,° the
superlative rascal!   80

LANCELOT 'Sfoot, I can no longer endure the rogue.—Master Dampit,
I come to take my leave once again, sir.

DAMPIT Who? My dear and kind Sir Lancelot, the only gentleman
of England, let me hug thee; farewell and a thousand.°

LAMPREY Composed of wrongs and slavish flatteries.   85

LANCELOT Nay, gentlemen, he shall show you more tricks yet; I'll
give you another taste of him.

LAMPREY Is't possible?

LANCELOT His memory is upon departing.°

DAMPIT Another cup of sack.   90

LANCELOT Mass, then 'twill be quite gone. Before he drink that, tell
him there's a country client come up and here attends for his
learned advice.

LAMPREY Enough.

DAMPIT One cup more and then let the bell° toll; I hope I shall be   95
weak enough by that time.

LAMPREY Master Dampit.

DAMPIT Is the sack spouting?

LAMPREY 'Tis coming forward, sir. Here's a countryman, a client of
yours, waits for your deep and profound advice, sir.   100

DAMPIT A coxcombry? Where is he? Let him approach; set me up a
peg higher.

LAMPREY You must draw near, sir.

DAMPIT Now, good man fooliaminy, what say you to me now?

LANCELOT Please your good worship, I am a poor man, sir—   105
DAMPIT What make you° in my chamber then?
LANCELOT I would entreat your worship's device° in a just and honest cause, sir.
DAMPIT I meddle with no such matters; I refer 'em to Master Noman's office.   110
LANCELOT I had but one house left me in all the world, sir, which was my father's, my grandfather's, my great-grandfather's; and now a villain has unjustly wrung me out and took possession on't.
DAMPIT Has he such feats?° Thy best course is to bring thy *ejectione firmae*,° and in seven year thou may'st shove him out by the law.   115
LANCELOT Alas, an't please your worship, I have small° friends and less money.
DAMPIT Hoyday! This gear will fadge well. Hast no money? Why, then, my advice is thou must set fire a'th'house and so get him out.   120
LAMPREY That will break° strife indeed.
LANCELOT I thank your worship for your hot counsel, sir.—Altering but my voice a little, you see he knew me not; you may observe by this that a drunkard's memory holds longer in the voice than in the person. But, gentlemen, shall I show you a sight? Behold   125
the little dive-dapper of damnation, Gulf the usurer, for his time worse than t'other.
        Enter Hoard with Gulf
LAMPREY What's he comes with him?°
LANCELOT Why, Hoard, that married lately the Widow Medler.
LAMPREY Oh, I cry you mercy, sir.°   130
HOARD Now, gentlemen visitants, how does Master Dampit?
LANCELOT Faith, here he lies e'en drawing in, sir, good canary as fast as he can, sir; a very weak creature, truly, he is almost past memory.
HOARD Fie, Master Dampit! You lie lazing abed here, and I come to invite you to my wedding dinner; up, up, up!   135
DAMPIT Who's this? Master Hoard? Who hast thou married in the name of foolery?
HOARD A rich widow.
DAMPIT A Dutch widow?
HOARD A rich widow; one Widow Medler.   140
DAMPIT Medler? She keeps open house.°
HOARD She did, I can tell you, in her t'other husband's days; open house for all comers; horse and man was welcome, and room enough for 'em all.

DAMPIT There's too much for thee then; thou may'st let out some°   145
to thy neighbours.

GULF What, hung alive in chains? Oh spectacle! Bed-staffs of steel?
O monstrum horrendum, informe, ingens, cui lumen ademptum!°
Oh Dampit, Dampit, here's a just judgement shown upon usury,
extortion, and trampling villainy.   150

LANCELOT This is ex'lent, thief rails upon the thief.

GULF Is this the end of cut-throat usury, brothel, and blasphemy?
Now may'st thou see what race a usurer runs.

DAMPIT Why, thou rogue of universality, do not I know thee? Thy
sound is like the cuckoo, the Welsh ambassador;° thou cowardly   155
slave that offers to fight with a sick man when his weapon's down.°
Rail upon me in my naked bed?° Why, thou great Lucifer's little
vicar, I am not so weak but I know a knave at first sight. Thou
inconscionable rascal! Thou that goest upon Middlesex juries,° and
will make haste to give up thy verdict because thou wilt not lose   160
thy dinner, are you answered?

GULF An't were not for shame—
Draws his dagger

DAMPIT Thou wouldst be hanged then.

LAMPREY Nay, you must exercise patience, Master Gulf, always, in
a sick man's chamber.   165

LANCELOT He'll quarrel with none, I warrant you, but those that are
bed-rid.

DAMPIT Let him come, gentlemen, I am armed; reach my close-stool
hither.

LANCELOT Here will be a sweet fray° anon; I'll leave you, gentlemen.   170

LAMPREY Nay, we'll along with you.—Master Gulf—

GULF Hang him, usuring rascal!

LANCELOT Push, set your strength to his, your wits to his.

AUDREY Pray, gentlemen, depart; his hour's come upon him.°—
Sleep in my bosom, sleep.   175

LANCELOT Nay, we have enough of him i'faith; keep him for the
house.
Now make your best.
For thrice his wealth I would not have his breast.

GULF A little thing would make me beat him, now he's asleep.   180

LANCELOT Mass, then 'twill be a pitiful day when he wakes. I would
be loath to see that day come.

GULF You overrule me, gentlemen, i'faith.
Exeunt

[5.1]

Enter Lucre and Witgood

WITGOOD Nay, uncle, let me prevail with you so much; i'faith, go,
now he has invited you.

LUCRE I shall have great joy there, when he has borne away the widow.

WITGOOD Why, la, I thought where I should find you presently.
Uncle, o'my troth 'tis nothing so.   5

LUCRE What's nothing so, sir? Is he not married to the widow?

WITGOOD No, by my troth, is he not, uncle.

LUCRE How?

WITGOOD Will you have the truth on't? He is married to a whore
i'faith.   10

LUCRE I should laugh at that.

WITGOOD Uncle, let me perish in your favour if you find it not so,
and that 'tis I that have married the honest woman.

LUCRE Ha! I'd walk ten mile a foot to see that i'faith.

WITGOOD And see't you shall, or I'll ne'er see you again.   15

LUCRE A quean i'faith? Ha, ha, ha!

Exeunt

[5.2]

Enter Hoard, tasting wine, the Host following in a livery cloak

HOARD Pup, pup, pup, pup! I like not this wine. Is there never a
better tierce° in the house?

HOST Yes, sir, there are as good tierce in the house as any are in
England.

HOARD Desire your mistress, you knave, to taste 'em all over; she has   5
better skill.

HOST [*aside*] Has she so? The better for her and the worse for you.
Exit [Host]°

HOARD Arthur!
[*Enter Arthur*]
Is the cupboard of plate° set out?

ARTHUR All's in order, sir.   10
[*Exit Arthur*]

194

HOARD I am in love with my liveries every time I think on 'em; they
    make a gallant show, by my troth.—Niece!
       [*Enter Niece*]

NIECE Do you call, sir?

HOARD Prithee show a little diligence and overlook the knaves
    a little; they'll filch and steal today and send whole pasties   15
    home to their wives; an thou beest a good niece, do not see me
    purloined.

NIECE Fear it not, sir.—[*Aside*] I have cause; though the feast be
    prepared for you, yet it serves fit for my wedding dinner° too.
       [*Exit Niece.*] *Enter two Gentlemen* [*Lamprey and Spitch-*
       cock]

HOARD Master Lamprey and Master Spitchcock, two the most   20
    welcome gentlemen alive. Your fathers and mine were all free
    o'th'fishmongers.°

LAMPREY They were indeed, sir. You see bold guests, sir, soon
    entreated.

HOARD And that's best, sir.   25
       [*Enter Servant*]
    How now, sirrah?

SERVANT There's a coach come to th'door, sir.
       [*Exit Servant*]

HOARD My Lady Foxstone,° o'my life.—Mistress Jane Hoard,
    wife!—Mass, 'tis her ladyship indeed.
       [*Enter Lady Foxstone*]
    Madam, you are welcome to an unfurnished house, dearth of   30
    cheer, scarcity of attendance.

LADY FOXSTONE You are pleased to make the worst,° sir.

HOARD Wife!
       [*Enter Courtesan*]

LADY FOXSTONE Is this your bride?

HOARD Yes, madam.—Salute my Lady Foxstone.   35

COURTESAN Please you, madam, a while to taste the air in the garden?

LADY FOXSTONE 'Twill please us well.
       Exeunt [*Lady Foxstone and Courtesan*]

HOARD Who would not wed? The most delicious life;
    No joys are like the comforts of a wife.

LAMPREY So we bachelors think, that are not troubled with them.   40
       [*Enter Servant*]

SERVANT Your worship's brother with another ancient gentleman°
    are newly alighted, sir.

[*Exit Servant*]

HOARD   Master Onesiphorus Hoard. Why, now our company begins
to come in.

[*Enter Onesiphorus Hoard, Limber and Kix*]

My dear and kind brother, welcome i'faith.   45

ONESIPHORUS   You see we are men at an hour,° brother.

HOARD   Ay, I'll say that for you, brother; you keep as good an
hour to come to a feast as any gentleman in the shire.—What, old
Master Limber and Master Kix. Do we meet, i'faith, jolly
gentlemen?   50

LIMBER   We hope you lack guests,° sir.

HOARD   Oh, welcome, welcome! We lack still such guests° as your
worships.

ONESIPHORUS   Ah, sirrah brother, have you catched up Widow
Medler?   55

HOARD   From 'em all, brother; and I may tell you I had mighty
enemies, those that stuck sore; old Lucre is a sore fox, I can tell
you, brother.

ONESIPHORUS   Where is she? I'll go seek her out; I long to have a
smack at her lips.   60

HOARD   And most wishfully, brother, see where she comes.

[*Enter Courtesan and Lady Foxstone*]

Give her a smack now we may hear it all the house over.

Both [*Courtesan and Onesiphorus Hoard*] *turn back*

COURTESAN   Oh heaven, I am betrayed! I know that face.°

HOARD   Ha, ha, ha! Why, how now? Are you both ashamed? Come,
gentlemen, we'll look another way.   65

ONESIPHORUS   Nay, brother, hark you; come, y'are disposed to be
merry?

HOARD   Why do we meet else, man?

ONESIPHORUS   That's another matter; I was ne'er so 'fraid in my life
but that you had been in earnest.   70

HOARD   How mean you, brother?

ONESIPHORUS   You said she was your wife?

HOARD   Did I so? By my troth, and so she is.

ONESIPHORUS   By your troth, brother?

HOARD   What reason have I to dissemble with my friends, brother?   75
If marriage can make her mine, she is mine. Why?

ONESIPHORUS   Troth, I am not well of a sudden. I must crave pardon,
brother; I came to see you, but I cannot stay dinner i'faith.

HOARD   I hope you will not serve me so, brother.

LIMBER By your leave, Master Hoard—   80

HOARD What now? What now? Pray, gentlemen, you were wont to
  show yourselves wise men.

LIMBER But you have shown your folly too much here.

HOARD How?

KIX Fie, fie! A man of your repute and name.   85
  You'll feast your friends but cloy 'em first with shame.

HOARD This grows too deep; pray let us reach the sense.

LIMBER In your old age dote on a courtesan—

HOARD Ha?

KIX Marry a strumpet!   90

HOARD Gentlemen!

ONESIPHORUS And Witgood's quean!

HOARD Oh! Nor lands, nor living?

ONESIPHORUS Living!

HOARD [to Courtesan] Speak.   95

COURTESAN Alas, you know at first, sir,
  I told you I had nothing.

HOARD Out, out! I am cheated; infinitely cozened.

LIMBER Nay, Master Hoard—

                    Enter Witgood and Lucre

HOARD A Dutch widow, a Dutch widow, a Dutch widow!   100

LUCRE Why, nephew, shall I trace thee still a liar?
  Wilt make me mad? Is not yon thing the widow?

WITGOOD Why, la, you are so hard o'belief, uncle. By my troth,
  she's a whore.

LUCRE Then thou'rt a knave.   105

WITGOOD *Negatur argumentum*,° uncle.

LUCRE *Probo tibi*,° nephew: he that knows° a woman to be a quean
  must needs be a knave; thou say'st thou know'st her to be one;
  ergo, if she be a quean, thou'rt a knave.

WITGOOD *Negatur sequela majoris*,° uncle: he that knows a woman to   110
  be a quean must needs be a knave; I deny that.

HOARD Lucre and Witgood, y'are both villains; get you out of my
  house.

LUCRE Why, didst not invite me to thy wedding dinner?

WITGOOD And are not you and I sworn perpetual friends before   115
  witness, sir, and were both drunk upon't?

HOARD Daintily abused! Y'ave put a junt upon me.

LUCRE Ha, ha, ha!

HOARD A common strumpet!

WITGOOD Nay, now you wrong her, sir; if I were she I'd have the   120
   law on you for that; I durst depose for her she ne'er had common
   use nor common thought.

COURTESAN Despise me, publish me: I am your wife;
   What shame can I have now, but you'll have part?
   If in disgrace you share, I sought not you;   125
   You pursued me, nay, forced me;
   Had I friends would follow it,°
   Less than your action has been proved a rape.

ONESIPHORUS Brother!

COURTESAN Nor did I ever boast of lands unto you,   130
   Money, or goods; I took a plainer course
   And told you true I'd nothing.
   If error were committed, 'twas by you;
   Thank your own folly. Nor has my sin been
   So odious, but worse has been forgiven;   135
   Nor am I so deformed but I may challenge
   The utmost power of any old man's love.—
   She that tastes not sin before, twenty to one but she'll taste it after;
   most of you old men are content to marry young virgins and take
   that which follows; where, marrying one of us, you both save a   140
   sinner and are quit from° a cuckold for ever.
   'And more, in brief, let this your best thoughts win,
   She that knows sin knows best how to hate sin.'

HOARD Cursed be all malice! Black are the fruits of spite
   And poison first their owners. Oh, my friends,   145
   I must embrace shame to be rid of shame.
   Concealed disgrace prevents a public name.
   Ah, Witgood. Ah, Theodorus.

WITGOOD Alas, sir, I was pricked in conscience to see her well
   bestowed, and where could I bestow her better than upon your   150
   pitiful worship? Excepting but myself, I dare swear she's a virgin;
   and now, by marrying your niece, I have banished myself for ever
   from her. She's mine aunt now, by my faith, and there's no
   meddling with mine aunt, you know—a sin against my nuncle.

COURTESAN [kneeling] Lo, gentlemen, before you all   155
   In true reclaimèd form I fall.
   Henceforth for ever I defy
   The glances of a sinful eye,
   Waving of fans—which some suppose
   Tricks of fancy—treading of toes,   160

Wringing of fingers, biting the lip,
The wanton gait, th'alluring trip,
All secret friends and private meetings,
Close-borne letters and bawds' greetings,
Feigning excuse to women's labours   165
When we are sent for to th'next neighbour's,°
Taking false physic, and ne'er start
To be let blood, though sign be at heart,°
Removing chambers, shifting beds,°
To welcome friends in husbands' steads,   170
Them to enjoy, and you to marry,
They first served while you must tarry,
They to spend, and you to gather,
They to get, and you to father—
These and thousand thousand more,   175
New reclaimed, I now abhor.
LUCRE Ah, here's a lesson, rioter, for you.
WITGOOD [*kneeling*] I must confess my follies; I'll down too.
    And here for ever I disclaim
    The cause of youth's undoing, game,   180
    Chiefly dice, those true outlanders
    That shake out beggars, thieves, and panders,°
    Soul-wasting surfeits, sinful riots,
    Queans' evils, doctors' diets,°
    'Pothecaries' drugs, surgeons' glisters,°   185
    Stabbing of arms for a common mistress,°
    Ribbon favours, ribald speeches,°
    Dear perfumed jackets, penniless breeches,
    Dutch flapdragons, healths in urine,°
    Drabs that keep a man too sure in—   190
    I do defy you all.
    Lend me each honest hand, for here I rise
    A reclaimed man loathing the general vice.°
HOARD So, so, all friends. The wedding dinner cools.
    Who seem most crafty prove oft times most fools.   195
        [*Exeunt*]

NO WIT, NO HELP
LIKE A WOMAN'S

THE ACTORS IN THE COMEDY

Sir Oliver Twilight,° a rich old knight
Philip, his son, servant° to Mistress Grace
Sandfield, friend to Philip, servant to Mistress Jane
Master Sunset, true father of Mistress Grace
Master Low-water,° a decayed° gentleman   5
Sir Gilbert Lambston°
Master Weatherwise° ⎤
Master Pepperton°   ⎬ suitors to the Lady Goldenfleece
Master Overdone°   ⎦
Master Beveril, brother to Mistress Low-water   10
Dutch Merchant
Dutch Boy
Savourwit,° Sir Oliver's man
Footman
Pickadille,° Lady Goldenfleece's fool   15
Lady Twilight
Lady Goldenfleece,° a rich widow
Mistress Low-water
Mistress Grace, Sunset's daughter, but supposed Twilight's
Mistress Jane, Twilight's daughter, but supposed Sunset's   20

Prologue

How is't possible to suffice
So many ears, so many eyes?
Some in wit, some in shows
Take delight, and some in clothes;
Some for mirth they chiefly come,   5
Some for passion, for both some;
Some for lascivious meetings, that's their arrant;°
Some to detract, and ignorance their warrant.
How is't possible to please
Opinion tossed in such wild seas?°   10
Yet I doubt not, if attention
Seize you above, and apprehension
You below, to take things quickly,°
We shall both make you sad and tickle ye.°

[1.1]

*Enter Philip, Sir Oliver Twilight's son, with Savourwit, his
father's man*

PHILIP I am at my wit's ends, Savourwit.

SAVOURWIT And I am even following after you as fast as I can,
sir.

PHILIP My wife will be forced from me, my pleasure!

SAVOURWIT Talk no more on't, sir. How can there be any   5
    Hope i'th'middle when we're both at our
    Wits' end in the beginning? My invention°
    Was ne'er so gravelled since I first set out upon't.°

PHILIP Nor does my stop stick only in this wheel,°
    Though it be a main vexation, but I'm grated°   10
    In a dear absolute friend, young Master Sandfield.

SAVOURWIT Ay, there's another rub, too.

PHILIP   Who supposes
    That I make love to his affected mistress,°
    When 'tis my father works against the peace
    Of both our spirits and woos unknown to me.°   15
    He strikes out sparks of undeservèd anger°
    'Twixt old steel friendship and new stony hate,°
    As much forgetful of the merry hours
    The circuits of our youth hath spent and worn,
    As if they had not been, or we not born.   20

SAVOURWIT See where he comes.

    Enter Sandfield

SANDFIELD   Unmerciful in torment!
    Will this disease never forsake mine eye?°

PHILIP It must be killed first if it grow so painful.
    Work it out strongly at one time that th'anguish°
    May never more come near thy precious sight.   25
    If my eternal sleep will give thee rest,
    Close up mine eyes with opening of my breast.

SANDFIELD I feel thy wrongs at midnight and the weight
    Of thy close treacheries. Thou hast a friendship
    As dangerous as a strumpet's that will kiss   30
    Men into poverty, distress, and ruin;
    And to make clear the face of thy foul deeds,°

Thou work'st by seconds.°
    [*Draws his sword*]

PHILIP Then may the sharp point of an inward horror
  Strike me to earth and save thy weapon guiltless.   35

SANDFIELD Not in thy father?°

PHILIP How much is truth abused when 'tis kept silent.

SANDFIELD Oh, defend me friendship!

SAVOURWIT True, your anger's in an error all this while, sir;
  But that a lover's weapon ne'er hears reason,°   40
  'Tis out still like a mad man's. Hear but me, sir.
  'Tis my young master's injury, not yours,
  That you quarrel with him for, and this shows
  As if y'would challenge a lame man the field
  And cut off 's head because he has lost his legs.   45
  His grief makes him dead flesh, as it appeared
  By off'ring up his breast to you; for believe it, sir,
  Had he not greater crosses of his own,
  Your hilts could not cross him.

SANDFIELD   How?

SAVOURWIT   Not your hilts, sir.°
  Come, I must have you friends; a pox of weapons.   50
  There's a whore gapes for't; put it up i'th'scabbard.°

SANDFIELD Thou'rt a mad slave.
    [*Puts up his sword*]

SAVOURWIT   Come, give me both your hands.
    [*He clasps their hands*]
  Y'are in a quagmire both; should I release you now,
  Your wits would both come home in a stinking pickle;°
  Your father's old nose would smell you out presently.   55

PHILIP Tell him the secret which no mortal knows
  But thou and I, and then he will confess
  How much he wronged the patience of his friend.

SAVOURWIT Then thus the marigold opens at the splendour
  Of a hot constant friendship 'twixt you both.   60
  'Tis not unknown to your ear, some ten years since,
  My mistress, his good mother, with a daughter°
  About the age of six, crossing to Jersey,°
  Was taken by the Dunkirks, sold both, and separated,
  As the last news brings hot—the first and last°   65
  So much discovered; for in nine years' space
  No certain tidings of their life or death,

Or what place held 'em, earth, the sea, or heaven,
Came to the old man's ears, the knight my master,
Till about five months since a letter came   70
Sent from the mother, which related all
Their taking, selling, separation,
And never meeting; and withal required
Six hundred crowns for ransom, which my old master
No sooner heard the sound, but told the sum,   75
Gave him the gold and sent us both aboard.°
We landing by the way, having a care°
To lighten us of our carriage, because gold
Is such a heavy metal, eased our pockets°
In wenches' aprons. Women were made to bear,   80
But for us gentlemen 'tis most unkindly.°

SANDFIELD Well, sir?
PHILIP   A pure rogue still!
SAVOURWIT   Amongst the rest, sir,
'Twas my young master's chance there to dote finely°
Upon a sweet young gentlewoman, but one
That would not sell her honour for the Indies,   85
Till a priest struck the bargain, and then half a crown°
Dispatched it.
To be brief, wedded her and bedded her,
Brought her home hither to his father's house,
And with a fair tale of mine own bringing up°   90
She passes for his sister that was sold.

SANDFIELD Let me not lose myself in wond'ring at thee.
But how made you your score even for the mother?°
SAVOURWIT Pish, easily; we told him how her fortunes
Mocked us as they mocked her. When we were o'th'sea,   95
She was o'th'land, and as report was given,
When we were landed, she was gone to heaven.
So he believes two lies one error bred:°
The daughter ransomed and the mother dead.

SANDFIELD Let me admire thee and withal confess   100
My injuries to friendship.
PHILIP   They're all pardoned.
     [*They embrace*]
These are the arms I bore against my friend.
SAVOURWIT But what's all this to th'present? This discourse
Leaves you i'th'bog still.

PHILIP   On, good Savourwit.

SAVOURWIT For yet our policy has crossed ourselves;°   105
    For the old knave, my master, little thinking her
    Wife to his son, but his own daughter still,
    Seeks out a match for her.

PHILIP   Here I feel the surgeon
    At second dressing.

SAVOURWIT   And he's entertained°
    Even for pure need, for fear the glass should crack   110
    That is already broken, but well soldered,°
    A mere sot for her suitor, a rank fox,
    One Weatherwise, that woos by the almanac,
    Observes the full and change, an arrant mooncalf.°
    And yet, because the fool demands no portion   115
    But the bare down of her smock, the old fellow,°
    Worn to the bone with a dry covetous itch
    To save his purse and yet bestow his child,
    Consents to waste [her on] lumps of almanac stuff°
    Kned with May-butter.—Now, as I have thought on't,   120
    I'll spoil him in the baking.

SANDFIELD   Prithee, as how, sirrah?

SAVOURWIT I'll give him such a crack in one o'th'sides,
    He shall quite run out of my master's favour.

PHILIP I should but too much love thee for that.

SAVOURWIT   Thus then,
    To help you both at once, and so good night to you.   125
    After my wit has shipped away the fool,°
    As he shall part I'll buzz into the ear
    Of my old master that you, sir, Master Sandfield,
    Dearly affect his daughter and will take her
    With little or no portion. Well stood out in't.°   130
    Methinks I see him caper at that news
    And in the full cry, oh! This brought about°
    And wittily dissembled on both parts,
    You to affect his love, he to love yours,°
    I'll so beguile the father at the marriage,   135
    That each shall have his own, and both being welcomed°
    And chambered in one house, as 'tis his pride
    To have his children's children got successively°
    On his forefathers' feather beds, in the day times,
    To please the old man's eyesight, you may dally   140

And set kiss on the wrong lip; no sin in't;°
Brothers and sisters do't, cousins do more.
But pray take heed you be not kin to them.°
So in the night time, nothing can deceive you;°
Let each know his own work and there I leave you.   145
SANDFIELD Let me applaud thee.
PHILIP   Blessed be all thy ends,
That mak'st armed enemies embracing friends.
About it speedily.
          Exit [Philip with Sandfield]
SAVOURWIT   I need no pricking.
I'm of that mettle, so well paced and free,°
There's no good riders that use spur to me.°   150
          Enter Grace Twilight
Oh, are you come?
GRACE   Are any comforts coming?°
SAVOURWIT I never go without 'em.°
GRACE Thou sport'st joys that utterance cannot perfect.°
SAVOURWIT Hark, are they risen?
GRACE   Yes, long before I left 'em.°
And all intend to bring the widow homeward.   155
SAVOURWIT Depart then, mistress, to avoid suspect.
Our good shall arrive time enough at your heart.
          [Exit Grace]
Poor fools that ever more take a green surfeit
Of the first fruits of joys. Let a man but shake the tree,
How soon they'll hold up their laps to receive comfort!°   160
The music that I struck made her soul dance.
Peace.
          *Enter the Lady Widow Goldenfleece with Sir Gilbert Lamb-
          ston, Master Pepperton, Master Overdone, suitors. After them
          the two old men, Sir Oliver Twilight and Master Sunset,
          with their daughters, Grace Twilight, [and] Jane Sunset*
[Aside] Here comes the Lady Widow, the late wife
To the deceased Sir Avarice Goldenfleece,
Second to none for usury and extortion,
As too well it appears on a poor gentleman,   165
One Master Low-water, from whose estate
He pulled that fleece that makes his widow weight.
Those are her suitors now, Sir Gilbert Lambston,
Master Pepperton, Master Overdone.

LADY GOLDENFLEECE Nay, good Sir Oliver Twilight, Master
   Sunset,   170
   We'll trouble you no farther.
SUNSET, SIR OLIVER   No trouble, sweet madam.
SIR GILBERT We'll see the widow at home;° it shall be our charge,
   that.
LADY GOLDENFLEECE It shall be so indeed.
   Thanks, good Sir Oliver, and to you both°   175
   I am indebted for those courtesies
   That will ask me a long time to requite.
SIR OLIVER Ah, 'tis but your pleasant condition to give it out so,
   madam.
LADY GOLDENFLEECE Mistress Grace and Mistress Jane, I wish you
   both   180
   A fair contented fortune in your choices,°
   And that you happen right.
GRACE, JANE   Thanks to you, good madam.
GRACE [aside] There's more in that word 'right' than you
   imagine.°
LADY GOLDENFLEECE I now repent, girls, a rash oath I took,
   When you were both infants, to conceal a secret.   185
GRACE What does't concern, good madam?
LADY GOLDENFLEECE   No, no.
   Since you are both so well, 'tis well enough.
   It must not be revealed; 'tis now no more
   Than like mistaking of one hand for t'other.°
   A happy time to you both.
GRACE, JANE   The like to you, madam.   190
GRACE [aside] I shall long much to have this riddle opened.
JANE [aside] I would you were so kind to my poor kinswoman
   And the distressed gentleman her husband,
   Poor Master Low-water, who on ruin leans.
   You keep this secret as you keep his means.   195
LADY GOLDENFLEECE Thanks, good Sir Oliver Twilight. Welcome,
   sweet Master Pepperton; Master Overdone, welcome.
     Exeunt, leaving Sir Oliver with Savourwit
SIR OLIVER And goes the business well 'twixt those young lovers?
SAVOURWIT Betwixt your son and Master Sunset's daughter
   The line goes even, sir.
SIR OLIVER   Good lad, I like thee.°   200
SAVOURWIT But, sir, there's no proportion, height, or evenness

Betwixt that equinoctial and your daughter.°
SIR OLIVER 'Tis true, and I'm right glad on't.
SAVOURWIT   Are you glad, sir?
There's no proportion in't.
SIR OLIVER   Ay, marry I am, sir.
I can abide no word that ends in portion;   205
I'll give her nothing.
SAVOURWIT   Say you should not, sir,
As I'll ne'er urge your worship 'gainst your nature,
Is there no gentleman, think you, of worth and credit,
Will open's bed to warm a naked maid?
A hundred gallant fellows, and be glad   210
To be so set awork. Virginity
Is no such cheap ware as you make account on,°
That it had need with portion be set off,
For that sets off a portion in these days.
SIR OLIVER Play on, sweet boy.   215
Oh, I could hear this music all day long,
When there's no money to be parted from.
Strike on, good lad!
SAVOURWIT Do not wise men and great often bestow
Ten thousand pound in jewels that lie by 'em?   220
If so, what jewel can lie by a man
More precious than a virgin? If none more precious,
Why should the pillow of a fool be graced
With that brave spirits with dearness have embraced?°
And then, perhaps, ere the third spring come on,   225
Sends home your diamond cracked, the beauty gone;
And more to know her, 'cause you shall not doubt her,
A number of poor sparks twinkling about her.°
SIR OLIVER Now thou play'st Dowland's *Lachrymae* to thy
   master.°
SAVOURWIT But shall I dry your eyes with a merry jig now,   230
And make you look like sunshine in a shower?
SIR OLIVER How, how, my honest boy, sweet Savourwit?
SAVOURWIT Young Master Sandfield, gallant Master Sandfield—
SIR OLIVER Ha! What of him?
SAVOURWIT   —Affects your daughter strangely.°
SIR OLIVER Brave Master Sandfield!—Let me hug thy zeal   235
Unto thy master's house.—Ha, Master Sandfield!
But he'll expect a portion.

SAVOURWIT   Not a whit, sir,
  As you may use the matter.
SIR OLIVER Nay, an the matter fall into my using,
  The devil a penny that he gets of me.   240
SAVOURWIT He lies at the mercy of your lock and key, sir;
  You may use him as you list.
SIR OLIVER   Say'st thou me so?
  Is he so far in doing?
SAVOURWIT   Quite over head and ears, sir.
  Nay more, he means to run mad and break his neck
  Off some high steeple if he have her not.   245
SIR OLIVER Now bless the young gentleman's gristles; I hope
  To be a grandfather yet by 'em.
SAVOURWIT   That may you, sir,
  To, marry, a chopping girl with a plump buttock,
  Will hoist a farthingale at five years' old
  And call a man between eleven and twelve   250
  To take part of a piece of mutton with her.°
SIR OLIVER Ha, precious wag! Hook him in finely, do.
SAVOURWIT Make clear the way for him first; set the gull going.°
SIR OLIVER An ass, an ass, I'll quickly dash his wooing.
SAVOURWIT [aside] Why now the clocks   255
  Go right again. It must be a strange wit
  That makes the wheels of youth and age so hit;°
  The one are dry, worn, rusty, furred, and soiled;
  Love's wheels are glib, ever kept clean, and oiled.
         Exit [*Savourwit*]
SIR OLIVER I cannot choose but think of this good fortune;   260
  That gallant Master Sandfield!
         Enter Weatherwise
WEATHERWISE [aside]   Stay, stay, stay!
  What comfort gives my almanac today?
         [*Reads his almanac*]
  Luck, I beseech thee. 'Good days', 'evil days', 'June', 'July'; speak
  a good word for me now, and I have her. Let me see, 'the fifth
  day, 'twixt hawk and buzzard;° the sixth day, backward and   265
  forward'—that was beastly to me, I remember; 'the seventh day,
  on a slippery pin; the eighth day, fire and tow; the ninth day, the
  market is marred'—that's long of the hucksters, I warrant you; but
  now 'the tenth day'—luck, I beseech thee now before I look into't;
  'the eleventh day,° against the hair'°—a pox on't! Would that   270

hair had been left out—'against the hair'! That hair will go nigh to
choke me; had it been against anything but that, 'twould not have
troubled me because it lies cross i'th'way. Well, I'll try the fortune
of a good face yet, though my almanac leave me i'th'sands.°

SIR OLIVER [*aside*] Such a match too. I could not wish a better.   275

WEATHERWISE [*aside*] Mass, here he walks!—Save you sweet Sir
Oliver.—Sir Oliver Twilight!

SIR OLIVER Oh, pray come to me a quarter of a year hence; I have
a little business now.

WEATHERWISE How, a quarter of a year hence? What, shall I come   280
to you in September?

SIR OLIVER Nor in November neither, good my friend.

WEATHERWISE Y'are not a mad knight; you will not let your
daughter hang past August, will you? She'll drop down under tree
then. She's no winter fruit, I assure you, if you think to put her   285
in crust° after Christmas.

SIR OLIVER Sir, in a word, depart; my girl's not for you;
I gave you a drowsy promise in a dream,
But broad awake now, I call't in again.
Have me commended to your wit; farewell, sir.   290
    [*Exit Sir Oliver*]

WEATHERWISE Now the devil run away with you, and some lousy
fiddler with your daughter. May Clerkenwell° have the first cut
of her, and Hound's Ditch° pick the bones. I'll never leave the
love of an open-hearted widow for a narrow-eyed maid again; go
out of the road way like an ass to leap over hedge and ditch; I'll   295
fall into the beaten path again and invite the widow home to a
banquet. Let who list seek out new ways, I'll be at my journey's
end before him.
My almanac told me true, how I should fare;
Let no man think to speed against the hair.   300
    Exit

[1.2]

Enter Mistress Low-water

MISTRESS LOW-WATER Is there no saving means? No help
   religious
  For a distressed gentlewoman to live by?
  Has virtue no revenue?° Who has all then?
  Is the world's lease from hell, the devil head-landlord?
  Oh, how was conscience, the right heir, put by?   5
  Law would not do such an unrighteous deed,
  Though with the fall of angels't had been fee'd.°
  Where are our hopes in banks? Was honesty°
  A younger sister without portion left?
  No dowry in the Chamber beside wantonness?°   10
  Oh, miserable orphan!
  'Twixt two extremes runs there no blessèd mean,
  No comfortable strain that I may kiss it?°
  Must I to whoredom or to beggary lean,
  My mind being sound? Is there no way to miss it?   15
  Is't not injustice that a widow laughs°
  And lays her mourning part upon a wife?°
  That she should have the garment, I the heart;°
  My wealth her husband left her and me her grief?°
  Yet stood all miseries in their loathed'st forms   20
  On this hand of me, thick like a foul mist,
  And here the bright enticements of the world°
  In clearest colours, flattery, and advancement,
  And all the bastard glories this frame jets in,
  Horror nor splendour, shadows fair nor foul,   25
  Should force me shame my husband, wound my soul.
     Enter Mistress Jane, Sunset's daughter.
  Cousin, y'are welcome. This is kindly done of you
  To visit the despised.
JANE   I hope not so, coz.
  The want of means cannot make you despised;
  Love not by wealth but by desert is prized.   30
MISTRESS LOW-WATER Y'are pleased to help it well, coz.
JANE   I am come to you,
  Beside my visitation, to request you
  To lay your wit to mine, which is but simple,

And help me to untie a few dark words
Made up in knots—they're of the widow's knitting,   35
That ties all sure—for my wit has not strength
Nor cunning to unloose 'em.
MISTRESS LOW-WATER   Good, what are they?°
Though there be little comfort of my help.
JANE She wished Sir Oliver's daughter and myself
Good fortune in our choices, and repented her   40
Of a rash oath she took when we were both infants,
A secret to conceal; but since all's well,
She holds it best to keep it unrevealed.
Now what this is, heaven knows.
MISTRESS LOW-WATER   Nor can I guess.
The course of her whole life, and her dead husband's,   45
Was ever full of such dishonest riddles
To keep right heirs from knowledge of their own.
And now I'm put i'th'mind on't, I believe
It was some piece of land or money given°
By some departing friend upon their deathbed,   50
Perhaps to yourself, and Sir Oliver's daughter
May wrongfully enjoy it, and she hired°
—For she was but an hireling in those days—
To keep the injury secret.   ⟩
JANE   The most likeliest
That ever you could think on.
MISTRESS LOW-WATER   Is it not?   55
JANE Sure, coz, I think you have untied the knot;
My thoughts lie at more ease. As in all other things,
In this I thank your help, and may you live
To conquer your own troubles and cross ends,
As you are ready to supply your friends.   60
MISTRESS LOW-WATER I thank you for the kind truth of your
     heart,
In which I flourish when all means depart.
[Aside] Sure in that oath of hers there sleeps some wrong°
Done to my kinswoman.
     Enter Footman
JANE   Who'd you speak withal?
FOOTMAN The gentlewoman of this house forsooth.   65
JANE Whose footman are you?
FOOTMAN   One Sir Gilbert Lambston's.

JANE Sir Gilbert Lambston's? There my cousin walks.
FOOTMAN Thank your good worship.
          [*Exit Jane*]
MISTRESS LOW-WATER   How now, whence are you?
FOOTMAN This letter will make known.
          [*Gives letter to her*]
MISTRESS LOW-WATER   Whence comes it, sir?
FOOTMAN From the knight, my master, Sir Gilbert Lambston.   70
MISTRESS LOW-WATER Return't; I'll receive none on't.
          [*Throws down letter*]
FOOTMAN   There it must lie then;
    I were as good run to Tyburn afoot and hang myself
    At mine own charges as carry it back again.
          Exit [*Footman*]
MISTRESS LOW-WATER Life, had he not his answer? What strange
    impudence
    Governs in man, when lust is lord of him.   75
    Thinks he me mad? 'Cause I have no moneys on earth,
    That I'll go forfeit my estate in heaven
    And live eternal beggar? He shall pardon me,
    That's my soul's jointure; I'll starve ere I sell that.
    Oh, is he gone, and left the letter here!   80
    Yet I will read it, more to hate the writer.
          [*Reads*]
    'Mistress Low-water. If you desire to understand your own com-
    fort, hear me out, ere you refuse me. I'm in the way now to double
    the yearly means that first I offered you; and to stir you more to
    me, I'll empty your enemy's bags to maintain you; for the rich   85
    widow, the Lady Goldenfleece, to whom I have been a longer suitor
    than you an adversary, hath given me so much encouragement
    lately, insomuch that I am perfectly assured the next meeting strikes
    the bargain. The happiness that follows this 'twere idle to inform
    you of; only consent to my desires, and the widow's notch shall lie 90
    open to you. Thus much to your heart; I know y'are wise. Farewell.
    Thy friend to his power, and another's, Gilbert Lambston.'
    In this poor brief what volumes has he thrust°
    Of treacherous perjury and adulterous lust!
    So foul a monster does this wrong appear   95
    That I give pity to mine enemy here.°
    What a most fearful love reigns in some hearts
    That dare oppose all judgement to get means,

And wed rich widows only to keep queans.
What a strange path he takes to my affection,   100
And thinks't the near'st way—'twill never be—°
Goes through mine enemy's ground to come to me.
This letter is most welcome; I repent now
That my last anger threw thee at my feet;
My bosom shall receive thee.
            Enter Sir Gilbert Lambston
SIR GILBERT [*aside*]   'Tis good policy too   105
To keep one that so mortally hates the widow;°
She'll have more care to keep it close herself.
And look what wind her revenge goes withal,
The self-same gale whisks up the sails of love.
I shall loose much good sport by that.°   110
—Now, my sweet mistress.
MISTRESS LOW-WATER   Sir Gilbert! You change suits oft,°
You were here in black but lately.
SIR GILBERT My mind ne'er shifts though.
MISTRESS LOW-WATER [*aside*]   A foul mind the whilst.—
But sure, sir, this is but a dissembling glass
You sent before you; 'tis not possible   115
Your heart should follow your hand.
SIR GILBERT   Then may both perish.
MISTRESS LOW-WATER Do not wish that so soon, sir. Can you
    make
A three-months' love to a rich widow's bed,
And lay her pillow under a quean's head?
I know you can't, howe'er you may dissemble't;   120
You have a heart brought up better.
SIR GILBERT   Faith, you wrong me in't;
You shall not find it so. I do protest to thee
I will be lord of all my promises,
And ere't be long, thou shalt but turn a key
And find 'em in thy coffer; for my love,   125
In matching with the widow, is but policy
To strengthen my estate and make me able
To set off all thy kisses with rewards;
That the worst weather our delights behold,
It may hail pearl and shower the widow's gold.   130
MISTRESS LOW-WATER You talk of a brave world, sir.
SIR GILBERT   'Twill seem better

When golden happiness breaks forth itself
Out of the east port of the widow's chamber.°
MISTRESS LOW-WATER And here it sets.
SIR GILBERT   Here shall the downfall be;
Her wealth shall rise from her and set in thee.   135
MISTRESS LOW-WATER You men have th'art to overcome poor
    women.
    Pray give my thoughts the freedom of one day,
    And all the rest take you.
SIR GILBERT   I straight obey.
    [*Aside*] This bird's my own.
        Exit Sir Gilbert Lambston
MISTRESS LOW-WATER There is no happiness but has her season,   140
    Wherein the brightness of her virtue shines;°
    The husk falls off in time that long shuts up
    The fruit in a dark prison; so sweeps by
    The cloud of miseries from wretches' eyes,
    That yet, though fallen, at length they see to rise;   145
    The secret powers work wondrously and duly.
        Enter Master Low-water
LOW-WATER Why, how now, Kate?
MISTRESS LOW-WATER   Oh, are you come, sir? Husband,
    Wake, wake, and let not patience keep thee poor;
    Rouse up thy spirit from this falling slumber.
    Make thy distress seem but a weeping dream,   150
    And this the opening morning of thy comforts.
    Wipe the salt dew off from thy careful eyes,
    And drink a draught of gladness next thy heart
    T'expel the infection of all poisonous sorrows.
LOW-WATER You turn me past my senses.
MISTRESS LOW-WATER   Will you but second   155
    The purpose I intend I'll be first forward.
    I crave no more of thee but a following spirit;°
    Will you but grant me that?
LOW-WATER   Why, what's the business
    That should transport thee thus?
MISTRESS LOW-WATER   Hope of much good,
    No fear of the least ill; take that to comfort thee.   160
LOW-WATER Yea?
MISTRESS LOW-WATER Sleep not on't; this is no slumbering
    business;

217

'Tis like the sweating sickness; I must keep°
Your eyes still wake, y'are gone if once you sleep.
LOW-WATER I will not rest then till thou hast thy wishes.   165
MISTRESS LOW-WATER Peruse this love paper as you go.
LOW-WATER A letter?
          Exeunt

[1.3]

*Enter Sir Oliver Twilight, with Master Sandfield, Philip,
and Savourwit*

SIR OLIVER Good Master Sandfield, for the great affection
     You bear toward my girl, I am well pleased
     You should enjoy her beauty. Heaven forbid, sir,
     That I should cast away a proper gentleman,
     So far in love, with a sour mood or so.   5
     No, no;
     I'll not die guilty of a lover's neck-cracking.°
     Marry, as for portion, there I leave you, sir,
     To the mercy of your destiny again;
     I'll have no hand in that.
SANDFIELD   Faith, something, sir;   10
     Be't but t'express your love.
SIR OLIVER   I have no desire, sir,
     To express my love that way, and so rest satisfied.
     I pray take heed in urging that too much
     You draw not my love from me.
SANDFIELD   Fates foresee, sir.
SIR OLIVER Faith, then you may go; seek out a high steeple   15
     Or a deep water; there's no saving of you.
SAVOURWIT [*aside*] How naturally he plays upon himself!°
SIR OLIVER Marry, if a wedding dinner, as I told you,
     And three years' board, well lodged in mine house,
     And eating, drinking, and a sleeping portion°   20
     May give you satisfaction, I am your man, sir;
     Seek out no other.
SANDFIELD   I am content to embrace it, sir,
     Rather than hazard languishment or ruin.
SIR OLIVER I love thee for thy wisdom; such a son-in-law

Will cheer a father's heart. Welcome, sweet Master Sandfield.   25
Whither away, boys? Philip?

PHILIP   To visit my love, sir,
Old Master Sunset's daughter.

SIR OLIVER   That's my Philip.
Ply't hard, my good boys both, put 'em to't finely.
One day, one dinner, and one house shall join you.

PHILIP, SANDFIELD That's our desire, sir.
          Exeunt [Philip and Sandfield]

SIR OLIVER   Pish! Come hither, Savourwit.   30
Observe my son and bring me word, sweet boy,
Whether h'as a speeding wit or no in wooing.

SAVOURWIT That will I, sir.—[*Aside*] That your own eyes might tell
   you.
I think it speedy, your girl has a round belly.
          Exit Savourwit

SIR OLIVER How soon the comfortable shine of joy   35
Breaks through a cloud of grief!
The tears that I let fall for my dead wife
Are dried up with the beams of my girl's fortunes.
Her life, her death, and her ten years' distress,
Are even forgot with me; the love and care   40
That I ought her, her daughter sh'owes it all;°
It can but be bestowed, and there 'tis well.°
          Enter Servant
How now, what news?

SERVANT There's a Dutch merchant, sir, that's now come over,
Desires some conference with you.

SIR OLIVER   How? A Dutch merchant?   45
Pray send him in to me.—What news with him, trow?
          [*Exit Servant.*] *Enter Dutch Merchant with a little Dutch Boy*
          in great slops

DUTCH MERCHANT Sir Oliver Twilight?

SIR OLIVER That's my name indeed, sir.
I pray be covered, sir; y'are very welcome.°

DUTCH MERCHANT This is my business, sir. I took into my
   charge   50
A few words to deliver to yourself
From a dear friend of yours that wonders strangely
At your unkind neglect.

SIR OLIVER   Indeed? What might he be, sir?

DUTCH MERCHANT Nay, y'are i'th'wrong gender now;
   'Tis that distressed lady, your good wife, sir.   55
SIR OLIVER What say you, sir? My wife?
DUTCH MERCHANT   Yes, sir, your wife!
   This strangeness now of yours seems more to harden
   Th'uncharitable neglect she taxed you for.
SIR OLIVER Pray, give me leave, sir. Is my wife alive?
DUTCH MERCHANT Came any news to you, sir, to th'contrary?   60
SIR OLIVER Yes, by my faith, did there.
DUTCH MERCHANT   Pray how long since, sir?
SIR OLIVER 'Tis now some ten weeks.
DUTCH MERCHANT   Faith, within this month, sir,
   I saw her talk and eat; and those in our calendar
   Are signs of life and health.
SIR OLIVER   Mass, so they are in ours.
DUTCH MERCHANT And these were the last words her passion threw
   me: 65
   'No grief', quoth she, 'sits to my heart so close
   As his unkindness and my daughter's loss.'
SIR OLIVER You make me weep and wonder, for I swear
   I sent her ransom, and that daughter's here.
DUTCH MERCHANT Here! That will come well to lighten her of one
   grief.   70
   I long to see her for the piteous moan
   Her mother made for her.
SIR OLIVER   That shall you, sir.—Within there!
       [*Enter Servant*]
SERVANT Sir?
SIR OLIVER   Call down my daughter.
SERVANT   Yes, sir.
       [*Exit Servant*]
SIR OLIVER Here's strange budgelling! I tell you, sir,
   Those that I put in trust were near me too—   75
   A man would think they should not juggle with me—
   My own son and my servant, no worse people, sir.
DUTCH MERCHANT And yet, ofttimes, sir, what worse knave to a
   man
   Than he that eats his meat?
SIR OLIVER   Troth, you say true, sir.
   I sent 'em simply, and that news they brought,°   80
   My wife had left the world; and with that sum°

I sent to her, this brought his sister home.
Look you, sir, this is she.
    Enter Grace
DUTCH MERCHANT   If my eye sin not, sir,
Or misty error falsify the glass,
I saw that face at Antwerp in an inn   85
When I set forth first to fetch home this boy.
SIR OLIVER How? In an inn?
GRACE [*aside*]   Oh, I am betrayed, I fear.
DUTCH MERCHANT How do you, young mistress?
GRACE   Your eyes wrong your tongue, sir,
And makes you sin in both; I am not she.
DUTCH MERCHANT No? Then I never saw face twice.—Sir Oliver
    Twilight,   90
I tell you my free thoughts, I fear y'are blinded.°
I do not like this story; I doubt much
The sister is as false as the dead mother.
SIR OLIVER Yea! Say you so, sir? I see nothing lets me°
But to doubt so too then.—   95
So, to your chamber; we have done with you.
GRACE [*aside*] I would be glad you had. Here's a strange
    storm.—
Sift it out well, sir; till anon I leave you, sir.
    [*Exit Grace*]
DUTCH MERCHANT Business commands me hence, but as a pledge
Of my return I'll leave my little son with you,   100
Who yet takes little pleasure in this country
'Cause he can speak no English, all Dutch he.
SIR OLIVER A fine boy; he's welcome, sir, to me.
DUTCH MERCHANT Where's your leg and your thanks to the
    gentleman?
War es yu neighgen an you thonkes you?°   105
DUTCH BOY *Ick donck you, ver ew edermon vrendly kite.*
SIR OLIVER What says he, sir?
DUTCH MERCHANT He thanks you for your kindness.
SIR OLIVER Pretty knave!
DUTCH MERCHANT Had not some business held me by the way,   110
This news had come to your ear ten days ago.
SIR OLIVER It comes too soon now methinks; I'm your debtor.
DUTCH MERCHANT But I could wish it, sir, for better ware.
    [*Exit Dutch Merchant*]

SIR OLIVER We must not be our own choosers in our fortunes.
　　　Here's a cold pie to breakfast: wife alive,   115
　　　The daughter doubtful and the money spent!
　　　How am I juggled withal!
　　　　Enter Savourwit
SAVOURWIT　　　　　　It hits, i'faith, sir;
　　　The work goes even.
SIR OLIVER　　　　Oh, come, come, come, are you come, sir?°
SAVOURWIT [*aside*] Life, what's the matter now?
SIR OLIVER There's a new reckoning come in since.°   120
SAVOURWIT [*aside*] Pox on't! I thought all had been paid;
　　　I can't abide these after-reckonings.
SIR OLIVER I pray come near, sir; let's be acquainted with you.
　　　You're bold enough abroad with my purse, sir.
SAVOURWIT No more than beseems manners and good use, sir.   125
SIR OLIVER Did not you bring me word some ten weeks since,
　　　My wife was dead?
SAVOURWIT　　　　Yes, true, sir, very true, sir.
SIR OLIVER Pray stay and take my horse along with you.°
　　　And with the ransom that I sent for her
　　　That you redeemed my daughter?
SAVOURWIT　　　　　　　　Right as can be, sir;   130
　　　I never found your worship in a false tale yet.
SIR OLIVER I thank you for your good word, sir, but I'm like
　　　To find your worship now in two at once.
SAVOURWIT I should be sorry to hear that.
SIR OLIVER　　　　　　　　　　I believe you, sir.
　　　Within this month my wife was sure alive—   135
　　　There's six weeks bated of your ten-weeks' lie—
　　　As has been credibly reported to me
　　　By a Dutch merchant, father to that boy,
　　　But now come over, and the words scarce cold.
SAVOURWIT [*aside*] Oh strange!—'Tis a most rank untruth; where is
　　　he, sir?   140
SIR OLIVER He will not be long absent.
SAVOURWIT [*aside*]　　　　　　　All's confounded.—
　　　If he were here, I'll tell him to his face, sir;
　　　He wears a double tongue—that's Dutch and English.
　　　Will the boy say't?
SIR OLIVER　　　　'Las, he can speak no English.
SAVOURWIT [*aside*] All the better; I'll gabble something to him.—   145

Hoyste kaloiste, kalooskin ee vou, dar sune, alla gaskin?

DUTCH BOY *Ick wet neat watt hey zackt; Ick unverston ewe neat.*

SAVOURWIT Why la, I thought as much.

SIR OLIVER   What says the boy?

SAVOURWIT He says his father is troubled with an imperfection at
one time of the moon and talks like a madman.   150

SIR OLIVER What? Does the boy say so?

SAVOURWIT   I knew there was somewhat in't.
Your wife alive! Will you believe all tales, sir?

SIR OLIVER Nay, more, sir; he told me he saw this wench,
Which you brought home, at Antwerp in an inn;
Tells me I'm plainly cozened of all hands;°   155
'Tis not my daughter neither.

SAVOURWIT [*aside*]   All's broke out.—
How? Not your daughter, sir? I must to't again.
*Quisquinikin sadlamare, alla pisse kickin sows-clows, hoff tofte le
cumber shaw, bouns bus boxsceeno.*

DUTCH BOY *Ick an sawth no int hein clappon de heeke, I dinke ute zein*   160
zennon.

SAVOURWIT Oh *zein zennon*! Ah ha! I thought how 'twould prove
i'th'end. The boy says they never came near Antwerp, a quite
contrary way, round about by Parma.

SIR OLIVER What's the same *zein zennon*?   165

SAVOURWIT That is, he saw no such wench in an inn. 'Tis well I
came in such happy time to get it out of the boy before his father
returned again. Pray be wary, sir; the world's subtle. Come and
pretend a charitable business in policy, and work out a piece of
money on you!°   170

SIR OLIVER Mass, art advised of that?

SAVOURWIT The age is cunning, sir; beside, a Dutchman will live
upon any ground and work butter out of a thistle.°

SIR OLIVER Troth, thou say'st true in that; they're the best thri-
vers in turnips, artichokes, and cabbages; our English are not like   175
them.

SAVOURWIT Oh, fie, no, sir!

SIR OLIVER Ask him from whence they came, when they came
hither.

SAVOURWIT That I will, sir.—*Culluaron lagooso, lageen, lagan, ruffi,*   180
punkatee.

DUTCH BOY *Nimd aweigh de cack.*

SAVOURWIT What, what? I cannot blame him then.

SIR OLIVER What says he to thee?

SAVOURWIT The poor boy blushes for him; he tells me his father   185
came from making merry with certain of his countrymen, and he's
a little steeped in English beer. There's no heed to be taken of his
tongue now.

SIR OLIVER Hoyda! How com'st thou by all this? I heard him speak
but three words to thee.   190

SAVOURWIT Oh, sir, the Dutch is a very wide language. You shall
have ten English words even for one, as for example, *Gullder-goose*;
there's a word for you, master.

SIR OLIVER Why, what's that same *Gullder-goose*?

SAVOURWIT How do you and all your generation.   195

SIR OLIVER Why, 'tis impossible! How prove you that, sir?

SAVOURWIT 'Tis thus distinguished,° sir: *Gull*, how do you—*der*,
and—*goose*, your generation.

SIR OLIVER 'Tis a most saucy language;° how cam'st thou by't?

SAVOURWIT I was brought up to London in an eelship;°   200
There was the place I caught it first by th'tail.
[*Aside*] I shall be tripped anon; pox, would I were gone.—
I'll go seek out your son, sir, you shall hear
What thunder he'll bring with him.

SIR OLIVER   Do, do, Savourwit;°
I'll have you all face to face.

SAVOURWIT [*aside*]   Cuds me! What else, sir?   205
An you take me so near the net again,
I'll give you leave to squat me; I have 'scaped fairly.
We are undone in Dutch; all our three-months' roguery
Is now come over in a butter firkin.
          Exit Savourwit

SIR OLIVER Never was man so tossed between two tales!   210
I know not which to take, not which to trust;
The boy here is the likeliest to tell truth
Because the world's corruption is not yet
At full years in him; sure he cannot know
What deceit means, 'tis English yet to him.   215
And when I think again, why should the father
Dissemble for no profit? He gets none,
Whate'er he hopes for, and I think he hopes not.
The man's in a good case, being old and weary,°
He dares not lean his arm on his son's shoulder   220
For fear he lie i'th'dirt, but must be rather

Beholding to a stranger for his prop.
    Enter Dutchman [Dutch Merchant]

DUTCH MERCHANT I make bold once again, sir, for a boy here.

SIR OLIVER Oh, sir, y'are welcome. Pray resolve me one thing,
    sir;
  Did you within this month, with your own eyes,   225
  See my wife living?

DUTCH MERCHANT   I ne'er borrowed any.
  Why should you move that question, sir? Dissembling
  Is no part of my living.

SIR OLIVER   I have reason
  To urge it so far, sir—pray be not angry though—
  Because my man was here since your departure,   230
  Withstands all stiffly, and to make it clearer,
  Questioned your boy in Dutch, who, as he told me,
  Returned this answer first to him: that you
  Had imperfection at one time o'th'moon
  Which made you talk so strangely.   235

DUTCH MERCHANT How, how's this? *Zeicke yongon, ick ben ick quelt
medien dullek heght, ee untoit van the mon, an koot uramed?*

DUTCH BOY *Wee ek, heigh lieght in ze bokkas, dee't site.*

DUTCH MERCHANT Why la you, sir! Here's no such thing;
  He says he lies in's throat that says it.   240

SIR OLIVER Then the rogue lies in's throat, for he told me so,
  And that the boy should answer at next question
  That you ne'er saw this wench nor came near Antwerp.

DUTCH MERCHANT Ten thousand devils! *Zeicke hee ewe ek kneeght,
yongon, dat wee neeky by Antwarpon ne don cammen no seene de*   245
doughter dor?

DUTCH BOY *Ick hub ham hean sulka dongon he zaut, hei es an skallom
an rubbout.*

DUTCH MERCHANT He says he told him no such matter; he's a knave
  and a rascal.   250

SIR OLIVER Why, how am I abused! Pray tell me one thing, What's
  Gullder-goose in Dutch?

DUTCH MERCHANT How? *Gullder-goose*? There's no such thing in
  Dutch; it may be an ass in English.

SIR OLIVER Hoyda! Then am I that ass in plain English; I am grossly   255
  cozened, most inconsiderately.
  Pray let my house receive you for one night
  That I may quit these rascals, I beseech you, sir.

DUTCH MERCHANT If that may stead you, sir, I'll not refuse you.
SIR OLIVER A thousand thanks and welcome.   260
　　On whom can fortune more spit out her foam,
　　Worked on abroad and played upon at home.
　　　　Exeunt

[2.1]

Enter Weatherwise, the gull, meeting [Pickadille and] two or three [servants] bringing out a table

WEATHERWISE So, set the table ready; the widow's i'th'next room looking upon my clock with the days and the months and the change of the moon. I'll fetch her in presently.

[Exit Weatherwise]

PICKADILLE She's not so mad to be fetched in with the moon, I warrant you. A man must go roundlier to work with a widow than to woo her with the hand of a dial, or stir up her blood with the striking part of a clock; I should ne'er stand° to show her such things in chamber.°

Exeunt [Servants.] Enter Weatherwise with the widow [Lady Goldenfleece], Sir Gilbert Lambston, Master Pepperton, [and] Master Overdone

WEATHERWISE Welcome, sweet widow, to a bachelor's house here; a single man I, but for two or three maids that I keep.

LADY GOLDENFLEECE Why, are you double with them° then?

WEATHERWISE An exceeding good mourning° wit. Women are wiser than ever they were since they wore doublets.° You must think, sweet widow, if a man keep maids they're under his subjection.°

LADY GOLDENFLEECE That's most true, sir.

WEATHERWISE They have no reason to have a lock, but the master must have a key° to't.

LADY GOLDENFLEECE To him, Sir Gilbert. He fights with me at a wrong weapon° now.

WEATHERWISE *[aside]* Nay, an Sir Gilbert strike, my weapon falls;°
I fear no thrust but his. Here are more shooters,°
But they have shot two arrows without heads;°
They cannot stick i'th'butt yet. Hold out, knight,°
And I'll cleave the black pin i'th'midst o'th'white.°

Exit [Weatherwise]

LADY GOLDENFLEECE Nay, and he led me into a closet, sir, where he showed me diet drinks for several months,° as scurvigrass for April, clarified whey for June, and the like.

SIR GILBERT Oh, madam, he is a most necessary property, an't be but to save our credit, ten pound in a banquet.

LADY GOLDENFLEECE Go! Y'are a wag, Sir Gilbert.

SIR GILBERT How many there be in the world of his fortunes, that
prick their own calves with briers to make an easy passage for
others, or like a toiling usurer sets his son a-horse-back in cloth-
of-gold breeches while he himself goes t'th'devil a-foot in a pair of
old strossers.   35
But shall I give a more familiar sign?
His are the sweetmeats, but the kisses mine.
  [*Kisses her*]

OVERDONE Excellent!—[*Aside*] A pox o'your fortune.

PEPPERTON [*taking Overdone aside*] Saucy courting has brought all
modest wooing clean out of fashion. You shall have few maids   40
nowadays got without rough handling; all the town's so used to't,
and most commonly too they're joined° before they're married,
because they'll be sure to be fast° enough.

OVERDONE Sir, since he strives t'oppose himself against us,
Let's so combine our friendships in our straits,   45
By all means graceful to assist each other.
For I protest it shall as much glad me
To see your happiness and his disgrace,
As if the wealth were mine, the love, the place.

PEPPERTON And with the like faith I reward your friendship.   50
I'll break the bawdy ranks of his discourse
And scatter his libidinous whispers straight.
  [*To Lady Goldenfleece*] Madam!

LADY GOLDENFLEECE   How cheer you, gentlemen?

SIR GILBERT [*aside*]   Pox on 'em.
They waked me out of a fine sleep; three minutes
Had fastened all the treasure in mine arms.   55

PEPPERTON You took no note of this conceit, it seems, madam.

LADY GOLDENFLEECE Twelve trenchers, upon every one a
  month.°
January, February, March, April—

PEPPERTON Ay, and their posies° under 'em.

LADY GOLDENFLEECE Pray what says May? She's the spring lady.   60

PEPPERTON 'Now gallant May in her array
Doth make the field pleasant and gay.'

OVERDONE 'This month of June use clarified whey,
Boiled with cold herbs and drink alway'.

LADY GOLDENFLEECE Drink't all away, he should say.   65

PEPPERTON 'Twere much better, indeed, and wholesomer for his
liver.

SIR GILBERT September's a good one here, madam.

LADY GOLDENFLEECE Oh, have you chose your month; let's hear't,
Sir Gilbert.   70

SIR GILBERT 'Now mayst thou physics safely take,
And bleed and bathe for thy health's sake.
Eat figs and grapes and spicery,
For to refresh thy members dry'.°

LADY GOLDENFLEECE Thus it is still when a man's simple meaning   75
lights among wantons. How many honest words have suffered
corruption since Chaucer's days? A virgin would speak those words
then that a very midwife would blush to hear now, if she have
but so much blood left to make up an ounce of grace. And who is
this long on, but such wags as you that use your words like your   80
wenches. You cannot let 'em pass honestly by you, but you must
still have a flirt at 'em.

PEPPERTON You have paid some of us home, madam.

Enter Weatherwise

WEATHERWISE [*aside*] If conceit will strike this stroke, have at the
widow's plumtree. I'll put 'em down all for a banquet.—Widow   85
and gentlemen, my friends and servants, I make you wait long here
for a bachelor's pittance.

LADY GOLDENFLEECE Oh, sir, y'are pleased to be modest.

WEATHERWISE No, by my troth, widow, you shall find it otherwise.

Strike music. Enter banquet, and six of his tenants with the
twelve signs, made like banqueting-stuff. Aries, Taurus, Gemini,
Cancer, Leo, Virgo, Libra, Scorpio, Sagittarius, Capricorn,
Aquarius, and Pisces

LADY GOLDENFLEECE What, the twelve signs?   90

WEATHERWISE These are the signs of my love, widow.

LADY GOLDENFLEECE Worse meat would have served us, sir. By my
faith,
I'm sorry you should be at such charges, sir,
To feast us a whole month together here.

WEATHERWISE Widow, thou'rt welcome a whole month and ever.   95

LADY GOLDENFLEECE And what be those, sir, that brought in the
banquet?

WEATHERWISE Those are my tenants; they stand for fasting days.°

SIR GILBERT Or the six weeks in Lent.

WEATHERWISE   Y'are i'th'right, Sir Gilbert.
Sweet widow, take your place at Aries here;
That's the head sign. A widow is the head°   100

229

Till she be married.

LADY GOLDENFLEECE What is she then?

WEATHERWISE   The middle.°

LADY GOLDENFLEECE 'Tis happy she's no worse.
       [*She sits*]

WEATHERWISE Taurus, Sir Gilbert Lambston, that's for you.
   They say you're a good town-bull.

SIR GILBERT   Oh, spare your friends, sir.
       [*Sir Gilbert sits*]

WEATHERWISE And Gemini for Master Pepperton.   105
   He had two boys at once by his last wife.

PEPPERTON I hear the widow find no fault with that, sir.
       [*Pepperton sits*]

WEATHERWISE Cancer the Crab for Master Overdone,
   For when a thing's past fifty it grows crooked.°
       [*Overdone sits*]

LADY GOLDENFLEECE Now for yourself, sir.

WEATHERWISE   Take no care for me, widow;   110
   I can be anywhere. Here's Leo,
   Heart and back; Virgo, guts and belly.
   I can go lower yet, and yet fare better,
   Since Sagittarius fits me the thighs;°
   I care not if I be about the thighs,   115
   I shall find meat enough.
       [*Weatherwise sits*]

LADY GOLDENFLEECE   But under pardon, sir.°
   Though you be Lord o'th'feast and the conceit both,
   Methinks it had been proper for the banquet
   To have had the signs all filled, and no-one idle.

WEATHERWISE I know it had, but whose fault's that, widow?   120
   You should have got you more suitors to have stopped the
   gaps.

LADY GOLDENFLEECE Nay, sure, they should get us, and not we
      them.
   There be your tenants, sir; we are not proud;
   You may bid them sit down.

WEATHERWISE   By th'mass, it's true too.   125
   Then sit down tenants once° with your hats on,° but spare the
   meat, I charge you, as you hope for new leases. I must make my
   signs draw out a month yet, with a bit every morning to breakfast
   and at full moon with a whole one;° that's restorative. Sit round,

sit round, and do not speak, sweet tenants. You may be bold   130
enough, so you eat but little.

    [*Tenants sit*]

How like you this now, widow?

LADY GOLDENFLEECE   It shows well, sir;
And like the good old hospitable fashion.

PICKADILLE [*aside*] How! Like a good old hospital! My mistress
makes an arrant gull on him.   135

LADY GOLDENFLEECE But yet methinks there wants clothes for the
feet.°

WEATHERWISE That part's uncovered yet. Push! No matter for the
feet.

LADY GOLDENFLEECE Yes, if the feet catch cold the head will feel   140
it.

WEATHERWISE Why, then, you may draw up your legs° and lie
rounder together.°

SIR GILBERT He's answered you well, madam.

WEATHERWISE An you draw up your legs too, widow, my tenant will   145
feel you there, for he's one of the calves.°

LADY GOLDENFLEECE Better and better, sir; your wit fattens as
he° feeds.

PICKADILLE [*aside*] She's took the calf from his tenant and put it
upon his ground° now.   150

    [*Enter Servant*]

WEATHERWISE How now, my lady's man, what's the news, sir?

SERVANT Madam, there's a young gentleman below;
H'as earnest business to your ladyship.

WEATHERWISE Another suitor, I hold my life, widow.

LADY GOLDENFLEECE What is he, sir?

SERVANT   He seems a gentleman;   155
That's the least of him, and yet more I know not.

LADY GOLDENFLEECE Under the leave o'th'master of the house
here,
I would he were admitted.

WEATHERWISE With all my heart, widow; I fear him not.
Come cut and long tail.

    [*Exit Servant*]

SIR GILBERT [*aside*]   I have the least fear°   160
And the most firmness; nothing can shake me.

WEATHERWISE If he be a gentleman, he's welcome; there's a sign
does nothing, and that's fit for a gentleman.° The feet will be kept

warm enough now for you, widow; for if he be a right gentleman, he has his stockings warmed and he wears socks beside,° partly for   165
warmth, partly for cleanliness; and if he observe Fridays,° too, he comes excellent well. Pisces will be a fine fish dinner for him.

LADY GOLDENFLEECE Why then you mean, sir, he shall sit as he comes?°

WEATHERWISE Ay, an he were a lord he shall not sit above my   170
tenants. I'll not have two lords to them, so I may go look my rent in another man's breeches. I was not brought up to be so unmannerly.

    Enter Mistress Low-water [as a gallant gentleman, her husband
    like a serving-man after her]

MISTRESS LOW-WATER [*aside*] I have picked out a bold time.—
Much good do you, gentlemen.   175

WEATHERWISE Y'are welcome as I may say, sir.

MISTRESS LOW-WATER Pardon my rudeness, madam.

LADY GOLDENFLEECE   No such fault, sir;
You're too severe to yourself; our judgement quits you.
Please you to do as we do.

MISTRESS LOW-WATER   Thanks, good madam.

LADY GOLDENFLEECE Make room, gentlemen.

WEATHERWISE   Sit still, tenants.   180
I'll call in all your old leases and rack you else.°

ALL TENANTS Oh, sweet landlord!

MISTRESS LOW-WATER Take my cloak, sirrah.
    [*Gives cloak to Low-water*]
                      If any be disturbed,
I'll not sit, gentlemen. I see my place.

WEATHERWISE [*aside*] A proper woman turned gallant!° If the widow   185
refuse me, I care not if I be a suitor to him. I have known those who have been as mad, and given half their living for a male companion.

MISTRESS LOW-WATER How, Pisces! Is that mine? 'Tis a conceited°
banquet.   190
    [*Sits*]

WEATHERWISE If you love any fish, pray fall to, sir. If you had come sooner you might have happened among some of the flesh signs, but now they're all taken up; Virgo had been a good dish for you, had not one of my tenants been somewhat busy° with her.

MISTRESS LOW-WATER Pray let him keep her, sir; give me meat   195
fresh,

I'd rather have whole fish than broken flesh.°

SIR GILBERT What say you to a bit of Taurus?

MISTRESS LOW-WATER No, I thank you, sir;
The bull's too rank for me.

SIR GILBERT   How, sir?

MISTRESS LOW-WATER   Too rank, sir.   200

SIR GILBERT Fie, I shall strike you dumb like all your fellows.°

MISTRESS LOW-WATER What, with your heels or horns?

SIR GILBERT   Perhaps with both.

MISTRESS LOW-WATER It must be at dead low water,°
When I'm dead then.

LOW-WATER [aside] 'Tis brave, Kate,° and nobly spoken of thee.   205

WEATHERWISE This quarrel must be drowned.—Pickadille, my
lady's fool!

PICKADILLE You're your own man,° sir.

WEATHERWISE Prithee step in to° one o'th'maids.

PICKADILLE That I will, sir, and thank you too.   210

WEATHERWISE Nay, hark you, sir; call for my sun-cup presently; I'd
forgot it.

PICKADILLE How, your sun-cup?—[Aside] Some cup I warrant that
he stole out o'th'Sun Tavern.

          [Exit Pickadille]

LADY GOLDENFLEECE [aside] The more I look on him, the more I
thirst for't.°   215
Methinks his beauty does so far transcend,
Turns the signs back, makes that the upper end.°

WEATHERWISE How cheer you, widow? Gentlemen, how cheer
you?
Fair weather in all quarters.
The sun will peep anon; I have sent one for him.°   220
In the meantime I'll tell you a tale of these.°
This Libra here, that keeps the scales so even,
Was i'th'old time an honest chandler's widow,
And had one daughter which was called Virgo,
Which now my hungry tenant has deflowered.   225
This Virgo, passing for a maid, was sued to°
By Sagittarius there, a gallant shooter,
And Aries, his head rival; but her old crabbed°
Uncle Cancer here, dwelling in Crooked Lane,
Still crossed the marriage, minding to bestow her   230
Upon one Scorpio, a rich usurer.

The girl, loathing that match, fell into folly
With one Taurus, a gentleman in Townbull Street,°
By whom she had two twins, those Gemini there,
Of which two brats she was brought abed in Leo,   235
At the Red Lion about Tower Hill.
Being in this distress, one Capricorn,
An honest citizen, pitied her case and married her
To Aquarius, an old water-bearer,
And Pisces was her living ever after;   240
At Standard she sold fish, where he drew water.°

ALL It shall be yours,° sir.

LADY GOLDENFLEECE Meat and mirth too. Y'are lavish!
Your purse and tongue has been at cost today, sir.

SIR GILBERT You may challenge all comers at these twelve wea- 245
pons,° I warrant you.

    Enter clown [Pickadille, carrying the sun-cup, wearing no doublet,
    but wearing a veil over his face]

PICKADILLE Your sun-cup call you it! 'Tis a simple voyage that I
have made here. I have left my doublet within for fear I should
sweat through my jerkin, and thrown a cypress over my face for
fear of sun-burning.   250

WEATHERWISE How now, who's this? Why, sirrah!

PICKADILLE Can you endure it, mistress?

LADY GOLDENFLEECE Endure what, fool?

WEATHERWISE Fill the cup, coxcomb.

PICKADILLE Nay, an't be no hotter, I'll go put on my doublet again. 255
    Exit [Pickadille]

WEATHERWISE What a whoreson sot is this! [*To Low-water*] Prithee
fill the cup, fellow, and give't the widow.

MISTRESS LOW-WATER Sirrah, how stand you? Bestow your service
there upon her ladyship.

    [*Low-water gives Lady Goldenfleece the cup*]

LADY GOLDENFLEECE What's here? A sun?

WEATHERWISE   It does betoken, madam,   260
A cheerful day to somebody.

LADY GOLDENFLEECE [*aside*] It rises
Full in the face of yon fair sign, and yet°
By course he is the last must feel the heat.°
—Here, gentlemen, to you all,
For you know the sun must go through the twelve signs.   265
    [*Drinks*]

WEATHERWISE Most wittily, widow; you jump with my conceit
   right;
  There's not a hair between us.
LADY GOLDENFLEECE   Give it Sir Gilbert.°
SIR GILBERT I am the next through whom the golden flame
  Shines, when 'tis spent in thy celestial ram.
  The poor feet there must wait and cool a while.°   270
    [*Drinks*]
MISTRESS LOW-WATER We have our time, sir; joy and we shall
  meet;
  I have known the proud neck lie between the feet.°
WEATHERWISE So round it goes.
    [*Each drinks in turn.*] *Enter clown* [*Pickadille*]
PICKADILLE I like this drinking world well.
WEATHERWISE So fill't him° again.   275
PEPPERTON Fill't me? Why, I drunk last, sir.
WEATHERWISE I know you did, but Gemini must drink twice,
  Unless you mean that one of them shall be choked.
LADY GOLDENFLEECE [*aside*] Fly from my heart all variable
   thoughts.
  She that's enticed by every pleasing object   280
  Shall find small pleasure and as little rest.
  This knave hath loved me long; he's best and worthiest,°
  I cannot but in honour see him requited.—
  Sir Gilbert Lambston!
MISTRESS LOW-WATER How! Pardon me, sweet lady,
  That with a bold tongue I strike by your words;   285
  Sir Gilbert Lambston?
SIR GILBERT   Yes, sir, that's my name.
MISTRESS LOW-WATER There should be a rank villain of that name;
  Came you out of that house?
SIR GILBERT   How, sir slave!
MISTRESS LOW-WATER Fall to your bull; leave roaring till anon.
WEATHERWISE Yet again! An you love me, gentlemen, let's have no 290
  roaring here. If I had thought that, I'd have sent my bull to the
  Bear Garden.
PEPPERTON Why, so you should have wanted one of your signs.
WEATHERWISE But I may chance want two now, an they fall together
  by the ears.°   295
LADY GOLDENFLEECE What's the strange fire that works in these
   two creatures?

Cold signs both, yet more hot than all their fellows.°

WEATHERWISE Ho, Sol in Pisces! The Sun's in New Fish Street.
Here's an end of this course.

PICKADILLE Madam, I am bold to remember your worship for a   300
year's wages and a livery cloak.

LADY GOLDENFLEECE How, will you shame me? Had you not both
last week, fool?

PICKADILLE Ay, but there's another year past since that.

LADY GOLDENFLEECE Would all your wit could make that good,   305
sir.

PICKADILLE I am sure the sun has run through all the twelve signs
since, and that's a year; these° gentlemen can witness.

WEATHERWISE The fool will live,° madam.

PICKADILLE [aside] Ay, as long as your eyes are open,° I warrant   310
him.

MISTRESS LOW-WATER Sirrah!

LOW-WATER Does your worship call?

MISTRESS LOW-WATER Commend my love and service to the
widow;
Desire her ladyship to taste that morsel.   315
    [Gives him the letter]

LOW-WATER [aside] This is the bit I watched for all this while,
But it comes duly.
    [He gives the letter to Lady Goldenfleece]

SIR GILBERT And wherein has this name of mine offended,
That y'are so liberal of your infamous titles,
I but a stranger to thee? It must be known, sir,   320
Ere we two part.

MISTRESS LOW-WATER Marry, and reason, good sir.

LADY GOLDENFLEECE Oh, strike me cold!—This should be your
hand,° Sir Gilbert?

SIR GILBERT Why, make you question of that, madam? 'Tis one of   325
the letters I sent you.

LADY GOLDENFLEECE Much good do you, gentlemen.
    [Rising]

ALL How now? What's the matter?
    [All rise]

WEATHERWISE [to Pickadille] Look to the widow; she paints white;°
some aqua coelistis for my lady. Run, villain!   330

PICKADILLE Aqua Solister! Can nobody help her case but a lawyer,
and so many suitors here?

LADY GOLDENFLEECE Oh, treachery unmatched, unheard of!

SIR GILBERT How do you, madam?

LADY GOLDENFLEECE Oh, impudence as foul! Does my disease   335
    Ask how I do? Can it torment my heart
    And look with a fresh colour in my face?°

SIR GILBERT What's this! What's this!

WEATHERWISE I am sorry for this qualm, widow.

LADY GOLDENFLEECE He that would know a villain when he meets
    him,   340
    Let him ne'er go to a conjurer; here's a glass°
    Will show him without money and far truer.
    Preserver of my state, pray tell me, sir,
    That I may pay you all my thanks together,
    What blessed hap brought that letter to your hand   345
    To free me, so fast locked in mine enemy's power?°

MISTRESS LOW-WATER I will resolve you, madam. I have
    a kinsman
    Somewhat infected with that wanton pity
    Which men bestow on the distress of women,
    Especially if they be fair and poor;   350
    With such hot charity, which indeed is lust,
    He sought t'entice, as his repentance told me,
    Her whom you call your enemy, the wife
    To a poor gentleman, one Low-water.

LADY GOLDENFLEECE Right, right, the same.   355

LOW-WATER [aside] Had it been right,° 't'ad now been.

MISTRESS LOW-WATER And, according to the common rate of
    sinners,
    Offered large maintenance, which with her seemed nothing;
    For if she would consent, she told him roundly,
    There was a knight had bid more at one minute   360
    Than all his wealth could compass, and, withal,°
    Plucked out that letter as it were in scorn;
    Which, by good fortune, he put up in jest
    With promise that the writ should be returnable
    The next hour of his meeting. But, sweet madam,   365
    Out of my love and zeal, I did so practice
    The part upon him of an urgent wooer
    That neither he nor that returned more to her.

SIR GILBERT [aside] Plague o'that kinsman!

WEATHERWISE   Here's a gallant rascal!

LADY GOLDENFLEECE Sir, you have appeared so noble in this
    action,   370
  So full of worth and goodness, that my thanks
  Will rather shame the bounty of my mind
  Than do it honour.—Oh, thou treacherous villain!
  Does thy faith bear such fruit?
  Are these the blossoms of a hundred oaths   375
  Shot from thy bosom? Was thy love so spiteful
  It could not be content to mock my heart,
  Which is in love a misery too much,
  But must extend so far to the quick ruin
  Of what was painfully got, carefully left me;   380
  And, 'mongst a world of yielding, needy women,
  Choose no one to make merry with my sorrows
  And spend my wealth on, in adulterous surfeits,
  But my most mortal enemy? Oh despiteful!
  Is this thy practice? Follow it, 'twill advance thee.   385
  Go, beguile on. Have I so happily found
  What many a widow has with sorrow tasted,
  Even when my lip touched the contracting cup,°
  Even then to see the spider? 'Twas miraculous!°
  Crawl with thy poisons hence, and for thy sake   390
  I'll never covet titles and more riches,
  To fall into a gulf of hate and laughter.
  I'll marry love hereafter; I've enough,
  And wanting that, I have nothing. There's thy way.°
OVERDONE Do you hear, sir? You must walk.   395
PEPPERTON Hear't! Thrust him down stairs!
WEATHERWISE Out of my house, you treacherous, lecherous rascal!
SIR GILBERT All curses scatter you.
    [Exit Sir Gilbert]
WEATHERWISE Life, do you thunder here! If you had stayed a little
  longer, I'd have ripped out some of my bull out of your belly again.   400
PEPPERTON 'Twas a most noble discovery; we must love you forever
  for't.
LADY GOLDENFLEECE [to Weatherwise] Sir, for your banquet and
    your mirth, we thank you;
  You, gentlemen, for your kind company;
  [to Mistress Low-water] But, you, for all my merry days to come,   405
  Or this had been the last else.
MISTRESS LOW-WATER   Love and fortune

Had more care of your safety, peace, and state, madam.
WEATHERWISE [*aside*] Now, will I thrust in for't.
PEPPERTON [*aside*] I'm for myself now.
OVERDONE [*aside*] What's fifty years? 'Tis man's best time and
    season.   410
    Now the knight's gone, the widow will hear reason.
LOW-WATER [*aside*] Now, now! The suitors flatter; hold on, Kate;
    The hen may pick the meat, while the cocks prate.
       Exeunt

[2.2]

Enter Master Sandfield, Philip, Sir Oliver Twilight's son,
with Savourwit

PHILIP If thou talk'st longer, I shall turn to marble,
    And death will stop my hearing.
SANDFIELD   Horrible fortune!
SAVOURWIT Nay, sir, our building is so far defaced,
    There is no stuff left to raise up a hope.
PHILIP Oh, with more patience could my flesh endure   5
    A score of wounds and all their several searchings
    Than this that thou hast told me.
SAVOURWIT   Would that Flemish ram
    Had ne'er come near our house. There's no going home
    As long as he has a nest there and his young one,
    A little Flanders' egg new fledged; they gape   10
    For pork, and I shall be made meat for 'em.
PHILIP 'Tis not the bare news of my mother's life°
    —May she live long and happy—that afflicts me
    With half the violence that the latter draws,
    Though in that news I have my share of grief,   15
    As I had share of sin and a foul neglect;
    It is my love's betraying; that's the sting
    That strikes through flesh and spirit; and sense nor wit
    From thee, in whom I ne'er saw ebb till now,°
    Nor comforts from a faithful friend can ease me.   20
    I'll try the goodness of a third companion,

What he'll do for me.
　　　[*Draws his sword*]
SANDFIELD　　　　　　　Hold! Why, friend?°
SAVOURWIT Why, master, is this all your kindness, sir? Offer to steal
　　into another country and ne'er take your leave on's? Troth, I take
　　it unkindly at your hands,° sir; but I'll put it up° for once.　　　25
　　　[*Puts up the sword*]
　　Faith, there was no conscience in this, sir: leave me here to endure
　　all weathers, whilst you make your soul dance like a juggler's egg
　　upon the point of a rapier! By my troth, sir, y'are too blame in't;
　　you might have given us an inkling of your journey; perhaps others
　　would as fain have gone as you.　　　30
PHILIP Burns this clay lamp of miserable life,
　　When joy, the oil that feeds it, is dried up?
　　　Enter his mother [Lady Twilight] new landed, with a gentleman
　　　[Master Beveril], a scholar, and others.
LADY TWILIGHT He has removed his house.
BEVERIL　　　　　　　　　　　So it seems, madam.
LADY TWILIGHT I'll ask that gentleman.—Pray can you tell me, sir,
　　Which is Sir Oliver Twilight's?　　　35
PHILIP Few can better, gentlewoman.
　　It is the next fair house your eye can fix on.
LADY TWILIGHT I thank you, sir.—Go on.
　　　[*Exeunt servants*]
　　He had a son about some ten years since.
PHILIP That son still lives.
LADY TWILIGHT　　　　I pray how does he, sir?　　　40
PHILIP [*aside*] Faith, much about my health, that's never worse.—
　　If you have any business to him, gentlewoman,
　　I can cut short your journey to the house.
　　I'm all that ever was of the same kind.
LADY TWILIGHT Oh, my sweet son! Never fell fresher joy　　　45
　　Upon the heart of mother.—This is he, sir!
BEVERIL My seven-years' travel has even worn him out
　　Of my remembrance.
SAVOURWIT [*aside*]　　Oh, this gear's worse and worse!
PHILIP I am so wonder-struck at your blessed presence,
　　That through amazed joy I neglect my duty.　　　50
　　　[*Kneels*]
LADY TWILIGHT Rise, and a thousand blessings spring up with
　　thee!

SAVOURWIT [*aside*] I would we had but one in the mean time;
    Let the rest grow at leisure.
LADY TWILIGHT But know you not this gentleman yet, son?
PHILIP I take it's Master Beveril.
BEVERIL   My name's Beveril, sir.   55
PHILIP Right welcome to my bosom!
       [*Embraces Beveril*]
LADY TWILIGHT   You'd not think, son,
    How much I am beholding to this gentleman,
    As far as freedom; he laid out the ransom,
    Finding me so distressed.
PHILIP   'Twas worthily done, sir,
    And I shall ever rest your servant for't.   60
BEVERIL You quite forget your worth. 'Twas my good hap, sir,
    To return home that way after some travels;
    Where finding your good mother so distressed,
    I could not but in pity see her released.
PHILIP It was a noble charity, sir; heaven quit you!   65
SAVOURWIT [*aside*] It comes at last.
BEVERIL   I left a sister here,
    New married when I last took leave of England.
PHILIP Oh, Mistress Low-water!
BEVERIL   Pray, sir, how does she?
PHILIP So little comfort I can give you, sir,
    That I would fain excuse my self for silence.   70
BEVERIL Why, what's the worst, sir?
PHILIP   Wrongs has made her poor.
BEVERIL You strike my heart! Alas good gentlewoman!
PHILIP Here's a gentleman; you know him; Master Sandfield.
BEVERIL I crave pardon, sir.
PHILIP He can resolve you from her kinswoman.°   75
SANDFIELD Welcome to England, madam.
LADY TWILIGHT Thanks, good sir.
     [*They speak apart*]
PHILIP [*to Savourwit*] Now there's no way to 'scape; I'm compassed
    round;
    My shame is like a prisoner set with halberds.
SAVOURWIT Pish, master, master! 'Tis young flood again,°   80
    And you can take your time now; away quick!
PHILIP Push, thou'st a swimming head.
SAVOURWIT   Will you but hear me?

When did you lose your tide when I set forth with you?

PHILIP That's true.

SAVOURWIT Regard me then; though you have no feeling,   85
I would not hang by th'thumbs with a good will.°

PHILIP I hang by th'heart, sir, and would fain have ease.

SAVOURWIT Then this or none. Fly to your mother's pity,
For that's the court must help you; y'are quite gone
At common law, no counsellor can hear you;   90
Confess your follies and ask pardon for 'em.
Tell her the state of all things; stand not nicely;
The meat's too hard to be minced now;
She breeds young bones by this time.
Deal plainly; heaven will bless thee; turn out all   95
And shake your pockets after it. Beg, weep,
Kneel, anything; 'twill break no bones, man.
Let her not rest, take breathing time, nor leave thee,
Till thou hast got her help.

PHILIP   Lad, I conceive thee.

SAVOURWIT About it then; it requires haste; do't well;   100
There's but a short street between us and hell.

BEVERIL Ah, my poor sister!

LADY TWILIGHT   'Las, good gentlewoman!
My heart even weeps for her.—Ay, son, we'll go now.
    [*Philip*] *shogs his mother* [*and takes her to one side*]

PHILIP May I crave one word, madam?

LADY TWILIGHT   With me, son?
The more, the better welcome.

SAVOURWIT [*aside*]   Now, now luck!   105
I pray not often; the last prayer I made
Was nine-year-old last Bartholomew-tide; 'twould have been°
A jolly chopper, an 't'ad lived till this time.

LADY TWILIGHT Why do your words start back? Are they afraid
Of her that ever loved them?

PHILIP   I have a suit to you, madam.   110

LADY TWILIGHT You have told me that already; pray what is't?
If't be so great, my present state refuse it,
I shall be abler, then command and use it;
Whate'er't be, let me have warning to provide for't.

PHILIP [*kneeling*] Provide forgiveness then, for that's the want   115
My conscience feels. Oh, my wild youth has led me
Into unnatural wrongs against your freedom once.

    I spent the ransom which my father sent,
    To set my pleasures free, while you lay captive.
SAVOURWIT [*aside*] He does it finely, faith.
LADY TWILIGHT   And is this all now?   120
    You use me like a stranger; pray stand up.
PHILIP Rather fall flat; I shall deserve yet worse.
LADY TWILIGHT [*raising Philip*] Whate'er your faults are, esteem me
    still like a friend,°
    Or else you wrong me more in asking pardon
    Than when you did the wrong you asked it for,   125
    And since you have prepared me to forgive you,
    Pray let me know for what; the first fault's nothing.
SAVOURWIT [*aside*] 'Tis a sweet lady, every inch of her.
PHILIP Here comes the wrong then that drives home the rest.
    I saw a face at Antwerp that quite drew me   130
    From conscience and obedience; in that fray
    I lost my heart; I must needs lose my way;
    There went the ransom to redeem my mind;
    'Stead of the money I brought over her;
    And to cast mists before my father's eyes,   135
    Told him it was my sister, lost so long,
    And that yourself was dead. You see the wrong?
LADY TWILIGHT This is but youthful still. Oh, that word 'sister'
    Afflicts me when I think on't. I forgive thee
    As freely as thou didst it. For, alas,   140
    This may be called good dealing, to some parts
    That love and youth plays daily among sons.°
SAVOURWIT [*aside*] She helps our knavery well; that's one good
    comfort.
PHILIP But such is the hard plight my state lives in,
    That 'twixt forgiveness, I must sin again,   145
    And seek my help where I bestowed my wrongs.
    Oh, mother, pity once, though against reason!
    'Cause I can merit none; though my wrongs grieve you,
    Yet let it be your glory to relieve me.
LADY TWILIGHT Wherein have I given cause yet of mistrust,   150
    That you should doubt my succour and my love?
    Show me but in what kind I may bestow 'em.
PHILIP There came a Dutchman with report this day
    That you were living.
LADY TWILIGHT   Came he so lately?

PHILIP   Yes, madam.
   Which news so struck my father on the sudden   155
   That he grows jealous of my faith in both.°
   These five hours have I kept me from his sight
   And wished myself eternally so hid;
   And, surely, had not your blessed presence quickened
   The flame of life in me, all had gone out.   160
   Now to confirm me to his trust again,
   And settle much aright in his opinion,
   Say but she is my sister, and all's well.
LADY TWILIGHT You ask devotion like a bashful beggar
   That pure need urges, and not lazy impudence;   165
   And to express how glad I am to pity you,
   My bounty shall flow over your demand.
   I will not only with a constant breath
   Approve that, but excuse thee for my death.°
SAVOURWIT [aside] Why, here's a woman made as a man would wish   170
   to have her.
PHILIP Oh, I am placed higher in happiness
   Than whence I fell before!
SAVOURWIT [aside] We're brave fellows once again, and we can keep
   our own.   175
   Now, hoffte toffte, our pipes play as loftily!°
BEVERIL My sister fled!
SANDFIELD Both fled; that's the news now. Want must obey;
   Oppressions came so thick, they could not stay.
BEVERIL Mean are my fortunes, yet had I been nigh   180
   Distress nor wrong should have made virtue fly.
LADY TWILIGHT Spoke like a brother worthy such a sister.
BEVERIL Grief's like a new wound; heat beguiles the sense,
   For I shall feel this smart more three days hence.
   Come, madam, sorrow's rude and forgets manners.   185
        [Exeunt all but Savourwit]
SAVOURWIT Our knavery is for all the world like a shifting° bank-
   rupt; it breaks° in one place and sets up in another; he tries all
   trades from a goldsmith to a tobacco seller; we try all shifts from
   an outlaw to a flatterer; he cozens the husband and compounds
   with the widow; we cozen my master and compound with my   190
   mistress; only here I turn o'th'right hand from him; he is known
   to live like a rascal, when I am thought to live like a gentleman.
        Exit

[2.3]

Enter Kate [Mistress Low-water] with her man-husband
[Low-water, both disguised as before]

MISTRESS LOW-WATER I have sent in one to th'widow.

LOW-WATER Well said,° Kate,
Thou ply'st thy business close. The coast is clear yet.

MISTRESS LOW-WATER Let me but have warning,
I shall make pretty shift with them.   5

LOW-WATER That thou shalt, wench.
        Exit [Low-water. Enter Servant]

SERVANT My lady, sir, commends her kindly to you,
And for the third part of an hour, sir,
Desires your patience.
Two or three of her tenants out of Kent   10
Will hold her so long busied.

MISTRESS LOW-WATER   Thank you, sir.
'Tis fit I should attend her time and leisure.
        [Exit Servant]
Those were my tenants once, but what relief
Is there in what hath been or what I was?
'Tis now that makes the man. A last year's feast°   15
Yields little comfort for the present humour;
He starves that feeds his hopes with what is past.
        [Enter Low-water]
How now?

LOW-WATER They're come, newly alighted.

MISTRESS LOW-WATER Peace, peace! I'll have a trick for 'em; look   20
you second me well now.

LOW-WATER I warrant thee.

MISTRESS LOW-WATER I must seem very imperious, I can tell you.
Therefore, if I should chance to use you roughly, pray forgive me
beforehand.   25

LOW-WATER With all my heart, Kate.

MISTRESS LOW-WATER You must look for no obedience in these
clothes;° that lies in the pocket of my gown.°

LOW-WATER Well, well, I will not then.

MISTRESS LOW-WATER I hear 'em coming; step back a little, sir.   30

Enter Master Weatherwise, Master Pepperton, and Master Overdone, suitors

Where be those fellows? Who looks out there? Is there ne'er a knave i'th'house to take those gentlemen's horses? Where wait you today? How stand you like a dreaming goose in a corner? The gentlemen's horses, forsooth!

LOW-WATER Yes, an't like your worship.   35

[*Exit Low-water*]

PEPPERTON What's here? A strange alteration!

WEATHERWISE A new lord? Would I were upon my mare's back again then.

MISTRESS LOW-WATER Pray, gentlemen, pardon the rudeness of these grooms;

I hope they will be brought to better fashion.   40

In the meantime y'are welcome, gentlemen.

ALL We thank you, sir.

WEATHERWISE [*aside*] Life, here's quick work! [*Taking out almanac*] I'll hold my life he's struck the widow i'th'right planet. *Venus in cauda!*° I thought 'twas a lecherous planet that goes to't with° a   45
caudle.

[*Enter Low-water*]

MISTRESS LOW-WATER How now, sir?

LOW-WATER The gentlemen's horses are set up,° sir.

PEPPERTON No, no, no, we'll away!

WEATHERWISE We'll away.   50

MISTRESS LOW-WATER How! By my faith, but you shall not yet, by your leave! Where's Bess? Call your mistress, sir, to welcome these kind gentlemen, my friends.

[*Exit Low-water*]

PEPPERTON How! Bess?

OVERDONE Peg?°   55

WEATHERWISE Plain Bess!° I know how the world goes then; he has been a-bed with Bess i'faith; there's no trust to these widows; a young horsing° gentleman carries 'em away clear.

[*Enter Low-water*]

MISTRESS LOW-WATER Now where's your mistress, sir; how chance she comes not?   60

LOW-WATER Sir, she requests you to excuse her for a while; she's busy with a milliner about gloves.

MISTRESS LOW-WATER Gloves?

WEATHERWISE Hoyda! Gloves,° too!

MISTRESS LOW-WATER Could she find no other time to choose gloves 65
but now when my friends are here?

PEPPERTON No, sir, 'tis no matter; we thank you for your good will,
sir; to say truth, we have no business with her at all at this time
i'faith, sir.

MISTRESS LOW-WATER Oh, that's another matter: yet stay, stay, 70
gentlemen, and taste a cup of wine ere you go.

OVERDONE No, thank you, sir.

MISTRESS LOW-WATER Master Pepperton, Master Weatherwise,
will you, sir?

WEATHERWISE I'll see the wine in a drunkard's shoes first, and 75
drink't after he has brewed it.° But let her go; she's fitted i'faith.
[Aside] A proud surly sir here, he domineers already; one that will
shake her bones, and go to dice with her money, or I have no skill
in a calendar. Life! He that can be so saucy to call her Bess already
will call her prating quean a month hence. 80

     Exeunt [*suitors*]

LOW-WATER They have given thee all the slip.

MISTRESS LOW-WATER   So, a fair riddance.
There's three rubs gone; I've a clear way to th'mistress.°

LOW-WATER You'd need have a clear way, because y'are a bad pricker.°

MISTRESS LOW-WATER Yet if my bowl take bank, I shall go nigh
To make myself a saver;° 85
Here's alley room enough; I'll try my fortune.°
I am to begin the world like a younger brother;°
I know that a bold face and a good spirit
Is all the jointure he can make a widow.°
And't shall go hard, but I'll be as rich as he, 90
Or at least seem so, and that's wealth enough;
For nothing kills a widow's heart so much
As a faint bashful wooer; though he have thousands,
And come with a poor water-gruel spirit
And a fish-market face, he shall ne'er speed. 95
I would not have himself left a poor widower.°

LOW-WATER Faith, I'm glad I'm alive to commend thee, Kate.
I shall be sure now to see my commendations delivered.

MISTRESS LOW-WATER I'll put her to't i'faith.

LOW-WATER   But soft ye, Kate.
How an she should accept of your bold kindness? 100

MISTRESS LOW-WATER A chief point to be thought on, by my faith.
Marry, therefore, sir, be you sure to step in,

For fear I should shame myself and spoil all.

LOW-WATER Well, I'll save your credit then for once,
But look you come there no more.   105

MISTRESS LOW-WATER Away, I hear her coming.

LOW-WATER   I am vanished.

Exit [Low-water.] Enter Widow [Lady Goldenfleece]

MISTRESS LOW-WATER How does my life, my soul, my dear sweet
madam?

LADY GOLDENFLEECE I have wronged your patience; made you
stand too long here.   110

MISTRESS LOW-WATER There's no such thing i'faith, madam; y'are
pleased to say so.

LADY GOLDENFLEECE Yes, I confess I was too slow, sir.

MISTRESS LOW-WATER Why, you shall make me amends for that
then with a quickness° in your bed.   115

LADY GOLDENFLEECE That were a speedy mends, sir.

MISTRESS LOW-WATER Why, then you are out of my debt; I'll cross
the book° and turn over a new leaf° with you.

LADY GOLDENFLEECE So, with paying a small debt I may chance
run into a greater.°   120

MISTRESS LOW-WATER My faith, your credit will be the better then.
There's many a brave gallant would be glad of such fortune and
pay use for't.

LADY GOLDENFLEECE Some of them have nothing else to do; they
would be idle, an 'twere not for interest.°   125

MISTRESS LOW-WATER I promise you, widow, were I a setter-up,°
such is my opinion of your payment,° I durst trust you with all
the ware° in my shop.

LADY GOLDENFLEECE I thank you for your good will;° I can have
no more.   130

MISTRESS LOW-WATER [*aside*] Not of me, i'faith, nor that neither,
an you know all.—Come make but short service,° widow, a kiss
and to bed, I'm very hungry i'faith, wench.

LADY GOLDENFLEECE What are you, sir?

MISTRESS LOW-WATER Oh, a younger brother has an excellent   135
stomach,° madam, worth a hundred of your sons and heirs° that
stay their wedding stomachs° with a hot bit° of a common
mistress,° and then come to a widow's bed like a flash of
lightning.° Y'are sure of the first of me,° not of the five hundredth
of them. I never took physic yet in my life; you shall have the   140
doctor continually with them, or some bottle for his deputy; out

flies your moneys for restoratives and strengthenings; in me 'tis saved in your purse and found in your children; they'll get° peevish pothecaries' stuff, you may weigh 'em by th'ounces; I, boys of war, brave commanders, that shall bear a breadth in their shoulders and a weight in their hips, and run over a whole country with a pound o'beef and a biscuit in their belly. Ho, widow, my kisses are virgins, my embraces perfect, my strength solid, my love constant, my heat comfortable; but to come to the point, inutter-able.° 150

LADY GOLDENFLEECE But soft ye, soft ye; because you stand so strictly
Upon your purity, I'll put you to't, sir.
Will you swear here you never yet knew woman?°

MISTRESS LOW-WATER Never, as man e'er knew her, by this light, widow.

LADY GOLDENFLEECE What, what, sir?—[*Aside*] 'Shrew my heart, he moves me much. 155

MISTRESS LOW-WATER Nay, since you love to bring a man on's knees,
I take into the same oath thus much more,
That y'are the first widow, or maid, or wife,
That ever I in suit of love did court
Or honestly did woo. How say you to that, widow? 160

LADY GOLDENFLEECE Marry, I say, sir, you had a good portion° of chastity left you, though ill fortune run away with the rest.

MISTRESS LOW-WATER That I kept for thee, widow; she's of fortune, and all her strait-bodied daughters;° thou shalt have't, widow.
    [*Kisses her*]

LADY GOLDENFLEECE Push, what do you mean? 165

MISTRESS LOW-WATER I cannot bestow't better.

LADY GOLDENFLEECE I'll call my servants.

MISTRESS LOW-WATER By my troth, you shall not, madam.
    Enter Master Low-water

LOW-WATER Does your worship call, sir?

MISTRESS LOW-WATER Ha, pox! Are you peeping? 170
    Throws somewhat at him [*who exits*]
    [*Aside*] He came in a good time, I thank him for't.

LADY GOLDENFLEECE What do you think of me? You're very forward, sir.

MISTRESS LOW-WATER Extremity of love.

LADY GOLDENFLEECE   You say y'are ignorant,

It should not seem so surely by your play;
For aught I see you may make one yourself:°   175
You need not hold the cards to any gamester.°
MISTRESS LOW-WATER That love should teach men ways to wrong
    itself!
LADY GOLDENFLEECE Are these the first fruits of your boldness, sir?
    If all take after these, you may boast on 'em.
    There comes few such to market among women;   180
    Time you were taken down, sir.—Within, there!°
MISTRESS LOW-WATER [aside] I've lost my way again.
    There's but two paths that leads to widows' beds,
    That's wealth or forwardness, and I've took the wrong one.
        Enter Servant, with the suitors [Weatherwise, Pepperton, and
        Overdone]
SERVANT He marry my lady? Why, there's no such thought yet.   185
    [*Exit Servant*]
MISTRESS LOW-WATER [aside] Oh, here they all are again, too.
LADY GOLDENFLEECE Are you come, gentlemen? I wish no better
    men.
WEATHERWISE Oh, the moon's changed now!
LADY GOLDENFLEECE See you that gentleman yonder?
PEPPERTON Yes, sweet madam.   190
LADY GOLDENFLEECE Then pray be witness all of you; with this kiss
        [*Kisses Mistress Low-water*]
    I choose him for my husband.
ALL SUITORS A pox on't!
LADY GOLDENFLEECE And with this parted gold, that two hearts
    join.°
        [*Breaks a piece of gold and gives half to Mistress Low-water*]
MISTRESS LOW-WATER Never with chaster love than this of mine.   195
LADY GOLDENFLEECE And those that have the hearts to come to
    th'wedding,
    They shall be welcome for their former loves.
        Exit [Lady Goldenfleece]
PEPPERTON No, I thank you; y'ave choked me already.
WEATHERWISE I never suspected mine almanac 'till now. I believe
    he plays cogging John with me; I bought it at his shop; it may learn 200
    the more knavery by that.
MISTRESS LOW-WATER Now indeed, gentlemen, I can bid you
    welcome;
    Before 'twas but a flourish.

WEATHERWISE Nay, so my almanac told me there should be an
eclipse,° but not visible on our horizon but about the western   205
inhabitants of Mexicana and California.

MISTRESS LOW-WATER Well, we have no business there, sir.

WEATHERWISE Nor we have none here, sir, and so fare you well.

Exit [Suitors]

MISTRESS LOW-WATER You save the house a good labour, gentlemen; the fool carries them away in a voider.° Where be these   210
fellows?

Enter Servants [with Low-water and Pickadille]

SERVANT Sir?

PICKADILLE Here, sir.

SERVANT What's your worship's pleasure?

MISTRESS LOW-WATER Oh, this is something like.

[*To Low-water*]   Take your ease, sir;°   215
Here are those now more fit to be commanded.

LOW-WATER [*aside*] How few women are of thy mind; she thinks it
too much to keep me in subjection for one day, whereas some
wives would be glad to keep their husbands in awe all days of their
lives, and think it the best bargain that e'er they made.   220

[*Exit Low-water*]

MISTRESS LOW-WATER I'll spare no cost for th'wedding, some
device too,
To show our thankfulness to wit and fortune;
It shall be so.—Run straight for one o'th'wits.°

PICKADILLE How! One o'th'wits? I care not if I run on that account;
are they in town, think you?   225

MISTRESS LOW-WATER Whither run'st thou now?

PICKADILLE To an ordinary for one of the wits.

MISTRESS LOW-WATER Why to an ordinary above a tavern?

PICKADILLE No, I hold your best wits to be at ordinary, nothing so
good in a tavern.   230

MISTRESS LOW-WATER And why, I pray, sir?

PICKADILLE Because those that go to an ordinary dine better for
twelve pence than he that goes to a tavern for his five shillings; and
I think those have the best wits that can save four shillings and
fare better too.   235

MISTRESS LOW-WATER So, sir, all your wit then runs upon victuals.

PICKADILLE 'Tis a sign 'twill hold out the longer then.

MISTRESS LOW-WATER What were you saying to me?

SERVANT   Please, your worship,

251

I heard there came a scholar over lately
With old Sir Oliver's lady.   240
MISTRESS LOW-WATER [aside] Is she come?—
     What is that lady?
SERVANT   A good gentlewoman,
     Has been long prisoner with the enemy.
MISTRESS LOW-WATER I know't too well, and joy in her release.
     Go to that house then straight, and in one labour   245
     You may bid them, and entreat home that scholar.°
SERVANT It shall be done with speed, sir.
          [Exit servant]
PICKADILLE I'll along with you, and see what face that scholar has
     brought over; a thin pair of parbreaking sea-water green chops, I
     warrant you.   250
          [Exit Pickadille]
MISTRESS LOW-WATER Since wit has pleasured me, I'll pleasure wit;
     Scholars shall fare the better. Oh, my blessing!
     I feel a hand of mercy lift me up
     Out of a world of waters, and now sets me
     Upon a mountain, where the sun plays most,   255
     To cheer my heart even as it dries my limbs.
     What deeps I see beneath me, in whose falls
     Many a nimble mortal toils
     And scarce can feed himself. The streams of fortune
     'Gainst which he tugs in vain still beat him down,   260
     And will not suffer him, past hand to mouth,°
     To lift his arm to his posterity's blessing.
     I see a careful sweat run in a ring
     About his temples, but all will not do,
     For till some happy means relieve his state   265
     There he must stick and bide the wrath of fate!
     I see this wrath upon an uphill land;
     Oh, blessed are they can see their falls, and stand!
          Enter [Servant with] Beveril
     How now?
SERVANT With much entreating, sir; he's come.   270
          [Exit Servant]
MISTRESS LOW-WATER Sir y'are—[aside] my brother! Joys come
     thick together!
          [Embraces him]
     Sir, when I see a scholar, pardon me,

I am so taken with affection for him°
That I must run into his arms and clasp him.

BEVERIL Art stands in need, sir, of such cherishers;   275
I meet too few; 'twere a brave world for scholars
If half a kingdom were but of your mind, sir;
Let ignorance and hell confound the rest.

MISTRESS LOW-WATER Let it suffice, sweet sir; you cannot think
How dearly you are welcome.

BEVERIL   May I live   280
To show you service for't.

MISTRESS LOW-WATER   Your love, your love, sir,
We go no higher, nor shall you go lower.
Sir, I'm bold to send for you, to request
A kindness from your wit for some device
To grace our wedding; it shall be worth your pains,   285
And something more t'express my love to art;
You shall not receive all in bare embracements.

BEVERIL Your love I thank, but pray, sir, pardon me,
I've a heart says I must not grant you that.

MISTRESS LOW-WATER No, what's your reason, sir?

BEVERIL   I'm not at peace   290
With the lady of this house; now you'll excuse me;
She's wronged my sister, and I may not do't.

MISTRESS LOW-WATER The widow knows you not.

BEVERIL I never saw her face to my remembrance.
Oh, that my heart should not feel her wrongs so much,   295
And yet live ignorant of the injurer!

MISTRESS LOW-WATER Let me persuade thee, since she knows you not,
Make clear the weather; let not griefs betray you;
I'll tell her y'are a worthy friend of mine,
And so I tell her true, thou art indeed.   300
Sir, here she comes.
        Enter Widow [Lady Goldenfleece]

LADY GOLDENFLEECE What, are you busy, sir?

MISTRESS LOW-WATER Nothing less, lady; here's a gentleman
Of noble parts, beside his friendship to me;
Pray, give him liberal welcome.

LADY GOLDENFLEECE   He's most welcome.   305

MISTRESS LOW-WATER The virtues of his mind will deserve largely.

LADY GOLDENFLEECE [*aside*] Methinks his outward parts deserve as
much then;

A proper gentleman it is.

MISTRESS LOW-WATER   Come, worthy sir.

BEVERIL I follow.

> [*Exeunt all but Beveril*]
>   Check thy blood
> For fear it prove too bold, to wrong thy goodness.   310
> A wise man makes affections but his slaves;
> Break 'em in time, let 'em not master thee.
> Oh, 'tis my sister's enemy, think of that!
> Some speedy grief fall down upon the fire,
> Before it take my heart; let it not rise   315
> 'Gainst brotherly nature, judgement, and these wrongs.
> Make clear the weather.
> Oh, who could look upon her face in storms!
> Yet pains may work it out; griefs do but strive
> To kill this spark; I'll keep it still alive.   320

> [*Exit*]

[3.1]

Enter the three late suitors, Weatherwise, Pepperton, and Overdone, joined with Sir Gilbert Lambston

WEATHERWISE Faith, Sir Gilbert, forget and forgive;
There's all our hands to a new bargain of friendship.
PEPPERTON Ay, and all our hearts to boot, Sir Gilbert.
WEATHERWISE Why, la you! There's but four suitors left on's in all
th'world, and the fifth has the widow; if we should not be kind to   5
one another, and so few on's i'faith, I would we were all raked up
in some hole or other.
SIR GILBERT Pardon me, gentlemen, I cannot but remember
Your late disgraceful words before the widow
In time of my oppression.   10
WEATHERWISE Puh, Saturn reigned then, a melancholy, grumbling
planet; he was in the third house° of privy enemies and would have
bewrayed all our plots; beside, there was a fiery conjunction in the
dragon's tail° that spoiled all that e'er we went about.
SIR GILBERT Dragon or devil, somewhat 'twas, I am sure.   15
WEATHERWISE Why, I tell you, Sir Gilbert, we were all out of our
wits in't; I was so mad at that time myself, I could have wished
an hind-quarter of my bull out of your belly again, whereas now
I care not if you had eat tail and all; I am no niggard in the way
of friendship; I was ever yet at full moon in good fellowship,   20
and so you shall find if you look into the almanac of my true
nature.
SIR GILBERT Well, all's forgiven for once; hands apace, gentlemen.
WEATHERWISE Ye shall have two of mine to do you a kindness; yet
when they're both abroad, who shall look to th'house° here?   25
   [*Clasps hands with Sir Gilbert*]
PEPPERTON, OVERDONE Not only a new friendship, but a friend.°
   [*Clasps hands with Sir Gilbert*]
SIR GILBERT But upon this condition, gentlemen,
You shall hear now a thing worth your revenge.
WEATHERWISE An you doubt that
You shall have mine beforehand; I've one ready;°   30
I never go without a black oath about me.
SIR GILBERT I know the least touch of a spur in this

Will now put your desires to a false gallop,
By all means slanderous in every place
And in all companies, to disgrace the widow,   35
No matter in what rank, so it be spiteful
And worthy your revenges; so now I;°
It shall be all my study, care, and pains,
And we can lose no labour; all her foes°
Will make such use on't, that they'll snatch it from us   40
Faster than we can forge it, though we keep
Four tongues at work upon't and never cease.
Then for the indifferent world, faith, they're apter
To bid a slander welcome than a truth;°
We have the odds of our side. This in time   45
May grow so general, as disgrace will spread,
That wild dissension may divide the bed.

WEATHERWISE, PEPPERTON Excellent!

OVERDONE A pure revenge; I see no dregs in't.

SIR GILBERT Let each man look to his part now, and not feed   50
Upon one dish, all four on's, like plain maltmen;°
For at this feast we must have several kickshaws
And delicate made dishes, that the world
May see it is a banquet finely furnished.

WEATHERWISE Why, then let me alone for one of your kickshaws;   55
I have thought on that already.

SIR GILBERT   Prithee how, sir?

WEATHERWISE Marry, sir, I'll give it out abroad that I have lain with
the widow myself, as 'tis the fashion of many a gallant to disgrace
his new mistress when he cannot have his will of her, and lie with°
her name in every tavern though he ne'er came within a yard° of   60
her person; so I, being a gentleman, may say as much in that kind
as a gallant; I am as free by my father's copy.°

SIR GILBERT This will do excellent, sir.

WEATHERWISE And moreover I'll give the world thus much to
understand beside, that, if I had not lain with the widow in the   65
wane of the moon at one of my Seven Stars'° houses, when Venus
was about business of her own and could give no attendance, she
had been brought abed with two roaring boys° by this time, and
the Gemini being infants, I'd have made away with them like a
stepmother and put mine own boys in their places.°   70

SIR GILBERT Why, this is beyond talk; you out-run your master.°

    Enter clown [*Pickadille*]

PICKADILLE [*aside*] Whoop! Draw home° next time; here are all the
old shooters that have lost the game at pricks!° What a fair mark
had Sir Gilbert on't, if he had shot home before the last arrow
came in.° Methinks these show to me now, for all the world, like   75
so many lousy beggars turned out of my lady's barn, and have
ne'er a hole to put their heads in.°

WEATHERWISE Mass, here's her ladyship's ass; he tells us anything.

SIR GILBERT Ho, Pickadille!

PICKADILLE What, Sir Gilbert Lambston!   80
Gentlemen, outlaws all, how do you do?°

SIR GILBERT How! What dost call us? How goes the world at home,
lad? What strange news?

PICKADILLE This is the state of prodigals as right as can be;° when
they have spent all their means on brave feasts, they're glad to   85
scrape to a servingman for a meal's meat.
So that whilom, like four prodigal rivals,
Could goose or capon, crane or woodcock choose,
Now're glad to make up a poor meal with news;
A lamentable hearing!   90

WEATHERWISE He's in passion up to the eyebrows for us.

PICKADILLE Oh, Master Weatherwise, I blame none but you.
You are a gentleman deeply read in Pond's Almanac;°
Methinks you should not be such a shallow fellow;
You knew this day, the twelfth of June, would come°   95
When the sun enters into the Crab's room,
And all your hopes would go aside, aside.

WEATHERWISE The fool says true i'faith, gentlemen. I knew 'twould
come all to this pass; I'll show't you presently.
[*Takes out almanac*]

PICKADILLE If you had spared but four of your twelve signs now,°   100
You might have gone to a tavern and made merry with 'em.

WEATHERWISE H'as the best moral meaning of an ass that e'er I
heard speak with tongue—look you here, gentlemen: [*reading
almanac*] 'Fifth day, neither fish nor flesh.'

PICKADILLE No, nor good red herring,° an you look again.   105

WEATHERWISE [*reading*] 'Sixth day, privily° prevented.'

PICKADILLE Marry, faugh!

WEATHERWISE [*reading*] 'Seventh day, shrunk in the wetting.'

PICKADILLE Nay, so will the best ware° bought for love or money.

WEATHERWISE [*reading*] 'The eighth day, over head and ears.'   110

PICKADILLE By my faith, he come home in a sweet pickle then.

WEATHERWISE [*reading*] 'The ninth day, scarce sound at heart.'

PICKADILLE What o'pox ailed it?

WEATHERWISE [*reading*] 'The tenth day, a courtier's welcome.'

PICKADILLE That's a cup of beer and you can get it.   115

WEATHERWISE [*reading*] 'The eleventh day, stones against the wind.'

PICKADILLE Pox of an ass! He might have thrown 'em better.

WEATHERWISE Now the twelfth day, gentlemen, that was our day.
    [*Reading*] 'Past all redemption.'

PICKADILLE Then the devil go with't.   120

WEATHERWISE Now you see plainly, gentlemen, how we're used,
    The calendar will not lie for no man's pleasure.

SIR GILBERT Push, y'are too confident in almanac posies.

PEPPERTON Faith, so said we.

SIR GILBERT They're mere delusions.   125

WEATHERWISE How! You see how knavishly they happen,° sir.

SIR GILBERT Ay, that's because they're foolishly believed, sir.

WEATHERWISE Well, take your courses, gentlemen, without 'em,
    and see what will come on't; you may wander like masterless men;°
    there's ne'er a planet will care a half-penny for you. If they look   130
    after you, I'll be hanged, when you scorn to bestow two pence° to
    look after them.

SIR GILBERT How, a device at the wedding, say'st thou!

PICKADILLE Why, have none of you heard of that yet?

SIR GILBERT 'Tis the first news i'faith, lad.   135

PICKADILLE Oh, there's a brave travelling scholar entertained into
    the house o'purpose, one that has been all the world over and some
    part of Jerusalem;° h'as his chamber, his diet, and three candles
    allowed him after supper.

WEATHERWISE By my faith, he need not complain for victuals then,   140
    whate'er he be.

PICKADILLE He lies in one of the best chambers i'th'house, bravely
    matted; and to warm his wits as much, a cup of sack and an *aqua*
    vitae bottle stands just at his elbow.

WEATHERWISE He's shrewdly hurt, by my faith; if he catch an ague   145
    of that fashion, I'll be hanged.

PICKADILLE He'll come abroad anon.

SIR GILBERT Art sure on't?

PICKADILLE Why, he ne'er stays a quarter of an hour in the house
    together.   150

SIR GILBERT No? How can he study then?

PICKADILLE Pha, best of all; he talks as he goes° and writes as he
runs; besides, you know 'tis death to a traveller to stand long in
one place.

SIR GILBERT It may hit right, boys!—Honest Pickadille, thou wast   155
wont to love me.

PICKADILLE I'd good cause, sir, then.

SIR GILBERT Thou shalt have the same still; take that.

    [*Gives him money*]

PICKADILLE Will you believe me now; I ne'er loved you better in
my life than I do at this present.   160

SIR GILBERT Tell me now truly; who are the presenters? What
parsons° are employed in the device?

PICKADILLE Parsons! Not any, sir; my mistress will not be at the
charge; she keeps none but an old Welsh vicar.

SIR GILBERT Prithee, I mean, who be the speakers?   165

PICKADILLE Troth, I know none but those that open their mouths.
Here he comes now himself; you may ask him.

    Enter Master Beveril

WEATHERWISE Is this he? By my faith, one may pick a gentleman
out of his calves, and a scholar out on's cheeks;° one may see by
his looks what's in him. I warrant you there has ne'er a new   170
almanac come out these dozen years, but he has studied it over and
over.

SIR GILBERT Do not reveal us now.

PICKADILLE Because you shall be sure on't, you have given me a
ninepence here, and I'll give you the slip for't.°   175

    Exit [*Pickadille*]

SIR GILBERT Well said; now the fool's pleased, we may be bold.

BEVERIL [*aside*] Love is as great an enemy to wit
    As ignorance to art; I find my powers
    So much employed in business of my heart
    That all the time's too little to dispatch   180
    Affairs within me. Fortune, too remiss,
    I suffer for thy slowness; had I come
    Before a vow had chained their souls together,
    There might have been some hope, though ne'er so little;
    Now there's no spark at all, nor e'er can be,   185
    But dreadful ones struck from adultery;
    And if my lust were smothered with her will,
    Oh, who could wrong a gentleman so kind,

A stranger made up with a brother's mind?
SIR GILBERT Peace, peace, enough, let me alone to manage it.   190
    [*To Beveril*] A quick invention and a happy one
    Reward your study, sir.
BEVERIL   Gentlemen, I thank you.
SIR GILBERT We understand your wits are in employment, sir,
    In honour of this wedding.
BEVERIL   Sir, the gentleman
    To whom that worthy lady is betrothed   195
    Vouchsafes t'accept the power of my good will in't.
SIR GILBERT I pray resolve us then, sir,
    For we're friends that love and honour her,
    Whether your number be yet full or no
    Of those which you make choice of for presenters.   200
BEVERIL First, 'tis so brief, because the time is so,
    We shall not trouble many; and for those
    We shall employ, the house will yield in servants.
SIR GILBERT Nay, then, under your leave and favour, sir,
    Since all your pains will be so weakly graced,   205
    And wanting due performance lose their lustre,
    Here are four of us gentlemen, her friends,
    Both lovers of her honour and your art,
    That would be glad so to express ourselves,
    And think our service well and worthily placed.   210
BEVERIL My thanks do me no grace for this large kindness;
    You make my labours proud of such presenters.
SIR GILBERT She shall not think, sir, she's so ill beloved,
    But friends can quickly make that number perfect.
BEVERIL She's bound t'acknowledge it.
SIR GILBERT   Only thus much, sir,   215
    Which will amaze her most, I'd have't so carried,
    As you can do't, that neither she, nor none,
    Should know what friends we were till all were done.
WEATHERWISE Ay, that would make the sport.
BEVERIL   I like it well, sir.
    My hand and faith amongst you, gentlemen;   220
    It shall be so disposed of.
SIR GILBERT   We are the men then.
        [*Beveril clasps each by the hand*]
BEVERIL Then look you, gentlemen, the device is single,
    Naked, and plain, because the time's so short

And gives no freedom to a wealthier sport;
'Tis only, gentlemen, the four elements   225
In liveliest forms, earth, water, air, and fire.
WEATHERWISE Mass, and here's four of us too.
BEVERIL   It fits well, sir.
This the effect: that whereas all those four
Maintain a natural opposition
And untruced war, the one against the other,   230
To shame their ancient envies they should see
How well in two breasts all these do agree.
WEATHERWISE That's in the bride and bridegroom; I am quick, sir.
SIR GILBERT In faith, it's pretty, sir; I approve it well.
BEVERIL But see how soon my unhappiness and your kindness°   235
Is crossed together.
SIR GILBERT   Crossed! I hope not, sir.
BEVERIL I can employ but two of you.
PEPPERTON   How comes that, sir?
BEVERIL Air and the fire should be by me presented,
But the two other in the forms of women.
WEATHERWISE [aside] Nay, then we're gone again; I think these
    women   240
Were made to vex and trouble us in all shapes.
SIR GILBERT Faith, sir, you stand too nicely.
WEATHERWISE   So think I, sir.
BEVERIL Yet when we tax ourselves, it may the better
Set off our errors when the fine eyes judge 'em;°
But water certainly should be a woman.   245
WEATHERWISE By my faith, then he is gelded since I saw him last;
he was thought to be a man once° when he got his wife with child
before he was married.
BEVERIL Fie, you are fishing in another stream,° sir.
WEATHERWISE But now I come to yours, an you go to that,° sir; I   250
see no reason then, but fire and water should change shapes and
genders.
BEVERIL How prove you that, sir?
WEATHERWISE Why, there's no reason but water should be a man,
because fire° is commonly known to be a quean.   255
BEVERIL So, sir, you argue well.
WEATHERWISE Nay more, sir; water will break in at a little
crevice,° so will a man if he be not kept out; water will undermine,
so will an informer; water will ebb and flow, so will a gentle-

man;° water will search any place, and so will a constable, as lately   260
he did at my Seven Stars° for a young wench that was stole; water
will quench fire, and so will Wat the barber;° *ergo*, let water wear
a codpiece-point.

BEVERIL Faith, gentlemen, I like your company well.

WEATHERWISE Let's see who'll dispute with me at the full o'th'   265
moon.

BEVERIL No, sir; an you be vainglorious of your talent, I'll put you
to't once more.

WEATHERWISE I'm for you, sir, as long as the moon keeps in this
quarter.   270

BEVERIL Well, how answer you this then? Earth and water are both
bearers, therefore they should be women.

WEATHERWISE Why, so are porters and peddlers, and yet they are
known to be men.

BEVERIL I'll give you over° in time, sir; I shall repent the bestowing   275
on't° else.

WEATHERWISE If I that have proceeded in five and twenty such
books of astronomy should not be able to put down a scholar now
in one thousand six hundred thirty and eight,° the dominical letter
being G,° I stood for a goose.   280

SIR GILBERT Then this will satisfy you though that be a woman;
Oceanus, the sea, that's chief of waters,
He wears the form of a man, and so may you.

BEVERIL Now I hear reason, and I may consent.

SIR GILBERT And so, though earth challenge a feminine face,   285
The matter of which earth consists, that's dust,
The general soul of earth is of both kinds.

BEVERIL Fit yourselves, gentlemen, I've enough for me.
Earth, water, air, and fire, part 'em amongst you!

WEATHERWISE Let me play air;° I was my father's eldest son.   290

BEVERIL Ay, but this air never possessed the lands.

WEATHERWISE I'm but disposed to jest with you, sir; 'tis the same
my almanac speaks on, is't not?

BEVERIL That 'tis, sir.

WEATHERWISE Then leave it to my discretion to fit both the part   295
and the person.

BEVERIL You shall have your desire, sir.

SIR GILBERT   We'll agree
Without your trouble now, sir; we're not factious,
Or envy one another for best parts,

Like quarrelling actors that have passionate fits;   300
We submit always to the writer's wits.
BEVERIL He that commends you may do't liberally,
For you deserve as much as praise can show.
SIR GILBERT We'll send to you privately.
BEVERIL   I'll dispatch you.
SIR GILBERT [aside] We'll poison your device.
        Exit [Sir Gilbert]
PEPPERTON [aside]   She must have pleasures,   305
Shows, and conceits, and we disgraceful doom.
        [Exit Pepperton]
WEATHERWISE [aside] We'll make your elements come limping
        home.
        Exeunt [Weatherwise and Overdone]
BEVERIL How happy am I in this unlooked-for grace,
This voluntary kindness from these gentlemen!
        Enter Mistress Low-water and her man-husband [Low-water,
        both disguised]
'Twill set off all my labours far more pleasing   310
Before the widow, whom my heart calls mistress,
But my tongue dares not second it.
LOW-WATER [aside to Mistress Low-water] How say you now, Kate?
MISTRESS LOW-WATER I like this music well, sir.
BEVERIL   Oh unfortunate!
Yet though a tree be guarded from my touch,   315
There's none can hinder me to love the fruit.
MISTRESS LOW-WATER [aside to Low-water] Nay, now we know
your mind, brother, we'll provide for you.
        Exit [the Low-waters]
BEVERIL Oh, were it but as free as late times knew it,
I would deserve, if all life's wealth could do it.   320
        Exit

[4.1]

*Enter at Sir Oliver's house, himself, old Sunset, his redeemed
lady [Lady Twilight], Master Sandfield, the Dutch
Merchant, Philip, Sir Oliver's son, and Savourwit, aloof off,
and servants*

SIR OLIVER Oh, my reviving joy! Thy quickening presence
  Makes the sad night of threescore and ten years
  Sit like a youthful spring upon my blood.
  I cannot make thy welcome rich enough
  With all the wealth of words.

LADY TWILIGHT   It is expressed, sir,   5
  With more than can be equalled; the ill store
  Lies only on my side, my thanks are poor.

SIR OLIVER Blessed be the goodness of his mind forever
  That did redeem thy life; may it return
  Upon his fortunes double! That worthy gentleman,   10
  Kind Master Beveril, shower upon him, heaven,
  Some unexpected happiness to requite him
  For that my joy unlooked for! Oh, more kind°
  And juster far is a mere stranger's goodness
  Than the sophistic faith of natural sons!   15
  Here's one could juggle with me, take up the ransom,
  He and his loose companion.

SAVOURWIT [*aside*]   Say you me so, sir?
  I'll eat hard eggs for that trick!

SIR OLIVER   Spend the money°
  And bring me home false news and empty pockets!
  In that young gallant's tongue there you were dead   20
  Ten weeks before this day, had not this merchant
  Brought first the truth in words, yourself in substance.

LADY TWILIGHT Pray let me stay you here, ere you proceed, sir.
  Did he report me dead, say you?

SIR OLIVER   Else you live not.

LADY TWILIGHT See now, sir, you may lay your blame too
    rashly,   25
  When nobody looked after it; let me tell you, sir,°
  A father's anger should take great advice°
  Ere it condemn flesh of so dear a price.

264

He's no way guilty yet, for that report
The general tongue of all the country spread,   30
For being removed 'far off I was thought dead.

PHILIP Can my faith now be taken into favour, sir?
Is't worthy to be trusted?

SAVOURWIT [aside]   No, by my troth, is't not;
'Twould make shift to spend another ransom yet.

SIR OLIVER Well, sir, I must confess y'ave here dealt well with
    me;   35
And what is good in you I love again.

SAVOURWIT [aside] Now am I half ways in, just to the girdle,
But the worst part's behind.

SIR OLIVER   Marry, I fear me, sir,°
This weather is too glorious to hold long.

LADY TWILIGHT I see no cloud to interpose it, sir,   40
If you place confidence in what I have told you.

SIR OLIVER Nay, 'tis clear sky on that side; would 'twere so
All over his obedience. I see that,
And so does this good gentleman.

LADY TWILIGHT   Do you, sir?

SIR OLIVER That makes his honesty doubtful.

LADY TWILIGHT [to Dutch Merchant]   I pray, speak, sir.   45
The truth of your last kindness makes me bold with you.

DUTCH MERCHANT The knight, your husband, madam, can best
    speak;
He truliest can show griefs whose heart they break.

LADY TWILIGHT I'm sorry yet for more; pray let me know't, sir,
That I may help to chide him, though 'twould grieve me.   50

SIR OLIVER Why then prepare for't. You came over now
In the best time to do't you could pick out;
Not only spent my money, but to blind me,
He and his wicked instrument—

SAVOURWIT [aside]   Now he fiddles me!

SIR OLIVER Brings home a minion here, by great chance known; 55
Told me she was his sister; she proves none.

LADY TWILIGHT This was unkindly done, sir. Now I'm sorry
My good opinion lost itself upon you;
You are not the same son I left behind me;
More grace took him. Oh, let me end in time,   60
For fear I should forget myself and chide him!
Where is she, sir? Though he beguiled your eyes,°

He cannot deceive mine; we're now too hard for him.
For since our first unfortunate separation,
I've often seen the girl—[*aside*] would that were true—   65
By many a happy accident, many a one;
But never durst acknowledge her for mine own,
And therein stood my joys distressed again.

SIR OLIVER You rehearse miseries, wife.—Call the maid down.

SAVOURWIT [*aside*] She's been too often down to be now called
   so;°   70
She'll lie down shortly and call somebody up.°

LADY TWILIGHT He's now to deal with one, sir, that knows
   truth;
He must be shamed or quit; there's no mean saves him.°

SIR OLIVER I hear her come.

LADY TWILIGHT [*aside to Philip*] You see how hard 'tis now   75
To redeem good opinion, being once gone;
Be careful then, and keep it when 'tis won.
Now see me take a poison with great joy,
Which but for thy sake I should swoon to touch.
       Enter Grace

GRACE [*aside*] What new affliction? Am I set to sale   80
For any one that bids most shame for me?

SIR OLIVER Look you! Do you see what stuff they've brought me
   home here?

LADY TWILIGHT Oh, bless her, eternal powers! My life, my
   comforts,
My nine-years' grief, but everlasting joy now!
Thrice welcome to my heart; 'tis she indeed.   85
       [*Embraces Grace*]

SIR OLIVER What, is it?

PHILIP   I'm unfit to carry a ransom!

SAVOURWIT [*aside to Grace*] Down on your knees to save your belly
   harmless;
Ask blessing, though you may never mean to use it,°
But give't away presently to a beggar-wench.
       [*Grace kneels*]

PHILIP My faith is blemished; I'm no man of trust, sir.   90

LADY TWILIGHT Rise with a mother's blessing.
       [*Grace rises*]

SAVOURWIT [*aside*] All this while sh'as rise with a son's.°

SIR OLIVER But soft ye, soft ye, wife!

I pray take heed you place your blessing right now.
This honest Dutchman here told me he saw her 95
At Antwerp in an inn.
LADY TWILIGHT True, she was so, sir.
DUTCH MERCHANT Sir, 'tis my quality, what I speak once,
I affirm ever; in that inn I saw her;
That lets° her not to be your daughter now.
SIR OLIVER Oh, sir, is't come to that!
SUNSET Here's joys ne'er dreamed on! 100
SIR OLIVER Oh, Master Sunset, I am at the rising
Of my refulgent happiness!—Now, son Sandfield,
Once more and ever!
SANDFIELD I am proud on't, sir.
SIR OLIVER [to Philip] Pardon me, boy, I have wronged thy faith too
much.
SAVOURWIT [aside] Now may I leave my shell and peep my head
forth. 105
SIR OLIVER Where is this Savourwit, that honest whoreson,
That I may take my curse from his knave's shoulders?
SAVOURWIT Oh, sir, I feel you at my very blade here;
Your curse is ten stone weight, and a pound over.
SIR OLIVER Come, thou'rt a witty varlet and a trusty. 110
SAVOURWIT You shall still find me a poor faithful fellow, sir,
If you have another ransom to send over
Or daughter to find out.
SIR OLIVER I'll do thee right, boy;
I ne'er yet knew thee but speak honest English;
Marry, in Dutch I found thee a knave lately. 115
SAVOURWIT That was to hold you but in play a little,
Till farther truths came over, and I strong;°
You shall ne'er find me a knave in mine own tongue;
I have more grace in me; I go out of England
Still when I take such courses; that shows modesty, sir. 120
SIR OLIVER Anything full of wit and void of harm
I give thee pardon for, so was that now.
SAVOURWIT Faith, now I'm quit, I find myself the nimbler
To serve you so again, and my will's good.
[Aside] Like one that lately shook off his old irons, 125
And cuts a purse at bench to deserve new ones.°
SIR OLIVER Since it holds all the way so fortunate still,
And strikes so even with my first belief,

267

This is the gentleman, wife, young Master Sandfield here,
A man of worthy parts, beside his lands,   130
Whom I make choice of for my daughter's bed.
SAVOURWIT [*aside*] But he'll make choice there of another
   bedfellow.°
LADY TWILIGHT I wish 'em both the happiness of love, sir.
SIR OLIVER 'Twas spoke like a good lady! An your memory
   Can reach it, wife, but 'tis so long ago, too,   135
   Old Master Sunset he had a young daughter
   When you unluckily left England so,
   And much about the age of our girl there,
   For both were nursed together.
LADY TWILIGHT   'Tis so fresh
   In my remembrance, now y'have wakened it,   140
   As if twelve years were but a twelve-hours' dream.
SIR OLIVER That girl is now a proper gentlewoman,
   As fine a body, wife, as e'er was measured
   With an indenture cut in farthing steaks.°
SUNSET Oh, say not so, Sir Oliver, you shall pardon me, sir.   145
   I'faith, sir, you are too blame.
SIR OLIVER   Sings, dances, plays,
   Touches an instrument with a motherly grace.
SUNSET 'Tis your own daughter that you mean that by.
SAVOURWIT [*aside*] There's open Dutch indeed, an he could take
   it!°
SIR OLIVER This wench, under your leave—
SUNSET   You have my love in't.   150
SIR OLIVER Is my son's wife that shall be.
SAVOURWIT [*aside*]   Thus I'd hold with't;°
   Is your son's wife that should be Master Sandfield's.
LADY TWILIGHT I come in happy time to a feast of marriages.
SIR OLIVER And now you put's i'th'mind, the hour draws on
   At the new-married widow's; there we're looked for;   155
   There will be entertainments, sports, and banquets;
   There these young lovers shall clap hands together;
   The seed of one feast shall bring forth another.°
SUNSET Well said, Sir Oliver.
SIR OLIVER   Y'are a stranger, sir,
   Your welcome will be best.
DUTCH MERCHANT   Good sir, excuse me.   160
SIR OLIVER You shall along i'faith; you must not refuse me.

268

[Exeunt all except] Mother [Lady Twilight], Sister [Grace],
Philip, and Savourwit

PHILIP Oh, mother, these new joys that sets my soul up,
   Which had no means, nor any hope of any,
   Has brought me now so far in debt to you,
   I know not which way to begin to thank you.   165
   I am so lost in all, I cannot guess
   Which of the two my service most constrains,
   Your last kind goodness or your first dear pains.

LADY TWILIGHT Love is a mother's duty to a son,
   As a son's duty is both love and fear.°   170

SAVOURWIT I owe you a poor life, madam, that's all;
   Pray call for't when you please; it shall be ready for you. .

LADY TWILIGHT Make much on't, sir, till then.

SAVOURWIT *[aside]*   If buttered sack will.

LADY TWILIGHT Methinks the more I look upon her, son,
   The more thy sister's face runs in my mind.   175

PHILIP Belike she's somewhat like her; it makes the better, madam.

LADY TWILIGHT Was Antwerp, say you, the first place you found
      her in?

PHILIP Yes, madam. Why do you ask?

LADY TWILIGHT   Whose daughter were you?

GRACE I know not rightly whose, to speak truth, madam.

SAVOURWIT *[aside]* The mother of her was a good twigger the whilst. 180

LADY TWILIGHT No? With whom were you brought up then?

GRACE   With those, madam,
   To whom, I've often heard, the enemy sold me.

LADY TWILIGHT What's that?

GRACE Too often have I heard this piteous story
   Of a distressed mother I had once,   185
   Whose comfortable sight I lost at sea;
   But then the years of childhood took from me
   Both the remembrance of her and the sorrows.

LADY TWILIGHT *[aside]* Oh, I begin to feel her in my blood!
   My heart leaps to be at her.—What was that mother?   190

GRACE Some said an English lady, but I know not.

LADY TWILIGHT What's thy name?

GRACE   Grace.

LADY TWILIGHT   May it be so in heaven,
   For thou art mine on earth. Welcome dear child,
   Unto thy father's house, thy mother's arms,

After thy foreign sorrows.
    [*Embracing Grace*]
SAVOURWIT [*aside*]   'Twill prove gallant!   195
LADY TWILIGHT What, son! Such earnest work; I bring thee joy
    now
    Will make the rest show nothing, 'tis so glorious.
PHILIP Why, 'tis not possible, madam, that man's happiness
    Should take a greater height than mine aspires.
LADY TWILIGHT No, now you shall confess it; this shall quit thee   200
    From all fears present, or hereafter doubts,
    About this business.
PHILIP   Give me that, sweet mother.
LADY TWILIGHT Here take her then, and set thine arms a-work;
    There needs no 'fection, 'tis indeed thy sister.°
PHILIP My sister!
SAVOURWIT [*aside*] Cuds me, I feel the razor!   205
LADY TWILIGHT Why, how now, son? How comes a change so
    soon?
PHILIP Oh, I beseech you, mother, wound me anywhere
    But where you pointed last. That's present death!
    Devise some other miserable torment,
    Though ne'er so pitiless, and I'll run and meet it.   210
    Some way more merciful let your goodness think on,
    May steal away my joys, but save my soul.
    I'll willingly restore back every one
    Upon that mild condition; anything
    But what you spake last will be comfortable.   215
LADY TWILIGHT Y'are troubled with strange fits in England here.
    Your first suit to me did entreat me hardly
    To say 'twas she, to have old wrath appeased,
    And now 'tis known your sister, y'are not pleased.
    How should I show myself?
PHILIP   Say 'tis not she.   220
LADY TWILIGHT Shall I deny my daughter?
PHILIP   Oh, you kill me
    Beyond all tortures!
LADY TWILIGHT   Why do you deal thus with me?
PHILIP She is my wife; I married her at Antwerp;
    I have known the way unto her bed these three months.
SAVOURWIT [*aside*] And that's too much by twelve weeks for a
    sister.
              225

LADY TWILIGHT I understand you now, too soon, too plain.

PHILIP Oh, mother, if you love my peace forever,
Examine her again, find me not guilty.

LADY TWILIGHT 'Tis now too late, her words make that too true.

PHILIP Her words? Shall bare words overthrow a soul?   230
A body is not cast away so lightly.°
How can you know 'tis she? Let sense decide it;
She then so young, and both so long divided.

LADY TWILIGHT She tells me the sad story.

PHILIP   Does that throw me?°
Many a distress may have the face of yours   235
That never was kin to you.

LADY TWILIGHT   But, however, sir,
I trust you are not married.

PHILIP   Here's the witness,
And all the wealth I had with her; this ring
That joined our hearts together.
          [Shows the ring]

LADY TWILIGHT   Oh, too clear now!
Thou'st brought in evidence to o'erthrow thyself;   240
Had no one word been spoke, only this shown,
'T'had been enough to approved her for mine own.
See here, two letters that begun my name
Before I knew thy father; this I gave her,
And, as a jewel, fastened to her ear.   245

GRACE Pardon me, mother, that you found it stray;°
I kept it till I gave my heart away.

PHILIP Oh, to what mountain shall I take my flight
To hide the monster of my sin from sight!

SAVOURWIT [aside] I'll to Wales presently; there's the best hills   250
To hide a poor knave in.

LADY TWILIGHT Oh, heap not desperation upon guilt!
Repent yet and all's saved; 'twas but hard chance;
Amongst all sins heaven pities ignorance;°
She's still the first that has her pardon signed;°   255
All sins else see their faults, she's only blind.
Go to thy chamber, pray, leave off, and win;
One hour's repentance cures a twelve-month's sin.

GRACE Oh, my distressed husband, my dear brother!
          Exit [Lady Twilight] with her daughter [Grace]

PHILIP Oh, Savourwit! Never came sorrow yet   260

271

To mankind like it; I'm so far distressed
I've no time left to give my heart attendance,
Too little all to wait upon my soul!
Before this tempest came, how well I stood,
Full in the beams of blessedness and joy!   265
The memory of man could never say
So black a storm fell in so bright a day.
I am that man that even life surfeits of;
Or if to live, unworthy to be seen
By the savage eyesight; give's thy hand;   270
Commend me to thy prayers.

SAVOURWIT [*aside*]   Next time I say 'em.

PHILIP Farewell, my honest breast, that craves no more°
Than possible kindness; that I've found thee large in,°
And I must ask no more; there wit must stay,
It cannot pass where fate stops up the way.   275
Joy thrive with thee; I'll never see thee more.

SAVOURWIT What's that, sir?
Pray come back, and bring those words with you;
You shall not carry 'em so out of my company.
There's no last refuge, when your father knows it;   280
There's no such need on't yet; stay but till then,
And take one with you that will imitate you
In all the desperate onsets man dare think on.
Were it to challenge all the wolves in France
To meet at one set battle, I'd be your half in't;   285
All beasts of venom—what you had a mind to,
Your part should be took still. For such a day
Let's keep ourselves in heart, then am I for you.
In the meantime, to beat off all suspicion,
Let's to the bridehouse too; here's my petition.   290

PHILIP Thou hast a learning art when all hopes fly;
Let one night waste, there's time enough left to die.

SAVOURWIT A minute's as good as a thousand year, sir,
To pink a man's heart like a summer suit.°
          Exeunt

[4.2]

Enter two or three Servants placing things in order, with
Pickadille, the clown, like an overseer

PICKADILLE Bestir your bones nimbly, you ponderous beef-but-
tocked knaves; what a number of lazy hinds do I keep company
withal! Where's the flesh-colour velvet cushion now for my lady's
pease-porridge-tawny-satin bum? You attendants upon revels!

FIRST SERVANT You can prate and domineer well because you have   5
a privileged° place, but I'd fain see you set your hand to't.

PICKADILLE Oh, base bone-pickers, I set my hand to't! When did
you e'er see a gentleman set his hand to anything, unless it were
to a sheepskin and receive a hundred pound for his pains?

SECOND SERVANT And afterward lie in the Counter for his pleasure.   10

PICKADILLE Why, true, sir; 'tis for his pleasure indeed; for, spite of
all their teeths, he may lie i'th'hole° when he list.

FIRST SERVANT Marry, and should for me.

PICKADILLE Ay, thou wouldst make as good a bawd as the best jailor
of them all; I know that.   15

FIRST SERVANT How, fool?

PICKADILLE Hark! I must call you knave within; 'tis but staying
somewhat the longer for't.°

Exeunt

[4.3]

*Loud music. Enter the new-married widow [Lady
Goldenfleece], and Kate [Mistress Low-water], her husband,
both changed in apparel [but Mistress Low-water still in
disguise], arm in arm together; after them Sir Oliver
Twilight, Master Sunset, and the Dutch Merchant;
after them the mother [Lady Twilight], Grace, the daughter
sad, with Jane Sunset; after these, melancholy Philip,
Savourwit, and Master Sandfield [and Low-water, still
disguised]*

MISTRESS LOW-WATER This fair assembly is most freely welcome.
ALL Thanks to you, good sir.
LADY GOLDENFLEECE [*to Lady Twilight*] Come my long-wished-for
    madam,
    You and this worthy stranger take best welcome;
    Your freedom is a second feast to me.   5
MISTRESS LOW-WATER [*aside to Low-water*] How is't with my
    brother?
LOW-WATER The fit holds him still;
    Nay, love's more violent.
MISTRESS LOW-WATER   'Las, poor gentleman!
    I would he had my office without money;°
    If he should offer any, I'd refuse it.   10
LOW-WATER I have the letter ready;
    He's worthy of a place that knows how to use it.
MISTRESS LOW-WATER That's well said.—
    Come ladies; gentlemen; Sir Oliver; good;
    Seat yourselves; shall we be found unreadiest?   15
    What is yon gentleman with the funeral face there?
    Methinks that look does ill become a bride-house.
SIR OLIVER Who does your worship mean, sir? My son Philip?
    I am sure he had ne'er less reason to be sad.
    Why are you sad, son Philip?
PHILIP   How, sir, sad?   20
    You shall not find it so, sir.
SAVOURWIT [*aside to Philip*]   Take heed he do not then.
    You must beware how you carry your face in this company; as far
    as I can see, that young bridegroom has hawk's eyes; he'll go nigh
    to spell sister in your face;° if your nose were but crooked enough

to serve for an S, he'd find an eye° presently, and then he has more 25
light for the rest.

PHILIP I'll learn then to dissemble.

SAVOURWIT Nay, an you be to learn that now, you'll ne'er sit in a
branched-velvet gown° as long as you live; you should have took
that at nurse° before your mother weaned you; so do all those that 30
prove great° children° and batten well. Peace, here comes a scholar
indeed; he has learned it,° I warrant you.

Enter Master Beveril with a pasteboard

LADY GOLDENFLEECE Kind sir, you're welcome; you take all the
pains, sir.

MASTER BEVERIL I wish they were but worthy of the grace
Of your fair presence and this choice assembly. 35
Here is an abstract, madam, of what's shown,°
Which I commend to your favour.

LADY GOLDENFLEECE Thank you for't, sir.

BEVERIL [*aside*] I would I durst present my love as boldly.

MISTRESS LOW-WATER [*aside*] My honest brother! 40

LADY GOLDENFLEECE Look thee here, sweetheart.

MISTRESS LOW-WATER What's there, sweet madam?

BEVERIL Music, and we're ready.

> *Loud music a while. A thing like a globe opens of one side
> o'th'stage and flashes out fire, then Sir Gilbert, that presents
> the part, issues forth with yellow hair and beard, intermingled
> with streaks like wild flames, a three-forked fire in's hand;
> and, at the same time, Air [Weatherwise] comes down hanging
> by a cloud, with a coat made like an almanac, all the twelve
> moons set in it, and the four quarters; winter, spring, summer,
> and autumn, with change of weathers: rain, lightning, and
> tempest, etc. And from under the stage, at both ends, arises
> Water [Overdone] and Earth [Pepperton], two persons; Water
> with green flags° upon his head standing up instead of hair,
> and a beard of the same, with a chain of pearl. Earth with a
> number of little things like trees, like a thick grove, upon his
> head, and a wedge of gold in his hand, his garment of clay
> colour. The Fire speaking first; the scholar [Beveril] stands
> behind, gives him the first word, which he now follows.*

BEVERIL [*whispering*] 'The flame of zeal—'

SIR GILBERT [*as Fire*]   'The wicked fire of lust
Does now spread heat through water, air, and dust.' 45

BEVERIL [*aside*] How! He's out° in the beginning!—'The wheel of
time—'

WEATHERWISE [*aside*] The devil set fire o'th'distaff.°

SIR GILBERT 'I that was wont in elder times to pass
 For a bright angel, so they called me then,   50
 Now so corrupted with the upstart fires
 Of avarice, luxury, and inconstant heats,
 Struck from the bloods of cunning clap-fallen daughters,
 Night-walking wives, but, most, libidinous widows,
 That I, that purify even gold itself,   55
 Have the contemptible dross thrown in my face,
 And my bright name walk common in disgrace.
 How am I used o'late, that I am so handled,
 Thrust into alleys, hospitals, and tubs!°
 I was once a name of comfort, warmed great houses   60
 When charity was landlord; I have given welcome
 To forty russet yeomen at a time°
 In a fair Christmas-hall. How am I changed!
 The chimneys are swept up, the hearth as cold
 As the forefathers' charity in the son.   65
 All the good hospitable heat now turns
 To my young landlord's lust, and there it burns.
 Rich widows, that were wont to choose by gravity
 Their second husbands, not by tricks of blood,
 Are now so taken with loose Aretine flames°   70
 Of nimble wantonness and high-fed pride,
 They marry now but the third part of husbands,
 Boys, smooth-faced catamites, to fulfil their bed,
 As if a woman should a woman wed.
 These are the fires o'late my brightness darks,   75
 And fills the world so full of beggarly sparks.'°

BEVERIL [*aside*] Heart!° How am I disgraced! What rogue should this
 be?

LADY GOLDENFLEECE By my faith, monsieur Fire, y'are a hot
 whoreson!

MISTRESS LOW-WATER [*aside*] I fear my brother is beside his wits,
 He would not be so senseless to rail thus else.   80

WEATHERWISE (*as Air*) 'After this heat, you madams, fat and
 fair,°
 Open your casements wide and take in air;
 But not that air false women make up oaths with,°
 No, nor that air gallants perfume their clothes with;°
 I am that air that keeps about the clouds;   85

None of my kindred was smelt out in crowds;°
Not any of our house was ever tainted,
When many a thousand of our foes have fainted.°
Yet some there are that be my chief polluters,
Widows that falsify their faith to suitors,   90
And will give fair words when the sign's in Cancer,°
But, at the next remove, a scurvy answer;
Come to the poor men's houses, eat their banquet,
And at night with a boy tossed in a blanket;
Nay, shall I come more near? Perhaps at noon,°   95
For here I find a spot full in the moon.°
I know youth's trick; what's she that can withstand it
When Mercury reigns, my lady's chamber planet?°
He that believes a widow's words shall fail
When Venus' gown-skirts sweeps the Dragon's tail.°   100
Fair weather the first day she makes to any,
The second cloudy, and the third day rainy;
The fourth day a great storm, lightning and thunder;
A bolt strikes the suitor, a boy keeps her under.'
BEVERIL [*aside*] Life! These are some counterfeit slaves crept in their
    rooms°   105
O'purpose for disgrace; they shall all share with me.
Heart! Who the devil should these be?
        Exit Beveril
LADY GOLDENFLEECE   My faith, gentlemen,
    Air has perfumed the room well.
SIR OLIVER   So methinks, madam.
SAVOURWIT [*aside*] A man may smell her meaning two rooms
    off,°
Though his nose wanted reparations,   110
And the bridge left at Shoreditch as a pledge
For *rosa solis* in a bleaking-house.
MISTRESS LOW-WATER Life! What should be his meaning in't?
LOW-WATER   I wonder.
OVERDONE (*as Water*) 'Methinks this room should yet retain such
    heat,
Struck out from the first ardour and so glow yet,   115
You should desire my company, wish for water,
That offers here to serve your several pipes°
Without constraint of mill or death of water house.°
What if I sprinkled on the widow's cheeks

A few cool drops to lay the guilty heat   120
That flashes from her conscience to her face;
Would't not refresh her shame? From such as she
I first took weakness and inconstancy;
I sometimes swell above my banks and spread;°
They're commonly with child before they're wed;   125
In me the Sirens sing before they play,
In her more witchcraft, for her smiles betray;
Where I'm least seen, there my most danger lies—
So, in those parts hid most from a man's eyes:
Her heart, her love, or what may be more close;   130
I know no mercy, she thinks that no loss;
In her, poor gallants; pirates thrive in me;
  I help to cast away and so does she.'
LADY GOLDENFLEECE Nay, an you can hold nothing, sweet
    sir Water,°
    I'll wash my hands o'you ever hereafter.   135
PEPPERTON (*as Earth*) 'Earth stands for a full point; me you should
    hire°
To stop the gaps of water, air, and fire;°
I love muck well, but your first husband better.°
Above his soul he loved it, at his end
Did fearfully witness it; at his last gasp   140
His spirit flamed as it forsook his breast,
And left the sparkles quarrelling 'bout his lips;°
Now of such metal the devil makes him whips.
He shall have gold enough to glut his soul;
And as for earth, I'll stop his crane's throat full;°   145
The wealth he left behind him, most men know,
He wrung inconscionably from the rights
Of poor men's livings; he drunk dry their brows.°
That liquor has a curse, yet nothing sweeter;
When your posterity drinks, then 'twill taste bitter.'   150
SIR GILBERT 'And now to vex, 'gainst nature, form, rule, place,
    See once four warring elements all embrace.'

> [*They embrace.*] *Enter four* [*persons including Beveril*] *at sev-
> eral corners, addressed like the four winds, with wings, etc.,
> and dance all to the drum and fife; the four Elements seem to
> give back*° *and stand in amaze; the South Wind has a great
> red face, the North Wind a pale bleak one, the Western Wind
> one cheek red and another white, and so the Eastern Wind.*

At the end of the dance, the Winds shove off the disguises of
the other four [the Elements], which seem to yield and almost
fall off of themselves at the coming of the Winds; so all the
four old suitors are discovered. Exeunt all the Winds but one,
which is the scholar [Beveril] in that disguise; so shows all

LADY GOLDENFLEECE How! Sir Gilbert Lambston! Maste
  Overdone!
  All our old suitors! You have took pains, my masters.

SIR GILBERT We made a vow we'd speak our minds to you.   155

WEATHERWISE And I think we're as good as our words though, it
  cost some of our purses; I owe money for the clouds yet, I care
  not who knows it; the planets are sufficient enough to pay the
  painter, an I were dead.

LADY GOLDENFLEECE Who are you, sir?   160

BEVERIL [*removing his disguise*] Your most unworthy servant.

LADY GOLDENFLEECE Pardon me, is't you, sir?

BEVERIL My disgrace urged my wit to take some form
  Wherein I might both best and properliest
  Discover my abusers and your own,   165
  And show you some content, before y'had none.

LADY GOLDENFLEECE Sir, I owe much both to your care and love,
  And you shall find your full requital worthy.
  [*To the suitors*] Was this the plot now your poor envy works out?
  I do revenge myself with pitying on you.—   170
  Take Fire into the buttery, he has most need on't;
  Give Water some small beer, too good for him;
  Air, you may walk abroad like a fortune teller;°
  But take down Earth and make him drink i'th'cellar.
    [*Exeunt Suitors*]

MISTRESS LOW-WATER The best revenge that could be.

LADY TWILIGHT   I commend you, madam.   175

SIR OLIVER I thought they were some such sneakers.

SAVOURWIT The four suitors! And here was a mess of mad elements!

MISTRESS LOW-WATER Lights, more lights there! Where be these
  blue-coats?
    [*Enter servants with lights*]

LADY GOLDENFLEECE You know your lodgings, gentlemen, tonight.   180

SIR OLIVER 'Tis bounty makes bold guests, madam.

LADY GOLDENFLEECE [*to Lady Twilight*] Good rest, lady.

SIR OLIVER A most contentful night begin a health, madam,
  To your long joys, and may the years go round with't.

LADY GOLDENFLEECE As many thanks as you have wished 'em
    hours, sir,   185
  Take to your lodging with you.
MISTRESS LOW-WATER A general rest to all.
       Exeunt [all but Philip and Savourwit]
PHILIP I'm excepted.
SAVOURWIT Take in another to you then; there's room enough
  In that exception, faith, to serve us both.   190
  The dial of my sleep goes by your eyes.
      [Exeunt]°

[5.1]

[Enter] Widow [Lady Goldenfleece] and Mistress Low-water°

LADY GOLDENFLEECE Now like a greedy usurer alone,
  I sum up all the wealth this day has brought me,
  And thus I hug it.
    [Embraces her]
MISTRESS LOW-WATER Prithee!
LADY GOLDENFLEECE   Thus I kiss it.
    [Kisses her]
MISTRESS LOW-WATER I can't abide these kissings.
LADY GOLDENFLEECE   How, sir? Not?
  I'll try that sure, I'll kiss you out of that humour.°   5
MISTRESS LOW-WATER Push, by my troth, I cannot.
LADY GOLDENFLEECE   What cannot you,
  sir?
MISTRESS LOW-WATER Not toy, nor bill and imitate house
  pigeons;
  A married man must think of other matters.
LADY GOLDENFLEECE How, other matters, sir? What other
  matters?
MISTRESS LOW-WATER Why, are there no other matters that belong
  to't?   10
  Do you think y'have married only a cock-sparrow,°
  And fit but for one business like a fool?
  You shall not find it so.
LADY GOLDENFLEECE   You can talk strangely, sir.
  Come, will you to bed?
MISTRESS LOW-WATER   No, faith, will not I.
LADY GOLDENFLEECE What, not to bed, sir?   15
MISTRESS LOW-WATER An I do, hang me! Not to bed with you!
LADY GOLDENFLEECE How, not to bed with me! Sir, with
  whom else?
MISTRESS LOW-WATER Why, am not I enough to lie with
  myself?
LADY GOLDENFLEECE Is that the end of marriage?
MISTRESS LOW-WATER   No, by my faith,°
  'Tis but the beginning, yet death is the end on't   20
  Unless some trick come i'th'middle and dash all.

LADY GOLDENFLEECE Were you so forward lately, and so
    youthful,
  That scarce my modest strength could save me from you,
  And are you now so cold?
MISTRESS LOW-WATER   I've thought on't since.
  It was but a rude part in me, i'faith,   25
  To offer such bold tricks to any woman,
  And by degrees I shall well break myself from't;
  I feel myself well chastened since that time,
  And not the third part now so loosely minded.
  Oh, when one sees their follies, 'tis a comfort;   30
  My very thoughts take more staid years upon 'em.
  Oh, marriage is such a serious divine thing!
  It makes youth grave and sweetly nips the spring.
LADY GOLDENFLEECE If I had chose a gentleman for care
  And worldly business, I had ne'er took you;   35
  I had the offers of enough more fit
  For such employment; I chose you for love,
  Youth, and content of heart, and not for troubles;
  You are not ripe for them; after y'have spent
  Some twenty years in dalliance, youth's affairs,   40
  Then take a book in your hand and sum up cares;
  As for wealth now, you know that's got to your hands.
MISTRESS LOW-WATER But had I known't had been so wrongfully
    got,
  As I heard since, you should have had free leave
  To have made choice of another master for't.   45
LADY GOLDENFLEECE Why, can that trouble you?
MISTRESS LOW-WATER   It may too soon; but go;
  My sleeps are sound; I love not to be started
  With an ill conscience at the fall of midnight,
  And have mine eyes torn ope with poor men's curses;
  I do not like the fate on't, 'tis still apt   50
  To breed unrest, dissension, wild debate,
  And I'm the worst at quarrels upon earth,
  Unless a mighty injury should provoke me.
  Get you to bed, go.
LADY GOLDENFLEECE Not without you, in troth, sir.
MISTRESS LOW-WATER If you could think how much you wrong
    yourself
   In my opinion of you, you would leave me now   55

With all the speed you might; I like you worse
For this fond heat, and drink in more suspicion of you.
You high-fed widows are too cunning people
For a poor gentleman to come simply to.   60
LADY GOLDENFLEECE What's that, sir?
MISTRESS LOW-WATER   You may make a youth on him.°
'Tis at your courtesy, and that's ill-trusted;°
You could not want a friend, beside a suitor,
To sit in your husband's gown and look over your writings.°
LADY GOLDENFLEECE What's this?   65
MISTRESS LOW-WATER I say there is a time when women
Can do too much and understand too little.
Once more, to bed; I'd willingly be a father
To no more noses than I got myself;
And so good night to you.   70
LADY GOLDENFLEECE [aside] Now I see the infection.
A yellow poison runs through the sweet spring°
Of his fair youth already; 'tis distracted;
Jealous of that which thought yet never acted.—
Oh, dear sir! On my knees I swear to thee.   75
       [Kneels]
MISTRESS LOW-WATER I prithee use them in thy private
    chamber
As a good lady should; spare 'em not there;
'Twill do thee good; faith, none 'twill do thee here.
LADY GOLDENFLEECE [rising] Have I yet married poverty and
    missed love?
What fortune has my heart? That's all I craved,   80
And that lies now a-dying; it has took
A speeding poison, and I'm ignorant how;
I never knew what beggary was till now.
My wealth yields me no comfort in this plight;
Had want but brought me love, I'd happened right.   85
       Exit Widow [Lady Goldenfleece]
MISTRESS LOW-WATER So, this will serve now for a preparative
To ope the pores of some dislike at first;°
The physic will pay't home.
       Enter Master Low-water
                        How dost thou, sir?
How goes the work?
LOW-WATER   Your brother has the letter.

MISTRESS LOW-WATER I find no stop in't then; it moves well
    hitherto;   90
  Did you convey it closely?
LOW-WATER   He ne'er set eye of me.
    [*Enter Beveril*] *above* [*with a letter*]
BEVERIL I cannot read too often.
MISTRESS LOW-WATER [*to Master Low-water*] Peace, to your office.
BEVERIL What blessed fate took pity of my heart,
  But with her presence to relieve me thus!
  All the large volumes that my time hath mastered   95
  Are not so precious to adorn my spirit
  As these few lines are to enrich my mind.
  I thirst again to drink of the same fountain.
  [*Reads*] 'Kind Sir, I found your care and love so much in the
  performance of a little, wherein your wit and art had late employ-   100
  ment, that I dare now trust your bosom with business of more
  weight and eminence. Little thought the world that, since the
  wedding dinner, all my mirth was but dissembled and seeming
  joys but counterfeit. The truth to you, sir, is, I find so little signs
  of content in the bargain I made i'th'morning, that I began   105
  to repent before evening prayer; and to show some fruits of
  his wilful neglect and wild disposition, more than the day
  could bring forth to me, h'as now forsook my bed; I know no cause
  for't.'
MISTRESS LOW-WATER [*aside*] But I'll be sworn I do.   110
BEVERIL [*reads*] 'Being thus distressed, sir, I desire your comfortable
  presence and counsel, whom I know to be of worth and judgement,
  that a lady may safely impart her griefs to you and commit 'em to
  the virtues of commiseration and secrecy.—Your unfortunate
  friend, The Widow Wife.—I have took order for your private   115
  admittance with a trusty servant of mine own, whom I have placed
  at my chamber door to attend your coming.'—He shall not wait
  too long and curse my slowness.
LOW-WATER [*aside*] I would you'd come away then.
BEVERIL How much am I beguiled in that young gentleman!   120
  I would have sworn h'ad been the perfect abstract
  Of honesty and mildness; 'tis not so.
MISTRESS LOW-WATER [*aside*] I pardon you, sweet brother; there's
  no hold
  Of what you speak now; you're in Cupid's pound.
BEVERIL Blessed be the secret hand that brought thee hither;   125

But the dear hand that writ it ten times blessed.
    [Exit Master Beveril above]
LOW-WATER That's I still; h'as blessed me now ten times at
  twice.
  Away, I hear him coming.
MISTRESS LOW-WATER   Strike it sure now.
    Exit [Mistress Low-water]
LOW-WATER I warrant thee, sweet Kate; choose your best—
    Enter Master Beveril
BEVERIL Who's there?   130
LOW-WATER Oh, sir, is't you? Y'are welcome then;
  My lady still expects you, sir.
BEVERIL   Who's with her?
LOW-WATER Not any creature living, sir.
BEVERIL   Drink that;
    [Gives money]
  I've made thee wait too long.
LOW-WATER   It does not seem so now, sir.
  Sir, if a man tread warily as any   135
  Wise man will, how often may he come
  To a lady's chamber and be welcome to her!
BEVERIL Thou giv'st me learnèd counsel for a closet.
LOW-WATER Make use on't, sir, and you shall find no loss in't.
    [Exit Beveril]
  So, you are surely in, and you must under.°   140
    Enter Kate [Mistress Low-water] with all the guests: Sir Oliver,
    Master Sunset, Wife [Lady Twilight], Daughter [Grace],
    Philip, Sandfield, [Jane, Dutch Merchant] and Savourwit
MISTRESS LOW-WATER Pardon my rude disturbance, my wrongs
  urge it;
  I did but try the plainness of her mind,
  Suspecting she dealt cunningly with my youth,
  And told her the first night I would not know her;°
  But minding to return, I found the door   145
  Warded suspiciously, and I heard a noise,
  Such as fear makes, and guiltiness at th'approaching
  Of an unlooked-for husband.
ALL   This is strange, sir.
MISTRESS LOW-WATER Behold, it's barred; I must not be kept out!
SIR OLIVER There is no reason, sir.
MISTRESS LOW-WATER   I'll be resolved in't.   150

If you be sons of honour, follow me!
> *Break open door; rush in*

SAVOURWIT Then I must stay behind, for I think I was begot
i'th'woodyard,° and that makes everything go so hard° with me.

MISTRESS LOW-WATER [*within*] That's he; be sure on him.
> *Enter confusedly [Mistress Low-water] with the widow [Lady*
> *Goldenfleece], and her brother [Beveril] the scholar [and the*
> *rest]*

SIR OLIVER Be not so furious, sir.   155

MISTRESS LOW-WATER She whispered to him to slip into her
closet.

What, have I taken you? Is not my dream true now?
Unmerciful adulteress, the first night!

SIR OLIVER Nay, good sir, patience!

MISTRESS LOW-WATER   Give me the villain's heart
That I may throw't into her bosom quick;°   160
There let the lecher pant.

LADY TWILIGHT   Nay, sweet sir!

MISTRESS LOW-WATER Pardon me; his life's too little for me.

LADY GOLDENFLEECE How am I wrongfully shamed? Speak
your intent, sir,

Before this company; I pursue no pity.

MISTRESS LOW-WATER This is a fine thievish juggling, gentlemen!   165
She asks her mate that shares in guilt with her.
Too gross, too gross!

BEVERIL [*aside*]   Rash mischief!

MISTRESS LOW-WATER   Treacherous sir,
Did I for this cast a friend's arm about thee,
Gave thee the welcome of a worthy spirit,
And lodged thee in my house, nay, entertained thee   170
More like a natural brother than a stranger,
And have I this reward? Perhaps the pride
Of thy good parts did lift thee to this impudence.
Let her make much on 'em; she gets none of me.
Because thou'rt deeply read in most books else,   175
Thou wouldst be so in mine; there it stands for thee;
> [*Pointing to Lady Goldenfleece*]

Turn o'er the leaves, and where you left, go forward;
To me it shall be like the book of fate,
Ever clasped up.

SIR OLIVER   Oh, dear sir, say not so.

MISTRESS LOW-WATER Nay, I'll swear more; forever I refuse her;   180
  I'll never set a foot into her bed,
  Never perform the duty of man to her
  So long as I have breath.
SIR OLIVER What an oath was there, sir! Call't again.
MISTRESS LOW-WATER I knew by amorous sparks struck from their
    eyes   185
  The fire would appear shortly in a blaze,
  And now it flames indeed.—Out of my house,
  And take your gentleman of good parts along with you;
  That shall be all your substance; he can live
  In any emperor's court in Christendom.   190
  You know what you did, wench, when you chose him
  To thrust out me; you have no politic love!
  You are to learn to make your market, you!
  You can choose wit, a burden light and free,
  And leave the grosser element with me,   195
  Wealth, foolish trash, I thank you.—Out of my doors!
SIR OLIVER Nay, good sir, hear her.
LADY TWILIGHT, SUNSET Sweet sir!
MISTRESS LOW-WATER Pray, to your chambers, gentlemen; I should
    be here
  Master of what is mine.
SIR OLIVER   Hear her but speak, sir!   200
MISTRESS LOW-WATER What can she speak but woman's common
    language?
  She's sorry and ashamed for't; that helps nothing.
LADY GOLDENFLEECE Sir, since it is the hard hap of my life
  To receive injury where I placed my love—
MISTRESS LOW-WATER Why la, I told you what escapes she'd
    have.°   205
SIR OLIVER Nay, pray, sir, hear her forward.
LADY GOLDENFLEECE   Let our parting
  Be full as charitable as our meeting was,
  That the pale envious world, glad of the food
  Of others' miseries, civil dissensions,
  And nuptial strifes, may not feed fat with ours;   210
  But since you are resolved so wilfully
  To leave my bed and ever to refuse me,
  As by your rage I find it your desire,
  Though all my actions deserve nothing less,

Here are our friends, men both of worth and wisdom;   215
Place so much power in them to make an evenness
Between my peace and yours. All my wealth within doors,
In gold and jewels, lie in those two caskets
I lately led you to, the value of which
Amounts to some five thousand apiece;   220
Exchange a charitable hand with me
And take one casket freely; fare thee well, sir.

SIR OLIVER How say you to that now?

MISTRESS LOW-WATER   Troth, I thank her, sir!
Are not both mine already? You shall wrong me,
And then make satisfaction with mine own?   225
I cannot blame you, a good course for you.

LADY TWILIGHT I know 'twas not my luck to be so happy;
My miseries are no starters; when they come,°
Stick longer by me.

SIR OLIVER   Nay, but give me leave, sir;
The wealth comes all by her!

MISTRESS LOW-WATER   So does the shame,   230
Yet that's most mine; why should not that be too?

SIR OLIVER Sweet sir, let us rule so much with you:
Since you intend an obstinate separation
Both from her bed and board, give your consent
To some agreement reasonable and honest.   235

MISTRESS LOW-WATER Must I deal honestly with her lust?

LADY TWILIGHT Nay, good sir.

MISTRESS LOW-WATER Why, I tell you, all the wealth her husband
    left her
Is not of power to purchase the dear peace
My heart has lost in these adulterous seas;   240
Yet, let her works be base, mine shall be noble.

SIR OLIVER That's the best word of comfort I heard yet.

MISTRESS LOW-WATER Friends may do much.—Go, bring those
    caskets forth.
        [Exit servants]
I hate her sight; I'll leave her, though I lose by't.

SIR OLIVER Spoke like a noble gentleman i'faith!   245
I'll honour thee for this.

BEVERIL [aside]   Oh, cursèd man!
Must thy rash heat force this division?

288

MISTRESS LOW-WATER You shall have free leave now without all
    fear;
    You shall not need oiled hinges, privy passages,
    Watchings, and whisperings; take him boldly to you.   250
LADY GOLDENFLEECE Oh, that I had that freedom! Since my shame
    Puts by all other fortunes, and owns him
    A worthy gentleman, if this cloud were past him,
    I'd marry him, were't but to spite thee only,
    So much I hate thee now.   255
        Enter servants with two caskets, and the suitors [Sir Gilbert
        Lambston, Weatherwise, Pepperton, and Overdone]
SIR OLIVER Here come the caskets, sir; hold your good mind now,
    And we shall make a virtuous end between you.
MISTRESS LOW-WATER Though nothing less she merit but a curse
    That might still hang upon her and consume her still,
    As't has been many a better woman's fortune   260
    That has deserved less vengeance and felt more,
    Yet my mind scorns to leave her shame so poor.
SIR OLIVER Nobly spoke still.
SIR GILBERT   This strikes me into music—ha, ha!°
PEPPERTON Parting of goods before the bodies join?
WEATHERWISE This 'tis to marry beardless domineering boys! I   265
    knew 'twould come to this pass. Well fare a just almanac yet,° for
    now is Mercury going into the second house near unto Ursa
    Major, that great hunks,° the Bear at the bridge-foot in heaven,°
    which shows horrible bear baitings in wedlock; and the sun
    entering into th'Dog,° sets 'em all together by th'ears.   270
SIR OLIVER You see what's in't?
    [Opening the caskets]
MISTRESS LOW-WATER   I think 'tis as I left it.
LADY GOLDENFLEECE Then do but gage your faith to this assembly
    That you will ne'er return more to molest me,
    But rest in all revenges full appeased
    And amply satisfied with that half my wealth,   275
    And take't as freely as life wishes health.
SIR OLIVER La you, sir; come, come, faith, you shall swear that!
MISTRESS LOW-WATER Nay, gentlemen, for your sakes,
    Now I'll deal fairly with her.
SIR OLIVER I would we might see that, sir.
MISTRESS LOW-WATER   I could set her free,   280
    But now I think on't, she deserves it not.

SUNSET Nay, do not check your goodness, pray, sir; on with't.

MISTRESS LOW-WATER I could release her ere I parted with her,
　But 'twere a courtesy ill-placed, and set her
　At as free liberty to marry again   285
　As you all know she was before I knew her.

SIR OLIVER What, couldst thou, sir?

MISTRESS LOW-WATER But 'tis too good a blessing for her.
　Up with the casket, sirrah.

LADY GOLDENFLEECE   Oh, sir, stay!

MISTRESS LOW-WATER I have nothing to say to you.

SIR OLIVER   Do you hear, sir?   290
　Pray, let's have one word more with you for our money.

LADY GOLDENFLEECE Since y'have exposed me to all shame and
　sorrow,
　And made me fit but for one hope and fortune,
　Bearing my former comforts away with you,
　Show me a parting charity but in this;   295
　For all my losses pay me with that freedom,
　And I shall think this treasure as well given
　As ever 'twas ill-got.

MISTRESS LOW-WATER I might afford it you,
　Because I never mean to be more troubled with you;   300
　But how shall I be sure of the honest use on't,
　How you'll employ that liberty? Perhaps sinfully,
　In wantonness unlawful, and I answer for't;
　So I may live a bawd to your loose works still
　In giving 'em first vent. Not I, shall pardon me;   305
　I'll see you honestly joined ere I release you;
　I will not trust you for the last trick you played me;
　Here's your old suitors.

PEPPERTON   Now we thank you, sir.

WEATHERWISE My almanac warns me from all cuckoldy
　conjunctions.

LADY GOLDENFLEECE Be but commander of your word now, sir,   310
　And before all these gentlemen, our friends,
　I'll make a worthy choice.

SUNSET   Fly not ye back now.

MISTRESS LOW-WATER I'll try thee once. I am married to
　another;
　There's thy release!

SIR OLIVER   Hoyda! There's a release with a witness!°

Thou'rt free, sweet wench.

LADY GOLDENFLEECE   Married to another!   315
Then in revenge to thee,
To vex thine eyes 'cause thou hast mocked my heart,
And with such treachery repaid my love,
This is the gentleman I embrace and choose.
      [*Embraces Beveril*]

MISTRESS LOW-WATER Oh, torment to my blood, mine enemy!   320
None else to make thy choice of but the man
From whence my shame took head?

LADY GOLDENFLEECE   'Tis done to quit thee,
Thou that wrong'st woman's love, her fate can fit thee.°

SIR OLIVER Brave wench i'faith! Now thou hast an honest
      gentleman,
Rid of a swaggering knave, and there's an end on't.°   325
A man of good parts, this t'other had nothing.
Life, married to another!

SIR GILBERT   Oh, brave rascal with two wives!

WEATHERWISE Nay, an our women be such subtle animals, I'll lay
wait at the carrier's for a country chambermaid° and live still a
bachelor. When wives are like almanacs, we may have every year   330
a new one; then I'll bestow my money on 'em. In the meantime,
I'll give 'em over and ne'er trouble my almanac about 'em.

SIR GILBERT I come in a good time to see you hanged, sir,
And that's my comfort. Now I'll tickle you, sir.

MISTRESS LOW-WATER You make me laugh indeed.

SIR GILBERT   Sir, you remember   335
How cunningly you choked me at the banquet
With a fine bawdy letter?

MISTRESS LOW-WATER   Your own fist, sir.°

SIR GILBERT I'll read the statute book to you now for't.
Turn to the act in *Anno Jac. primo*,°
There lies a halter for your windpipe.

MISTRESS LOW-WATER   Fie, no.   340

SIR OLIVER Faith, but you'll find it so, sir, an't be followed.

WEATHERWISE So says my almanac, and he's a true man. Look you!
      [*Reads*] 'The thirteenth day, work for the hangman.'

MISTRESS LOW-WATER The fourteenth day, make haste; 'tis time
      you were there then.

WEATHERWISE How, is the book so saucy to tell me so?   345

BEVERIL Sir, I must tell you now, but without gall,

The law would hang you if married to another.

MISTRESS LOW-WATER You can but put me to my book, sweet
   brother,°
   And I've my neck-verse perfect, here and here.°
     [*Removes her disguise, revealing her breasts*]
   Heaven give thee eternal joy, my dear sweet brother.   350

ALL Who's here?

SIR GILBERT [*aside*] Oh devil! Herself! Did she betray me?
   A pox of shame, nine coaches shall not stay me.
    Exit Sir Gilbert

BEVERIL I've two such deep healths in two joys to pledge,
   Heaven keep me from a surfeit.

SIR OLIVER   Mistress Low-water!   355
   Is she the jealous cuckold all this coil's about?
   And my right worshipful servingman, is it you, sir?

LOW-WATER A poor wronged gentleman, glad to serve for his own,
   sir.

SIR OLIVER By my faith, y'have served the widow a fine trick   360
   between you.

MISTRESS LOW-WATER No more my enemy now, my brother's wife
   And my kind sister.

SIR OLIVER   There's no starting now from't;
   'Tis her own brother, did not you know that?

LADY GOLDENFLEECE 'Twas never told me yet.

SIR OLIVER   I thought you'd known't.   365

MISTRESS LOW-WATER What matter is't? 'Tis the same man was
   chose still,
   No worse now than he was. I'm bound to love you;
   Y'have exercised in this a double charity,°
   Which, to your praise, shall to all times be known:
   Advanced my brother and restored mine own.   370
   Nay, somewhat for my wrongs, like a good sister,
   For well you know the tedious suit did cost
   Much pains and fees; I thank you, 'tis not lost;
   You wished for love, and, faith, I have bestowed you
   Upon a gentleman that does dearly love you;   375
   That recompense I've made you; and you must think, madam,
   I loved you well, though I could never ease you,
   When I fetched in my brother thus to please you.

SIR OLIVER Here's unity forever strangely wrought.

LADY GOLDENFLEECE I see too late there is a heavy judgement   380

Keeps company with extortion and foul deeds,
And like a wind which vengeance has in chase
Drives back the wrongs into the injurer's face.
My punishment is gentle, and to show
My thankful mind for't, thus I'll revenge this,   385
With an embracement here, and there a kiss.°
     [*Embraces Mistress Low-water; kisses Beveril*]

SIR OLIVER Why now the bells they go trim, they go trim!°
  [*To Beveril*] I wished thee, sir, some unexpected blessing
For my wife's ransom, and 'tis fallen upon thee.

WEATHERWISE A pox of this! My almanac ne'er gulled me to this   390
  hour; the thirteenth day, work for the hangman, and there's nothing
  toward it;° I'd been a fine ass if I'd given twelve pence for a horse
  to have rid to Tyburn tomorrow. But now I see the error, 'tis false
  figured; it should be thirteen days and a half, work for the
  hangman, for he ne'er works under thirteen pence half-penny;°   395
  beside, Venus being a spot in the sun's garment shows there should
  be a woman found in hose and doublet.

SIR OLIVER Nay, faith, sweet wife, we'll make no more hours on't
  now, 'tis as fine a contracting time° as ever came amongst
  gentlefolks.—Son Philip, Master Sandfield, come to the book°   400
  here!

PHILIP [*aside to Savourwit*] Now I'm waked into a thousand miseries
  and their torments.

SAVOURWIT [*aside to Philip*] And I come after you, sir, drawn with
  wild horses; there will be a brave show on's anon, if this weather 405
  continue.

SIR OLIVER Come, wenches, where be these young gentlemen's
  hands now?

LADY TWILIGHT [*aside*] Poor gentleman, my son!—
  Some other time, sir.

SIR OLIVER   I'll have't now, i'faith, wife.   410
     [*Puts Philip's hand into Jane's and Sandfield's into Grace's*]

LADY GOLDENFLEECE What are you making here?

SIR OLIVER   I have sworn, sweet madam,
  My son shall marry Master Sunset's daughter,
  And Master Sandfield, mine.

LADY GOLDENFLEECE   So you go well, sir;
  But what make you this way then?
     [*Points to Jane*]

SIR OLIVER   This? For my son.

LADY GOLDENFLEECE Oh, back, sir, back! This is no way for him.   415
SUNSET, SIR OLIVER How?
LADY GOLDENFLEECE Oh, let me break an oath to save two souls,
Lest I should wake another judgement greater!
You come not here for him, sir.
SIR OLIVER   What's the matter?
LADY GOLDENFLEECE Either give me free leave to make this match,   420
Or I'll forbid the banns.
SIR OLIVER   Good madam, take it.
LADY GOLDENFLEECE Here, Master Sandfield, then—
SIR OLIVER Cuds bodkins!
LADY GOLDENFLEECE Take you this maid.
    [Gives Jane to Sandfield]
SANDFIELD You could not please me better, madam.   425
SIR OLIVER Hoyda! Is this your hot love to my daughter, sir?
LADY GOLDENFLEECE Come hither, Philip; here's a wife for you.
    [Gives Grace to Philip]
SIR OLIVER Zunes, he shall ne'er do that; marry his sister!
LADY GOLDENFLEECE Had he been ruled by you, he had married
    her,
But now he marries Master Sunset's daughter,   430
And Master Sandfield, yours; I've saved your oath, sir.
PHILIP Oh, may this blessing hold!
SAVOURWIT [aside]   Or else all the liquor runs out.
SIR OLIVER What riddle's this, madam?
LADY GOLDENFLEECE A riddle of some fourteen years of age now.
You can remember, madam, that your daughter   435
Was put to nurse to Master Sunset's wife.
LADY TWILIGHT True, that we talked on lately.
SIR OLIVER   I grant that, madam.
LADY GOLDENFLEECE Then you shall grant what follows. At that
    time
You likewise know old Master Sunset here
Grew backward in the world, till his last fortunes°   440
Raised him to this estate.
SIR OLIVER   Still this we know too.
LADY GOLDENFLEECE His wife, then nurse to both her own and
    yours,
And both so young, of equal years, and daughters,
Fearing the extremity of her fortunes then
Should fall upon her infant, to prevent it,   445

294

She changed the children, kept your daughter with her,
And sent her own to you for better fortunes.
So long, enjoined by solemn oath unto't
Upon her death bed, I have concealed this;
But now so urged, here's yours, and this is his.   450

SAVOURWIT Whoop, the joy is come of our side!

WEATHERWISE Hey,° I'll cast mine almanac to the moon too, and
strike out a new one for the next year.

PHILIP It wants expression, this miraculous blessing!

SAVOURWIT Methinks I could spring up and knock my head   455
Against yon silver ceiling now for joy.

WEATHERWISE By my faith, but I do not mean to follow you there,
so I may dash out my brains against Charles' Wain and come down
as wise as a carman.

SIR OLIVER I never wondered yet with greater pleasure.   460

LADY TWILIGHT What tears have I bestowed on a lost daughter,
And left her behind me.

LADY GOLDENFLEECE   This is Grace,
This Jane; now each has her right name and place.

SUNSET I never heard of this.

LADY GOLDENFLEECE   I'll swear you did not, sir.

SIR OLIVER How well I have kept mine oath against my will.   465
Clap hands and joy go with you. Well said, boys!

PHILIP [to Grace] How art thou blessed from shame and I from ruin.

SAVOURWIT I from the baker's ditch, if I'd seen you in.°

PHILIP Not possible the whole world to match again
Such grief, such joy, in minutes lost and won.   470

BEVERIL Whoever knew more happiness in less compass?
Ne'er was poor gentleman so bound to a sister
As I am, for the wittiness of thy mind;°
Not only that thy due, but all our wealth
Shall lie as open as the sun to man   475
For thy employments; so the charity
Of this dear bosom bids me tell thee now.

MISTRESS LOW-WATER I am her servant for't.

LADY GOLDENFLEECE   Hah, worthy sister!
The government of all I bless thee with.

BEVERIL Come, gentlemen, on all perpetual friendship.   480
Heaven still relieves what misery would destroy;
Never was night yet of more general joy.
        [Exeunt]

Epilogue

WEATHERWISE° Now let me see what weather shall we have now;
  [*Takes out almanac*]
Hold fair now, and I care not.—Mass, full moon, too,
Just between five and six this afternoon.
This happens right. [*Reading*] 'The sky for the best part clear,
Save here and there a cloud or two dispersed.'   5
That's some dozen of panders and half a score
Pickpockets; you may know them by their whistle,
And they do well to use that, while they may,
For Tyburn cracks the pipe and spoils the music.°
What says the destiny of the hour this evening?   10
Hah. [*Reading*] 'Fear no colours!' By my troth, agreed then,°
The red and white looks cheerfully; for know ye all,°
The planet's Jupiter; you should be jovial;°
There's nothing lets it but the sun i'th'Dog;°
Some bark in corners that will fawn and cog,   15
Glad of my fragments for their ember week;°
The sign's in Gemini too, both hands should meet;°
There should be no noise i'th'air, if all things hap,°
Though I love thunder when you make the clap.
Some faults perhaps have slipped, I am to answer;°   20
And if in anything your revenge appears,
Send me in with all your fists about mine ears.
  [*Exit*]

EXPLANATORY NOTES

ABBREVIATIONS

Barber   *A Trick to Catch the Old One*, ed. Charles Barber, Fountainwell Drama Texts (Berkeley, 1968).

Bullen   *The Works of Thomas Middleton*, ed. A. H. Bullen, 8 vols. (New York, 1964; first pub. Boston, 1885–6).

Chambers   Chambers, E. K., *The Elizabethan Stage*, 4 vols. (Oxford, 1965; first pub. 1923).

Dyce   *The Works of Thomas Middleton*, ed. Alexander Dyce, 5 vols. (London, 1840).

Eccles   Mark Eccles, as quoted in Levin.

Frost   *The Selected Plays of Thomas Middleton*, ed. David L. Frost (Cambridge, 1978).

Henke   Henke, James T., *Courtesans and Cuckolds: A Glossary of Renaissance Dramatic Bawdy* (New York, 1979).

Henning   *A Mad World, My Masters*, ed. Standish Henning, Regents Renaissance Drama Series (Lincoln, Nebr., 1965).

Johnson   *No Wit, No Help Like a Woman's*, ed. Lowell E. Johnson, Regents Renaissance Drama Series (Lincoln, Nebr., 1976).

Lawrence   *Jacobean and Caroline Comedies*, ed. Robert G. Lawrence (London, 1973).

Levin   *Michaelmas Term*, ed. Richard Levin, Regents Renaissance Drama Series (Lincoln, Nebr., 1966).

Linthicum   Linthicum, M. C., *Costume in the Drama of Shakespeare and his Contemporaries* (Oxford, 1936).

Loughrey   *Thomas Middleton: Five Plays*, ed. Bryan Loughrey and Neil Taylor, Penguin Classics (Harmondsworth, 1988).

Mad   *A Mad World, My Masters.*

N&Q   *Notes & Queries.*

No Wit   *No Wit, No Help Like a Woman's.*

o   Octavo.

OED   *Oxford English Dictionary.*

PQ   *Philological Quarterly.*

Partridge   Partridge, Eric, *Shakespeare's Bawdy* (London, 1969).

Price 1   G. R. Price, as quoted in Levin.

Price 2   *Thomas Middleton: Michaelmas Term and A Trick to Catch the Old One*, ed. G. R. Price, Studies in English Literature No. 91 (The Hague, 1976).

q   Quarto.

Q1   First Quarto.

Q2	Second Quarto.
Rubinstein	Rubinstein, Frankie, *A Dictionary of Shakespeare's Sexual Puns and their Significance*, 2nd edn. (London, 1989).
Salgado	*Four Jacobean City Comedies*, ed. Gamini Salgado (Harmondsworth, 1975).
Sampson	*Thomas Middleton*, ed. M. W. Sampson, Masterpieces of the English Drama (New York, 1915).
S.D.	Stage Direction.
SP	*Studies in Philology*.
Shakespeare	*The Complete Works of Shakespeare*, ed. Hardin Craig and David Bevington (Brighton, 1973).
Stow	Stow, John, *A Survey of London*, introd. and notes by C. L. Kingsford, 2 vols. (Oxford, 1971; first pub. 1908).
Sugden	Sugden, E. H., *A Topographical Dictionary* (Manchester, 1925).
Term	*Michaelmas Term*.
Tilley	Tilley, M. P., *Dictionary of Proverbs in England in the Sixteenth and Seventeenth Centuries* (Ann Arbor, 1950).
Trick	*A Trick to Catch the Old One*.
Watson	*A Trick to Catch the Old One*, ed. G. J. Watson, The New Mermaids (London, 1968).

A Mad World, My Masters

The title of the play, 'A Mad World, My Masters', was a proverbial phrase dismissive of the craziness of life (see Tilley W880).

The Actors in the Comedy
This list is derived from the Second Quarto (1640).

1 *Progress*: (1) self-aggrandizement; (2) state procession.

2 *Follywit*: Middleton frequently uses 'wit' combinations for the names of major characters; cf. Savourwit in *No Wit* and Allwit in *A Chaste Maid in Cheapside*. These characters are 'witty' (in the full sense of the term) but flawed, as Follywit's name indicates.

   nephew: grandson.

3 *Penitent Brothel*: called Penitent Once-Ill in S.D.s beginning 4.1 and 4.4 (coinciding with his reformation) in Q.

4 *Mawworm*: an intestinal worm, a parasite; its activities induce peevishness (Frost).

5 *Hoboy*: a corruption of 'hautboy', a reed instrument in a military band.

6–7 *Inesse . . . brothers*: these are the eldest brothers from different families one of whom holds his lands *in esse* (i.e. in actual possession) one *in posse* (i.e. in anticipated possession). Each would be a prime source of revenue for the Courtesan.

8 *Harebrain*: variously called Hargrave and Shortrod in the later stages of
Q. Hares exhibit in the spring a proverbial madness stimulated by sexual
jealousy (Frost).

9 *Gunwater*: probably a jocular euphemism for 'urine' (s.v. 'pistol' in
Partridge); Q calls him Gumwater in Act 4.

11 *Rafe*: Ralph.

19 *Frank*: a diminutive of 'Frances', combining with Gullman to produce the oxymoron 'honest cheater' (Frost); cf. Penitent Brothel and
Follywit.

1.1 Q does not divide the play into scenes. Although I have given the
probable location of each scene throughout this edition of the four
plays—here, the setting is (in all likelihood) a London street—readers
should bear in mind that the Jacobean stage was non-locational and
relatively bare of scenery or any other indication of place. Nor would the
reader of the early editions of these plays be informed as to location.
Place can often be inferred from the dialogue, but in some cases a claim
that has the confidence of its bald assertion is in fact in response as much
to the vagueness or absence of direction within the scene as to any
explicit indication of where it takes place.

s.d. *others his comrades*: an unspecified number of followers attend
Follywit in addition to those named.

4 *forecast*: someone who schemes for the future.

7 *civil fortunes*: respectable career in society.

8 *upo'th'*: like other similar contractions in Middleton this is pronounced
as a single syllable 'upoth' rather than two unstressed or elided syllables
'upo the' (cf. 'i'th' ' and 'o'th' ').

7-9 This passage is an imitation of Falstaff's speech in *1 Henry IV*,
3.3.16-23 in which he jokingly disavows responsibility for his own
behaviour: 'Company, villainous company, hath been the spoil of me'
(3.3.12). Frost suggests that Follywit's speech enables the boy actor to
parody an adult rival in Shakespeare's company.

12 *well given*: well disposed.

13 *all in black*: soberly dressed.

swore . . . Sundays: when uttering the names of God in public worship
(Frost).

13-14 *never . . . stomach*: presumably, drinking on an empty stomach to
induce vomiting (Frost).

15 *blown . . . colours*: blossomed into colourful attire—as opposed to going
all in black.

26 *Mass*: by the mass; an exclamation like 'byrlady', which continued to be
used by Protestants despite the Reformation.

30 *countenance*: (1) facial expression; (2) repute; (3) financial credit.

31 *I . . . blushing*: I assure you that I will not blush.

32 *lost thy colours*: one duty of an ensign was to carry the flag or standard (the 'colours') in battle. To lose it to the enemy, as Parolles famously does in Shakespeare's *All's Well That Ends Well*, was a mark of shame.

34 *Lent . . . down*: your cheeks are pale. The flags that were flown on the tops of playhouses were taken down during Lent.

35–6 *blushing . . . purses*: Follywit means that he would not expect them to 'blush' (from drinking) or 'laugh' unless they had the money to enjoy themselves.

47 *poor*: a mere.

55–6 *is . . . hundred*: an allusion to James I's decree in 1603 requiring all landholders worth forty pounds a year to be knighted or else to suffer a fine. Follywit contrasts Sir Bounteous's more ancient and distinguished lineage.

65 *cut . . . way*: proverbial = avoid tediousness.

   down: to Sir Bounteous's country estate.

68 *French ruff*: a deep ruff, which, instead of extending at right angles to the neck, hung down from the top of a high stock which was fastened up to the chin (Linthicum 160). Frost notes that it was more fashionable than the English ruff.

69 *blue . . . clock*: blue coats were worn by servants, and second-hand ones could no doubt be bought at Westminster, site of the Court and Law Courts (Frost).

70 *colour*: quibble on 'pretext'.

72 *fathoms*: breadth of comprehension.

75 *probably*: convincingly, plausibly.

77 *a Roman captain*: Follywit is so called because he follows the custom of a Roman leader in allowing his troops to pillage what booty they can carry (Frost).

80 *first*: a term taken from heraldry, here meaning 'first rank'.

   pranks: the word at this time could convey, as it does now, the merely frolicsome; but it retained the stronger sense of acts outraging order and decency as in 'lewd, pestiferous, and dissentious pranks' (*1 Henry VI*, 3.1.15).

82 *tricks*: with a pun on 'card tricks'.

83 *last stamp*: the most up-to-date.

88 *I . . . riot*: I reproach him for youthful follies which are widespread and accepted (Frost).

89 *Time's comic flashes*: youth's absurd outbursts.

94 *With . . . suspect*: with a bizarre but warranted suspicion.

95 *his serious time*: transferred epithet; = his time seriously.

watch and ward: the action of watching and warding, the duties of a watchman or sentinel.

98 *her*: Mistress Harebrain's.

100 *who*: the Courtesan.

104 *To . . . aim*: a reference to the person in archery who stood near the target to report on the accuracy of the shot. Harebrain is 'giving aim' to his own cuckolding both by his excessive jealousy and by his employing a courtesan as his wife's moral tutor.

105 *forkèd*: as are the cuckold's horns.

107 *close*: (1) able to keep a secret; (2) lecherous (s.v. in Rubinstein).

110–11 *Holland Skirt*: editors (except Frost) emend Q to 'Holland shirt'. By so doing they ignore a likely bawdy double entendre in 'hole and skirt' (s.v. 'holland' in Partridge). 'Holland' was a linen fabric originally imported from the province of Holland. 'Skirt' was used to signify the bottom half of a woman's gown from 1355.

116 *bass*: with a pun on 'base'.

121 *court of conscience*: Court of Requests, established in 1517 to deal with small claims. But Penitent also means that the Courtesan, in refusing payment until he has got what he paid for, has a business ethic, a conscience.

122 *common place*: a brothel, with a pun on the Court of Common Pleas.

129 *keeper*: punning on 'game-keeper'.

132 *proud*: (1) fine; (2) arrogant; (3) sexually aroused.

145–52 *Fifteen . . . gone*: these lines allude to the practice of gratifying the male taste for virgins by simulating a hymen by means of surgical sewing (Frost).

147–9 *There's . . . done*: a thrust at Sir Bounteous's sexual incompetence.

151 *once*: once more.

154 *British*: probably Bretons (Frost).

156 *politic conveyance*: cunning management.

157 *religious eyebrow*: demure expression.

167 *'Twill . . . own*: i.e. 'have it your own way'.

183 *well-placed*: Q reads 'plac'st'.

184 *prick*: write (with a pun on 'penis' as the one-syllable word that offends).

1.2 A room in Harebrain's house in London.

1 *recovered*: remembered.

2 *He-cats*: tom cats, i.e. casual philanderers.

4 *be at charge*: bear the expense.

10 *fixed . . . month*: this circumlocution alludes to the practice of raising and restricting evil spirits within the circumference of a circle; the evil is to be perpetrated within a month (Frost).

16 *Addressed . . . practice*: (1) prepared for the trick; (2) bribed.

19 *purloined*: robbed. Repetition of the word suggests that Harebrain sees the sexual significance of 'loin'. Frost sees a more elaborate possibility where 'pur' = the knave in the card game 'Post and Pair' and 'to loin' = 'to copulate' and hence a pun on 'loined by a knave'.

19–20 *merry Greeks*: common term for roisterers.

20–1 *kept . . . key*: Italians were proverbially jealous. Harebrain may have chastity belts in mind.

28 *save*: protect.

34 *carried it well*: a triple pun: borne herself, men, and children well.

45 *Hero . . . Adonis*: poems famous for their frank eroticism, by Marlowe and Shakespeare respectively.

46 *mary-bone*: bone containing edible marrow, considered a great delicacy and held to be an aphrodisiac.

47 *Resolution*: *The First Book of the Christian Exercise Pertaining to Resolution* (1582) was a popular book of devotion written by the Jesuit, Robert Parsons.

58 *A . . . strain*: Frost suggests that the metaphor is a complicated one drawn from the breeding of livestock and plants. A simpler and more likely explanation is that 'strain' = 'tune' (*OED* III.12).

60–3 *I'll keep . . . own*: the sexual work ethic here is only thinly disguised. Harebrain claims that his is one of the few wives whose sexual favours are reserved for her husband.

60 *stint*: allotted (sexual) tasks.

61 *pension*: (sexual) payment for board and lodging.

62 *that's . . . one*: Q has 'thats bare one'.

69 *the Family*: the Anabaptist millennial sect called the 'Family of Love' notorious for its emphasis on sexual freedom. In his play of the same name, Middleton satirizes the alleged hypocrisy and sexual looseness of the sect's members.

89 *coted scriptures*: probably a copy of the scriptures with annotations, popular with Puritan sects (Frost).

96 *all nations*: everybody. But we recall the Mother's itemization of her daughter's international clients at 1.1.153.

97 *home*: incisively (for the sexual pun on this word and on 'to the quick' see Rubinstein 210 where she uses this example).

quick: the tenderest or most vital part. 'To touch to the quick' remains proverbial (see Tilley Q13).

98   *reach*: conclude.

102   *Against*: when.

104   *master's side*: an allusion to the name of the most comfortable of the four 'wards' or divisions in the London Counters, or debtors' prisons: the master's, the knight's, the twopenny, and the hole, in descending order of cost (Frost). The 'master' here is the husband, of course, and gives rise to the puns of line 106.

112   *to the third pile*: to the bone. Three pile was a velvet of triple thickness.

121   *sense*: (1) reason; (2) sensuality.

134   *requital*: punishment *on* and *by* women, as they both get and give the disease (syphilis).

135   *pit-hole*: (1) hell; (2) pudendum.

153   *end*: with a double entendre.

154   *alteration*: this continues the innuendo. Harebrain's other (alternative) name in Q is Shortrod (cf. Shortyard in *Term*).

155   *refrain*: i.e. from weeping.

159   *sweet fruit*: (1) of repentance; (2) of sexual dalliance.

2.1   The scene takes place in a room in Sir Bounteous's country house in one of the Home Counties, perhaps Berkshire, as Sir Bounteous talks of attending the assizes at Newbury (4.3.96).

4–5   *Polcut . . . Colewort*: if 'polcut' is a variant of 'polecat', then both surnames convey notions of a noxious smell, the one animal, the other vegetable (colewort = cabbage).

8   *linen stockings*: legwear of servants.

8–9   *threescore . . . day*: a running footman ran before his master's coach, covering considerable distances (Frost).

15   *city*: the financial district of London. There are a fair number of references to this area in these plays.

16   *followed*: (1) admired; (2) prosecuted; (3) pursued for debts.

18   *free . . . mercers*: the joke here involves our reading 'free of' to mean 'free with' as well as 'free from' and (possibly) 'a Free Man of' (the Mercers' Guild). Lord Owemuch lives up to his name.

    cross: (1) thwart; (2) cancel his debts.

19   *turn . . . leaf*: (1) begin again; (2) open a fresh account.

35   *seven . . . hour*: an excessive speed indicative of the hardships of the job.

41   *confine*: the Footman is continually walking away.

44   *large*: abundance of.

49 *progressive*: alluding to the Footman's coming and going, and perhaps to his long-winded style of speaking.

57–8 *i'th'cue . . . i'th'nick*: ostensibly, both phrases mean 'so perfectly' or 'so opportunely'. They also refer bawdily to the penis and pudendum.

58 *like me*: Q has a second 'like me'. But this kind of repetition is not one of Sir Bounteous's habits; it seems likely that it is a compositor's error.

60 *'tis gone . . . on't*: following 'nick' and 'cue' this clause may be glancing at Sir Bounteous's impotence.

63–4 *chief . . . gold*: steward.

68 *Travailed*: (1) travelled; (2) laboured in childbirth. This was a popular pun in Jacobean English; 'travel' was often spelt and pronounced 'travail'.

70 *No bastard*: no wine and no illegitimate children (a common pun).

76 *woodcock*: Sir Bounteous plays on the sense of 'simpleton'.

80 *lord's*: Q reads 'love's', which is a little excessive even for Sir Bounteous.

83 *music*: resident band of musicians.

89 *Your . . . effected*: a pompous circumlocution supposedly in keeping with Follywit's new status.

97 *knowledge*: acquaintance.

113 *present suit*: immediate request.

127 *Imberbis juvenis*: beardless youth.

128 *midwife's*: midwife was a cant term for an effeminate man.

128–9 *there's . . . a-coming*: an allusion to the proverb 'Long hair and short wit' (see B. J. and H. W. Whiting. *Proverbs, Sentences and Proverbial Phrases* (Cambridge, Mass.: Harvard UP, 1963), H23).

135 *generously*: (1) gallantly; (2) magnanimously; (3) liberally.

136–7 *H'es . . . cleanly*: he has played many tricks adroitly.

143 s.d. *A . . . tune*: Music was very common in plays performed by children in the private theatres. We know that in the Blackfriars Theatre there was a music room, a curtained space above the stage in the tiring-house façade, where the musicians would have been located. Such might be the case here. On Sir Bounteous's command, the curtain would be drawn back and the 'consort' revealed to the audience. This interpretation is supported by: (1) the absence of an entrance for the musicians in the s.d., and (2) the use of an organ—an instrument difficult to bring on stage.

s.d. *honour*: bow.

s.d. *seems to foot*: is seen to dance to.

148 *in ordinary*: belonging to the regular staff.

154–5 *Walloon . . . Welshman*: Frost notes that the Flemish were famous for their musicianship and the Welsh for their bragging.

155 S.D. *A . . . organs*: a song sung, no doubt, by one or more of the 'consort' accompanied by the organ.

2.2 The ante-chamber or open area outside Follywit's room ('*toward his lodging*') in Sir Bounteous's country house.

5 *curtains*: of the bed-canopy.

6 *prodigal child*: appropriate for Follywit's history.

15 *They're dreamers*: Q reads 'their dreames', which editors other than Dyce and Bullen retain.

gi'n't: given it (see also 3.2.46).

17 *chambers*: Q reads 'champers'. It is possible that Sir Bounteous means 'gun-chambers'.

19 *even*: Q reads 'ev'n'. In all cases, both in prose and verse, I have standardized to 'even'. The accent on the word's second syllable is too slight to worry about its effect on scansion in a passage of verse.

29 *distinctions*: Frost suggests a pun on the nonce-word 'de-stink-shuns' (i.e. 'farts'). Its likelihood is increased by Follywit's injunction in the next line to 'whelm your nose'.

33 *hold . . . meat*: restrict me to coarse fare.

34 *dag's end*: at a distance (dag = a kind of pistol).

fit: punish.

35 *Under . . . leave*: in the guise of a lord.

41 *lap . . . lead*: bury him (lead = the lining of a wooden coffin).

2.3 A room in the Courtesan's house in London.

2.4 A room in Sir Bounteous's country house.

3 *[GUNWATER]*: who the 'gaping rascal' is here is indicated in Follywit's subsequent remark.

20–1 *honestest . . . Lincolnshire*: perhaps a reference to Nottinghamshire's Robin Hood whose men dressed in Lincoln green. Lincolnshire, however, had a reputation for festivity (see Sugden).

40–1 *spur . . . horse*: an allusion to the proverb, 'Do not spur a free (i.e. willing) horse' (Tilley H638).

43 *conscience*: moral.

46 *bound*: (1) tied up; (2) legally obligated.

48 *[not]*: Frost's insertion of the negative makes the passage more sensible.

49–50 *at Westminster*: at Court rather than on the battlefield (Frost).

50–1 *knight . . . Windsor*: one of a body of military pensioners residing within the precincts of Windsor Castle.

63 *stand upon*: insist upon, with the common Renaissance pun on tumescence (or in Sir Bounteous's case the lack of it) following 'stiff from'.

71 *bound . . . securities*: punning on entering a legal obligation on one's own recognizance.

81 *of all other*: more than anyone else.

88 *lie . . . by't*: (1) remain with the spoils; (2) brazen it out.

90 *hazard a windpipe*: run the risk of being hanged.

2.5 A room in the Courtesan's house in London.

5 *a saver*: make money (from the brothers' purses).

13 *your own wish*: Q has 'her own wish'.

21 *conveyed*: craftily managed.

25 *take . . . you*: explain yourself to me.

37 *college*: the chartered body of the Royal College of Physicians founded in 1518. It was the examining and qualifying body for the medical profession.

47-9 *make . . . company*: make it possible for her to enjoy your company as you both desire.

2.6 Follywit's bedchamber in Sir Bounteous's country house.

S.D. Our knowledge of the layout and procedures of the stage in the Jacobean private theatres is still not exhaustive. It is possible that Follywit was concealed behind the curtains that hung over the third door at the back of the stage in the centre (if there was a third door). Or that he was in a curtained recess at the rear of the stage. The least likely possibility is that he was in a portable curtained booth brought on especially for this scene.

1 Q has Sir Bounteous (who must be *within*, though that is not indicated) calling for Gunwater, with a number of unattached (*within*)s for the following cries for help until Follywit shouts for the Footman in line 6.

2 *Singlestone*: one testicle, hence = a eunuch. Cf. Cockstone in *Term*, Lady Foxstone and Sir Gilbert Lambston in *No Wit*, and Laxton in *The Roaring Girl*. 'Singlestone' and 'Laxton' suggest sexual impoverishment, the others lechery.

4 *Ewen*: yewen, i.e. made from the wood of the yew—hence 'wooden' or perhaps 'oafish'.

5 *Simcod*: 'Sim' is the abbreviation for 'Simon', a name used generically for 'person'; 'cod' = (colloquially) scrotum. Cf. Singlestone.

30 *Suchman*: such a one as Singlestone. (Frost suggests rather implausibly that the word is a mistake for 'Suckman'.)

39 *hard bound*: (1) tied fast; (2) constipated.

49 *use to*: are accustomed to frequent.

50 *conveyances*: (1) passage-ways; (2) cunning tricks.

63 *enter into bond*: (1) be tied up; (2) submit to legal bond. Until 1642 peers and members of the House of Commons could not be summoned to appear in court, or be sued for debt, or be subject to direct taxation.

112 *counsellor's double fee*: the chief counsel in a legal action commanded a double fee.

3.1 A room in Harebrain's house in London.

26 *deflowers . . . deflowered*: cf. *Romeo and Juliet*, 4.5.36–7: 'There she lies, | Flower as she was, deflowered by him'.

34 *scrivener*: notary (presumably to take down her will). Frost notes that scriveners often doubled as money-lenders, which helps to explain the ensuing exchange about 'bonds'.

37 *loose*: with purgatives.

41 *for*: for fear of.

71 *giddy flames*: foolish fits of passion.

73 *Thrice*: many times (and again on line 92).

82 *'tis*: she is.

105–6 *apply . . . luxury*: judge all by the standard of its own lecherousness (Frost).

106 *it*: its. The usual genitive form of 'it' was 'his', but 'it' was sometimes used.

108 *squire*: pimp.

109 *of the stamp*: loose, available—like current coins in circulation ready to receive impressions (of men).

known: i.e. carnally.

3.2 The Courtesan's bed-chamber.

S.D. *viols, gallipots*: glass and earthenware jars used by apothecaries for ointments and medicines.

S.D. *plate*: metal utensils.

17 *loose liver*: (1) one who lives loosely; (2) one who loosens the liver (hence 'purgation' on the next line). Physicians had a reputation for impiety.

17–18 *put . . . purgation*: Frost offers two meanings: (1) put you to an inner cleansing; (2) put on you the onus to clear yourself of the accusation.

22 *What art thou?*: What is the matter with you?

24–5 *Rosamond . . . Harry*: Tilley (G467) records this phrase as proverbial in the sixteenth century; it was probably a line from a lost ballad. Rosamond Clifford, mistress of Henry II, was poisoned by Queen Eleanor.

44 *good will*: (1) inclination; (2) sexual desire.

45–6 *surfeit of Venus*: too much sex.

54 *ingredients*: the 'quacksalving terms' are taken from contemporary *materia medica*; the elements share in common their great rarity and cost, and alleged ability to cure nearly any disease (Henning).

liquor of coral: a solution of coral in water.

54–5 *clear . . . succinum*: spermaceti or white amber.

55 *unicorn's horn*: horn of the rhinoceros, passed off as derived from the unicorn.

55–6 *magisterium perlarum*: precipitate of pearls from an acid solution, another costly medicine

58 *Ossis . . . cervi*: small bones in the heart of a female deer (thought to be beneficial to pregnant women).

aurum potabile: gold held in a state of minute subdivision in some volatile oil and taken as a cordial.

62 *spirit of diamber*: a stomachic and cordial containing ambergris, musk, and other aromatics.

69–70 *olei succini . . . cinnamoni*: oils of yellow amber, mace, cinnamon.

71 *oil of mace*: with a pun on the maces carried by the serjeants in an arrest of debtors.

79 *I . . . her*: (1) made her pregnant; (2) caused her to have a fit; (3) dealt with her appropriately.

cock o'th'game: game-cock ('game' = sexual indulgence).

80 *spurs*: (1) knight's spurs; (2) testicles.

81 *they're hatched*: i.e. his spurs are engraved.

81–2 *cost . . . angel*: (1) cost you a gold coin; (2) damaged your reputation (angel = good angel).

98 *of her*: in her.

100–1 *facility in taking*: the Courtesan is adept sexually (i.e. at taking a man) and is also a clever swindler (bleeding her clients dry). (Frost notes that the 'taker up' was the gang member whose task was to soften up the victim.)

103 *Diversa . . . scabierum*: 'Ulcers as they be of many sorts, so are they cured after divers manners' (Pliny, *Natural History*, xxvi. 14, trans. P. Holland, 1601).

107 *running scab*: I have adopted Q2's addition of 'scab' here.

broad: because an intelligencer spreads information.

108 *scald*: (1) paltry, contemptible; (2) scabby. Taken with 'white' and 'pander' = afflicted with venereal disease.

111 *mine*: my case.

112 *busy . . . head*: presumably, the constable was beating him about the head.

113 *covet the head*: (1) constables covet the position of headborough (a minor parish official); (2) scabs tend to form on top of the head (particularly as a result of venereal disease).

114 *derived him*: traced his pedigree. Frost suggests a play on the medical meaning of 'derive' which = reduce inflammation.

118 *power . . . downward*: through laxatives, enemas, and emetics.

128 *Put up*: (1) put away your purses; (2) stop interfering with me sexually (because 'put up' commonly meant 'sheathe your sword').

131 *an't . . . once*: if it ever comes to that.

151 *Hercules' Pillars*: Gibraltar and Mt. Abyla (in mythology placed there by Hercules), on either side of the Strait of Gibraltar, the traditional limits of navigation (*non plus ultra* = no farther).

169–70 *prick-eared . . . hair*: the doubles entendres here are straightforward enough: jealousy is alert to sounds of copulation.

171 *faint liver*: a coward.

174 s.d. *Enter . . . listening*: Penitent Brothel and Mistress Harebrain are copulating off-stage. Presumably the curtains around the Courtesan's bed are drawn shut with Harebrain listening outside them, and known to be doing so by the Courtesan. We are to imagine Mistress Harebrain's voice to be too soft to be heard by her husband.

175 *flesh . . . end*: (unconsciously) punning on the sexual activity taking place.

183 *trod*: the delaying 'huh' after this word draws attention to a possible alternative bawdy conclusion. Cf. 'tread their husbands' (3.3.106).

186 *right my humour*: it suits my inclination perfectly.

187 *ride*: a bawdy pun.

190 *I . . . that*: we are to imagine that Mistress Harebrain has affirmed her love for her husband.

203–5 *lay . . . upon't*: the Courtesan's request here suggests the action taking place off-stage.

211 *Bound*: constipated.

221–4 *And to . . . St. John's*: the names of the Courtesan's 'relatives' continue the bawdy play. An 'uncle' is a pimp, an 'aunt' a bawd, and the 'cousins' are prostitutes. 'Winchcomb' = wench's comb; 'Lipsalve' = an ointment for sores; 'Lickit' = one who fellates; 'Horseman' = one who 'rides' a man.

224 *St. John's*: a church in Clerkenwell, a district in north London notorious for thieves and prostitutes.

240 *conjure*: the stress is on the second syllable.

246–7 *When plots . . . spread*: this horticultural metaphor thinly conceals the bawdy punning.

3.3 A room in Follywit's house in London.

4 *at all adventures*: whatever the risks.

13 *set him forward*: advance him.

25–6 *shrode pull*: a 'shrewd pull' or 'sharp assault'. Frost suggests a pun on 'shroud pall'; i.e. Follywit is pretending to have had a premonition of death.

31 *preposterous*: putting the last first; i.e. the Courtesan (the last) will become the chief beneficiary of Sir Bounteous's will over the claims of Follywit (the first).

32 *the thirds*: a widow was entitled to a third of her husband's real property.

33 *entailed land*: land that would have restrictions on its transference (with a pun on 'tail').

35 *thought-acting*: able to commit an act only in thought (i.e. he is physically impotent).

37 *(When . . . shame)*: hence only 'thought-acting'.

38 *blanched*: whitened by cosmetics; but see note on 'scald' (3.2.108).

39 *gravely*: solemnly, with a pun on the 'grave' of 'graveyard'.

47 *Most . . . indeed*: coaches were often used for assignations and prostitution.

58–9 *key . . . backward*: stealthily; Italians had a reputation for lust and perversity. They were reputed to favour anal intercourse. Cf. note on 1.2.20–1.

60–2 *there remaining . . . performance*: if fortune does not 'smile' upon Sir Bounteous's sexual performance, he will order a 'caudle' (a spicy, restorative drink) to invigorate it.

61 *send down*: swallow.

63 *'tis mine own*: I've thought of something.

70 *walk . . . conceit*: go down in his estimation.

75 *'tis in grain*: fast-dyed (i.e. the plan will hold). 'Grain' = the red dye derived from the *coccus* insect; when dried it has a granular appearance.

79 *friend's house*: the dress.

80 *there's . . . you*: there's a part of my plan for you to savour (with perhaps a bawdy reference to the enjoyment of the 'friend'). Henning suggests that this remark may be directed at the audience.

92 *horse-keeper*: in 1554 Frances Brandon married Adrian Stokes, her master of the horse, on the death of her husband, Henry Grey, Duke of Suffolk. It was a *cause célèbre*. (It should also be remembered that Leicester was Queen Elizabeth's Master of the Queen's Horse.)

94 *set him up*: stimulate him, give him an erection.

100 *upper bodies*: the bodice (hence the breasts). At this time, the bodice resembled the male doublet.

104–5 *beaver to th'bum*: top to tail.

105 *an Amazonian time*: an age of masculine women.

106 *tread*: mount sexually.

106–7 *couple ... behind*: locks of false hair wound round the hatband, apparently indicating that the 'woman' is available (Frost).

108 *to a hair*: (1) to a nicety; (2) a quibble on the false hair.

111 *I'll ... back*: because from behind Follywit looks convincing as a woman.

113 *Dost ... clay?*: Follywit may be pretending dismay at being classed as a mere mortal ('clay' = human flesh); perhaps he is punning on 'clay' meaning 'cowardly'.

113–14 *clay ... holes*: (1) as a building material; (2) as a penis.

119 *court*: (1) courtyard; (2) royal court; (3) court of law.

124 *you ... nigh*: it is more than possible.

125 *put in*: (1) land; (2) enter (sexually) (cf. 'shoot in' on line 128).

130 *Putney and Cue*: small towns west of London on the Surrey bank of the Thames, both well-known pleasure haunts. Cue = Kew (but see note on 2.1.57–8). Middleton also makes indecent use of the initials.

136 *Inns o'Court man*: law student, resident at one of London's Inns of Court.

137 *two-shilling*: standard price for the average whore.

140 *bonny ... scribes*: a difficult phrase. 'Scribs' = 'scrubs' or 'skinflints'. In this context, Middleton may be thinking of 'scrub' meaning 'claw' or 'scratch' and hence of a woman as a 'clawer' or 'scratcher'. (Cf. the proverb, 'One mule does scrub another' (Tilley M1306).) 'Bony scribes' perhaps refers back to panderism and may mean 'pimps'. ('Scribe' could mean 'penman' (*OED* sb. 6) and 'pen' could mean 'penis'.)

141–2 *Hang ... hang 'em*: a not entirely coherent response from Mawworm; he seems to be continuing Follywit's contempt for base bribes.

4.1 Penitent Brothel's bedroom.

20 *a hundred*: I have adopted Bullen's insertion of the indefinite article.

21 *German clock*: the first clocks were imported from Germany and were mechanically very complicated.

24 *strike*: a quibble on 'copulate'.

27 *know*: stay in.

29 *bear*: Q reads 'better.'

30 *at a stand*: (1) idle; (2) tumescent.

36 *has . . . bone?*: the palpability of evil spirits was a key question for theologians.

41 *Come . . . delight?*: either (1) Is it delight that has changed you so? or (2) What has changed you so, Delight?

46 *All . . . thee*: I will give you everything.

48 *our*: Q reads 'her' which makes some sense, but I have adopted Dyce's emendation.

49 *fadom*: (1) embrace; (2) penis.

58–9 *seared . . . cheerful*: other editors have emended Q's 'seared' to 'seized' and 'Sear' to 'Seize'. Would the compositor have misread the manuscript twice? 'Sear' can mean (figuratively) 'burn', 'scorch' (*OED* v. 4); 'with rigour' suggests energetic, even violent coupling, and 'veins most cheerful' alludes to tumescence.

69 *conjure*: affect (by invocation).

71 S.D. *Succubus . . . exit*: a stamp of the foot was the usual signal for the trap-door on the stage to be opened.

4.2 A room in Sir Bounteous's country house.

8 *'Tis . . . ear*: I need to whisper it to you.

9 *taste*: (1) understand; (2) relish.

12 *sound*: not infected by sexual disease.

13 *feared*: doubted.

15 *linen . . . jaw*: to hide the effects of syphilis (so Gunwater suspects).

21 *Monsieur's days*: Francis, Duke of Anjou, brother of the French king, Charles IX, commonly called Monsieur by the English, was a persistent suitor of Elizabeth in the 1570s and 1580s. His invocation here is obscure. He was heartily disliked by the English as a prospective husband for Elizabeth mainly because of his Catholicism, but also because of his sickly appearance and chronic ill-health (to which Sir Bounteous may be referring in his remark about the linen cloth about the jaws).

22–3 *Our . . . fire*: this is a reference to: (1) the iron age, the period of human culture characterized by the smelting of iron and its almost universal use in industry; (2) the treatment for venereal disease, which consisted in part of a heat treatment in 'sweating tubs'.

23 *tried*: purified by fire (*OED* v. 3).

25 *we seldom . . . it*: either (1) we hardly ever take medicine unless it be for the pox; or (2) we hardly ever have sex (physic) without getting the pox.

4.3 A room ('closet') in Sir Bounteous's country house.

12–13 *admit . . . service*: as a lover.

24 *Flower-de-luce*: the Fleur-de-Lis was a popular sign for a tavern, but Follywit presumably does not mean one of the four London taverns with that name (as Frost maintains) as the scene is set in Sir Bounteous's country house in Berkshire (see note at beginning of 2.1).

29–30 *induction*: introduction. 'Overworn phrase' and 'action toward the middle region' suggest a quibble on the term meaning a particular kind of opening scene to a play, usually an allegorical dumb-show.

30–1 *his . . . region*: presumably an attempt on Gunwater's part to fondle the disguised Follywit's 'middle region'.

31 *saucy nibbling motion*: the nips of lascivious impulses.

39 *onyx . . . silexque*: onyx with its compounds and silica. The phrase formed part of a mnemonic verse in Lily's Latin grammar, *Brevissima Institutio* (1540), 'The third Exception of Nouns increasing short, being the Doubtful Gender'.

49 *sirrah*: Sir Bounteous presumably thinks Gunwater is still present.

50 *bumbasted*: stuffed (from having eaten well).

57 *scent*: sense of smell.

71 *wild boar*: the worst creature because it roots up the vineyard of Israel, Psalm 80: 13, and therefore becomes an image of Satan (Frost).

77 *engross her*: buy her up wholesale = swallow her up.

86 *supplied*: with a sexual innuendo.

92 *waft*: unsavoury whiff (Bullen).

93 *distaste the vessel*: destroy the savour of the woman. ('Vessel' was a Puritan word meaning a person filled with some quality.)

4.4 A room in Harebrain's house.

31 *beaver band*: beaver-skin hat band.

49 *Spring souls*: let souls spring.

50 *Harebrain*: Q reads 'Hargraue'.

whose: Penitent's.

52 *thy enticement*: my enticement of you (through his employment of the Courtesan).

66 *that*: that which (his whore).

81 *right*: true, righteous.

90 *break strife*: conventional phrase for taking a meal (also an appropriate one for Penitent in his new circumstances).

4.5 A street in London.

4 *that*: that which.

10 *turn over*: i.e. a new leaf.

17 *object*: (1) that which is worth contemplation or perusal (*OED* sb. II. 9); (2) that which is worth winning or gaining (*OED* sb. I. 4).

20 *By . . . lady*: Q reads 'ladies' for 'lady' which is followed by all editors (assuming that Follywit is addressing the women in the audience) except Frost. 'Lady' seems the more likely reading considering the Mother's opening remark, which makes more sense as a reply than as a form of polite greeting.

24 *in good time*: how opportune.

41 *made*: wealthy.

43 *hole*: hides.

43-4 *choice of*: particular about.

52-4 *When . . . mouthful*: an allusion to paying black market prices for meat forbidden to be sold during Lent (Henning).

55 *at first*: before the Fall.

simple of herself: pure.

58 *outcry . . . man*: (1) outrage a man's modesty; (2) proclaim a man a cuckold.

68 *maid*: Q reads 'man', which makes a kind of sense; but Dyce's emendation is persuasive.

72 *fear*: frighten.

81 *With you*: as far as you're concerned.

none: there are none.

85 *the way's . . . you*: the way is prepared for you (by the Mother's rhetoric and the daughter's broken hymen).

88 *curious*: (1) virtuoso; (2) prying.

96 *know no fiction*: know that I am telling the truth.

97 *'bove the waste*: over uncultivated land; i.e. Follywit's estate is so large that it would take a day's travelling to see it all.

102 *clap hands*: the Mother witnesses the legally binding betrothal ceremony of the clasping of hands. (Hence Follywit's appellation, 'Mother'.)

107 *clap't up*: conclude it quickly.

127 *get some charges*: profit.

130 *and clip enough*: (1) embrace enough (possessions); (2) embrace each other enough (Frost).

5.1 A room in Sir Bounteous's country house.

1 *blue coats*: see note on 1.1.69.

3 *friend*: sweetheart, lover. Cf. the proverb 'All is well, Jack shall have Jill'.

4 *puts in*: makes a claim.

8 *Harebrain*: Q reads 'Shortrod'.

copiously: extremely (an affected term, as is 'compendiously').

12–13 *Harebrain*: Q reads 'Shortrod'.

16 *In octavo*: briefly ('octavo' is a small size of book)—responding to 'compendiously'.

30 *fearful fools*: fearful about the plague. When deaths due to plague reached a certain number per week the theatres were closed.

where to play: the City Fathers were under constant pressure from the Puritan community to ban theatrical production.

39 *[MAWWORM]*: all editions follow Q's '*SERVANT*'. But it hardly seems likely that one of Sir Bounteous's servants should possess this kind of information.

greatest share: the greatest number of shares in the company (enabling him to make a living from acting).

41 *Put . . . hat*: persons of equal social rank kept on their hats in each other's company.

43 *least feathers*: the poor, who would have the least number of hats or hat plumes (a sign of wealth).

48–9 *took all quietly*: (1) took everything that happened without complaining; (2) stole everything without being detected (the pun is repeated in 'bear things bravelier away').

53 *boys*: who would play the female roles.

56 *works out restraints*: deals with prohibitions against performances by travelling theatrical companies.

legs: bows.

58 *of*: for.

61 *thou rollest . . . fellows*: an allusion to the proverb, 'A rolling stone gathers no moss' (Tilley S885). But if 'moss' means 'wealth', Sir Bounteous is misapplying the proverb.

fellows: all editions follow Q's 'fellow'. It seems more likely that Sir Bounteous is not singling out a particular person among Follywit's companions.

66 *The Slip*: the play's name is punned upon remorselessly in this scene: among the less accessible meanings are (1) the skirt of a garment; (2) a coin.

68 *Cover*: put out eating utensils.

69 *lurcher*: (1) glutton; (2) petty thief, cheat. It is not clear to whom Sir Bounteous is speaking, the players or the servants, but the pun suggests he is addressing the players.

74 *light*: (1) wanton; (2) light-fingered.

76 *dissemble it*: to whom is Sir Bounteous speaking? If it is to himself, his immediate attack on them must be intended to show a comic lack of restraint.

83 *under one hood*: cf. the proverb, 'He carries (bears) two faces under one hood' (Tilley F20).

84-5 *Yes . . . double*: an obscure remark whose general meaning seems to be 'I could swear my eyes had seen two faces'.

93 *Soft*: Q reads 'post' which later editors emend to 'pox'. 'Post' for 'pox' requires an inspired misreading by the compositor. Examination of Middleton's Trinity College manuscript of *A Game at Chess* suggests that 'post' might well be mistaken for 'soft', an appropriate introduction to a remark that is an aside. Here, 'soft' = stay a moment.

95 *Would . . . me?*: Is there something you want with me?

105 *you ne'er . . . me*: a jibe at Sir Bounteous's impotence.

110 *little*: trivial.

116 *bare*: bare-headed.

120 *And*: but.

127 *Excellent well, sir*: in Q1 this phrase is missing although there is another speech prefix for Sir Bounteous's name before 'What else lack you?' suggesting that a reply from Follywit has dropped out. Q2 inserts this one.

5.2 A room in Sir Bounteous's house.

8 *Ireland*: a well-known refuge for English debtors.

21 *bold Beacham*: 'As bold as Beauchamp' (Tilley B162) is an old proverb founded on the exploits of Thomas, 1st Earl of Warwick.

25 *Term*: the year was divided into four terms appointed for the sitting of the London courts of law. (See note on *Term*, *The Actors in the Comedy* 22-4.)

28 *nimble conceit*: clever invention.

34-5 *send . . . supper*: although it was fairly common for prostitutes to dine with the players at the theatre after the play, the wording here suggests that the Courtesan would be summoning Follywit to her. The following lines, however, indicate that their love-making takes place in the theatre.

36 *good conceit*: favourable opinion.

parts: the actors' theatrical and private parts.

36-7 *two-penny room*: a covered upper room of the theatre, which had seats and could be used for entertainment after a performance; it was a disreputable part of the house, frequented by whores (Frost).

37–8 *less . . . gentlemen*: gallants liked to sit on the stage to watch a perform-ance, often crowding out the actors. The 'less compass' here, however, that the actors are found in the next morning = the arms of the prostitutes.

41 *shifts*: (1) changes of costume; (2) linen smocks; (3) stratagems.

79 *auspicious*: a malapropism for 'suspicious'.

96 *lay*: charge.

103 *Smug . . . horse*: an allusion to a scene from *The Merry Devil of Edmonton* (not in the extant version) in which Smug plays St George riding upon a white horse.

114 *lets*: hinders, prevents.

136 *in a wood*: mad, confused.

138 *[HAREBRAIN]*: Q has '*Nub*' as the speech prefix. Most editors (except Frost) correct to '*Gun*' even though he says nothing else in this scene and never addresses his master in this manner.

156 *taste*: relish, appreciate.

188 *kneeling . . . play*: it was the custom for the players at the close of the play to kneel and pray publicly for their patrons, though in all likelihood the ceremony by this time had been discontinued in the public theatres.

234 *come . . . at all*: the final line of the nursery rhyme, 'Girls and Boys Come Out to Play'.

235 *prize*: Q reads 'peece', a straightforward misreading of the manuscript.

243 *thou art . . . him*: 'to be beforehand' means 'to draw money in advance'. The Courtesan has done this by selling her virginity many times over before the 'final' sale to Follywit; so she conned him before he conned her.

245 *Owemuch his*: Owemuch's.

257 *what . . . fool*: what kind of fool is she.

273 *pledge*: a drinking metaphor: Sir Bounteous 'began the toast' by being the first to drink from the 'cup' (i.e. by having the Courtesan as his mistress before her marriage to Follywit).

Michaelmas Term

The Actors in the Comedy
This list is derived from Dyce.

1 *Easy*: suggesting his weak, gullible good nature.

2–3 *Rearage, Salewood*: indicating impecuniousness (Rearage = 'in ar-rears') following the sale of their ancestral estates.

4 *Cockstone*: see note on 'Singlestone', *Mad*, 2.6.2.

5 *Ephestian Quomodo*: Levin guides us through the scholarly investigation of Quomodo's name as a Latin pun on 'Howe' (William Howe), a broker convicted by the Court of the Star Chamber on 18 June 1596 for a swindle similar to Quomodo's. Price (2) suggests that 'Ephestian' is intended to recall: (1) Hephaestion, friend to Alexander the Great; and (2) Hephaestus, the cuckolded god.

woollen draper: cloth merchant.

7–8 *Shortyard, Falselight*: it was a common practice for dishonest shop-keepers to give short measure and to keep their shops so dimly lit that their customers could not see that they were being cheated.

7 *Blastfield*: literally = infect (an estate) with disease (cf. Salewood).

8 *Idem*: the 'same', i.e. built on the same lines as Quomodo (but also literally the same as Falselight, who plays the role).

9 *Andrew Lethe*: 'Lethe' is the name of the underworld's river of forget-fulness. In his quest for social advancement Lethe chooses to forget his real ancestry and makes much of an affectation of forgetfulness as an 'aristocratic' trait. Baldwin Maxwell ('Middleton's *Michaelmas Term*', *PQ* 22 (1943), 29–35) maintains that Lethe is a caricature of one of those Scotsmen (from Leith perhaps) who followed King James to London when he assumed the crown: hence 'Andrew' and 'Gruel', names recalling the patron saint of Scotland and Scotland's national dish (oatmeal porridge). William Power argues that the character of Andrew Lethe is part of a campaign waged by Middleton against James I ('Thomas Middleton vs. King James I', *N&Q* 202 (1957), 526–34).

12 *Dustbox, a scrivener*: scriveners (public scribes and notaries) often carried boxes filled with sand to blot ink.

14 *Thomasine*: diminutive, feminine form of 'Thomas' (cf. Frank in *Mad*).

16 *Country Wench*: in Q she is called 'Courtesan' in speech headers after the play's second scene, and 'Courtesan' or 'Harlot' in S.D.s after 3.1.

20 *tirewoman*: hairdresser; her name puns on 'combings' (Price 1) and is also an indication of her sexual activity (s.v. 'come' in Partridge).

21 *Judge*: Michaelmas Term, perhaps?

22, 24 *Michaelmas . . . Trinity Term*: Hilary was the winter term, Easter the early spring term, Trinity the late spring term. Michaelmas was the autumn term (beginning on 9 October), the first one of the legal year, and the longest, hence the others' 'father' (*Induction*, 37). It was also the busiest of the four terms because of the harvest and the end-of-the-year litigations. Country litigants would come to London after bringing in the harvest; the money they earned from it would finance their lawsuits.

Induction The location is a London street.

4 *weed*: the whitish cloak whose colour represents his (whitish) country conscience which he now must abandon; white = the liturgical colour for Michaelmas (Price 2).

5 *civil*: citified.

6 *civil black*: black, the devil's colour, was also the colour of the gowns of civil and guild officials and lawyers.

9 *free*: unconstrained.

13 *fat*: rich.

14 *The . . . hall*: crops from their country estates serve to finance the suits of country litigants in courts of law.

15 *Come they up*: the country litigants coming up to London for the Term.

18 *well boiled*: in malt liquors.

19 *no legs*: from the effects of venereal disease.

21 *Such another*: another witticism as clever as this one.

26 *cools*: draws to an end.

27 *fools*: those whom he has beggared.

29 *Thou*: the boy.

31 s.d. *fellow poor*: Price (2) notices the similarity between this character and Lethe. Might they not have been played by the same actor?

33 *for*: for the lack of.

34 *Crept . . . Terms*: become well-off in the course of three terms of litigation. Lethe has exploited the opportunities offered him in the busiest times of the year in the city, i.e. during the law terms.

36 *gale . . . hither*: cf. the proverb 'What wind blew you hither?' (Tilley W441).

42 *When . . . off*: when you have robbed them of all their wealth.

44 *neglect*: (1) failure to perform a duty (which might bring about a law-suit); (2) failure to come to trial (whose delay will increase expenses).

47 *'em*: the cups (the clients' wealth).

48 *bottom*: lees, dregs.

49 *lamb*: victim (a client) (Levin).

50 *skin*: to make parchment for legal documents (Levin).

54 *sixteen times about*: for 16 terms, i.e. 4 years.

57–8 *proud . . . meats*: the cold leftovers are acceptable to them, such is their pride (sarcastic).

58 *returns*: these were days on which writs and mandates had to be returned to court; there were eight in Michaelmas Term (Sampson).

63 *few*: straws. Just as birds need many straws to build a nest, so lawyers need many clients to build their wealth.

nests: the Q spelling, 'neasts', indicates the rhyme (Levin).

64 *small*: small amount of.

65 *gentlemen*: at any performance of the Paul's Boys at their theatre in the Song School there would have been a fair number of lawyers in the audience.

66 *ours*: the actors' (the Children of St Paul's). *Michaelmas Term* was one of four plays written by Middleton between 1604 and 1608 to be first presented by the Children; the other three were *Mad*, *Trick*, and *The Phoenix*.

sixpenny fees: sixpence was one of the standard fees charged for a seat in a 'private' room in the gallery for the wealthier patrons (see Chambers, ii. 534).

67 *two hours*: Chambers (ii. 21) notes that the Children began playing at 4 p.m. after prayers and had to be finished by 6 p.m.

68 *suits*: (1) law-suits; (2) suits of clothes (i.e. the theatre-goers themselves).

hang: linger (Levin).

call we: Qs and editions other than Levin's read 'we call'.

75 *Sat sapienti*: a shortened form of the proverbial expression *dictum sapienti sat est* ('a word to the wise is sufficient') found in Plautus's *Persa* and Terence's *Phormio* (Levin).

1.1 Q does not divide the play into scenes. Dyce was the first editor to do so. The scene is located in the middle aisle of St Paul's Cathedral (see 1.1.138).

s.d. The Jacobean theatre had a door for the actors on each side of the stage at the rear (but see note on *Mad*, 2.6. s.d.).

8 *last of November*: Michaelmas Term ended on 28 November.

9 *venturing*: (1) ventursome; (2) fornicating ('venture' was slang for prostitute).

11 *meddle with*: (1) have anything to do with; (2) have intercourse with (because of her venereal disease).

15-16 *some . . . look on*: proverbial (Tilley H692).

17 *North*: Scotland.

19 *pass so*: pass as a virgin.

22 *venture . . . firing*: take the risk (of venereal disease).

25 *newly fallen*: in the uncorrected copy of Q1 and in Q2 the 'newly' is missing. Levin observes that the compositor must have consulted his manuscript at this point. (Cf. *Trick*, 4.4.191).

30 *vacation*: preceding Michaelmas Term (Sampson).

31 *fetch him*: from the dead.

41 *inned*: lodged (in the stable of an inn).

since: not long since (i.e. I have just arrived in London).

47 *possessed*: persuaded, convinced.

52 *Essex*: a rural county north-east of London whose farmers had a reputation for gullibility (Sugden). Londoners thought of Essex as a distant Arcadia.

55 *at first*: paramount.

61 *crept . . . warmth*: see note on *Induction*, 34.

64 *cast*: (1) discarded (clothes); (2) cleaned out (ditches).

66 *mother only me*: only the mother favours me.

69 *Being . . . father's*: more certain regarding parentage (Sampson).

70 *'Men . . . love'*: in Q1–2 the line begins with double quotation marks ('gnomic pointing') to indicate an aphoristic sentence. Cf. 1.1.180.

73 *warned me*: ordered me to keep away from.

74 S.D. Rearage and Cockstone strike up a conversation again when Lethe enters so they must have moved to another part of the stage.

75 *spirits*: diabolical associates, familiars.

88 *Whom . . . wife*: because of the size of his penis; 'yard' = (1) a measuring rod; (2) a slang term for penis.

90–1 *There . . . abundance*: tradesmen's wives were a prime target for licentious gallants. (Sampson is the first editor to supply the 'in' before 'abundance'.)

98 *Dives into seasons*: probes into occasions, seizes opportunities (Levin).

103 *mark*: target in archery, hence 'shoot' and 'cleave'.

104 *heir*: with a pun on 'hair' (Levin).

105 *title*: to his lands.

106 *some*: Q reads 'some some'.

prison: for debt.

118 *that 'tis*: Dyce's punctuation seems marginally preferable to Q's 'that, 'tis' or Levin's 'that! 'Tis'.

122 *shape of gallantry*: dress of a gallant (Levin).

124 *Keep . . . him*: keep pace with him.

131 *bed*: Elizabethan men slept together as a habit of friendliness (Sampson). However, the tone of this suggests sexual dealings of some kind.

139 *Against*: opposite.

Saint Andrew's: Price (2) suggests that this church was the one to be found in Holborn, a residential district popular with the Inns of

Chancery lawyers, many of whom would have been in the audience. Holborn had something of an unsavoury reputation.

142 *back door*: through which debtors could escape their creditors (or lovers husbands).

143 *necessary*: useful.

147 *Who's this?*: Q1 reads 'Whose 'tis?' Price and Levin emend to 'Who? 'Tis!' conjecturing that the compositor misread the manuscript question mark as terminal 's'. Q2's correction, however, seems the most sensible and has been adopted here.

black angels: devils; cf. *Induction*, 6.

151 *Walter*: pronounced 'water' (and so cheapening the gruel) (Price 1). Levin instances the mercer, Walter Chamlet (watered camlet) in Middleton's and Webster's *Anything for a Quiet Life*. Weatherwise makes the same pun in *No Wit*, 3.1.262.

153 *Not hither?*: did he not bring him to London (to be brought up)?

154 *below*: in inferior circumstances out of London.

155 *strange*: strangers'.

158 *receivèd parts*: recognized talents (Levin).

164 *make . . . ready*: prepare our (elaborate and courtly) greetings.

166 *laid*: laid low, prostrated (Levin), dead (laid to rest).

167–8 *dry mutton*: eaten as part of the treatment of syphilis.

168 *swell . . . toad*: proverbial (Tilley T362).

176 *dear*: choice.

180 '*Esteem . . . metal*': see note on 1.1.70.

dizzy metal: dizzying substance (Price 1).

183 *remember me*: remind me of them by giving me another gift.

188 *knights*: see note on *Mad*, 1.1.55–6.

194 *horn*: of the hunters in the deer park (see line 200) (Levin).

201 *dogs*: in the hunt (Levin).

202 *take pain*: Levin restores Q1's 'pain' (over Q2's 'pains'). The original word makes the joke sharper.

fit for dogs: because they eat vomit.

207 *Easily remembered*: because of the horn's association with cuckoldry.

210 *runs full against*: utterly opposes.

211 *run upon*: (1) oppose; (2) pursue sexually.

213 *command*: have for the asking.

death of sturgeon: Bullen suggests that this phrase is an oath, Sampson that it means 'keg of sturgeon', and Levin that the text is corrupt. It may simply be Lethe's absurdly grandiloquent way of saying that he can provide her with an expensive fish (the source of caviar).

215 *scullery*: kitchen, presumably at Court (Eccles).

217 *friend*: sweetheart, lover.

221 *keeps aloof off*: remains withheld (Levin).

222 *copulation*: (1) union; (2) sexual congress.

223 *a mere*: sheer (Price 1).

230 *third sister*: and hence less likely to get the marriage dowry that would make her marriageable.

233–4 *that . . . night*: the sexual threat here is made clear by the secondary slang meaning for 'purse' of 'pudendum'.

234–7 *You . . . you!*: Price (1) notes that these lines are addressed to the women in the audience.

236 *ransom home*: from pawn (Sampson).

237 *recover your smocks*: punning on 'recover' as 'mount again'.

253–4 *i'th'mornings*: gentlemen ate gruel for breakfast.

254 *first*: see note on *Mad*, 1.1.80.

255–6 *tooth-drawer*: dentistry was regarded as a very menial occupation, proverbially pursued by thin and meagre people (see Tilley T434).

259 *on't*: Q reads 'out', which is just possible. However, as Levin notes, Price's conjecture that we are dealing with a turned 'n' is very plausible.

vacant time: vacation (Sampson).

260 *laid his life*: died.

263 *place*: of employment (Levin).

266 *of worship*: prominent, important.

272 *poorer name*: gruel.

drenched in Lethe: (1) replaced so often by Lethe (the new name); (2) drowned in the river of forgetfulness.

273 *understand*: recognize.

275 *pass*: deliver.

277 *And . . . raiment*: stain my new identity with the news of my birth.

290 *needy quality*: a skill for those who have to earn their living.

297 *sixpence British*: Baldwin Maxwell suggests that this is a reference to a new coin first minted in 1604 which designated James I as King of Great Britain ('Middleton's *Michaelmas Term*', *PQ* 22 (1943), 32). A Scots sixpence had about the value of an English halfpenny (Price 2).

303 *so*: provided that.

braver: better dressed.

1.2 A street in London.

   8 *these latter days*: these degenerate recent times (just before the Apocalypse).

11 *wars*: punning on 'whores' (s.v. 'war' in Rubinstein).

   beaten: experienced (Price 1).

13 *loose-bodied*: suggesting moral laxity.

14 *thou shalt*: Q has 'thou that shalt'.

19 *spark of humility*: because he will share her with others (Eccles).

25 *Bound*: (1) obliged; (2) tied.

26 *go*: (1) be; (2) copulate.

28 *Nay . . . you*: (sarcastic) not you and a thousand like you.

29 *Deny*: refuse (Dyce).

34 *dissemble*: all editions except Levin's accept Q's 'dissembler'. As Levin points out, however, the logic of the discussion between Hellgill and the Country Wench requires the emendation.

39 *break*: default, go bankrupt (Levin).

42 *out . . . maid*: you are (1) imprisoned by your virginity; (2) not a real citizen of London because you lack a trade (in this case, prostitution).

43 *lattice*: (1) the window-blind of the brothel; (2) the hymen.

44 *coarser beauties*: (1) whores; (2) penises.

46 *gilded flies*: rich men (those with gold).

49 *weeds*: cf. note on *Induction* 4.

   pants: in which the virtuous country lass breathes hard as she toils (Price 2).

54–5 *you . . . dressed*: you know that a woman not clothed respectably is food for all men ('dressed' = (1) clothed; (2) prepared for table).

2.1 A room in a tavern (Levin suggests the Horn).

   1 *I . . . room*: in order to change his luck.

   4 *put up all*: pocket all the winnings; Price (1) suggests a play on 'put up with any insult'.

   9 *Alsup*: all-sup, suggesting his hospitality (Price 1).

12 *second to*: close to, nearest.

19 *dear*: costly.

34 *such*: such gamesters, men about town (Price 1).

35 *keep me*: let me keep.

35–6 *Set 'em all*: bet the lot.

39 *ride down*: from London to the country.

47 *He's . . . friends*: presumably Lethe will leave the game when he is winning with the excuse that he has to visit friends.

51 *pass*: give up my turn to throw the dice (Levin). Shortyard then puns on the more general sense of 'go' or 'pass by', implying that it is a wonder Lethe should be considered acceptable in society.

54–5 *The . . . stay*: Rearage has lost again to Lethe.

54 *angels*: (1) the fallen angels; (2) coins.

57 *Let's . . . smock*: Sampson adduces the proverb 'wrapped in his mother's smock' (Tilley M1203) to support his suggestion that Easy is talking about Lethe's run of good luck. More likely, Easy is commenting on Lethe's effeminacy.

58 *pea*: as there is nothing between a pea and its pod, so there was nothing between Lethe and his outer clothing (Price 1).

62 *shift*: (1) shirt; (2) clever stratagem.

64 *I could—*: Levin suggests that Easy loses again at this point and threatens to do himself some physical harm. It is more likely that Easy is reflecting on his previous losses before Lethe moved away.

67 *purge*: loss (Price 1).

68 *up*: to London from Essex (Levin).

69 *quarter*: landlords collected their rent four times a year.

73 *Gum*: an appropriate name for a mercer (a dealer in silks and other fabrics) as gum was used to make the silk seem glossier.

76 *said*: done.

83 *knew*: Q has 'know'.

86 *will*: ask.

90–1 *whoresons*: the city merchants.

93–101 *a man . . . once*: a sustained double entendre (where head = prepuce, bow = vagina, and gun = penis) glancing wryly at the aggressiveness of women and at their capacity to achieve multiple orgasms.

102–3 *setting . . . losses*: revealing by your looks that you have lost.

104 *bones*: of which dice were made.

108 *use*: accustom (Levin).

122 *surfeits . . . brows*: riots on the money earned by the sweat of his father's brow (Price 1).

128 *service time*: throughout the time of divine service.

144 *Diseases*: syphilis (known as the 'bone-ache').

146 *That . . . well*: a marriageable virgin will make an attractive buy.

146–7 *Her . . . mine*: Q transposes 'mine' and 'thine' and does not indicate that the lines are spoken as an aside. All editions retain Q's version despite the obvious difficulties of interpretation. It seems likely that the pronouns were confused by the compositor (a suggestion Levin makes but does not act on).

146 *firstlings*: first acts, preliminaries (hence her virginity).

155 *keeps . . . even*: pays his debts on time (Price 1).

156 *watch*: am careful.

166 *Tenants!*: coming to pay their rent (hence his enthusiasm).

173 *rest beholding*: remain obligated.

2.2 A street in the Holborn district of London.

s.d. *that*: the Country Wench.

4 *under carved ceilings*: in the homes of the wealthy (Levin).

17–18 *left . . . unsought*: have not left unsearched all the places where the gentry dwell.

18 *keeps*: dwells (Dyce).

hear: of her.

20 *worth*: be unto.

30 *One minute*: one moment's pleasure.

31 *in mine*: in my maid (i.e. his daughter).

33 *present form*: a farm labourer's clothing (Price 1).

36 *serve . . . disguise*: disguised as a servant.

2.3 Quomodo's shop in London.

2–3 *for a need*: in an emergency, at a pinch (hence Thomasine's anger).

9 *came up*: to London.

countrymen: Scotsmen, presumably. 'Country' was an ambiguous word in seventeenth-century English as it frequently meant a region, district or county.

9–10 *give their words*: stand as surety.

15 *broker's*: a contemptuous term applied to various kinds of petty dealers or agents (Levin).

18–19 *cast of manchets*: a few small loaves or rolls of fine white bread (Dyce). This would be a cheap gift (Price 2).

20 *errand*: Q has 'errant'.

25 *out upon him*: a mild expression of abhorrence or reproach (cf. 'fie upon him') for which Mother Gruel apologizes ('sir-reverence' = begging your pardon).

37 *happy in suits*: fortunate in our petitions at Court (Eccles).

37–8 *bring . . . rooms*: show us through the Court (Levin).

38–9 *pop . . . again*: feed us the choicest meat until we burst.

40 *honourable napkin*: a napkin from the Court would presumably have the royal coat of arms stamped or embroidered on it.

43 *hold our credit*: judge our reputation.

55 *fool*: Q reads 'foote'.

56 *living*: rent from his lands (Levin). But Rearage's financial situation is precarious.

56–7 *snatching diet*: grabbing at whatever food he can lay his hands on. Price (2) suggests that it would be left-overs from the Court kitchen.

58 *cloth*: the arras (tapestry) or other hangings at Court.

59 *company of puppets*: before the curtain (cloth) rises.

60 *there*: at Court.

64 *garden*: many Londoners had small vegetable gardens (Levin).

65–6 *take it standing*: a double entendre.

73 *By your leave*: please leave us (Price 1).

76 *buck . . . struck*: deer (Easy) to be brought down.

80 *feared me*: feared for me (lest I slip) (Price 1).

84 *scholar*: because he can speak so 'poetically' (Levin).

91 *Three Knaves*: as Levin points out, this parody of a sign-board refers to the three knaves of the plot, Quomodo, Falselight and Shortyard.

92–4 *Do . . . Blastfield*: Quomodo pretends not to recognize Shortyard at first because of the 'misty weather' in his shop. But the opening question, 'Do you hear, sir?', does not seem to be directed at either Shortyard or Easy. Levin's stage direction (a form of which I have adopted) offers a sensible solution.

92 *What lack you*: a shopkeeper's usual greeting (Sampson).

95 S.D. *above*: on the upper stage—a balcony at the first gallery level in the tiring-house façade—where she can see what is going on on the stage below without being seen by the other characters. Thomasine's entrance at this particular juncture enables her to witness Easy's entrapment from the beginning.

109 *bonds lie forfeit*: debts are overdue.

114 *take the forfeiture*: foreclose.

117 *age*: space.

129–30 *I . . . him*: I was anticipating hearing this from him.

134 *bedfellow*: cf. note on 1.1.131.

140–1 *carry . . . occasion*: convey my immediate need (Levin).

148 *walk*: leave, depart (Dyce).

162 *Brentford*: Brentford (a town eight miles west of London) was a place for assignations, and the nurse-child was certainly illegitimate; but the

327

absurd idea of the two tradesmen going together on such an errand is the point (Price 2).

171 *take . . . cloth*: take the loan in goods instead of in cash.

178 *diseased*: dis-eased, worried.

185–6 *raise . . . exchange*: get twice its value in trade (Levin).

187 *harvest*: for 'reaping' profits (Levin). Cf. *Induction*, 12.

188 *chamber . . . hall gowns*: apparel for private rooms and for the great hall (Price 2).

190 *take . . . again*: be sure you understand me.

193 *hawks' . . . paper*: 'commodities' were often items that were out of demand, worthless, or hard to sell. Hawks were kept hooded until launched at their prey.

199–201 *as . . . executed*: these and lines 333–4 have tempted commentators to date the composition of the play at the time of the public execution of Francis Clarke on 29 November 1603, or at that of Sir Everard Digby on 30 January 1605/6. Executions were commonplace, however, and Middleton may well have no particular one in mind.

200 *found no eyes*: did not weep.

202 *rip . . . can*: does all he can to help the executioner disembowel him (a stage in the execution for treason) (Levin).

203 *no man*: because he is both cruel and impotent.

217 *I'm . . . sir*: playing on the meaning of his name (Levin).

219 *star mark*: the mark of the merchant or weaver from whom Quomodo purchased the cloth; it is not in the pattern, but on the bundle or case (Price 2).

222 *brother*: similarly inclined colleague (cf. 'brethren' in line 224).

     Stilliard-down: false balance (Sampson) (steelyard = scale for weighing).

225 *to be cursed*: because of their excessive rate of interest.

225–6 *their . . . throats*: their profit is at the expense of the poor (lie in the throat = 'stick in the craw').

226 *discharged*: released, by signing a promissory note for the loan (Levin).

237 *without*: unless.

253 *three hundred pound*: in rent.

255 *how . . . soe'er*: however doubtfully.

258 *down*: to his Essex estate.

271 *Hold there*: keep to that position.

285 *damn*: be damned.

290 *hand*: to shake; but Quomodo takes the word in the sense of 'hand-writing' or 'signature' (Levin).

296 *wild*: Weald (district in Kent).

306 *return*: pay back.

308 *piece*: Q reads 'price'. Price keeps the Q reading on the ground that a compositor's misreading of 'piece' (in Middleton's handwriting) as 'price' would be unlikely; but the identical error occurs in *No Wit*, 1.2.49, where 'piece' must be the true reading (Levin).

317 *it*: the import, significance of what I'm saying.

318 *ready . . . hands*: (1) ready for your signatures; (2) at your service.

to: for.

321 *It*: the privilege of signing the bond first.

325 *take . . . of*: precede.

332 *felling of trees*: Price instances this as another example of Quomodo's 'malign nature' and adduces evidence from William Harrison's *A Description of England*, ed. F. J. Furnivall (London, 1877), which complains about the deforestation of Elizabethan England.

333 *keep Christmas*: with the traditional Yule log (Dyce).

334 *quart'ring out*: being quartered (after having been hanged and drawn).

335 *own blood*: since he is signing away his inheritance, his lifeblood (Price 1).

he: Price argues that the omission of the pronoun in Q1 (uncorr.) and Q2 is one of Middleton's traits as a writer.

339 *Roman hand*: the 'Roman' or 'Italian' style of handwriting was replacing the native 'English' script (Price 1).

341 *R's . . . E's*: this emendation to Q's 'R' and 'E' (to recover the puns on 'arse' and 'ease') was first suggested by K. Deighton, *The Old Dramatists: Conjectural Readings* (London, 1896), 168, and was adopted in W. H. Williams's *Specimens of the Elizabethan Drama* (Oxford, 1905), which reprints part of this scene (Levin).

347 *coin*: money for the cloth.

349 *By . . . little*: some room, please.

354 *passage*: route, crossing (across the English Channel).

is stopped: perhaps by a Spanish blockade (Sampson), or by an edict of the English government prohibiting export (Eccles).

367–8 *new setter-up*: one just beginning in the trade.

370 *Idem*: see note on The Actors in the Comedy, 8.

371 *we . . . by't*: our trade demands that we can only buy it back from you at considerably less than what we sold it to you for.

373 *stand*: insist.

378 *Over your head*: another play on his name (Levin).

382 *want twenty*: lacks twenty (of the hundred) = 80.

389 *I'll . . . gentleman*: by greeting her with a kiss.

395 *proper springall*: Dyce first suggested this emendation. Q reads 'proper, springfull'.

400 *Vim . . . salutem*: 'Let me salute vigour, life, and hope'. The awkward Latin may be intended to show Sim's ignorance (Price 1).

401 *there*: in his speaking Latin.

402 *Templar*: because he is at one of the Inns of Court.

404 *grace*: virtue.

407 *Livery*: the Woollen Drapers' Company.

409–10 *make me away*: make away with me, murder me. Doctors had a reputation for atheism and amorality.

411 *cloth gowns*: those worn by lawyers.

414 S.D. *for*: disguised as.

421 *for me*: at that price (Price 1).

429 *keys*: to his strongbox (Levin).

431 *[now have I]*: this phrase (or one like it) is not in Q and must have dropped out. I have acted on Levin's suggestion that the compositor may have overlooked a phrase like this because it repeats words from the preceding line.

433 *Cozenage*: cheating (punning on the Inns of Court).

3.1 The Country Wench's lodging in London.

   S.D. *points*: ties the laces.

   S.D. *tirewoman*: see note on The Actors, 20.

1–6 *You talk . . . their parents*: Hellgill's lines are addressed to the audience. It is possible that the Country Wench, the Tailor and Mistress Comings do not enter until Hellgill's 'behold their parents', but it is more effective as theatre to have him comment on them as they help the Country Wench preen herself.

1 *You . . . itself*: the sense seems to be that the Country Wench's new appearance as a Gentlewoman (her alteration) manifests a defining activity (the thing itself) of the socially ambitious woman. Hellgill may also be implying that the art of fashion confers authenticity on the practitioner—clothes creating essence.

6 *parents*: the Tailor and the Tirewoman.

7 *wire*: the whole headdress, not just the supporting frame (Price 2).

15 *narrow-eared*: pressing closely to the ears.

18 *Italian*: see note on *Mad*, 3.3.58–9.

28 *red*: rouge.

34 *But . . . me!*: (sarcastic) what a fine job you're doing finding me a servant.

NOTES TO PAGES 101-3

36 S.D. *[Servant]*: Hellgill's probably (Dyce).

45 *There's . . . already*: see note on *Mad*, 1.1.55–6.

47 *we'll . . . likings*: we'll see how we like each other.

50 *our . . . month*: a reference presumably to a monthly payment made by a gallant to his mistress.

52–3 *and that . . . vacation*: because we (as prostitutes) work a full year.

54–5 *imperfect creatures*: women in general.

58 *serves*: (1) works (for); (2) copulates.

76 *when . . . all*: when all's said and done (Levin).

78 *consume*: pine away (Levin).

81 *salute*: kiss.

90 *place there*: position at court.

91 *come*: into the court's intimate circles (with a possible bawdy secondary meaning).

94 *you . . . on*: because they were talking of the fool.

95 *stay there awhile*: Rearage, Salewood, and the Country Wench are conversing apart.

99 *leave*: stop, cease.

102 *Here*: probably to Hellgill's Servant (Levin).

107 *flies*: male predators (cf. 1.2.46).

108–9 *Wit . . . fool*: the meaning of these lines hinges on the contrast between the Country Wench's inexperience and the men's sophistication. Nothing can match a prolonged experience of the world to learn the 'wit' of deep knavery. And yet, in the end, it's merely the wit of a 'spent fool', someone sexually and materially depleted.

111 *put up*: tolerate.

113 *two screens*: Rearage and Salewood (blocking the 'fire' of the Country Wench's passion).

116 *defacer*: by giving her partner the pox (which frequently scarred the face).

120 *place*: at court.

121 *him*: Lethe.

122 *'Tis . . . end*: that's what we intend.

124 *promise*: see 2.3.117–19.

126 *I . . . now*: we are to understand here that Easy has also entered into the successive bonds; Shortyard merely avoids saying *we*, which would be a frightening reference to Easy's liability. Later Easy explicitly admits his liability for £700 (Price 2).

132 *haunt*: where he spends his time (Levin).

135 *famed*: made famous (by his boasting) (Levin).

144 *hole*: (1) loophole; (2) pudendum.

145 *right*: title to her (Levin).

147 *part*: role (Price 1).

148–9 *gives . . . women*: repents the sin of sex.

149 *by myself*: from my own experience.

151 *nation*: there seems little doubt that the 'nation' Shortyard is addressing is the English, represented by Rearage and Salewood, who are excluding the Scottish 'stranger', Lethe.

159 *them*: the Scottish foreigners.

beg offices: a thrust at the way in which the Scots were given positions at Court under James I (Eccles).

there: in Hell.

160 *out*: out of preferment (Price 1).

161 *'em*: the offices.

162 *to us*: here Easy and Shortyard move in to court her (Levin).

163 *and worse*: Q has 'and a worse'.

164 *us*: Lethe and her (Price 1).

171 *infallible . . . side*: it's not clear what this phrase means precisely; the text may be corrupt. Shortyard seems to be saying that the Country Wench has proven Lethe to be a coward.

172 *why . . . coward?*: Q has no mark of punctuation after 'why', but this rhetorical question directed at the Country Wench makes more sense if we take 'why' to be an asseveration.

173–4 *You'll . . . first*: the Country Wench's 'courage' enables her to accept the punishment for prostitution (whipping).

176–7 *he . . . face*: the public whipping officer wore a mask (Sampson).

177–8 *Common Council*: London's governing body.

178 *Henry . . . days*: 1509–47.

181 *piece of stuff*: harlot (jocular).

189 *an . . . not*: if you do not drink to the toast.

194 *barrel*: i.e. body (Sampson).

196 *cast*: see note on 1.1.64.

196–7 *drabs . . . month*: as Levin suggests, this seems to be a reference to a monthly medicinal purging.

198 *make . . . to*: confide in you about; Shortyard then takes the word 'privy' in the sense of 'lavatory'.

202 *makes for me*: is to my advantage (Price 1).

205 *well*: well off (Price 1).

207 *mother*: hysteria.

217 *let . . . so*: send it with such a message (Price 1).

228 *she*: Thomasine.

232 *cast of manchets*: see note on 2.3.18–19.

236–7 *nay . . . arms*: presumably Lethe makes a threatening gesture.

250 *bear that mind*: hold that opinion (Levin).

254 *toward*: contemplating.

256 *I'll send . . . bones*: I'll infect you with syphilis (cf. note on 2.1.144). (Price notes the pun on 'banes'.)

256–7 *another . . . purse*: so that you will become poor.

260 *common filth*: whore.

possessed: haunted.

261 *'fraid*: Levin's emendation 'frayed' is attractive. But Q's 'fraide' complements 'possesst' on the previous line and should be retained.

262 *rest*: remain.

263 *use*: practice (of a bawd).

265 *leapt*: sprang.

267 *hither*: in the service of this woman (Price 1).

3.2 A street in London near St Paul's.

4 *Paul's*: see note on 1.1.

14 *past it*: past grace, a reprobate (Price 1).

3.3 A street in London near St Paul's.

2 *shapes*: the bodily forms which a spirit can assume.

10–11 *mad state*: foolish, dangerous position (Sampson).

13 *stand . . . law*: challenge the suit in court (Levin).

16 S.D. *[within]*: the Boy has run ahead of Easy, while pretending to look for Blastfield, in order to warn them (Price 2).

18 *Is . . . Paul's*: he is referring to Shortyard (alias Blastfield).

20 *his hour*: when Blastfield was due at St Paul's (Levin).

23 *a-striking*: arresting officers clapped their victims on the shoulder, hence the Boy's cry for a surgeon for Easy's shoulder.

32 *sir; I know*: Q has no mark of punctuation between these words. Price's position for the semicolon seems the best one.

43 *been in*: been talking about (Levin).

46 *citizens*: for bail.

3.4 Quomodo's shop.

6 *Livery*: see note on 2.3.406.

10 *lecher*: Q has 'leather'.

11 *Whose . . . down*: punning on tumescence and the lack of it.

16 *Row*: probably Goldsmith's Row (fashionable and expensive) in Cheapside (Dyce).

30 *Why*: there is no comma after *why* in Q.

52 *courtesy*: indulgence, discretion.

56 *good*: well-to-do.

61 *carrier's*: each messenger from the provinces had fixed headquarters at a London inn, where a man expecting money from the country would go to receive it (Sampson).

74 *gull*: the context suggests 'throat' or 'gullet'. *OED* records the meaning 'trickster' for the first time in 1700.

81 *Defend me!*: a shortened form of 'God defend me!'

82 *proceeded*: advancing to a higher degree (in a university).

83–4 *some bach'lors . . . standing*: the image compares debtors in prison to university students at various stages in their length of 'imprisonment'.

88 *subsidy*: the tax levied by Parliament on land and goods; here equivalent to 'highly assessed', wealthy (Price 2).

89 *spite on's heart*: despite his malign disposition.

90 *take all*: his store of crowns.

91 *Much!*: this is a contemptuously ironical expression meaning the opposite of what it says, referring perhaps to Easy's store of crowns, or more likely to the unlikelihood of Shortyard's 'performing' what Easy wants him to. Cf. our expression 'fat chance'.

98 *account*: (1) repute; (2) financial standing.

100 *save them harmless*: see they lose nothing by it (Levin).

101 *No words*: keep silent.

108 *word*: his word of honour not to escape.

124 *dreamt*: Q reads 'dream'.

126 *bring*: Q has 'ring'.

state: financial standing (Sampson).

127 *your day*: the date your loan was due.

131 *that's*: breaking one's word (Price 1).

note: thing worth noting (Price 1).

133 *charge*: financial responsibility.

136 *broke*: made obedient.

145 *To . . . ring*: it was the custom to engrave a little rhyme or 'posy' of love inside a finger ring.

147 *bonds abroad*: debts outstanding (Levin).

148 *medicine*: remedy. The posy's jingle functions as a mnemonic for the sentiment.

149 *entered*: explored the subject.

151–2 *too far . . . within*: either absconded, or imprisoned (Levin).

155 *bands*: Q has 'bonds'.

156 *But . . . lands*: this difficult line seems to imply that Easy's situation differs from that of the 'desperate debtor' by having lands to fall back on. The 'at first' may mean that his ownership of his lands will not last long given the extent of his debts.

157 *But . . . disinherit*: the debts (bastards) I get in the future will soon be paid off (disinherited).

165 *lie*: in prison.

171 *subsidy-men*: men of sufficient wealth to be listed in the tax rolls (*King's Books*) for a special *subsidy* assessment in addition to regular taxes (Sampson).

   forty pounds: the amount of the special subsidy assessment.

174 *alderman's deputies*: city officials (Levin).

179 *owe*: own.

181 *That . . . sir*: Easy has just finished explaining the situation to them.

188 *That's . . . refuge*: that's your only hope (Price 1).

196 *Not now*: don't abandon me now (Price 2). But any reconstruction of a conversation between Easy, Shortyard, and Falselight is hypothetical.

197 *t'other*: other than 'Gentleman', presumably. We have to assume that Shortyard and Falselight profess not to hear what the Boy says at line 189.

200 *otherwise*: in some other situation (Levin).

206 *Body . . . Quomodo*: as security, he gives them the right, if he defaults, to take his property or imprison his *body*; this to take precedence over Quomodo's claim on him (Levin).

222 *recullisance*: recognizance, a document acknowledging a debt and the security that is forfeit upon default (Price 2).

227–8 *The . . . you*: Quomodo will demand the £700 from us (as your bailsmen), and then we must take your forfeiture (Levin).

235 *'To . . . sins'*: see note on 1.1.70.

237 *drink'st up*: take in, suffer.

238–9 *Yet . . . jealousy*: I'm not able to warn you because Quomodo (the crafty man) is violently suspicious.

239 *rape*: seize violently (with a pun on 'reap'). Q1 (uncorr.) and Q2 read 'reape'.

jealousy: suspicion.

3.5 The location of this scene is not made clear. A London street would suffice.

1 *letter's made up*: the letter is never mentioned by Quomodo and perhaps was not sent to him; instead, Rearage conspires with the Country Wench's father (Price 2).

3 *stands . . . sheet*: this is a reference to a punishment imposed by the church courts for a variety of offences (from slander to adultery) in which the penitent, dressed only in a white sheet, appeared before the congregation to beg its forgiveness.

5 *shame*: shameful disclosures (Levin).

12 *I'll . . . you*: I'll concede that to you.

13 *'Tis . . . now*: thanks for nothing (Sampson).

16 *bawdy*: having jurisdiction over sexual offences (Levin).

19 *fetch her out*: arrest her.

21 *look how*: just as.

22 *watchmen . . . suit*: they will follow the Constable's lead (in disregarding the offence).

24 *made away*: see note on 2.3.408–9.

26 *jaunts*: fatiguing or troublesome journeys (Levin).

31–2 *he . . . head*: he was surrendered to satisfy the accumulated charges for his board (Sampson).

35 *Manners . . . meaning*: Easy must take Shortyard's question to suggest that Easy is insulting him by hoping that the horse would defecate on him.

41 *move . . . you*: ask you that.

42 *in a mind*: of one mind.

57 *I*: Q has 'I' followed by a comma, which some editors (because of the comma) translate as 'Ay'. 'I' (even if it were followed by a comma) makes more sense as a reply to Easy's question.

58 *I am where I am then*: in another disguise (Levin).

59 *of all hands*: on all accounts (Price 1).

60 *Content*: agreed.

let's trace him: Price points out that Rearage and Salewood have been conversing to one side and have now agreed to try to seek out Lethe's latest place of concealment for the Country Wench.

63 *called upon*: summoned by death (Sampson).

4.1 Quomodo's shop.

3 *quite*: completely.

14 *far*: far away (Levin).

20 *assurance*: the security of his lands. As Price (2) notes, Easy, terrified by the thought of imprisonment, has conveyed all his lands to the 'wealthy citizens', Falselight and Shortyard.

24 *hoisted*: taxed beyond my means.

27 *Curts'ing*: politely offering it to each other (Eccles).

29 *Templar*: see note on 2.3.401.

30–1 *any abroad*: illegitimate children.

31 *marks*: folds in horses' incisor teeth which disappeared with age (Sampson).

33 *they . . . in*: even when young they failed to produce offspring (hence they were inveterately sexually incapable).

stand about: (1) spend time upon; (2) bother to have an erection over.

35–6 *make . . . will*: if they want to have children, let them use their own devices.

39 *bow wide*: in archery the distance arrows fell from the target was measured in bow-lengths (Bullen).

41 *wax and parchment*: sealed legal obligations (Sampson).

54 *house*: Quomodo is likely flaunting his new ownership of Easy's house in Essex, not his own in London where the scene is taking place.

56–8 *Confusion . . . begged*: Levin suggests that these lines might possibly be an aside; but it is much more likely (as he also says) that Easy now openly turns on Quomodo.

57 *ware*: merchandise (Quomodo's cloth).

58 S.D. Q does not give an exit for Thomasine. I have adopted Levin's suggestion that she should leave with Easy.

62–3 *Hug . . . lift*: 'hug', 'shift' and 'lift' are terms from wrestling, success at which depends upon skill not strength.

62 *away*: be off.

68 *'em*: the trees on his Essex estate.

72 *I*: see note on 3.5.57.

75 *laugh . . . down*: the name of a card game (Dyce).

83 *same weapon*: cozenage.

84 *and . . . word*: it being a well-known saying.

84–5 *what's . . . belly*: proverbial (see Tilley D316).

89 *took the course*: thought of the way to accomplish it.

89 *keys*: see note on 2.3.428.

91 *scrivener*: scriveners were held in as much contempt as usurers. 'An usurer is one that puts his money to the unnatural act of generation, and the scrivener is his bawd' (Tilley U28).

93 *wide*: elastic, indulgent.

97 *searchers*: appointed to examine corpses and report the cause of death (Dyce). Price points out that Quomodo intends to bribe the two women, who are assistants of the parish clerk, to report his death as due to plague.

99 *sickness*: the plague (Sampson).

102 *November . . . eye*: 'raining' tears.

102-3 *fall . . . body*: autumn; a withering or drooping from grief (Price 1).

105-6 *affection . . . disposing*: regard for my commands (Sampson).

4.2 The Country Wench's lodging in London.

9 *unjust*: mistaken.

11 *ware*: (1) goods; (2) male and female genitals.

12-13 *make . . . great*: dispose of it in large quantities, wholesale (Sampson).

13 *wholesale*: a pun on 'hole sale' (Q reads 'hole-sale').

19 *distant*: far from the decorous thoughts of a lady.

21-2 *but . . . side*: she seems to mean that this is every prostitute's boast (Price 1).

26 *corruption . . . first*: corruption originates in the act of generation itself.

4.3 Outside Quomodo's shop.

5 *called upon*: see note on 3.5.63.

7 *want . . . expressed*: lack words to express myself (Sampson).

9 *Men . . . die*: they die before they can enjoy the fruits of their labour (Levin).

15 *good confidence*: being too trusting, credulousness.

18 *For*: as for.

19 *entailed*: fixed irrevocably, as an inheritance (Levin).

20 *it*: the stupidity.

37 *burial,*: Levin inserts the comma here, turning 'of mine honesty' into a minor oath paralleled by Winnifred's 'o'my fidelity'. Without the comma (as in Q), 'honesty' = Quomodo (as Price suggests). Equally plausibly, however, 'honesty' could = chastity (Thomasine's). With or without the comma an actor could convey the phrase's comic application.

42 *hanging moon*: the rainy crescent moon that 'will not hold water' (Price 1).

44 *'em*: the Country Wench and Lethe.

52 *if . . . right*: if the rumours are true.

56 *'t'as*: it (sex between them) has.

57 *show . . . woman*: weep.

58–9 *weep a stroke*: shed a tear.

73–4 *seven hundred pound*: Susan's dowry.

76 *in will*: in getting what I want.

4.4 Outside Quomodo's shop.

s.d. *Beadle*: beadles were frequently employed as marshals at a funeral.

1 *What . . . live*: how people loved me when I was alive.

2 *wringing*: Q reads 'ringing'. But, as Levin observes, it is hard to imagine the servants tolling bells as their way of mourning Quomodo's 'death'.

3 *take water*: travel by boat (Eccles).

10 *time*: for the funeral.

11 *worshipful Livery*: members of Quomodo's Drapers' Company.

Hospital Boys: the Boys of Christ's Hospital. Price (2) notes that Thomasine has engaged the Boys to lead the cortège, singing psalms. They are followed by the coffin, then the Beadle, then the mourners.

12 *bestow . . . me*: spend lavishly on me in the way she appoints my funeral.

37 *hear*: Q has 'feare'.

41 *'twere long first*: it took a long time (Sampson).

44 *foot*: of Quomodo's land.

45 *tricks*: (1) social accomplishments; (2) sexual techniques.

54 *[OLD WOMAN]*: Q reads 'MOTHER', but there is no reason to think that this character is one of the play's two mothers. She is much more likely to be, as Price notes, a neighbour or perhaps a hired mourner.

60 *'em*: the dead husbands.

63 *Lend . . . hand*: to help her up from her 'feigned swoon'. Perhaps her 'I have troubled you' is directed at the Old Woman as it is she who replies. Price, following Sampson, argues that Thomasine is already on her feet (she has pointed after the coffin) and speaks these lines exclusively to Easy, so that the Old Woman's reply is a comic misappropriation.

71 *offends*: by watching (Levin).

5.1 Quomodo's shop.

s.d. *writings*: Quomodo's legal papers, which Sim inherited (Levin). These would include, as Price notes, the conveyances on Easy's property to the Citizens (subsequently transferred to Quomodo and Sim) as well as the preliminary bonds made by Blastfield and Easy.

7 *son*: with a pun on 'sun'.

11–12 *Knaves . . . 'em*: the subtle plans of the minds of rogues are betrayed by the fools to whom they are entrusted.

15 *bleed*: bleeding was thought to be therapeutic for a number of illnesses.

16 *shapes*: disguises.

20 *deputy*: see note on 3.4.174.

22 *execution . . . ears*: cropping ears was a punishment for a number of minor offences.

23 *that office*: of the public executioner who also cropped ears.

32 *little scroll*: single paper.

35 *known before 'em*: ranked higher than them (in knavery).

37 *found*: discovered, found out.

39 *Fresh warders*: more guards.

40 *the other*: Easy has already had them arrest Falselight.

45 *The . . . bears*: this line either looks back to the previous one or forward to the one following. If the former, then it refers to the mind's tendency to outwit itself; if the latter, to the head losing its ears as punishment.

46 *corn*: grain (= wealth).

47 *Sweet . . . Blastfield*: Q has this phrase tacked on to Shortyard's speech which does not make any sense. A reasonable emendation is to give it to Easy who continues to use Shortyard's alias sarcastically (cf. line 41). Price changes 'Blastfield' to 'Easy' thus keeping the line with Shortyard.

50–1 *one thing*: sexual performance.

56 *read there*: Thomasine reads these papers during Quomodo's soliloquy.

57 *Did . . . all*: even if he had nothing.

60 *Saint Antholin's*: St Antholin's Church in Budge Row, known as a Puritan stronghold (Sugden).

63 *months*: missing in Q.

67 *Every . . . cannot*: not every goldsmith can.

69 *owe*: admit.

76 *house*: Quomodo's shop.

77 *Hospital money*: singers' fee (Levin).

mine own: as Levin notes, this is the fee he charged for officiating at the funeral.

93 *thither*: there, on the memorandum (Price 1).

94 *little Quomodo*: Thomasine.

95–6 *Nineteen . . . fourpence*: Thomasine first counts out in shillings £5 for the Hospital (twenty shillings to the pound) and then 3s. 4d. (40 pence) for the beadle.

100 *Who? 'Tis Easy!*: Q1 reads 'Whose? tis Easy' and Q2 'Who's? this Easy'. Neither reading makes much sense. Dyce's emendation 'Whose this? 'Tis Easy' makes sense but weakens the line of verse. Price's emendation seems the best.

106 *any*: anyone.

111 *Had-land*: slang name for a prodigal (Sampson). Cf. *Trick*, 1.2.4.

119 *Horner*: because he has cuckolded Quomodo.

5.2 A London street.

4 *bribe*: to release him.

8 *enjoy me*: as your wife.

12 *How . . . prove*: Levin notes that this last line is not very complimentary to Susan and therefore requires an aside.

how . . . prove: how soon the affections spring up for someone else.

5.3 The scene is located in the Judge's house.

3 *just*: correct.

6 *richly hired*: bribed at great expense.

arms: coat of arms.

7 *from*: as inherited from (Levin).

33 *I . . . am*: I am found to be myself (Levin), with the further implication (of which Quomodo is unconscious) that his real nature has been exposed.

34 *shifts*: (1) tricks; (2) disguises.

41 *apprehends*: understands.

42 *I . . . shall*: I think I shall arrest (apprehend) you.

46 *set down*: planned.

49 *shine*: sunshine.

66 *memory*: with the knowledge of her infidelity.

75 *lands*: Levin points out that the lands in Essex must still belong to Quomodo as the memorandum only covers the shop's contents.

80 *resolve*: explain.

82 *To my thought*: as I thought (Sampson).

88 *abject line*: vile course (Price 1) ('line' = lineage).

96 *brought forth*: committed.

101 *for*: before, in preference to.

105 *at first*: at time of the seduction.

111 *out*: disappear.

115 *virgin*: this is Susan whom Rearage has married.

117 *sin he follows*: Lethe's lust (Levin).

119 Something has dropped out here.

125 *Christmas*: implying the licentious festivities of that season (Price 1).

140 *Again*: in preparation for.

153 *villain*: (1) villain; (2) peasant.

158 The text is corrupt here. As Price suggests, something like 'then were' has dropped out.

A Trick to Catch the Old One

The Actors in the Comedy
This list is derived (with modifications) from Dyce.

1 *Theodorus*: derived from the Greek for 'gift from God'. Witgood + Theodorus = cleverness is God's gift to man (see W. Power, 'Middleton's Way with Names', *N&Q*, NS 7 (1960), 26+).

2 *Pecunius*: (1) wealthy; (2) avaricious.

3 *Walkadine*: derived from the Greek for 'terrible strength'; like his brother's, a Puritan name in actual use.
   Hoard: a suitable name for a usurer.

4 *Onesiphorus*: derived from the Greek meaning 'profit bearer'.

5 *Limber*: sexually so—or desiring to be—despite his age (with a pun on 'limp').

6 *Kix*: the dry stem of various herbaceous plants (hence a dry, sapless person). Middleton uses the name again for the impotent and sterile Sir Oliver Kix in his most famous City Comedy *A Chaste Maid in Cheapside* (*c*.1613).

7 *Tristram*: an ironic misappropriation of the name of the legendary lover, from the story of Tristram and Iseult.
   Lamprey: an eel-like fish thought to be a strong aphrodisiac.

8 *Spitchcock*: a fried or broiled eel.

9 *Dampit*: (1) = damned pit (Hell); (2) an allusion to Dampit's generally drunken, sodden state.

9–10 *Usurers*: Dampit is more important as a usurer than as a lawyer (his ostensible profession).

10 *Gulf*: a whirlpool (that which devours or swallows up).

14 *Sir Lancelot*: an ironic misappropriation of the name of King Arthur's friend and Guinevere's lover (cf. Sir Tristram).

17 *Gentlemen*: in Q Lucre and Walkadine Hoard are accompanied (confusingly) by a number of miscellaneous Gentlemen as well as named characters. In the first scene of the play, Watson, in his edition, on the basis of the exchanges between them, substitutes Limber and Kix for the unnamed Gentlemen accompanying Lucre. In the first scene of the fourth act, Q's speech headers indicate that the Gentlemen speakers accompanying Hoard are mainly Lamprey and Spitchcock. I have taken my cue from these two scenes and throughout substituted Lamprey and Spitchcock for the unnamed Gentlemen accompanying Hoard, and Limber and Kix for the unnamed Gentlemen accompanying Lucre. For a difficulty for this arrangement, see the notes on 4.5.128 and 130.

18 *Courtesan*: in this case, not a common prostitute but a kept mistress (Loughrey) (but see 1.1.66).

21 *Foxstone*: another bawdy name ('stone' = testicle). Cf. Singlestone in *Mad World*.

1.1 Q does not divide the play into scenes. The scene is set in a town in Leicestershire, probably on a street.

1 *that's all*: that means everything.

2–3 *What . . . downlands?*: the landscape is 'feminized'. Uplands and downlands represent breasts and womb.

2 *meadows*: a metonym for the cows which feed in the meadows.

4 *pit*: (1) Hell; (2) pudendum.

6 *consumes*: (1) his money; (2) his health.

  Long-acre: this term for a long narrow field of one acre was employed allusively for 'estate or patrimony' (Loughrey).

7 *about*: in circumference.

7–8 *he . . . conscience*: he who tries to find Lucre's conscience.

16 *before a stranger*: before an outsider does.

22–3 *sojourn . . . mercers*: rely upon their wits for the wherewithal to live (accommodation and clothing).

24 *out . . . law*: not punishable by law (Watson); but the phrase is deliberately ambiguous suggesting that Witgood may in fact embrace illegality.

30 *round-webbed*: probably an allusion to the shape created by the hooped farthingale.

31 *dryest*: withers.

40 *invention*: the Courtesan, around whom Witgood has suddenly thought of a plan (Loughrey).

44 *weapon*: words (Loughrey).

  Stay: with a pun on 'remain chaste' (see Henke).

51–2 *it . . . something*: something may come of it.

343

52 *perfect*: fully formed (Loughrey).

63 *resolute*: full of resolve (Loughrey).

65 *bots*: a disease in the digestive tract of horses caused by worms (here used as an expletive, cf. 'pox').

66 *mad host*: fun-loving innkeeper.

   bawd: innkeepers often doubled as pimps and procurers. But see note on The Actors, 18.

74 *wants*: deficiencies.

75 *set . . . state*: (1) play my role with such vigour; (2) show such confident boldness in the value of my land.

77 *shall go nigh*: shall make every effort.

81 *hasty*: urgent.

86 *officious to deserve*: anxious to earn my good will.

88 *lets . . . him*: leaves it up to God to take care of him.

90 *'Tis . . . world*: so it is the world over.

90–2 *an old . . . it*: an old man's love for his relatives is as perfunctory as his lovemaking (over before it's begun) with his wife.

96 *gift*: power.

98 S.D. Q does not have any S.D. here. Speech headers for the new speakers in Q = 1, 2, 3. But it is clear from the dialogue that the 'worshipful seniors' are Onesiphorus Hoard, Limber, and Kix. See note on The Actors, 17.

100 *common rioter*: notorious profligate.

102 *you . . . yourselves*: because you will have been hoodwinked by my plot (Loughrey).

106–7 *His . . . brother*: Lucre and Walkadine Hoard.

114–15 *beating the bargain*: haggling.

120 *his . . . niece*: Sam Freedom, Lucre's wife's son by a previous marriage, and Joyce (who eventually marries Witgood).

123 *fall in*: (1) reconcile; (2) fall into bed (s.v. 'fall' in Partridge).

   A scholar: Moneylove.

132 *viol*: with a pun on 'vial' as vagina (s.v. 'viol' in Henke).

   consort: (1) concert; (2) husband; i.e. she will be ready to play (sexually) with others as in a musical consort.

135 *A . . . match*: agreed, if there is a marriage.

1.2 Another street in the same town.

3 *laying*: searching.

4 *Hadland*: see note on *Term*, 5.1.111.

5 *of thine own*: inn-keepers would also keep guests' horses in their stable (Loughrey).

9 *in ... teeth*: despite yourself.

10-11 *contra ... professionem*: against your will and profession.

15 *ginger*: considered an aphrodisiac (Barber).

18 *pigs ... parson*: a reference to the parson being paid tithes in kind.

19-20 *Will ... again?*: Witgood is suggesting that a rich widow will make her suitor act like a trained animal in order to please her.

26 *all unmanned*: completely without male attendants (Loughrey).

29 *tongue ... T*: (1) capital T; (2) large penis (s.v. 'tongue' in Rubinstein). Henke suggests a reference to cunnilingus, s.v. 'tongue'. Witgood continues the bawdy punning in the 'case stands thus' where 'case' = pudendum.

45-6 *hole ... in*: with a secondary bawdy sense ('head' = prepuce).

49 *hic ... hostis*: a meaningless alliterative phrase punning on 'host' and 'enemy'.

51 *Park End*: this is probably not a reference to a real place in contemporary London.

53 *let off*: fired (though Barber notes that this use isn't recorded in the *OED* until 1714).

full time: perfectly in time (with each other).

56 *which ... seen*: which will never be surpassed (where 'more' = better).

1.3 A street in London.

9 *witness*: witnesses.

12 *any man's case*: open to anyone (Loughrey).

stand ... bawd: act as pimp (in his own cheating).

13 *wipes his nose*: cheats him.

16 *of a Jew*: i.e. it is not a Christian act (for the Western Renaissance the Jew epitomized lack of feeling). Jews were traditionally associated with usury.

17 *beaten ... bird*: the context suggests that Lucre is talking about having reached a final settlement in the negotiations ('price to a pound') in which he has beaten down the price.

19 *evening*: last stages.

24 *defeat*: defraud.

lap: enfold.

27-8 *vulnera dilacerata*: lacerated wounds. The 'poet' cannot be traced (Watson).

31 *want it*: suffer the resulting deprivation.

32 *lie by't*: (1) suffer the consequences; (2) lie by her; (3) be imprisoned (Loughrey).

67 *month*: Q has 'mouth'.

68 *again*: back.

69 *of*: on.

70 *naked*: unprotected.

longest . . . life: for as long as he lives.

71 *box*: (1) blow; (2) case.

1.4 A street in London, perhaps in Holborn.

3 *writings*: Widow Medler's fake documents which the Host gives Lucre (2.1.33).

9 *lost . . . ears*: (1) the deaf; (2) the criminal (with his cropped ears).

10 *trampler of time*: Dampit's later insistent use of this phrase to describe his frenzied activity is self-gratulatory. But 'infamous' here suggests someone who tramples on people's rights in his headlong pursuit of wealth. 'Trampler' was also a cant term for attorney.

11-12 *uneven . . . cloak*: Dampit is affecting poverty.

13 *brothel-vomiting*: Q reads 'brothell, vomiting' but *OED* cites only one instance of the word used adjectivally. Here, the hyphenated term means (1) someone who vomits (habitually) in brothels; (2) someone who spews forth the language of the brothel; (3) someone whom even the brothels vomit up.

13-14 *these . . . extant*: these days.

14-15 *stealing . . . house*: stealing a guard-dog is a good indication of Dampit's venomous mettle.

16-17 *He . . . stealing*: this may simply be a sarcastic reference to the commandment 'Thou shalt not steal'. *OED*, however, offers another meaning for 'commandment': 'The offence of inducing another to transgress the law'.

18-19 *set . . . ears*: (1) set the dogs fighting; (2) put people at odds with one other (hence the Host's reply).

22 *staked his masty*: presumably, Dampit had arranged a dog-fight, and had staked the dog itself as his wager (Barber).

27-8 *If . . . once*: once you introduce the devil.

29 *devil . . . footmen*: the devil looks after his own (continuing the trampling image in 'footmen').

31 *the . . . thee*: continuing the curse of 'A pox search thee' (Loughrey).

32 *walk so low*: are so small. Gulf then takes 'low' in the sense of 'humbly'.

34 *poets tell us*: e.g. Seneca, in whose plays this is one of the recurrent moral maxims (Barber). Most editors replace Q's 'poets tell' with 'poet tells' but this doesn't seem necessary.

46 *picklocks*: a cant term for thieves, as Dampit switches from the officers of the law to the law's transgressors.

50 *examiner's office*: where the depositions of witnesses were taken down.

54 *cellar*: to obtain drink.

55–6 *motions . . . Holborn*: presumably Dampit is referring to the glimpses people get of him and his kind as they dart about their business in Fleet Street and Holborn. In Fleet Street they seem like a puppet show ('motions'); in Holborn, something more ethereal. Dampit's rhapsodic account verges on incoherence. Watson reminds us that both these streets were haunts of sharpers.

63 *soused*: Q has 'souc'st': Price suggests 'birched' and Watson 'swindled'. *OED* gives 'soaked' which seems an appropriate sense for Dampit's extravagant use of language, especially in the boating context of the next line.

2.1 A room in Lucre's house.

7 *uncle's pen'worth*: the profit due to a relative (but 'to uncle', as Watson notes, was a slang term for 'to cheat').

8 *half in half*: 50 per cent profit.

reclaiming: (1) reformation; (2) demanding the return of the mortgage.

11 *last translation*: the most recent slang.

29–30 *Yesterday . . . us*: yesterday was our first taste of London.

30–1 *term business*: legal transactions which could only be dealt with while the law courts sat during one of the four terms (see note on *Michaelmas Term*, The Actors, 22–3).

33 *writings*: the Host has presumably brought fake legal documents for Lucre's perusal giving the details of the Widow Medler's fictitious estate.

34 *Medler*: (1) medlar was a fruit rotten before it was ripe and a slang term for prostitute and pudendum; (2) to meddle with = to have intercourse with.

46 *love covers faults*: presumably there is a bawdy innuendo here since faults are cracks, fissures (Loughrey); as the faults are the man's the words may refer to the woman covering the man in coupling.

50 *seat*: (1) estate; (2) love-seat (pudendum).

51 *take . . . you*: let me understand you fully.

61 *ere . . . down*: (1) before she goes down to the country; (2) before she has sex.

65   *give . . . gift*: grant her that (Sampson).

72–3 *I'll fit thee*: I'll provide everything you need; I'll satisfy your requirements.

84   *resolve*: explain.

87   *non-suited*: denied marriage suits.

88   *non-performance*: failure to make good on promises (both financial and sexual).

105 *That . . . still*: that's what I always said.

107 *goes current*: is in general circulation (Watson).

115 *coat . . . ears*: (1) stripped of my livery, i.e. dismissed; (2) stripped preparatory to whipping.

116 *much*: editors replace Q's 'much' with 'such'. But Q makes sense and matches the 'many' in 'many suitors'.

123 *lie*: lodge.

133 *that doubtful point*: Witgood's economic circumstances.

140 *cloak companions*: fashionable servants who treated their masters in a casual manner (Loughrey).

141 *since . . . cloaks*: Linthicum (27) notes that servants stopped wearing their traditional garb, blue coats, in the early seventeenth century. Wearing cloaks the same colour as their masters' caused confusion and resentment.

157 *he . . . then*: he is not then such a fool as he appears.

     deceives: Q has 'decaves'.

174 *put . . . him*: call him 'your worship'.

201 *it kept*: so Q; most editions unnecessarily change to 'kept it'.

216 *countenance*: moral and financial support.

221 *uncle's house*: an 'uncle's house' was particularly appropriate for sexual assignations as 'aunts' (= bawds) could be found there (Loughrey).

226 *Cole Harbour*: a group of tenements located near London Bridge, considered a haven for criminals. It was also notorious for hasty marriages. ('Cole' is slang for 'cheat' or 'sharper'.)

227 *interest in*: claim on.

236 *our . . . together*: with double entendre (pursued in the next line).

238–9 *take me handsomely*: interpret me correctly.

248 *clapped . . . suddenly*: settled it quickly.

250–1 *forty . . . forth*: £40 I need for getting myself fitted out.

266 *with . . . scabbard*: and hence peacefully.

267 *wit . . . pommel*: the amount of wit in the knob on the hilt of a sword (Watson).

282 *father's*: stepfather's.

284 *copy*: (1) pattern, example; (2) copyhold, right (pursued in 'charter').

   charter: incorporating a trade guild.

287 *Y'are . . . busy*: can you spare me a moment? (but 'busy' also has a bawdy meaning) (Loughrey).

304–5 *They . . . have it*: (1) they know the certainty of his inheritance; (2) they know he has my money and must have sex with them (s.v. 'it' in Partridge).

307 *about*: most editors follow Q2's 'about' rather than Q1's 'above'. Watson, however, argues for Q1, but it seems more likely that Lucre is making an inclusive comment on 'goodly rooms'.

311 *strike*: (1) come to an agreement; (2) perform sexually (s.v. in Partridge) (see also 'strike the stroke in' on line 317).

   above: in the upstairs rooms.

319 *thousand*: a £1,000.

323 *again*: when.

326 *standing cup*: bowl with a foot or pedestal (and punning on tumescence). Q reads 'stranding'.

339–40 *twelve companies*: the twelve trade guilds of London (Mercers, Grocers, Drapers, Fishmongers, Goldsmiths, Skinners, Merchant Taylors, Haberdashers, Salters, Ironmongers, Vintners, Clothworkers).

342 *He*: Witgood.

   to: compared to.

346 *will*: with a pun on 'sexual desire'.

347 *violent*: vehement (Loughrey).

349 *heir*: with a pun on (pubic) hair.

350 *enough in you*: (1) enough spirit; (2) enough semen.

352 *make . . . on't*: use either a heavy arrow or a slender one, i.e. proverbially, to accept the venture (Lawrence). Following Mistress Lucre's 'if you once come to put it forth', however, the sense of 'bolt' and 'shaft' as 'penis' (s.v. 'bolt' in Rubinstein and Henke) should not be overlooked.

2.2 A street in London.

6 *affected*: disposed, inclined.

18 *countenance*: support, advocate.

19 *pass*: accomplish the matter.

36 *phrase*: manner of speaking.

46 *mar your phrase*: spoil your eloquent flattery.

59 *open*: Watson notes that another name for a medlar was an 'openarse'. (See also note on 2.1.34.)

64 *he*: Witgood.

71 *makes for me*: works in my favour.

3.1 Although Price places this scene confidently in the 'common room' of Witgood's inn, it could just as easily be another London street scene.

21 *content*: paid.

shame . . . us: shame on us for having harassed you earlier (Loughrey).

22 *sure*: betrothed.

26 *Would . . . with*: I wish you owed us as much as we would dare to lend you without security (Barber).

55 *play . . . it*: bashfully pretend to demur and then accept the offer—the phrase is proverbial.

97 *Term*: Witgood is playing with the two senses of *suitor*. During the court sessions, when London was full of litigants, not only the lawyers but also the prostitutes did very well for themselves (Watson).

102 *him*: Lucre.

117 *I . . . happiness*: i.e. in marriage with Joyce.

124 *blue-coats*: see note on *Mad*, 1.1.69.

128 *to . . . of*: to speak with.

129 *saving myself harmless*: provided it does not get me into trouble.

130 *thou . . . me*: I shall be more generous to you.

133 *poor*: used ironically—three clients at the rate of a brace of royals each day would have brought in a fabulous sum of money (Loughrey).

134–6 *What . . . clutches*: in fact the Host has been tricked by the Widow and Witgood (Loughrey).

138 *his*: Witgood's.

149 *their . . . actions*: of Witgood and Lucre.

160 *overthrown*: (1) overcome; (2) thrown on my back.

160–1 *'tis . . . withstand*: (1) we can withstand only very little; (2) only a very small penis fails to tempt us.

162 *neither*: Witgood and Hoard.

163 *affection*: prejudice.

164 *drive it home*: (1) make it certain; (2) ensure sexual consummation.

166 *party*: an interested party.

168 *him*: Hoard.

169 *t'other*: Witgood.

173–4 *executions . . . due body*: not only are his goods to be forfeit but he will be imprisoned for debt (Loughrey).

185 *Within . . . conscience*: cf. 1.1.7–8.

194 *at the bound*: on the rebound.

200 *join . . . to land*: (1) join the estates; (2) copulate (s.v. 'join' in Henke).

202 *There*: in Witgood.

204 *him*: Hoard.

206–7 *chin . . . hair*: a penniless youth.

210 *deserve*: requite.

215 *My . . . expressed*: my joy is so great I cannot express it adequately.

216 *remember*: remind.

217 *suddenly*: soon.

220 *same purpose*: marriage.

224 *single*: alone.

228–9 *Cole Harbour*: see note on 2.1.226.

243 *to the rest*: sexual satisfaction.

247 *serve for*: deal with.

252 *days*: delays. The language of usury: days were 'grace days' tacked on to the stipulated loan time.

253–4 *she's . . . followed*: she has many admirers.

258–9 *weigh down*: outweigh in wealth as in a pair of scales, with a sexual innuendo as in 'jointure' and 'possess' (Loughrey).

3.2 A room in Hoard's house.

12 *private charge*: command to deliver the letter privately (Price).

3.3 The common room of a tavern.

1 *Dick*: who would be *within* as is William later.

2 *Pomegranate*: the name of a room in the inn; rooms were named, not numbered, in inns at this time ('Pomgarnet' is used in *1 Henry IV*, 2.4.41).

23 *bear me down*: insist (lit. = overthrow me in debate).

29 *bound*: opportunity; but see note on 3.1.194.

35 *'tis . . . door*: and therefore convenient to make their escape (Loughrey).

49 *Against*: when.

52 *'Las*: Q reads 'asse'.

62 *I'll do thy*: Q reads 'I be do thy'.

66 *making*: match-making.

71 *'tis much if*: I'd be surprised if (Loughrey).

87 *To boat*: this is a slip by Witgood, since he ought not to know that she had taken boat; he says it to make sure that the Host will be able to track down the fugitives (Barber). It is possible, however, to imagine Witgood 'deducing' the Courtesan's means of escape.

102 *thirsts*: Q has 'thrifts'.

104 *on*: on frustrating (Loughrey).

110 *mere*: performed without the help of anyone else (Loughrey).

111 *nearly*: closely (Loughrey).

112 *took*: gained refuge in.

3.4 A room in Dampit's house.

    2 *anno '99*: Stow (ii. 19) records a great storm in London in January 1589 in which the gates of St Paul's were blown down. Although there was no storm remarkable enough to be recorded for 1599, emendation is probably unnecessary.

    3–4 *Poovies' new buildings*: the Povies are presumably business rivals of Dampit. The buildings cannot be identified with certainty, though it is on record that in 1607 a William Povey was forced to dismantle a wooden building in St Paul's Churchyard which contravened building regulations (Loughrey).

29–30 *help . . . unready*: help you to undress.

31 *Audrey-prater*: a nonce word analogous to 'Margery-prater', a cant term for a hen (Lawrence).

35 *cony-catching*: the catching of the cony (or rabbit)—the deceit practised by the confidence-man.

44 *cavern-fed*: Q has 'cauerne-sed' (with the long 's') which editors usually transcribe as 'cavernesed', arguing that the word is a drunken invention on Dampit's part. It seems more likely that the compositor mistakenly substituted a long 's' for an 'f' (a frequent occurrence in this century, as Price points out), especially as 'cavern-fed' (equally a drunken invention) balances 'kitchen-stuff' in the previous lines. Here, the word presumably means that Audrey has been fed a vile diet of foolishness in her childhood.

45 *bawdreaminy*: another bizarre coinage of Dampit's; it is probably intended to convey the notion that Audrey spends her time in licentious dreams (see Henke for further variations).

56 *Proserpine*: Roman name for Persephone, queen of the underworld, who spends half the year as Pluto's consort and half the year on earth. Barber suggests that Dampit is referring to his landlady, to whom Audrey is servant. He may mean one of the local prostitutes.

61 *is here*: Q has 'here is'.

65 *burn horns*: Dampit's ramblings here must allude either to the ink-wells to be found in the Inns of Court or to the translucent horn used to protect leaves of paper when reading (Watson). Henke (s.v. 'burn') offers: infect the penis with venereal disease.

4.1 The common room of the tavern at Cole Harbour.

s.d. *he*: Hoard.

7 *slips*: neglects, overlooks.

22 *You . . . his*: because they are married.

27 *Upon calm conditions*: on condition that he behaves calmly.

29 *So*: so long as.

entrance: pronounced as three syllables.

34 *watched the hour*: waited for the opportunity.

51 *friends*: Q reads 'friend'. Here = relations, members of my family.

53 *flattered*: too favourably represented (Watson).

54 *touch*: test.

56 *scarce . . . needs*: hardly able to supply himself with his basic requirements.

67 *dry oak*: Hoard.

77 *[LIMBER]*: see note on The Actors, 17.

84–6 *In . . . present*: Lucre does not know that the wedding ceremony has already taken place and therefore wishes her to stay single and also in the same state of mind (i.e. to marry Witgood) (Loughrey).

105 *do mountains*: do anything to win back the widow (Loughrey).

4.2 A room in Lucre's house.

1 *son-in-law*: stepson.

2 *Oh . . . lamentation*: this line seems to be a variant on the old tune 'O man in desperation' mentioned in Nashe's *Summer's Last Will and Testament*, 1600, and Peele's *The Old Wives' Tale*, 1590 (Watson).

8 *Highgate*: now inside London, but it used to be a village outside (a suitable place for a country house).

15 *regardless . . . form*: unconcerned about his appearance.

16 *how now*: Q has 'how'.

firm: confirmed (Loughrey).

33 *merely . . . you*: plotted with no other object than to spite you (Loughrey).

35 *carry*: win.

62 *No*: Lucre's reply suggests that Witgood had stressed 'give' in the preceding line (Loughrey).

68 *so well*: Q reads 'to well'.

75 *Go to*: Lucre's wife obviously reacts against the mention of her humble origins (Loughrey).

76 *raising of paste*: Henke suggests this phrase also means 'causing a man to ejaculate'.

83 *them*: Lucre and Hoard.

85 *envy*: the stress is on the second syllable.

93 *Since . . . in*: another variant on the cozen/cousin pun where 'title' = 'kin'.

4.3 A street near Witgood's Inn.

17 *cast . . . at*: give up hope of.

37 *non plus ultra*: see note on *Mad*, 3.2.151.

57 *May . . . sir*: Price notes that the Host has probably come to report that the Widow has gone home with Hoard in spite of learning that Lucre has given up the mortgage to Witgood. (The Host continues to be ignorant of the Widow's identity.)

60 *Puritans*: and therefore strict in enforcement (Loughrey).

60–3 *Do . . . i'faith*: presumably the various creditors are speaking all at once.

4.4 A room in Hoard's house.

5 *spacious in content*: she has a great capacity to give (sexual) contentment ('spacious' continues the imagery suggested by 'large in possessions'). Henke suggests a pun: 'cuntent'.

6 *wise*: Q reads 'wife' (which is just possible).

7–8 *that's . . . me*: hinting at his own sexual inadequacy.

8–9 *She's . . . it*: (1) her beauty is priceless (just in her underwear) provided a man were sexually competent; (2) her sexual allure is great enough to generate a handsome income (provided she were properly marketed).

14–15 *entertain . . . qualities*: engage as servants those who have vocations and accomplishments.

17 *for nonce*: for that particular purpose.

19 *hang himself*: a traditional end for despairing usurers.

23 *of occupation*: with trades.

27 *cut his comb*: humiliate him (proverbial, see Tilley C256).

42 *There, boy*: as to a dog.

45 *countenance*: favour.

49 *within ourselves*: on our own lands.

52 *your*: Q has 'you'.

56 *Go . . . with*: proceed with.

61 *Polonian fashion*: close to the head (Watson suggests a pun on barber's pole).

80–1 *bear . . . it*: there is a covert allusion in this phrase to the cuckold's horns.

87 *precontract*: a legally binding betrothal agreement which would nullify Hoard's marriage.

102 *inconsiderate grant*: thoughtless promise (Loughrey).

112 *compound*: bargain. We never learn what form of bargaining Hoard has in mind. From the Courtesan's reply it would have to have involved an acknowledgement of the validity of the pre-contract, followed by some kind of expensive bribe, as opposed merely to settling Witgood's 'petty' debts. Her plan provides for a release, perhaps with no acknowledgement of the validity of the pre-contract, though it's not clear in what way her plan is 'nobler' than his offer to 'compound'.

119 *all inconveniences*: including scrapping the pre-contract.

120 *by . . . means*: only by this means.

127 *revenge*: payment of Witgood's debts will partly compensate for loss of the Widow (Price).

128 *release*: from the Courtesan's 'rash and unadvised words'.

130 *scrivener*: see note on *Term*, 4.1.91.

133 *deeper . . . state*: deeper than despair itself.

137 *he*: Witgood.

154 *give . . . talk*: proverbial.

177 *set . . . goose-giblet*: give tit for tat (Tilley H161).

181 *are . . . words*: are not debts stronger obligations than a promise of marriage? (Price).

183 *back-racket*: the return of a ball in tennis, hence metaphorically a verbal counter-thrust.

191 *Mulligrub's sister*: Mulligrub is an unpleasant character in Marston's *The Dutch Courtesan* (1605). To suffer from the mulligrubs was to experience a fit of the spleen, a bout of ill temper.

194 *all in all*: all things in all respects.

201 *in durance*: while a prisoner. But, as Price points out, although Witgood has been arrested he is not a prisoner.

211 *Tell me*: (1) say to me; (2) count.

212 *desperate debts*: 'bad' debts, not expected to be paid. Hoard offers to pay half of them (ten shillings in the pound); the creditors counter with two-thirds (a mark), which Hoard accepts.

212–13 *ne'er . . . accident*: which would never be paid except in the current circumstances (Loughrey).

221 *these presents*: the present document.

227 *in . . . of*: (1) in the possession of; (2) sexually employed by ('these villains will make the word as odious as the word "occupy"; which was an excellent good word before it was ill sorted', *1 Henry IV*, 2.4.146–9).

230 *manors*: Q has 'manor'.

235 *interchangeably*: reciprocally (with Witgood).

236 *these presents*: witnesses (those present; see also line 244).

237 *slipped*: let slip.

251 *something wanting*: a third of Witgood's debt (i.e. they aren't receiving full reimbursement).

262 *pig-haired*: short-haired (citizens wore their hair short).

262–3 *ram-headed*: with (a cuckold's) horns.

264 *By . . . league*: with Hoard, the Niece's guardian.

4.5 Dampit's bedroom.

S.D. *bed*. It is possible that Dampit's bed is on the inner stage behind curtains, which would be drawn back at his command in line 5. However, our uncertainty as to the existence of an inner stage should make us consider other possibilities. The bed could, for instance, have simply been thrust out onto the stage with Dampit in it.

1–4 Audrey's Song can be found in Thomas Ravenscroft's songbook 'Melismata' (1611) headed 'The Scriueners seruants Song of Holborne' and beginning 'My master is so wise'. The opening lines are missing from the play and run as follows: 'My master is so wise, so wise, that he's proceeded wittol, | My mistress is a fool, a fool, and yet 'tis the most get-all.' A. J. Sabol ('Ravenscroft's "Melismata" and the Children of Paul's', *Renaissance News*, 12 (1959), 3–9) finds it unaccountable that these opening lines should be missing from the play's text. But we should note that they: (*a*) accuse the husband of being a wittol, and (*b*) the wife of being wanton. Perhaps their omission is an indication that Middleton did not intend Dampit to be saddled with a wife. (See note on line 54.) We should note that the Song could conceivably have been a duet between Audrey and the Boy.

2 *pits*: taverns, brothels and women.

5 *Trahe, trahito*: Latin commands to 'draw' (curtains and drink). Q has the incorrect form 'traheto'.

S.D. *Enter Gentlemen*: in the dialogue that follows, between Spitchcock, Lamprey and Dampit, there are some lines not heard by Dampit.

6–7 *did . . . year*: previous editors have suggested that Lamprey's description indicates that Dampit's bed (at least) is chained to the chest containing his wealth. As Watson points out, there is no need for such a literal interpretation of these lines.

8 *steel bedstaffs*: Dampit's bed seems to have been strengthened with a frame of steel rods (Loughrey).

10 *conceit*: morbid symptom (Loughrey).

12 *trampler*: see note on 1.4.10.

26 *mullipood*: Watson constructs the meaning 'dirty toad' from 'mull' and 'pode'.

29–30 *tavern . . . head*: he is drunk.

49 *unfeathered*: hairless (as a result of the pox).

50 *cullisance*: a corruption of 'cognizance' = heraldic badge (Watson), i.e. a scab.

53 *pole of carnality*: the erect penis (Loughrey).

54 *My mistress*: some editors see this as a reference to Dampit's wife (whom we never meet). It does not seem very probable, however, that he would have a wife (or would want one), and this may either be a slip on Middleton's part or refer to Dampit's landlady as Barber suggests (see note on 3.4.56).

72 *pythagorical*: a jocular vulgarization of the Pythagorean doctrine of the transmigration of souls (see following note).

74 *he . . . cloak*: so that he will not be arrested (for debt).

79 *crawling*: sycophantic (also playing on lousiness, cf. the preceding line).
longer day: more time to pay his debts.

84 *farewell . . . thousand*: a thousand and one farewells.

89 *His . . . departing*: his memory is about to go (because of the drink).

95 *bell*: the funeral bell.

106 *make you*: are you doing.

107 *device*: advice (an obsolete variant, not a malapropism).

114 *feats*: crimes.

114–15 *ejectione firmae*: writ of ejection whereby a person ousted from an estate for years may recover possession of it (Watson).

116 *small*: few.

121 *break*: end contention (Barber).

128 *What's . . . him?*: Lamprey should of course know who Hoard is. In the play's third scene, Q has Lamprey and Spitchcock acting as peacemakers between Hoard and Lucre. See following note.

130 *Oh . . . sir*: an apology to Hoard, with whom Lamprey is well acquainted, for not recognizing him in a bridegroom's finery (Price). (The apology could just as well be directed at Lancelot. See note on The Actors, 17.)

141 *keeps open house*: is sexually hospitable (see notes to 2.2.59 and 2.1.221).

145 *let out some*: hire out (for copulation).

148 *O . . . ademptum*: 'O fearful monster, misshapen, huge, deprived of sight' (Virgil, *Aeneid*, iii. 658).

155 *like . . . ambassador*: Gwyn Williams ('The Cuckoo, the Welsh Ambassador', *Modern Language Review*, 51 (1956), 223–5) tells us that the

association of the cuckoo with the Welsh probably stemmed from the convention of using bird or beast as a love-messenger or messenger of friendship in Welsh poetry from the fourteenth to the sixteenth century. Loughrey and Taylor think that the allusion here is to the Welsh raiders who pillaged the Border counties in 'cuckoo-time', i.e. spring.

156 *when . . . down*: a double entendre.

157 *naked bed*: when I am naked in my bed.

159 *Middlesex juries*: London and Middlesex juries were hated for the unfair severity of their verdicts (Middlesex is a county in south-east England, bordering West and North London).

170 *sweet fray*: because of the contents of the close-stool.

174 *his . . . him*: he is on the point of death.

5.1 A room in Lucre's house.

5.2 A room in Hoard's house.

2 *tierce*: wine cask. But then the Host puns on the meaning from fencing— a (phallic) thrust. 'taste 'em all over' (5) suggests fellatio (s.v. 'tierce' in Henke).

7 S.D. *Exit [Host]*: probably the Host does not return to the stage. He nowhere indicates that he has learned the Widow's identity; he probably is still wearing the Widow's livery, though now functioning as Hoard's servant, while he awaits further effort by Witgood to regain the Widow. Middleton has to suppress the distracting episode of the Host's clamour when he discovers the Widow's identity and the risks to which Witgood has exposed him (Price).

9 *cupboard of plate*: a sideboard for the display of plate, or the service of plate itself (Watson).

19 *my . . . dinner*: having been married that morning, Joyce and Witgood plan to meet and reveal the marriage at Hoard's wedding dinner (Price).

21–2 *free o'th'fishmongers*: members of the Fishmongers' Company (with an obvious reference to the fish names, Lamprey and Spitchcock, see The Actors).

28 *Lady Foxstone*: she is introduced for the purposes of getting the Courtesan off the scene momentarily while Onesiphorus arrives, thus increasing the irony, and of adding a third female figure to the wedding party (Price).

32 *make the worst*: underrate your hospitality.

41 *with . . . gentleman*: Onesiphorus enters with both Limber and Kix, as the subsequent dialogue makes clear.

46 *at an hour*: punctual, on time.

51 *guests*: Q has 'guesse'.

358

52 *guests*: again, Q has 'guesse'.

63 *I . . . face*: the two knew each other in Leicestershire (Loughrey).

106 *Negatur argumentum*: argument is denied.

107 *Probo tibi*: I prove it to you.

knows: has carnal knowledge of.

110 *Negatur . . . majoris*: the conclusion of your major premiss is denied.

127 *follow it*: prosecute the case (Loughrey).

141 *quit from*: saved from the danger of becoming (Watson).

165–6 *Feigning . . . neighbour's*: pretending to assist a neighbour in her giving birth.

168 *though . . . heart*: even though the astrological signs are unpropitious for such treatment (i.e. she is using medical treatment as a mask for another escapade and has to go through with it, even though she has no need of it, in order to lend plausibility to the alibi).

169 *Removing . . . beds*: moving to different bedrooms (Loughrey).

182 *shake out*: produce by shaking.

184 *Queans' evils*: venereal diseases.

185 *glisters*: suppositories, enemas. Watson notes that Greene in *A Quip for an Upstart Courtier* sneers at this practice, one of the affectations of his upstart courtier.

186 *Stabbing of arms*: and then mingling the blood with the wine when drinking healths to women.

187 *Ribbon favours*: knots of ribbons given as favours to lovers (Loughrey).

189 *Dutch flapdragons*: the Dutch were supposed to be adept at the art of swallowing flaming raisins in wine.

healths in urine: another grotesque practice by gallants; the urine was mixed with wine.

193 *general vice*: all vices (Loughrey).

No Wit, No Help Like a Woman's

The Actors in the Comedy
The list is derived from the 1657 Octavo.

1 *Twilight*: and hence in his declining years, the evening of his life; cf. Sunset.

2 *servant*: suitor.

5 *Low-water*: a name suggesting poverty.

decayed: impoverished.

6 *Lambston*: = lamb's testicles. See note on 'Singlestone', *Mad*, 2.6.2.

7 *Weatherwise*: so-called because of his devotion to almanacs.

8 *Pepperton*: = having been infected venereally (s.v. 'pepper' in Rubinstein).

9 *Overdone*: worn out (sexually); cf. Mistress Overdone in *Measure for Measure*.

13 *Savourwit*: see note on 'Follywit', *Mad*, The Actors, 2.

15 *Pickadille*: = (1) an intricate, delicate edging on a collar; (2) intricate schemes.

17 *Goldenfleece*: riches (the Golden Fleece was the object of the quest of Jason and the Argonauts).

Prologue

7 *arrant*: a variant of errand (used for the rhyme).

9–10 *How is't . . . wild seas*: a conventional Jonsonian lament about the difficulty of pleasing audiences.

11–13 *attention . . . below*: the distinction is between spectators in the galleries of the theatre and those in the pit.

13 *take*: absorb.

14 *tickle ye*: amuse you.

1.1 O does not divide the play into scenes. The setting here is probably a street near Sir Oliver Twilight's house.

7 *invention*: inventiveness.

8 *since . . . upon't*: (1) since I was born; (2) since I began using it (my powers of invention).

9 *Nor . . . wheel*: this isn't the only impediment (the 'stop' was a block of wood thrust between a wheel's spokes to prevent it turning).

10 *grated*: harassed, aggravated (suggested by 'wheel' in the previous line, see *OED* v. 8, and continued in 'rub' in Savourwit's reply).

13 *affected mistress*: the woman he loves (i.e. Jane).

15 *woos*: on my behalf.

16 *He*: Sandfield.

17 *'Twixt*: O has ' 'Bwixt'.

22 *disease*: (1) annoyance; (2) illness.

24 *Work . . . time*: expel it vigorously all at once.

32 *make clear*: give a fair appearance to.

33 *seconds*: intermediaries (in this case, Sir Oliver).

36 *Not . . . father?*: is not your father one of your 'seconds'?

40 *lover's weapon*: (1) dagger; (2) penis (for which the whore 'gapes' at line 51).

ne'er: O reads 'now'.

49 *Your . . . him*: the implication seems to be that only by voluntarily offering up his breast to Sandford's sword (as a result of his 'greater crosses') could Philip lose in a duel between them.

51 *scabbard*: (1) sheath; (2) vagina.

54 *Your . . . both*: both your wits would.

62 *his*: Philip's.

63 *Jersey*: O reads 'Jerusey'. Editors have taken this to be Guernsey. But it is more likely to be Jersey, the Channel Island nearer the French coast, because: (1) Lady Twilight and Grace were taken by the 'Dunkirks' (French marauders) and (2) Philip and Savourwit landed somewhere 'by the way' (i.e. on the way) to Jersey, which must have been Guernsey, the Channel Island closer to England. On the other hand, the Dutch Merchant claims to have seen Grace in an inn at Antwerp, and Philip tells us that he met Grace there (2.2.130), so we should not expect too great a concern for a consistent geography in this play.

65 *last*: latest.

76 *him*: Philip.

77 *by the way*: Guernsey springs to mind; but Philip apparently meets and marries Jane in Antwerp.

79 *pockets*: with a pun on 'testes' (see Rubinstein).

81 *unkindly*: unnatural (for gentlemen to hold onto their wealth—and their semen).

83 *there*: Guernsey/Antwerp.

86 *half a crown*: the price paid the priest for marrying them.

90 *bringing up*: invention.

93 *made . . . mother*: satisfied (him) about the mother (lit. 'to make the score even' = to satisfy a debt or obligation).

98 *error*: wandering, journeying (by sea).

105 *For yet*: up until now.

108–9 *I . . . dressing*: I experience another feeling of anguish (i.e. when the doctor dresses a wound for the second time).

111 *but well soldered*: i.e. her appearance and manner are virginal.

114 *full and change*: the full and new moon.

mooncalf: (1) born fool; (2) monstrosity (produced by the influence of the moon at his birth).

116 *down*: (1) soft wool; (2) pulling down (of a garment).

119 *[her on]*: these words are missing in O. Dyce's insertion of them is obviously required.

126 *fool*: Weatherwise.

130 *Well . . . in't*: well done, congratulations (i.e. in anticipation).

132 *full cry, oh!*: = oh!

134 *You . . . yours*: the 'you' here continues to be Sandfield; 'he' (Philip) will love Grace as a sister.

136 *each/both*: Sandfield and Philip.

138 *got*: begot.

140–1 *you . . . lip*: this is directed at Sandfield.

143 *But . . . them*: do not do the 'more' that cousins do (again, directed at Sandfield).

144 *you*: Philip.

149 *well . . . free*: brisk and limber.

150 *There's . . . me*: knowledgeable employers know they do not need to exhort me to do something.

151 *comforts*: consolation, relief.

152 *'em*: i.e. comfits (sweetmeats).

153 *Thou . . . perfect*: an obscure remark. Perhaps: 'You make fun of joys (union with Philip) whose reality cannot be improved upon by words.'

154 *risen*: from their meal.

160 *comfort*: punning on the meaning 'semen'.

172 *at home*: to her house.

175 *you both*: Sir Oliver and Sunset.

181 *choices*: of husbands.

183 *There's . . . imagine*: O has this line spoken by both Grace and Jane. Johnson assigns it to Lady Goldenfleece believing that she's hinting at the secret. Dyce (correctly in my view) gives it to Grace who has already chosen 'rightly'.

189 *'tis . . . t'other*: because Grace and Jane are so alike in beauty and accomplishments.

200 *The . . . even*: the matter is moving straight on (Johnson); but the phrase also conveys the idea that they feel the same way about each other (i.e. friendship not love).

202 *equinoctial*: Weatherwise. The equinoctial line, the celestial or terrestrial equator, is curved.

212 *as . . . on*: as you describe.

224 *that*: that which.

with dearness: (1) lovingly; (2) with expensive gifts; (3) after trial and hazard.

227–8 *And . . . her*: the sense seems to be that Weatherwise will send Grace home complete with a number of new lovers ('poor sparks'). The clause, ' 'cause you shall not doubt her' is sarcastic (= 'you shall not suspect her capacity to attract lovers').

229 *Dowland's Lachrymae*: John Dowland (1563–1626), the English composer and lutenist, was most famous for his *Lachrymae* or 'Seaven Teares' pavane, published in 1605.

234 *strangely*: exceedingly.

251 *piece of mutton*: bout of love-making.

253 *gull*: Weatherwise.

257 *hit*: fit together.

264–70 *the fifth . . . day*: Weatherwise enumerates the days of his courtship of Grace in terms of his lack of progress with her (as the adverse comments of his almanac make clear).

265 *'twixt . . . buzzard*: as these are both birds of prey, Weatherwise means that there is no hope for him on that day (cf. our 'between a rock and a hard place').

270 *against the hair*: against the grain, contrary. There are fugitive obscene suggestions in most of Weatherwise's prognostications (including this one): moving backwards and forwards in a beastly fashion; the slippery pin (s.v. 'pin' in Rubinstein); fire and tow (s.v. 'distaff' in Partridge).

274 *i'th'sands*: in the lurch.

286 *in crust*: (1) in a pie; (2) sexually active ('crust' = a venereal scab; cf. the double entendre in 'drop down under a tree').

292 *Clerkenwell*: see note on *Mad*, 3.2.224.

293 *Hound's Ditch*: a street in London mainly devoted to the sale of second-hand clothes (Johnson notes the pun on 'hounds').

1.2 A room in Low-water's house.

3 *revenue*: the stress is on the second syllable.

7 *angels*: with a pun on angels as coins (see Glossary).

8 *banks*: seats of justice.

10 *Chamber*: the treasury of the City of London in which orphans' inheritances were deposited until they came of age. Middleton and his sister, Avis, received their inheritance from the Chamber (see Mark Eccles, ' "Thomas Middleton a Poett" ', *SP* 54 (1957), 517) (Johnson).

13 *strain*: harmonious melody (Johnson).

16 *a widow*: Lady Goldenfleece.

17 *wife*: Mistress Low-water.

18 *That . . . heart*: that she should pretend to be grieving (by wearing the mourning 'garment') whereas I truly am grieving (i.e. in the 'heart').

19 *husband*: O reads 'uncle'.

22 *here*: on the other hand.

37 *Good*: i.e. good soul, good woman (the vocative use).

49 *piece*: O reads 'price'. See note on *Term*, 2.3.307.

52 *hired*: bribed.

63 *hers*: Lady Goldenfleece's.

93 *brief*: letter (with a pun on the meaning 'summary').

96 *mine enemy*: Lady Goldenfleece.

101 *near'st way*: shortest route.

106 *keep*: as a mistress.

110 *loose*: O reads 'lose' but Johnson's emendation (where 'loose' = 'let loose') is clearly necessary.

111 *suits*: O has 'suiters'.

133 *east port*: O reads 'vast part' which makes minimal sense. Bullen's emendation picks up the sun metaphor.

141 *Wherein*: O has 'Herein'.

157 *following spirit*: willingness to help (Johnson).

163 *sweating sickness*: a disease (common in the fifteenth and sixteenth centuries) characterized by a high fever and profuse sweating and the possibility of death within 24 hours.

1.3 A room in Sir Oliver Twilight's house.

7 *neck-cracking*: suicide (by hanging).

17 *How . . . himself*: how well he takes up the theme again (of suicide).

20 *eating . . . portion*: (1) a living allowance; (2) accommodation.

41 *ought*: owed.

sh'owes: O reads 'shows'. Bullen's emendation follows the sense of 'ought'. Sir Oliver means that the love he owed to the mother belongs now entirely to the daughter.

42 *It*: the love and care owing the wife.

49 *covered*: see note on *Mad*, 5.1.68.

80 *simply*: (1) in good faith; (2) foolishly.

81 *that sum*: the amount of the ransom money. O has 'son' instead of 'sum'.

91 *blinded*: deceived.

94 *lets*: prevents.

105 The Dutch Merchant and the Dutch Boy speak a kind of pidgin English which is almost decipherable. Savourwit's Dutch is almost pure gibberish (words like 'pisse' surface occasionally).

118 *even*: smoothly.

120 *reckoning*: (1) account (of conduct); (2) bill.

128 *take . . . you*: let me catch up with you.

155 *Tells*: O has 'Tell'.

168-70 *Come . . . you*: they have come pretending to do you a good deed but intend to get money from you.

172-3 *live . . . thistle*: think up ways of making a profit in the most unpropitious circumstances (the Dutch were well known for their love of butter).

197 *distinguished*: divided into parts.

199 *saucy language*: because of the combination 'gull' and 'goose'.

200 *eelship*: presumably a vessel that fishes for eels. The Dutch were reputed to be very fond of eels.

204 *thunder*: of righteous indignation.

219 *in . . . case*: well off, used ironically (Johnson).

2.1 A room in Weatherwise's house.

7 *stand*: (1) tolerate; (2) achieve an erection.

8 *chamber*: (1) bedroom; (2) vagina.

11 *are . . . them*: are you their lover ('double' = coupled together).

12 *mourning*: Lady Goldenfleece is still in mourning ostensibly for her husband's death.

13 *doublets*: a recent fashion was for women to wear men's clothes. See also note on *Mad*, 3.3.100.

14 *under his subjection*: (1) under his rule; (2) lying underneath him.

16-17 *lock . . . key*: a common double entendre.

18-19 *at . . . weapon*: inappropriately (because his weapon = a penis, the 'key' of line 17).

20 *my weapon falls*: a double entendre.

21 *shooters*: with a pun on suitors which was pronounced the same (Johnson).

22 *arrows without heads*: this is in reference to the wooing efforts of Pepperton and Overdone (the context suggests a failure on their part to achieve an erection).

23 *butt*: (1) target; (2) vagina. But doubtless Weatherwise is also thinking of himself as their target.

24 *I'll . . . white*: a clear reference to a successful attempt at sexual intercourse. In archery the black pin was at the centre of the target in the white inner circle.

26 *diet . . . months*: the drink for each month's 'diet' (= prescribed food) is governed by his almanac.

42 *joined*: in sexual union.

43 *fast*: (1) quick; (2) bonded.

57 *upon . . . month*: one a month.

59 *posies*: versified epigrams painted on the back of wooden trenchers.

74 *members*: (1) limbs; (2) male and female sex organs.

97 *they . . . days*: because (at this stage) Weatherwise does not want them to partake of the banquet.

100 *head*: the first use in this line refers to Aries as the sign that dominates the head; the second 'head' = the head of the household.

101 *middle*: (1) because between husband and children; (2) the middle region of the body (see note on *Mad*, 4.3.30–1).

109 *thing*: penis.

114 *Since . . . thighs*: Sagittarius (governing the upper part of the legs) enables me to traverse the thighs.

116 *I . . . enough*: a bawdy double entendre (s.v. 'meat' in Henke).

126 *once*: this once.

hats on: see note on *Mad*, 5.1.41.

127–9 *I . . . one*: the sense seems to be that Weatherwise expects that the amount of food he has provided at this banquet would last his tenants a month.

136–7 *wants . . . feet*: a cover (i.e. guest) for Pisces (Johnson).

142 *draw . . . legs*: the better to receive a man (s.v. 'draw up' in Partridge).

142–3 *lie . . . together*: (1) curve yourself more (to keep warm); (2) lie closer together (with a lover).

146 *calves*: (1) according to his sign of the zodiac; (2) calf = fool.

148 *he*: the tenant.

149–50 *She's . . . ground*: she has transferred the tenant's foolishness to Weatherwise.

160 *Come . . . tail*: let all kinds come (proverbial); the 'kinds' are distinguished by penis size, 'cut' and 'long'.

163 *that's . . . gentleman*: because gentlemen are idle.

165 *wears socks beside*: the mark of a gentleman.

166 *observe Fridays*: by not eating meat.

168–9 *as he comes*: where there happens to be a vacant seat (presumably among Weatherwise's tenants).

181 *rack*: torture by stretching the joints by means of a special apparatus.

185 *A . . . gallant*: a gallant who looks like a beautiful woman.

189 *conceited*: fanciful, whimsical.

194 *busy*: (1) with eating; (2) with sexual play (s.v. 'business' in Henke).

197 *broken flesh*: a woman who is not a virgin (the deflowered Virgo).

201 *fellows*: other fish.

203 *dead low water*: when fish would be dead (and punning on her name).

205 *'Tis brave, Kate*: O has ' 'Tis a brave, Kate'.

208 *You're . . . man*: you are your own fool (as opposed to being 'my lady's').

209 *step in to*: (1) fetch; (2) penetrate (sexually).

215 *him*: Mistress Low-water.

217 *makes . . . end*: Lady Goldenfleece thinks that Mistress Low-water's beauty reverses the hierarchy of the table. Although 'he' is Pisces (who dominates the feet), 'he' should be Aries (who dominates the head).

220 *sun*: in the shape of the sun-cup.

221 *these*: the signs.

226 *maid*: virgin.

228 *head*: chief, and punning on Aries's domination of the head.

233 *Townbull Street*: a jocular substitute for Turnbull Street, an infamous quarter of the town (Bullen).

241 *sold fish*: prostituted herself.

   where: whereas.

242 *It . . . yours*: an exclamation of approval: 'the prize is yours'.

245–6 *twelve weapons*: the zodiacal signs.

262 *yon fair sign*: the disguised Mistress Low-water (who is the source of Lady Goldenfleece's warm feelings).

   yon: O has 'you'.

263 *By . . . heat*: i.e. the sun does not shine upon itself.

267 *There's . . . us*: there is no difference between us (with a pun on 'pubic hair').

270 *poor feet*: Mistress Low-water as Pisces.

272 *proud . . . feet*: Taurus (Sir Gilbert) dominates the neck; Pisces, the feet (Johnson).

275 *fill't him*: fill it for him.

282 *knave*: knight (but the other meaning is appropriate for Sir Gilbert).

294–5 *fall . . . ears*: quarrel.

297 *Cold signs both*: Taurus is cold and dry; Pisces moist and dry (Johnson).

308 *these*: O has 'this'.

309 *live*: thrive.

310 *as . . . open*: as long as you are alive (and available for gulling).

324 *hand*: handwriting.

329 *paints white*: turns pale.

337 *a fresh colour*: innocently.

341 *glass*: the letter.

346 *To free*: O reads 'From'. I have adopted Johnson's emendation.

356 *right*: i.e. ripe for sex, available for seduction.

361 *his*: Mistress Low-water's fictitious kinsman's.

388 *contracting*: of marriage.

389 *to . . . spider*: there was a belief that a spider in drink or food would poison those who consumed it only if they knew the spider was there.

394 *wanting*: lacking.

2.2 The street outside Sir Oliver Twilight's house.

12 *bare*: mere.

   my mother's life: the fact that my mother is alive.

19 *thee*: Savourwit.

22 S.D. *[Draws his sword]*: as indication that he is proposing to go abroad as a soldier of fortune.

25 *at your hands*: on your part.

   put it up: (1) sheathe the sword; (2) tolerate it.

75 *her kinswoman*: Jane Sunset.

80 *young flood*: flow of the tide up river.

86 *hang . . . thumbs*: a form of judicial punishment.

107 *Bartholomew-tide*: 24 August (St Bartholomew's Day).

123 *friend*: close relative.

141–2 *This . . . sons*: this may be thought good behaviour, in comparison with some of the antics which love and youth provoke sons daily to perpetrate.

156 *jealous*: suspicious.

169 *Approve*: confirm.

176 *hoffie toffie*: a made-up exclamation.

186 *shifting*: crooked, and constantly moving his place of business.

187 *breaks*: goes bankrupt.

2.3 A room in Lady Goldenfleece's house.

2 *Well said*: well done.

15 *'Tis . . . man*: punning on the literal sense of making (disguising herself as) a man.

27–8 *You . . . gown*: she means that she has left her obedience behind with her female clothes.

28 *these clothes*: her disguise as a man.

44–5 *Venus in cauda*: the planet Venus in the Dragon's tail. Such a conjunction increased the malevolent and lecherous aspects of the planet (Johnson). (See also note on 3.1.13–14.)

45 *goes to't with*: has sex with the aid of.

48 *set up*: stabled.

55 Q reads 'PEPPERT. OVERD. How Bess, Peg?' As both 'Bess' and 'Peg' are diminutives of 'Elizabeth', it seems advisable to distribute them between Pepperton and Overdone.

56 *Plain Bess*: custom forbade affectionate diminutives before marriage (Johnson).

58 *horsing*: (1) riding; (2) copulating.

64 *gloves*: customary gifts of the bride to the groom's men (Johnson).

75–6 *I'll . . . it*: presumably a drunkard might well use his shoe as a cup.

82 *There's . . . mistress*: in the game of bowls the 'mistress' or 'jack' was the small bowl that was the target for the bowlers. 'Rubs' were the impediments thrown up by uneven ground.

83 *pricker*: (1) one who provokes or incites; (2) (male) copulator. Mistress Low-water is 'bad' at both because she is female.

84–5 *if . . . saver*: (1) if my bowling ball uses the slope I will not have to throw so hard; (2) if my 'penis' ('bowl') is stored or hidden away ('take bank') I will not have to use it.

86 *alley*: a long narrow enclosure for playing at bowls.

87 *younger brother*: who would have no inheritance from his father and must needs be more aggressive in making his way in the world.

89 *he*: the younger brother.

96 *I . . . widower*: I would not have the younger brother marry someone who has no riches.

115 *quickness*: liveliness.

117–18 *cross the book*: cancel the debt.

118 *turn . . . leaf*: (1) make a fresh start; (2) open a new account; (3) make love again.

120 *greater*: by becoming pregnant.

125 *an . . . interest*: (1) if they did not dabble in usury; (2) if they were not sexually active.

126 *setter-up*: (1) one newly established financially (cf. note on *Term*, 2.3.336–7); (2) one who arouses someone sexually (s.v. 'set up' in Henke).

127 *payment*: satisfaction (financial and sexual).

128 *ware*: (1) goods; (2) penis.

129 *will*: with a pun on sexual inclination.

132 *make . . . service*: do not stand upon ceremony.

136 *stomach*: (1) appetite (including the sexual); (2) penis (see Partridge).

sons and heirs: the oldest sons in the family (the beneficiaries of primogeniture).

137 *stay . . . stomachs*: appease their (sexual) appetite.

hot bit: (1) of food; (2) of pudendum (infected with venereal disease).

137–8 *common mistress*: whore.

138–9 *like . . . lightning*: (1) because they have no staying power sexually; (2) because they bring the pox with them.

139 *first of me*: my virginity.

143 *get*: beget.

149–50 *inutterable*: (1) beyond words; (2) (in conjunction with 'point' as 'penis') inviolate ('utter' = ejaculate).

153 *knew*: carnally.

161 *portion*: (1) amount; (2) inheritance.

163–4 *That . . . daughters*: Mistress Low-water gives the richness of her chastity to Lady Goldenfleece and its moral off-shoots (i.e. the 'strait-bodied daughters').

175 *may . . . yourself*: you could be an experienced gallant.

176 *You . . . cards*: you are not inferior to any wooer.

181 *taken down*: (1) made detumescent; (2) humbled, taught a lesson.

194 *parted gold*: parted gold and a public kiss are betrothal customs (Johnson).

205 *eclipse*: a portent of disaster, even if it occurred in remote and barbaric places (Johnson).

210 *fool . . . voider*: there is no indication until this line that Pickadille is present during this scene. He comes in with Low-water at line 211, so if he were present he would have to leave with the suitors and reappear almost immediately. Perhaps Mistress Low-water is referring to Weatherwise when she speaks here of the 'fool'.

215 *something like*: how it should be.

223 *wits*: professional writers.

246 *bid them*: invite them (to the celebrations).

261 *past . . . mouth*: anything better than subsistence.

273 *affection*: O has 'affliction'.

3.1 A street near Lady Goldenfleece's house.

 12 *third house*: when Saturn is in the third house, Mercury is the Lord of the Ascendant and Saturn is in opposition to Mercury (Johnson).

13–14 *fiery . . . tail*: a comet (an evil omen) in conjunction with the Dragon's tail (a name given to the intersection of the orbit of the descending moon with the line of the sun's orbit) is astrologically maleficent.

 25 *house*: body.

 26 *Not . . . friend*: what is the distinction here? 'Friendship' may = (merely) 'friendly aid' (*OED* 4).

 30 *mine*: promise of revenge.

 37 *so now I*: I hereby vow to do so.

 39 *we . . . labour*: we will not be unsuccessful.

 44 *slander*: O reads 'slave'.

50–1 *not . . . dish*: not restrict ourselves to one theme.

 59 *lie with*: (1) tell lies about; (2) have sex with.

 60 *yard*: see note on *Term*, 1.1.88.

 62 *copy*: see note on *Trick*, 2.1.284.

 66 *Seven Stars*: the Pleiades, or the Virgins, a small but conspicuous cluster of stars in the constellation Taurus.

 68 *roaring boys*: (1) twin boy babies; (2) ruffianly young men.

 70 *and . . . places*: illegitimate children were thought to be more robust than those in marriage 'got 'tween asleep and wake' (*King Lear*, 1.2.15).

 71 *your master*: i.e. Sir Gilbert (since he proposed this way of revenging themselves). But Weatherwise has 'outrun' him by the malicious ingenuity of his invention.

 72 *Draw home*: pull the bow back as far as possible, i.e. be more vigorous in your love-making.

 73 *game at pricks*: in archery the 'prick' was the bull's-eye at the centre of the target. For the obvious innuendo cf. note on 2.1.24.

74–5 *if . . . in*: if he had seduced Lady Goldenfleece before her interest in Mistress Low-water.

 77 *hole . . . in*: see note on *Trick*, 1.2.45–6.

 81 *outlaws*: from Lady Goldenfleece's affection.

 84 *as . . . be*: in epitome.

 93 *Pond's Almanac*: Edward Pond began publishing almanacs in 1601; his annual publications were continuous from 1604–1709. The almanac

poesies, however, are recited by Weatherwise from Thomas Bretnor's 1611 almanac (Johnson).

95 *twelfth of June*: summer solstice, according to the old style calendar, when the sun entered the house of Cancer the Crab (Johnson).

100 *four . . . signs*: the four played by the wooers.

105 *nor . . . herring*: completing the proverb.

106 *privily*: stealthily, but Pickadille puns on 'privy', cf. note on *Term*, 3.1.198.

109 *ware*: as at 2.3.128 the pun is on 'penis' (in a detumescent state).

126 *how . . . happen*: how their maleficent predictions come true.

129 *masterless men*: vagrants, the seventeenth-century equivalent of today's unemployed (see A. L. Beier, *Masterless Men: The Vagrancy Problem in England 1560–1640*, London: Methuen, 1985).

131 *two pence*: the price of an almanac.

137–8 *and . . . Jerusalem*: deliberately nonsensical, unless we are supposed to think that the 'Holy City' would not be on the itinerary of any self-respecting, sophisticated, secular traveller.

152 *goes*: walks.

162 *parsons*: (1) persons; (2) ministers (of the church).

169 *cheeks*: Beveril has the lean cheeks of the scholar.

175 *give . . . for't*: disappoint you in exchange for it (where 'slip' puns on 'counterfeit coin'; cf. note on *Mad*, 5.1.66).

235 *unhappiness*: O has 'happiness'.

244 *Set off*: provide compensation for (hence, mask).

247 *he . . . once*: see note on *Term*, 2.1.93–101.

249 *you . . . stream*: you are talking about something else (and punning on sexual congress, s.v. 'fish' in Partridge).

250 *an . . . that*: if it comes to that.

255 *fire*: the fire of the pox.

258 *crevice*: (allusively) pudendum.

259–60 *so . . . gentleman*: in his finances.

261 *Seven Stars*: here, the name of a tavern.

262 *Wat, the barber*: 'Wat' is a diminutive of Walter; barbers functioned as doctors and administered to those suffering from the fires of lechery (Johnson).

275 *give you over*: yield to you.

276 *on't*: of time.

279 *one . . . eight*: although Thomas Middleton is given full credit for authorship on the title-page of the 1657 octavo edition of *No Wit* (the

first printed edition of the play), this edition was in fact a reprint of the slightly revised 1638 revival by James Shirley. A. H. Bullen was the first editor to point this out. He in turn owed his information to Dyce's discovery that Shirley, while in Dublin from 1636–40, had written a prologue—not published in the 1657 octavo—to a play called *No Wit to a Woman's* (see *Dramatic Works and Poems of James Shirley*, ed. William Gifford and Alexander Dyce (London, 1833), vi. 492–3). The only discernible revision that can be confidently ascribed to Shirley is this updating of Weatherwise's reference to the current year.

279–80 *dominical . . . G*: as a liturgical device, Sundays were given dominical letters. The first seven days of January were each assigned a letter, A to G, and the letter that fell on the first Sunday was the dominical letter for the year (Johnson).

290 *air*: with a pun on 'heir'.

4.1 A room in Sir Oliver Twilight's house.

13 *joy*: O reads 'joys'. Dyce's emendation agrees with the singular 'that' on the same line.

18 *eat . . . trick*: suffer for having been part of that plot.

26 *looked after*: deserved (lit. = 'searched for' OED 12.b).

27 *take great advice*: consider very carefully.

38 *behind*: (1) to come; (2) the buttocks (see Rubinstein).

62 *she*: O has 'he'.

70 *She's . . . so*: she has made love too often to be called a virgin.

71 *call somebody up*: give birth (where 'somebody' = a baby).

73 *mean*: middle course.

88 *may*: missing in O.

92 *a son's*: (1) Philip's blessing which = his child; (2) Philip's blessing after she has risen from bed after love-making.

99 *lets*: prevents, hinders.

117 *came over*: from Antwerp.

strong: in a strengthened position.

125–6 *Like . . . ones*: like a thief who, recently acquitted on one charge, begins stealing again in the courtroom itself.

132 *another bedfellow*: Jane Sunset.

144 *indenture . . . steaks*: servant's bond cut into tiny pieces.

149 *open Dutch*: as opposed to the double Dutch Savourwit spoke.

an . . . it: if he could understand it (primarily the unintended significance of Sir Oliver's use of 'motherly').

151 *Thus . . . with't*: in this way I would agree with it.

158 *another*: i.e. the consequent baptismal festivity.

170 *fear*: reverence.

204 *'fection*: affectation, pose.

231 *cast away*: condemned to death; English law required more than the testimony of one witness ('bare words') (Johnson).

234 *throw*: overthrow.

246 *found*: O has 'finde'.

254 *Amongst*: of.

255 *She's*: ignorance is.

272 *breast*: confidant.

273 *possible kindness*: the affection due a servant from a master.

294 *summer suit*: men's outer garments ornamented with perforations (and therefore only suitable for summer wear).

4.2 A room in Lady Goldenfleece's house.

 6 *privileged*: O has 'privilege'.

 12 *hole*: see note on *Mad*, 1.2.135 (here there is an obscene pun).

17–18 *I . . . for't*: the sense seems to be that being a knave (servant) in Lady Goldenfleece's house is one step towards becoming a bawd.

4.3 A room in Lady Goldenfleece's house.

 9 *office without money*: position (as husband) without charge.

23–4 *he'll . . . face*: he will see from your face that you have been sleeping with your sister.

25 *S . . . eye*: 'S' and 'I', the first two letters of 'sister'.

29 *branched-velvet gown*: embroidered (with leaves and branches) judge's gown.

30 *at nurse*: with your mother's milk.

31 *great*: (1) massive, bulky; (2) great-hearted, proud.

32 *learned it*: how to dissemble.

36 *abstract*: outline of the play's plot written up on the pasteboard.

43 S.D. *flags*: grass.

46 *out*: he is speaking the wrong lines.

48 *The . . . distaff*: Weatherwise is commenting on Sir Gilbert's transformation of the script. Beveril's wheel of time's distaff has been burnt up by the devil; i.e. what has been 'spun' (written) by Beveril has been replaced by the devil (Sir Gilbert).

59 *alleys*: for clandestine or coercive sex.

 tubs: sweating tubs used in the treatment for syphilis.

62 *russet yeomen*: countrymen dressed in reddish, homespun, woollen clothes.

70 *Aretine*: Pietro Aretino (1492–1556) was the author of scurrilous and obscene satires and poems. Here, the adjective invokes his erotic writings and the accompanying illustrations.

76 *beggarly sparks*: contemptible, weak gallants, the offspring of the unions between the women and their catamites.

77 *Heart!*: O reads 'Heat!'.

81 *fat*: plump, juicy.

83 *air*: breath.

84 *air*: scent.

86 *smelt . . . crowds*: the 'airs' of flatulence.

88 *have fainted*: from the noxious vapours produced by themselves (in the crowds).

91 *sign's in Cancer*: when Venus is in the house of Cancer women were thought to be fickle and inconstant (Johnson).

95 *more near*: closer to the truth.

    at noon: i.e. 'tossed in a blanket'.

96 *spot . . . moon*: when the moon is in Cancer women were thought to be at their most licentious.

98 *When . . . planet*: the appropriate sign for the bedchamber of the unfaithful because Mercury is associated with lies and deception.

100 *When . . . tail*: see note on 2.3.44–5.

105 *These . . . rooms*: presumably, Beveril does not recognize the four erstwhile suitors dressed for their roles in his play.

109 *A . . . off*: Lady Goldenfleece means the opposite of what she says.

117 *pipes*: throats.

118 *Without . . . house*: because Water is only a character in a play.

    water house: a building in which water is raised from a river or well into a 'conduit head' or reservoir to be conveyed by means of 'conduits' or pipes for domestic use (*OED*).

124 *I . . . spread*: an image of fertility, as the next line makes clear.

134 *sir Water*: see note on 3.1.262 ('Walter' was pronounced 'Water').

136 *full point*: full stop, final period.

137 *stop*: stop up.

138 *I . . . better*: (1) I love your first husband more than I love muck; (2) Your first husband loved muck more than I do. 'Muck' = (1) manure (which fertilizes the earth, as does the corpse of Lady Goldenfleece's husband); (2) money.

142 *And . . . lips*: is this a reference to frothing at the mouth in death?

145 *crane's throat*: the crane has a long neck, hence a large throat which = an excessive appetite for wealth.

148 *brows*: the sweat of their brows.

152 s.d. *give back*: fall back, retreat.

173 *fortune teller*: Weatherwise's costume is designed like that traditionally worn by astrologers and fortune tellers (Johnson).

192 s.d. O has '*Manent Widow and Mrs. Low-water*'.

5.1 A room in Lady Goldenfleece's house.

s.d. At the close of 4.3, O has an s.d. that leaves Lady Goldenfleece and Mistress Low-water on stage. At the beginning of Act 5 O's s.d. reads 'Widow and Mrs Low-water', indicating that the two have remained on stage between acts. However, this arrangement is hardly likely given that 4.3 ends with a short exchange between Philip and Savourwit which makes most sense as a coda to the scene after everyone else has exited.

5 *try*: test.

11 *cock-sparrow*: which was proverbially lecherous.

19 *end*: purpose (Mistress Low-water then puns on the other meaning).

61 *make a youth*: take advantage of his inexperience (Johnson).

62 *ill-trusted*: not to be trusted.

63–4 *You . . . writings*: the sense seems to be either: (1) Lady Goldenfleece would not want her erstwhile suitor to manage her former husband's business affairs; or (2) she may well intend to take a lover to replace her new husband.

72 *yellow poison*: jealousy.

87 *pores*: O reads 'powers' which makes sense. Dyce's emendation is, however, attractive, given the medical metaphor.

140 *under*: into a position of subjection (s.v. *OED adv.* 3a).

144 *know*: have sex with.

152–3 *begot i'th'woodyard*: conceived in the yard in which wood was stored (and hence not a 'son of honour').

153 *hard*: punning on wood being hard.

160 *quick*: alive.

205 *escapes*: evasions.

228 *starters*: lacking in perseverance (Johnson).

263 *This . . . music*: this makes me laugh.

266 *Well . . . yet*: the almanac continues to predict accurately.

268 *hunks*: 'Harry Hunks' was the name of a bear at Paris Garden (Bullen).

Bear . . . heaven: the Bear was a well-known tavern at the Southwark end of London Bridge (Sugden).

270 *Dog*: Sirius or the Dog-star has a pernicious influence (Johnson).

314 *with a witness*: (1) with a third party (as witness); (2) with a vengeance.

323 *fate*: O has 'hate'.

325 *Rid of*: being rid of.

329 *carrier's . . . chambermaid*: Weatherwise plans to accost a country girl new to the city.

337 *fist*: handwriting.

339 *Anno Jac. primo*: in the first year of James I (1603–4). This was an 'Acte to restrayne all persons from Marriage untill theire former Wyves and former Husbandes be deade' (Dyce).

348 *put . . . book*: require me to read.

349 *neck-verse*: by merely reciting Psalm 51: 1 in Latin a condemned man was entitled to the 'benefit of clergy', which put him outside civil law. Her breasts are Mistress Low-water's neck-verse (Johnson).

368 *exercised*: O has 'examin'd'.

386 *there*: O reads 'here'.

387 *trim*: ring properly.

391–2 *there's . . . it*: nothing has happened to make it come about (i.e. the hanging).

395 *thirteen pence half-penny*: a thief could be hanged if he stole more than that amount (Johnson).

399 *contracting time*: time for making a marriage contract.

400 *book*: marriage contract.

440 *Grew . . . world*: suffered worldly losses.

452 *Hey*: O has 'Hay'.

468 *baker's ditch*: as a punishment, dishonest bakers were dunked into water ditches (Johnson).

473 *wittiness*: O reads 'weakness'. Both Dyce and Bullen suggest 'wittiness' as an attractive emendation, but only Johnson acts on the suggestion.

Epilogue

1 *WEATHERWISE*: omitted in O.

9 *pipe*: windpipe.

11 *Fear no colours*: a military proverb meaning 'have no fear of hostile flags', with a pun on 'collars' as the hangman's ropes.

12 *red and white*: the audience, perhaps only its ladies; a conjunction of many-coloured Jupiter with the white and red Gemini results in

graceful, courteous, good-natured, and obliging people, just what Weatherwise wishes in the audience (Johnson).

13 *jovial*: punning on Jove (Jupiter).

14 *sun i'th'Dog*: see note on 5.1.270.

15–16 *Some . . . fragments*: Weatherwise compares hostile critics to barking dogs who will later crawl back to his table for bits of food.

16 *ember week*: a week of fasting.

17 *both . . . meet*: this is an invitation to the audience to applaud. Johnson notes that the Gemini twins have dominion over the hands.

18 *no*: not in O.

20 *answer*: here a line (ending with the word 'Cancer') has dropped out (Dyce).

GLOSSARY

a of, on (occasionally)

'a he

abstract plot synopsis, compendium, epitome

accidents incidents, events

admirable wonderful, marvellous

admiration wonder

admire marvel, wonder at

advance raise, promote

affects likes, loves, affects

again (sometimes) = before, in anticipation of

ague acute fever

air appearance

a-late recently

a-life dearly

All Hollandtide All Saints' Day, 1 November

alley a long narrow enclosure for playing bowls

aloof off at some distance away

an if/if it (on occasion)

ancient ensign

angel gold coin worth about 50 pence (so called because it was stamped with a design of St Michael slaying the dragon)

anon immediately, right away; coming!

answerable liable to be called to account

an't if it

Antwerp centre of the English wool trade in Flanders

apace quickly

apologies defences

apperil peril

appointed equipped

approve prove

aqua coelistis a cordial

aqua vitae liquor (usually whisky or brandy)

Aquarius the Water Bearer, the eleventh sign of the zodiac

Aries the Ram, the first sign of the zodiac

arrant manifest, notorious; warrant (*No Wit*, Prologue 8)

art cunning, artifice; learning

aspected influenced by or subjected to a particular aspect of the planets

aspic asp

assurances deeds, titles

a'th of the, on the

aught all that

aunt cant term for bawd

babliaminy babbler

bags money bags

balsamum balsam, an aromatic medicinal preparation

band collar

bands bonds

banes banns

banquet an elaborate dessert of sweetmeats, fruit and wine

Barnard's Inn an Inn of Chancery on the south side of Holborn

Barnet popular resort town 11 miles northwest of London

Barthol'mew-tide 24 August (the opening day of the annual fair held in West Smithfield)

bastard sweet Spanish wine

bated reduced

batten thrive, prosper

beadles minor (blue-coated) officials

Bear tavern at the Southwark end of London Bridge

Bear Garden famous bull-baiting pit in London

beaten well-worn

beaver hat made from beaver fur (fashionable and expensive)

beaver band beaver-skin hat band

Bedlam St Mary of Bethlehem in Bishopsgate, the hospital for the insane

bedstaffs staves laid loose across bedstead to support bedding

beginnings parentage

beguile disappoint, foil

beholding beholden

bench court of law

bents frames to extend dresses at the hips

beset assailed

beshrow beshrew

bestow expend, spend; marry off (*Term*, 5.3.126)

bill (verb) caress

bills advertisements

Blackfriars district in southwest London

blacks funeral hangings

blame blameworthy

blast blight, ruin

bleaking-house a hospital for sufferers of the pox

blood sensual appetite

bodkin long hairpin

body a'me body of me (a common exclamation)

bones dice

bounty hospitality; kindness; booty

brace two, a couple

brave fine, richly dressed; worthy (*Term*, 1.2.35)

braver more richly dressed

breaking deflowering

broadcloths fine black cloth used for men's clothes

brokers pawnbrokers

brothel cant term for whore

brow face

budgelling equivocating

bullbeggars hobgoblins, scarecrows

bully a familiar term of address

bum French farthingale (roll of material stiffened with wire and worn around the hips)

bunch pack

buss kiss

buttery store-room, for both liquor and food

buz a common interjection of impatience or contempt

buzz whisper

buzzard (1) an inferior bird of prey; (2) a foolish person

by-blow side-thrust

cabishes cabbages

cambric fine white linen

canary a light, sweet wine from the Canary Isles

Cancer the Crab, the fourth sign of the zodiac

canopy bed hangings

Capricorn the Goat, the tenth sign of the zodiac

careful full of care/woe

carman carter, carrier

carriage bearing, style

cassocks long loose cloaks (often worn by usurers)

cast vomit

cast soil besmirch, stain

caterpillar extortioner; parasite

catamites boys kept for sex

cates provisions, food

cattle chattels

caudles warm drink (wine or ale mixed with gruel) often used as an aphrodisiac

cauls webs

ceiled covered (walls and ceiling)

censure judgement

certify assure

chain of gold a steward's insignia of office

challenge claim

champ chew

champion champaign, unenclosed

champion grounds open fields

Chancery the Court of the Lord Chancellor of England, the highest court of judicature next to the House of Lords, formerly primarily a court of appeal

chandler maker or seller of candles

chargeable burdensome, expensive

charges expenses

chin-clout muffler worn by the lower classes and a mark of a prostitute

choice of particular about

chopping strong, healthy

chops jaws, sides of the face

circuits activities

circumference space

circumstance fact

citizen Londoner; tradesman (*Term*, 1.1.91)

clap-fallen infected with gonorrhoea

clarified whey watery part of milk with the impurities removed

cleanly cleverly, adroitly

clear pure

clip embrace

close secret; in hiding

close-stool chamber pot for defecating enclosed in a stool or box

closet private room, inner chamber

cloth of arras a rich tapestry fabric in which figures and scenes are often woven in colour

cloth o'gold a tissue consisting of threads, wires or strips of gold, generally interwoven with silk or wool

cloth o'tissue rich kind of cloth, often interwoven with gold and silver

cloven devilish

cloy disgust, weary (with an excess of something)

clubs rallying cry used to call out the London apprentices during a fight

coached by coach

coad's nigs God's nigs, a variant of the oath, 'God's nails'

codpiece flap or cover for the crotch in men's breeches

conceive have a conception of, understand

consume waste away (*Trick*, 3.1.16)

contentious bellicose, quarrelsome

cog flatter, fawn

cogging cheating

coil tumult

colour (verb) excuse, disguise

come about circulate, go round

comfortable sustaining, refreshing, cheering

command have for the asking

commenced graduated

commodious useful, accommodating

commodity profit

companions a term of contemptuous familiarity

compendiously briefly, concisely

complement number of servants

complemental hospitable

composure mixture, prescription

compound bargain

compounded put together

conceit invention; understanding; (verb) understand

cony-burrows rabbit warrens

confounded ruined

confusion ruin

conjure entreat

conjurer magician, wizard

consents agrees

conscience innermost thoughts; conscience

consort company of musicians; companion

construe read

contrived delicately made

contunded pounded

conveyances passages; tricks

cormorant insatiably greedy

corse corpse

counsellor legal advocate

Counters London prisons for debtors (Wood Street and the Poultry)

courtesan whore; kept mistress

cousin a familiar mode of address

cousin-german first cousin

covey set

coxcomb conceited fool

coxcombry conceited fools (a coinage)

coz a familiar mode of address

cozened cheated

crank cocky

credit reputation, prestige

cremitoried burnt, syphilitic

crinkling wrinkled

Crooked Lane a street which formerly ran from New Fish Street to St Michael's Lane in London

cross thwart, oppose

cross ends undesirable outcomes

crosses annoyances, vexations

crown top

crowns gold coins worth five shillings

cry you mercy beg your pardon

cuds bodkins mild oath (= God's little body)

cuds me mild oath (= God save me)

cullis strong, nourishing broth

curiously elaborately

curvet leap (of a horse)

custom trade; habit

cypress dark veil

dainty choice, valuable; handsome
dame mistress of a household
dashed splashed with mud
dauber plasterer
daunt overcome
decking dressing up
decorum decorous, seemly
deeds legal papers
defy renounce
delicate delectable, lovely
demise conveyance or transfer of an estate by will or lease
demur delay
depose give evidence on oath
desperate defaulted
despite contempt, scorn
despitefully insolently, shamefully
detaining withholding
device stratagem; entertainment
devices stratagems
diet food
dilacerate torn
discharge receipt
discover reveal
diseased upset, worried
dispatch settle quickly; go quickly
dispatchful deadly
dispend expend
dissolution undoing
distaff cleft stick used in spinning wool
distaste render offensive
distracted mad, insane
dive-dapper dabchick, a small diving waterfowl
dizzy giddy
divulged proclaimed
dog me follow
double deceitful
doublet a close-fitting body garment with or without sleeves
doubt fear; suspect (*Mad*, 3.1.69)
dove-holes dovecots
downfall the act of falling down (*No Wit*, 1.2.134)
drab whore
drawers tapsters, bartenders
dresser board table on which food was prepared
drink down outdrink
drink drunk drink until drunk

dumb shows sequences in mime and gesture in which the events of a succeeding scene were exhibited beforehand
Dunkirks privateers from Dunkirk
Dutch widow whore
duties polite greetings
e'er ever
effeminate voluptuous
embryon embryo
engross monopolize
enow enough
entertain receive, accept; entertainment (*Mad*, 1.2.85)
envy malice; (verb) bear malice
ergo therefore
errant thoroughgoing, unmitigated
estate (verb) furnish with an estate
esteem popularity
even evening
exceed are surpassing
except against make objection to
Exchequer court dealing with state revenues
executions seizures of goods
explete complete
exsiccate dried up
express show
extempore right, immediately
extremely categorically, vehemently, completely
extremity full amount
fact crime, deed
fadge succeed
fain obliged; gladly
falls collars
false gallop canter
fame good reputation, credit
familiar saucy
fancy love
farthingale woman's hooped skirt
fathom embrace; power
fearful timid; fearsome
feathers hat plumes (indicative of wealth)
featly deftly
felts hats
fetch out bring to light
fetched in taken in, deceived
fetches tricks, stratagems
fetching over cheating

firkin small cask

fish-market flat and watery(?) (*No Wit*, 2.3.95)

fits seizures, moods

fledged ready to fly

flight excursion (away from home)

flirt joke, jest, gibe

flout deride

fond foolish

fondly foolishly

fool the King's professional jester

fooliaminy fools (a coinage)

footcloth large richly-ornamented cloth laid over the back of a horse and hanging down onto the ground on each side

forborne endured

forepart front

formally in outward appearance

forsooth in truth (ironic, mocking, derisive)

frame world

fray frighten

free-breasted generous

freedom city limits

frolic frolicsome, sportive

frotting rubbing with perfume

froward presumptuous; refractory, naughty

furred encrusted

gage pledge

gale breeze

gallant a man of fashion and pleasure, a ladies' man

galleasses heavy low-built vessels larger than a galley

game sexual sport; gambling

gamester gambler; whoremonger

Ganymede ravishing youth abducted by Zeus to serve as his cupbearer and page (= effeminate youth)

gaped opened

gear business, affair

Gemini the Twins, the third sign of the zodiac

gentleman a person of considerable rank in the seventeenth century

geometrical ground-measuring

gernative addicted to 'girning' or grumbling

gilt gold, money (*Mad*, 2.2.28)

girt girded, wrapped

glib smooth, slippery

go to come, come

good fellow cant term for thief

goodman master

goosecap booby, simpleton

gossip godparent

grated harassed, aggravated

gravelled perplexed

green inexperienced, immature

gristles tender, delicate things; bones (*No Wit*, 1.1.245)

Guernsey one of the Channel Islands about 30 miles from the French coast

Guildhall London's City Hall

gulf voracious belly

gull dupe, fool

gullery trickery

gum substance applied to silk to make it glossy

habiliments clothing

habit clothing, outward appearance

halberd a shafted weapon with an axe-like cutting blade

half moon a wig in the shape of half-moon

hall law-court

handsomely cleverly

happily fortunately

hard at near-by

hartichalks artichokes

h'as he has

haunt lodging

hazard risk

heaviness sadness

hinds country bumpkins

hireling servant

his its (on occasion)

hit of remember

hobbyhorse buffoon

Holborn district in London with a poor reputation

hold my life wager my life

honest chaste

honesty chastity

Horn Fleet Street tavern

hospital charitable institution for abandoned foundlings and orphans

hoyda form of the exclamation, 'heyday'

hoys small coastal ships

hucksters grain speculators

humour whim; disposition (*Trick*, 2.1.180)

humours moods, temperaments

hunting meal cold meal, often lavish, taken during the hunt

idle frivolous, insubstantial

impeachment disparagement, accusation

impressier impression

in use customary

inconscionable extreme, abominable

indented made an agreement

indenture contract by which an apprentice was bound to his master

indifferent moderately, passably; impartial, unconcerned; immaterial (*Trick*, 2.1.23)

indifferences impartiality

industry occupation, employment

infortunity misfortune

Inns of Court residence halls for law students in London

intelligencers spies

interlude perform a play (in the interval of a feast)

interpose obstruct

invention device

inward intimate

iwis certainly

jack fellow

jar discord; impediment

Jersey Channel Island about 18 miles from the French coast

jets struts

jointure lands settled on the wife by the husband to be fully hers on the husband's death until she herself dies

juggle deceive, beguile

jump fit exactly, accord

junt trick

kersened christened

kersey coarse cloth

kickshaws elaborately made dishes of food

kind nature

kitchen-stuff slops, waste

knaves servants

kned kneaded

la an exclamation, meaningless in itself, usually accompanying an emphatic statement, sometimes rendered 'la you now'

lasts shapes, sizes

law-quillets legal technicalities, quibbles

laying out exercising, expenditure

leads roof

leash set of three

Leo the Lion, the fifth sign of the zodiac

let hindrance, impediment

let off fire off

lets hinders

lewd base, vile

liberal generous (sometimes with bawdy implications)

liberties suburbs outside the jurisdiction of civil authorities

Libra the Balance, the seventh sign of the zodiac

like (in stage directions) disguised as

likes pleases

litter straw

longitude length

long of/on because of

look what no matter what

lopped de-branched

lordships estates

'lot allot

lotium-water stale urine used as a hair-wash

louse remove lice from

luxury licentiousness

maintenance provider, 'meal-ticket'

make-match place in which to bring about a marriage

makeshift rogue, shifty person

maltmen brewers

mark coin worth two-thirds of a pound

marquess marchioness

marry by St Mary (an exclamation of surprise etc.)

masty mastiff

maw appetite, inclination

may-butter unsalted butter used for medicinal purposes

mealy spotted, flecked

mean moderation; course of action

mean season meanwhile

mechanic labouring
meddle be intimate with
mends amends
mercer dealer in silks and other fabrics
mere complete, absolute
mess a group of four
methinks it seems to me
Middleburgh a Dutch port and centre of international trade
minion mistress, loose woman
Mitre well-known London tavern (on the corner of Bread Street and Cheapside)
mock-face arrangement of hair (roughly resembling a face)
monkey-tailed lecherous
mortal deadly
motion proposal
motions promptings, urgings
mought might
moveables personal property
muckinder handkerchief, bib
murrain plague
mull-sack heated, sweetened, and spiced sherry
murrey mulberry coloured
muscadine a rich wine (thought to be an aphrodisiac when combined with eggs)
musical pleasant, undisturbed
muss muddle
musty-visage ill-humoured, peevish
name reputation
napkins handkerchiefs
narrow-eared pressing closely to the ears
ne nor
neat handsome
ne'er never
Newbury a town in Berkshire
nibbled caught, tricked
nice delicate, over-refined
nigher hand nearer
nightgown dressing-gown
noble coin worth about 40 pence
noisome stinking
nonce the time being
Northamptonshire rural county in central England
notch store of wealth

nuncle uncle
nurse-child an infant lodged away from home with a wet-nurse
oars rowing boats
observances rules of conduct
o'erseen (1) deluded; (2) drunk
officers constables
on's of us
on't of it
opinion reputation
orange-tawny brownish yellow with a tinge of orange
ordinary meal in inn or tavern; eating-house (as distinct from a tavern)
o'th of the, on the
outcry proclaim
outdare outdo
outlanders foreigners
outlandish of foreign design
out-monies funds invested
overcharged overloaded
overseer steward
ox-browed cuckolded
pair of organs organ
parbreaking vomiting
parcel small group; piece (of land)
paring pruning
Parma Italian city
parsons persons
part role; proceeding (*Term*, 5.3.11)
passion lamentation
passion of me an exclamation
paste dough
pasties pies
pax pox
pea pooh
peevish foolish, trifling
perfumer fumigator of rooms
pestiferous plague-carrying
philosopher lover of wisdom
physic cathartic, purge
pickle wretched state
piety pity
pig-eater term of endearment
piles rocks
pillions back saddles (for a second rider)
pin peg
pink pierce
Pisces the Fishes, the twelfth sign of the zodiac

players strolling players
plumtree pudendum
ply'st work vigorously
pointed sharpened, sharp
poise weigh
pole rod (five-and-a-half yards)
policy crafty calculation
politicly craftily, cunningly
polittian negotiator
portion dowry
portly in a dignified manner, imposingly
portmantua travelling bag
possess give possession to (*Term*, 4.1.79)
Poultry London prison for debtors
powd'ring seasoning
pox syphilis
pox of an imprecation
praemunire sheriff's writ
prating idle chattering
prattle chatter; copulate
prefer recommend
pregnant resourceful, quick-witted
present immediate
presently immediately
preserves preservatives
prevented forestalled
pricking spurring
prigging pilfering, haggling
prithee I pray thee
privy furtive, sly, secret; intimate, familiar
probably plausibly
proceeded advancing to a higher degree at a university; studied (*No Wit*, 3.1.277)
prodigious amazing; monstrous
profess claim to practise
promoter informer
proper handsome
property attribute, quality
prostitution prostitute
protest affirm
prove test; prosper
provident convenient
publish publicly denounce
pudding compressed tobacco resembling a sausage
puh pooh
puling whining
pumps footwear of servants

pung punk (prostitute)
punks prostitutes
pup pooh
purchase profit; booty (*Mad*, 2.4.66; 3.2.90)
pure complete, absolute (*No Wit*, 1.1.82)
push pish
put out invest
quacksalving characteristic of a quack
qualm feeling of sickness
quean whore, mistress
quickening enlivening
quid pro quo tit for tat
quit requite, reward; acquit, exonerate
quo'they indeed
racked rented at an extortionate rate
rank lustful, licentious
rapture paroxysm, fit
rarely exceptionally
rawly hardly, barely
reaches schemes, contrivances
Red Lion a tavern near the Tower of London
refocillation refreshment, tonic
refulgent radiant, resplendent
regardless of without regard for
resolved assured, convinced
respective respectful
'rest arrest
restraints prohibitions against acting
reversion contingent interest in future properties (metaphorically = leftovers)
Rhenish Rhine wine
ringworm syphilis
risse risen
rosa solis a cordial
rose nobles gold coins stamped with a rose, worth about 75 pence
round blunt, direct
rounded whispered
roundly bluntly, directly; completely, readily; in full (*Trick*, 4.4.158)
royals gold pieces worth about 75 pence
rub obstacle
rubbish land
ruffling rustling
sack white Spanish wine
Sagittarius the Archer, the ninth sign of the zodiac

sa ho a cry in hare-hunting and falconry
saving except for
savours stinks
saying report
scab rascal, scoundrel
scabiosity scabies, syphilis
scattered broke (financially)
Scorpio the Scorpion, the eighth sign of the zodiac
screen protect
scrivener notary
scrubbing scratching
scruple one-third of a dram
scullers sculling boats
scurvigrass spoonwort (thought to be a remedy for scurvy)
searchings surgical probings
season time
sect sex
seeded impregnated
sense feeling
serge durable woollen or worsted cloth often worn by the poor
sergeant sheriff's arresting officer
set fair stand a good chance of (*Trick*, 2.2.19)
set me cover my bet
several various, different
'sfoot mild oath (= God's foot)
shadow conceal
shaft arrow
shark petty swindle
sh'as she has
sheepskin loan papers
shift expedient provision; clothing (*Term*, Induction 33); change (of clothing) (*Term*, 4.1.62)
shogs jogs (to attract attention)
shooters suiters
Shoreditch parish in northeast London with an unsavoury reputation
'shrew beshrew
shroud shrewd, grievous
shrugging shivering
silly helpless, frail, simple
simple poor
single simple, plain (*No Wit*, 3.1.222)
sinks excretory organs
sirrah a slightly contemptuous mode of address used for one's inferiors

'sizes assizes
skills matters
skutcheons memorial shields bearing a coat of arms fixed at the entrance of the house of the deceased
sleight trick
'slid God's (eye-)lid (a mild oath)
slippery wanton, licentious
slops baggy trousers
'slud God's blood (a mild oath)
smack kiss
small beer weak, watered-down beer
smocks women's undergarments
snobbing sobbing
snuffers instruments for snuffing candles
solister variant of 'solicitor
solus alone
sophistic false, speciously reasoned
sophistication adulteration
sorts fits, is convenient
spacious large, ample
sparks flashy gallants
speed prosper
speeding productive, effective; quick, deadly (*No Wit*, 5.1.82)
spiny thin and dry
springall youth
spume foam
spur-royals gold coins worth about 80 pence with a sun and its rays resembling the rowel of a spur stamped on them
squall young minx (sometimes a term of endearment)
squat strike, slap
squire lover
stand for act as, represent
stand to stand by
Standard the great conduit (water fountain) in Cheapside
stands upon involves
starting shying away (*No wit*, 5.1.363)
state estate
stays corset
steaks pieces
steeped soaked, drunk
stick hesitate, scruple; haggle (*Trick*, 4.2.10)
sticks persists
still always, continually

stinkard one who stinks
stirring stimulating, provoking
stomach inclination; appetite
strait-bodied close fitting (clothes)
stranger foreigner
stretched most extended
stroke sexual thrust
strossers tight breeches
struck by passed by
stuff material; rubbish
succubus demon in the shape of a woman
suffered permitted
suffice satisfy
sufficient financially solvent, well-to-do
suits petitions
summoner minor official who summoned people to court
Sun tavern located in New Fish Street in London
sun-cup a drinking vessel in the shape of the sun
suspect suspicion
swag sink down
swagger act, behave insolently
swimming giddy
taffeta thin soft silk
take on lament
tarantula poisonous spider (reputed to turn all it touched to excrement)
taste hint
Taurus the Bull, the second sign of the zodiac
tax censure
t'ee thee
tell count
tenters wooden frame for stretching cloth (hence the rack)
thrice many times
throat, to lie in one's to lie vilely, infamously
thrum-chinned bearded (thrum = fringe of a piece of weaving)
thrummed thatched
tickle stir up, incite, beat, chastise
timorsome fearful
tires headdresses
title deed of property
tobacco shop a place to buy tobacco and a public resort for smoking

told counted
tongues speaks of
took order dealt
t'other the other, other
touch put to the test
tow flax on the distaff of a spinning wheel
towardly promising
town-bull womanizer, fornicator
toy whim, fancy; trifle; (verb) caress
trace follow
tract track
train draw, entice
translated transformed
trap adorn
trap-window hinged window or movable penthouse that was lowered to dim the light
trashed staggered through mud and mire
trencher wooden plate or shallow dish (common in wealthy homes before the introduction of pewter)
tried tested, proven
troth truly, indeed
trow do you believe; believe
trussed up bound, tied up; hanged
tubs sweating tubs (used in treatment for syphilis)
turn over reform
twigger whore
twine embrace
twits censures, upbraids
Tyburn gallows at the west end of Oxford Street in London
unbound dismissed (*Mad*, 2.6.20)
unconscionably extremely, abominably
underput whore
undo ruin
undoing ruin
undone ruined
unfledged without a beard
ungotten unborn
unkindness unnaturalness
unquenchable inextinguishable (of fire)
unshapen unformed, callow
unsought unsearched
untendered unpaid
unthrift prodigal, spendthrift
upo'th'nail at once, then and there